THE AMERICAN
LABOR FORCE

A VOLUME IN THE CENSUS MONOGRAPH SERIES

THE AMERICAN LABOR FORCE:

Its Growth
And Changing Composition

by

GERTRUDE BANCROFT

Bureau of the Census

for the
SOCIAL SCIENCE RESEARCH COUNCIL
in cooperation with the
U. S. DEPARTMENT OF COMMERCE
BUREAU OF THE CENSUS

JOHN WILEY & SONS, INC., NEW YORK
CHAPMAN & HALL, LIMITED, LONDON

FOREWORD

The statistical results compiled by the Bureau of the Census constitute a tremendous mass of detailed information about the population of the United States and its characteristics and economic activities. To meet the requirements of government agencies, business concerns, and investigators of social problems and to satisfy the needs of individual citizens, facts must be gathered and published, showing the distribution of the population in each large and small political unit with respect to age, sex, color, marital status, occupation, income, education, national origin, and other characteristics. This information provides the basis for apportionment of representatives in Congress, for answering many questions by direct reference, and for formulating many plans, at least in preliminary form.

It is the first business of the Bureau of the Census to put into print the census results that directly answer as many such questions as possible. Along with these results, similar data from one or two previous censuses are usually included. Limitations of time, space, and money prevent any extensive statement of the relations between particular results, the long-term trends of significant totals and subtotals, the shifting proportions of the people belonging to different categories, and various interesting and important relations such as those between income, occupation, and age. It is not that the Bureau of the Census fails in any sense to appreciate the value and need for such analyses, but rather that it must concentrate on its basic concern with the summary statistics that constitute its unique contribution to knowledge.

When plans for the 1950 Census were made, the need for more extensive analysis was recognized and a series of census monographs similar to those issued after the 1920 Census was proposed. Because of the pressures caused by the depression in the early 1930's and by defense and war in the early 1940's, plans for monographs based on those censuses could not be carried out. Late in the 1940's interested persons from business, research, and government agencies expressed the need for a series that would provide analyses of the most significant results of the 1950 Census. The Social Science Research Council, with the assistance of Russell Sage Foundation, took the lead in stimulating the formulation of suitable plans and in June 1950 appointed a Committee on Census Monographs to cooperate with the Bureau in organizing this project. The members of the Committee are:

Ralph G. Hurlin, Russell Sage Foundation (Chairman)

Robert W. Burgess, formerly Western Electric Company, since February 1953 Director of the Bureau of the Census

John D. Durand, United Nations

Ernest M. Fisher, Columbia University

F. F. Hill, Cornell University

Frederick F. Stephan, Princeton University

Conrad Taeuber, Bureau of the Census

Ralph J. Watkins, Dun & Bradstreet, Inc.

Paul Webbink, Social Science Research Council

J. Frederic Dewhurst, Twentieth Century Fund, and William F. Ogburn, University of Chicago, were members of the Committee during the first year and a half.

It is essential in any sound census monograph program to obtain the cooperation of authors with a broad understanding not only of the statistical information provided by the regular tabulations of the current census but also of the results of earlier censuses and other relevant knowledge and points of view from other sources and even from other countries. The preparation of a monograph should include broad exploration of new questions suggested by the new information, as well as narrowing the elements of doubt and controversy on old questions. The Social Science Research Council Committee early undertook, in consultation with leading figures in various professional fields, to develop a suggested list of monograph titles and authors and persuaded experts in the subject areas selected to undertake the preparation of memoranda outlining and discussing the topics proposed. Then, in 1951, arrangements were made for continuing cooperation between the Committee and the Bureau concerning the selection of topics, proposals of authors and consultants, and editorial supervision.

Throughout the conduct of the project there has been close collaboration with a number of interested Federal agencies and with universities and research organizations, which provided staff and facilities to help bring the project to completion. They and the Council, which also obtained necessary funds from the Rockefeller and Russell Sage Foundations, provided assistance without which the monographs could not have been prepared.

The task of preparing monographs is an essential part of the broad function of making the information secured by censuses fully available to satisfy the needs and interests of the community and to constitute a broad base for further studies in the social sciences. As Director of the Census and President of the Social Science Research Council, respectively, we wish to record our full approval of the monograph project. It is not implied, of course, that the views expressed in these reports are necessarily those of the Bureau of the Census, the Department of Commerce, or the

Social Science Research Council.   The views are those of the individual authors, each of whom has been given the freedom to interpret available materials in the light of his technical knowledge and competence.   This freedom of the individual authors is an essential element in making the most useful analyses and interpretations generally available to the community.

ROBERT W. BURGESS, DIRECTOR
BUREAU OF THE CENSUS

PENDLETON HERRING, PRESIDENT
SOCIAL SCIENCE RESEARCH COUNCIL

PREFACE

The student of the American labor force in the decade of the 1950's has enormous advantages over any of his predecessors who were working before World War II. Instead of decennial readings of the economic activity of the population, he has monthly readings, based on the Census Bureau's Current Population Survey. Information on the labor force status of the population by sex and moderately detailed age classes, is, at the time of writing, available on an annual average basis for about 15 years— a stock of observations it would have taken 150 years to acquire if we had had to rely only on the decennial counts. The monthly statistics on the labor force have become more and more comprehensive, so that with respect to a number of fields of labor force behavior they exceed decennial census data in scope. The flexibility of the labor force in a period of emergency or of prolonged full employment, its seasonal expansion and contraction, and its varying composition from month to month and year to year have been traced through almost all levels of national economic activity, except deep decline and depression. The differential activity of various population groups has been measured, and some of the reasons for differences have been uncovered. Much, too, has been learned about the course of employment and unemployment in periods of recovery, world-wide military conflict, localized conflict, cold war, and mild recession.

As a result of the work of my colleagues at the Census Bureau, the survey findings have been presented, summarized, and interpreted, both in haste to meet an all-powerful monthly publication date, and at greater leisure, in annual and special reports. They and other analysts in the U. S. Department of Commerce, the U. S. Department of Labor, the U. S. Department of Agriculture, the Federal Reserve Board, the Council of Economic Advisers, and elsewhere in and out of the Federal Government have used the current sample statistics to tell the unfolding story of the economy in the World War II and postwar years and to give light for the study of many types of problems. The farm worker, the aged worker, the youthful worker, the Negro in the labor market, the underemployed, the unemployed, the migrant, and perhaps more extensively and intensively than any other type—the working woman—have all been the subject of continuous investigation and research on the basis of the survey data.

I have assumed that most readers interested in the American labor force are familiar with the details of labor force history in the recent past and that a recapitulation would have only limited uses. Furthermore, certain population groups—the aged and youth, for example, whose labor force activity is of great interest and importance—are the subject of other monographs in this series. Instead, my objective has been to bring up to date the long-run trends and to search for further evidence on the factors determining labor force behavior, chiefly in the detailed information collected in the decennial censuses of 1940 and 1950. The work done by John D. Durand in his 1948 study for the Social Science Research Council, *The Labor Force in the United States, 1890–1960,* has laid the foundation for all who do research in this field. I have tried to extend his analysis on the basis of later data and have sought to determine how the unprecedented economic and demographic events that have occurred since 1940 have changed the patterns of labor force behavior of the American people.

A decennial census is a source of information—and a unique one—about the population in individual cities and labor market areas throughout the entire country. It presents the opportunity for testing the extent of variability about national averages. These area data also offer a challenge to the analyst who is searching for patterns and causes of differences in labor force participation, and who believes that in the characteristics of individual areas are the answers to many questions that cannot be attacked at the national level. It was readily shown that a growing uniformity among areas has developed, as a result perhaps of the widespread and powerful influences set in motion by World War II, but no important new relationships were revealed by my analysis of area data. However, for the sake of others who may want to continue along this line of research, some of the compilations of statistics for areas are included in Appendix D.

A word or two on that most vexing of all problems—the comparability of data from various sources. Labor force statistics from the 1950 Census of Population come from complete counts of the population 14 years old and over, a 20-percent sample, a 3⅓-percent sample, and a sample used for fertility tabulations which averaged 2.4 percent. Thus, figures on number and characteristics of persons in the labor force will vary because of sampling variability alone. The 1940 data are also complete counts and sample estimates—a 5-percent sample in that year. Some of them have been adjusted for defects in enumeration; some have not. Prior to 1940, we have statistics based on a "gainful worker" concept, some of which have been revised for comparability with later data and others not. Finally, in the Current Population Survey series, the labor force measurement differs from the decennial census levels because of the superior training and experience of the current survey interviewers (see Chapter 2 and Appendix A). To adjust all these figures to a single base would be a great service to the general user, but it would require a prodigious expenditure of clerical resources and the use of many arbitrary, mechanical procedures whose effects might be to bias the basic data. Instead, I have attempted to follow the rule of adjusting the data as far as possible for comparability in measuring changes over past time or in making projections into the future, but otherwise I have used unadjusted statistics from any available source to provide evidence on the question at hand. In most cases, the conclusions would be the same, regardless of the source used or adjustment applied, but the procedure puts a heavy burden on the reader to examine table titles and notes. For this, I offer my sympathy and my regrets.

Any writer in a field as broad and as rich in experts as the labor force field must expect a group of lively critics. Therefore, in acknowledging the assistance I have received, I am anxious that I do not seem to share responsibility as well. John D. Durand reviewed my manuscript with great care, making many priceless suggestions and warning me away from the pitfalls I had dug for myself. I should like to record my gratitude and my debt to him without in any way implicating him in the final version. Gladys L. Palmer read early and late drafts, giving me a helping hand when I needed it most. My thanks to her, and to Conrad Taeuber for his criticisms and his monumental patience, cannot be adequately expressed here. Leon R. Paley, Robert B. Pearl, and Robert L. Stein contributed advice and other aid, particularly in connection with assembling and interpreting the Current Population Survey data. Several people worked long and hard on the preparation of this volume: Murray Gendell, who gave valuable assistance on the labor force projections and the 1940–1950 comparisons; Marian L. Hester, who did most of the calculations, posted countless tables, and was a Girl Friday of unvarying good humor; Thurma I. Halle, who uncomplainingly typed and retyped nearly illegible copy; and Ingrid L. Millison and Mildred M. Russell, who carefully edited text and tables. My dependence on all these individuals they know, but perhaps not the full measure of my gratitude.

Gertrude Bancroft

Washington, D. C.
July 1958

CONTENTS

CHAPTER 1

ECONOMIC ACTIVITY OF THE
POPULATION

The present study is devoted mainly to an examination of the ways in which the economic activity of the American people has been changing and of the factors underlying the changes. As an introduction to that examination, this chapter sets forth the concepts to be used and provides measures of the segment of the population that contributes in varying degrees to the national product of economic goods and services—the "economically active" population.

More than one type of measure of economic activity is needed to give an adequate account of the complexity and variety of ways of earning a living in a country as large as the United States. Much of the economic activity is part-time or part-year work. In many sections of the country and in many industries (agriculture, fishing, logging, construction, food processing), work is highly seasonal because of the climate or because of the cycle for particular crops. Expansion and contraction of activities in summer and winter resort areas and fluctuations in trade because of holiday peaks are also responsible for a considerable amount of job shifting and part-year employment. For other reasons too, American workers do not stay on the same job, month after month or year after year; at least one in ten workers changes jobs during the course of a year, and a large proportion of the job changes are made to improve economic status.[1] There is also a high degree of mobility in and out of the labor force on the part of married women. This variety of work attachments of individuals results in combinations of job holding within families that are probably more complex here than in many other countries. It is for these reasons, too, that labor force analysts have been concerned with refining the various measures of economic activity. (See Appendix C.)

Economic activity as defined in this study means the activity of working or seeking to work for pay or for profit in the worker's own or his family

---

[1] According to a Census Bureau survey covering job histories of persons who worked in 1955, 42 percent of the job changes during the year were made to improve status, and 16 percent were due to the termination of a temporary job. See *Current Population Reports*, "Job Mobility of Workers in 1955," Series P–50, No. 70, table E.

enterprise (business, farm, or profession); it also includes work without pay in a family enterprise. Over the course of his lifetime, virtually every man, unless hopelessly handicapped by physical or mental illness, will be "economically active" in this sense. Perhaps four out of every five women will work at a paid job or in a family enterprise at some time in their lives.[2]

At any given time, however, the active population will be only a portion of the total of potential workers. Some will be too young or fully oc-cupied with their education, and some will be too old to work; ill health and disability will prevent the employment of others; and seasonal factors, determining the demand for workers in some industries and areas, will also affect the number of economically active. For women, the need and desire to make homes and care for children are powerful deterrents to eco-nomic activity. For both men and women, there are also variations in intensity of activity—the number of hours worked in a week or weeks worked in a year—that reflect these as well as other factors.

The most sharply focused picture of the economically active population is provided by statistics on the current labor force—those persons 14 years of age and over who, *during a specific calendar week,* had jobs (the employed), or were seeking them (the unemployed), or were on active duty in the Armed Forces. All persons who did any work at all for pay or profit, or who worked without pay in a family business or farm for 15 hours or more, are counted as employed. Persons absent from their jobs all week and not seeking other jobs are also counted as employed. Those who did not work but were looking for work are counted as unemployed.[3]

---

[2] In 1946, a Census Bureau survey found that almost four out of every five women in the working age population had done some kind of work during their lifetime. Since that date, there has been a grow-ing tendency for women in their middle years to work, even though they have not held paid jobs prior to marriage.

[3] Detailed definitions of the employment status categories follow:

The *employed* comprise those who, during the survey week, were either (1) "at work"—those who did any work for pay or profit, or worked without pay for 15 hours or more on a family farm or busi-ness; or (2) "with a job but not at work"—those who did not work and were not looking for work but had a job or business from which they were temporarily absent because of vacation, illness, industrial dispute, or bad weather, or because they were taking time off for various other reasons. Prior to 1957, the statistics also included in the group "with a job but not at work" persons on layoff who had definite instructions to return to work within 30 days of the date of layoff—now classified as unem-ployed—and persons waiting to report to new wage and salary jobs scheduled to start within the fol-lowing 30 days, now classified either as unemployed or (if in school during the survey week) as not in the labor force.

The *unemployed* include those who did not work at all during the survey week and were looking for work. Also included as unemployed are those who did not work at all during the survey week and—

1. Were waiting to be called back to a job from which they had been laid off; or
2. Were waiting to report to a new wage or salary job scheduled to start within the following 30 days (and were not in school during the survey week); or
3. Would have been looking for work except that they were temporarily ill or believed no work was available in their line of work or in the community.

Not in the labor force includes all civilians 14 years of age and over who are not classified as em-ployed or unemployed. These persons are further classified as "engaged in own home housework," "in school," "unable to work" because of long-term physical or mental illness, "in institutions," and "other." The "other" group includes for the most part retired persons, those reported as too old to

Although the term "labor force" may have many meanings in popular usage (e.g., in a narrow sense, the work force of a specific factory, or broadly, the entire population with work skills), the definition just cited has come to be accepted as the official technical definition, based on many years of research with the data from the Current Population Survey of the Census Bureau and from the 1940 and 1950 Decennial Censuses. In this volume, then, the "labor force" will continue to be used to describe the population that is economically active during a single calendar week.

The labor force in 1956

During 1956, in an average week, there were just over 70 million persons 14 years of age and over[4] in the American labor force, or two-fifths of the total population of 168 million[5] (table 1 and figure 1). The actual number who worked full time (defined as 35 hours or more during the week) in civilian jobs was only 50.6 million in an average week. Another 11 million worked part time; 4 million of these usually worked full time, and 7 million, the majority of them women, usually worked part time. Persons who usually worked full time but had less than 35 hours work during a given week are those who took time off for illness or holidays, or were unable to work a full week for such reasons as bad weather, slack work, or because they were laid off from their jobs. Persons who usually worked part time did so because of age or poor health, or because they had other commitments such as home housework and family care or attendance at school.

The balance of the labor force in the typical week in 1956 made no actual contribution to the civilian economy during the week, although they may have drawn pay for past work or unemployment benefits based on previous employment. About 3.2 million had jobs but were absent all week, chiefly because of vacation, illness, or other personal matters. They, along with 61.8 million at work, make up the employed group, which constituted 92.3 percent of the labor force in 1956. About 2.6 million persons or 3.6 percent of the labor force were unemployed, that is, out of work and seeking jobs, many of them entering the labor force for the first time. The

work, the voluntarily idle, and seasonal workers for whom the survey week fell in an offseason and who were not reported as unemployed. Persons doing only incidental unpaid family work (less than 15 hours) are also classified as not in the labor force.

[4] Children under 14 are excluded by definition from the labor force. Some of them do work on farms, however, and as newsboys, delivery boys, baby sitters, mother's helpers, helpers in stores, etc. Two surveys in 1950 gave their number (aged 10 to 13) at about 1,100,000 in August and 700,000 in October. In months when work is slack on farms, the number is probably much smaller.

[5] These statistics, and all others in this volume described as at "current survey levels," are from the monthly sample survey of the population conducted by the Bureau of the Census—the Current Population Survey. A detailed description of that survey of the concepts and methods used, and of the sampling design is available in *Current Population Reports*, "Concepts and Methods used in the Current Labor Force Statistics Prepared by the Bureau of the Census," Series P–23, No. 2, and "Expansion of the Current Population Survey Sample: 1956," P–23, No. 3.

remainder of the labor force, 2.8 million persons, was in the Armed Forces, stationed in this country or abroad, providing protection and security but for the most part not available for other contributions to the economy.

TABLE 1.—EMPLOYMENT STATUS OF THE POPULATION, BY SEX: ANNUAL AVERAGES, 1956

[Current survey levels]

Employment status	Total		Male		Female	
	Number (thousands)	Percent	Number (thousands)	Percent	Number (thousands)	Percent
Total, all ages.............	168,030	100.0	83,327	100.0	84,703	100.0
Labor force, 14 years old and over..	70,387	41.9	48,579	58.3	21,808	25.7
Not in labor force.................	97,643	58.1	34,748	41.7	62,895	74.3
LABOR FORCE						
Total........................	70,387	100.0	48,579	100.0	21,808	100.0
Armed Forces[1]......................	2,857	4.1	2,823	5.8	34	0.2
Civilian labor force...............	67,530	95.9	45,756	94.2	21,774	99.8
Employed......................	64,979	92.3	44,148	90.9	20,831	95.5
At work full time..............	50,641	71.9	36,530	75.2	14,111	64.7
At work part time..............	11,178	15.9	5,638	11.6	5,540	25.4
Usually work full time........	4,112	5.9	2,838	5.8	1,274	5.8
Usually work part time........	7,066	10.0	2,800	5.8	4,266	19.6
With a job but not at work......	3,160	4.5	1,980	4.1	1,180	5.4
Unemployed......................	2,551	3.6	1,608	3.3	943	4.3
NOT IN LABOR FORCE						
Total........................	97,643	100.0	34,748	100.0	62,895	100.0
Under 14 years old[2].................	47,852	49.0	24,404	70.2	23,448	37.3
14 years old and over.............	49,791	51.0	10,344	29.8	39,447	62.7
Keeping house.................	33,399	34.1	93	0.3	33,306	52.9
Going to school....................	6,593	6.8	3,289	9.5	3,304	5.3
Unable to work..................	1,943	2.0	1,127	3.2	816	1.3
In institutions[3]...................	1,444	1.5	879	2.5	565	0.9
Other..........................	6,412	6.6	4,956	14.3	1,456	2.3

Note: Annual averages are averages of observations for survey week in each month.

[1] Independent estimate of Armed Forces, including those stationed overseas.

[2] Excluded from labor force by definition. Special surveys in 1950 indicated an estimated 600,000 aged 10 to 13 working in agriculture and 500,000 in other industries in a peak summer month.

[3] Based on 1950 Census of Population.

Source: Derived from U. S. Bureau of the Census, *Current Population Reports*, Series P-50, No. 72, tables 1 and 17; *1950 Census of Population*, Vol. II, *Characteristics of the Population*, Part 1, U. S. Summary, table 50; unpublished estimates of the Bureau of the Census; and unpublished tabulations of Current Population Survey data.

Most of the employed workers in the United States (over 80 percent in 1956) work for wages or salaries,[6] the vast majority of them in nonagricultural industries (table 2 and figure 2). Self-employed workers, who operate their own unincorporated business or professions, constituted less than 10 percent of the total employed, and those who operated their own farms about 6 percent. Less than 2 million, or about 3 percent, were unpaid family workers—persons working without pay on their family farm or in their family business. These are family members who, during the week of reference, worked for 15 hours or more at tasks that contribute to the operation of the family enterprise. Needless to say, it is not always easy to distinguish, particularly in farm households, between work that

[6] The class-of-worker and industry designations relate to the job in which the person worked the greatest number of hours during the week. Approximately 3.7 million persons (5.5 percent of the total employed) worked at more than one job in July 1956.

contributes to the operation of the family enterprise and work that is incidental to the home management. Moreover, many farm women and children regard their farm work as part of their household chores and do not report it to the survey or census interviewer.

FIGURE 1.—EMPLOYMENT STATUS OF THE LABOR FORCE, BY SEX, IN AN AVERAGE WEEK: 1956

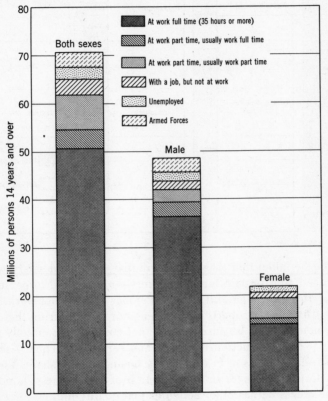

Note: Based on data in table 1.

TABLE 2.—TYPE OF INDUSTRY AND CLASS OF WORKER OF EMPLOYED PERSONS, BY SEX:
ANNUAL AVERAGES, 1956

[Current survey levels]

Type of industry and class of worker	Total		Male		Female	
	Number (thousands)	Percent	Number (thousands)	Percent	Number (thousands)	Percent
Total employed..............	64,979	100.0	44,148	100.0	20,831	100.0
Agriculture......................	6,585	10.1	5,278	12.0	1,307	6.3
Wage and salary workers.......	1,692	2.6	1,394	3.2	298	1.4
Self-employed workers.........	3,570	5.5	3,391	7.7	179	0.9
Unpaid family workers.........	1,323	2.0	493	1.1	830	4.0
Nonagricultural industries......	58,394	89.9	38,870	88.0	19,524	93.7
Wage and salary workers.......	51,877	79.9	33,934	76.8	17,943	86.1
Self-employed workers.........	5,936	9.1	4,863	11.0	1,073	5.2
Unpaid family workers.........	581	0.9	73	0.2	508	2.4

Source: Derived from U. S. Bureau of the Census, *Current Population Reports*, Series P–50, No. 72, table 12.

FIGURE 2.—PERCENT DISTRIBUTION OF EMPLOYED PERSONS, BY TYPE OF INDUSTRY, CLASS OF WORKERS, AND SEX: 1956

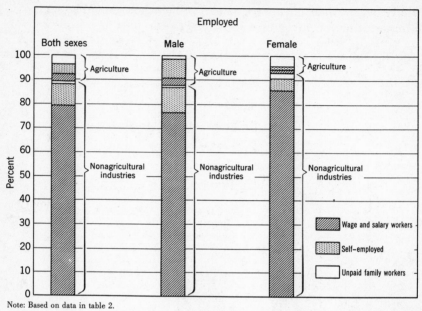

Note: Based on data in table 2.

It should be noted that these three groups—wage and salary workers, self-employed, and unpaid family workers—are limited to persons who actually perform some gainful work. Persons who do not work but who draw rent from their property or dividends or interest from their investments are not included because they are not contributing directly by their own labor to the production of goods and services. Thus, a man who supplies capital to his son to establish a business, who shares the profits but takes no part whatever in the operation of the business, is not in the labor force unless he has other activities that qualify him.

In 1956, in the average week, there were more than twice as many men as women in the civilian labor force (45.8 million versus 21.8 million) and in the labor force employed full time (38.5 million versus 15.3 million) (table 3). An equal number of men and women actually worked part time (5½ million), but most of these women usually worked part time whereas half the men on part-time schedules usually worked full time at their jobs.

In our society, "wage earners" traditionally have been thought of as adult men, but in 1956, men 20 to 64 years of age numbered only 40 million out of 67.5 million in the civilian labor force, or about 60 percent. Women in the same age group in the labor force numbered 18.8 million and constituted an important segment of the total (28 percent). Men and women 65 years and over made up 5 percent of the total civilian labor force, and boys and girls in their teens about 8 percent (tables 3 and 4).

TABLE **3.**—EMPLOYMENT STATUS OF THE CIVILIAN LABOR FORCE, BY AGE AND SEX: ANNUAL AVERAGES, 1956

[Current survey levels. Numbers in thousands]

Employment status and sex	Total, 14 years and over		14 to 19 years	20 to 64 years	65 years and over
	Number	Percent			
Both sexes.....................	67,530	100.0	5,274	58,830	3,426
Male..........................	45,756	67.8	3,097	40,055	2,604
Employed......................	44,148	65.4	2,801	38,827	2,520
Full time[1]...................	38,510	57.0	1,393	35,271	1,846
Agriculture................	4,162	6.2	372	3,319	471
Nonagricultural industries.......	34,348	50.8	1,021	31,952	1,375
Part time.....................	5,638	8.4	1,408	3,556	674
Usually work full time.........	2,838	4.2	149	2,525	164
Agriculture................	520	0.8	52	394	74
Nonagricultural industries.......	2,318	3.4	97	2,131	90
Usually work part time.........	2,800	4.2	1,259	1,031	510
Agriculture................	596	0.9	263	171	162
Nonagricultural industries.......	2,204	3.3	996	860	348
Unemployed....................	1,608	2.4	296	1,228	84
Female........................	21,774	32.2	2,177	18,775	822
Employed......................	20,831	30.8	1,963	18,063	805
Full time[1]...................	15,291	22.6	1,099	13,720	472
Agriculture................	606	0.9	78	490	38
Nonagricultural industries.......	14,685	21.7	1,021	13,230	434
Part time.....................	5,540	8.2	864	4,343	333
Usually work full time.........	1,274	1.9	103	1,140	31
Agriculture................	76	0.1	13	61	2
Nonagricultural industries.......	1,198	1.8	90	1,079	29
Usually work part time.........	4,266	6.3	761	3,203	302
Agriculture................	625	0.9	65	502	58
Nonagricultural industries.......	3,641	5.4	696	2,701	244
Unemployed....................	943	1.4	214	712	17

[1] Includes persons with a job but not at work all week, a small fraction (about one-tenth) of whom usually work part time.

Source: Derived from U. S. Bureau of the Census, *Current Population Reports*, Series P-50, No. 72, tables 8, 9, and 10, and unpublished tabulations of Current Population Survey data.

TABLE **4.**—AGE DISTRIBUTION OF MAJOR COMPONENTS OF THE CIVILIAN LABOR FORCE, BY SEX: ANNUAL AVERAGES, 1956

[Current survey levels]

Employment status and sex	Total, 14 years old and over	14 to 19 years	20 to 64 years	65 years and over
Both sexes....................	100.0	7.8	87.1	5.1
Male........................	100.0	6.8	87.5	5.7
Employed....................	100.0	6.3	88.0	5.7
Agriculture................	100.0	13.0	73.6	13.4
Nonagricultural industries...........	100.0	5.4	89.9	4.7
Unemployed.................	100.0	18.4	76.4	5.2
Female......................	100.0	10.0	86.2	3.8
Employed....................	100.0	9.4	86.7	3.9
Agriculture................	100.0	11.9	80.6	7.5
Nonagricultural industries...........	100.0	9.3	87.1	3.6
Unemployed.................	100.0	22.7	75.5	1.8

Source: Same as table 3.

In the central age group the vast majority of men typically were full-time workers, and 9 out of 10 worked in nonagricultural industries (table 5). Women in the 20 to 64 age group were also predominantly full-time workers (almost 75 percent), but a significant proportion (17 percent) usually worked part time. Among teen-agers the situation was reversed; a larger proportion of boys in the labor force than of girls usually worked

part time, for boys are more likely than girls to combine part-time work
with school or college attendance.

Youth and old age are both periods when part-time work may be preferred to full-time work, for obvious reasons. However, older men (65
and over) are much more likely to be working full time than are boys just
entering the labor force, according to 1956 experience. As far as women
are concerned, regular part-time work is equally common at both ends of
the age range.

TABLE 5.—PERCENT DISTRIBUTION OF THE CIVILIAN LABOR FORCE BY EMPLOYMENT STATUS,
BY AGE AND SEX: ANNUAL AVERAGES, 1956

[Current survey levels]

Employment status and sex	Total, 14 years old and over	14 to 19 years	20 to 64 years	65 years and over
Male..............................	100.0	100.0	100.0	100.0
Employed.........................	96.5	90.4	96.9	96.8
Full time[1].......................	84.2	45.0	88.0	70.9
Agriculture..................	9.1	12.0	8.2	18.1
Nonagricultural industries...........	75.1	33.0	79.8	52.8
Part time........................	12.3	45.4	8.9	25.9
Usually work full time..................	6.2	4.8	6.3	6.3
Agriculture..................	1.1	1.7	1.0	2.8
Nonagricultural industries...........	5.1	3.1	5.3	3.5
Usually work part time..................	6.1	40.6	2.6	19.6
Agriculture..................	1.3	8.5	0.4	6.2
Nonagricultural industries...........	4.8	32.1	2.2	13.4
Unemployed........................	3.5	9.6	3.1	3.2
Female..............................	100.0	100.0	100.0	100.0
Employed.........................	95.7	90.2	96.2	97.9
Full time[1].......................	70.2	50.5	73.1	57.4
Agriculture..................	2.8	3.6	2.6	4.6
Nonagricultural industries...........	67.4	46.9	70.5	52.8
Part time........................	25.5	39.7	23.1	40.5
Usually work full time..................	5.9	4.7	6.0	3.8
Agriculture..................	0.4	0.6	0.3	0.3
Nonagricultural industries...........	5.5	4.1	5.7	3.5
Usually work part time..................	19.6	35.0	17.1	36.7
Agriculture..................	2.9	3.0	2.7	7.0
Nonagricultural industries...........	16.7	32.0	14.4	29.7
Unemployed........................	4.3	9.8	3.8	2.1

[1] Includes persons with a job but not at work all week, a small fraction (about one-tenth) of whom usually work part
time.

Source: Same as table 3.

American agriculture relies to a much greater extent than do other
industries on young workers and workers past 65 (table 4). Over 25
percent of the male agricultural workers and 20 percent of the female
workers were in these age groups, many of them working as unpaid family
workers. At these ages it might be said to be either too early or too late
to seek other, more remunerative, types of work.

The foregoing description has concerned the employed segment of the
civilian labor force. The unemployed segment was close to a minimum
level in 1956 and was heavily weighted with young people who tend to
change jobs frequently and to report brief periods of looking for work
while they try to locate the jobs they prefer. About one in five of the
persons looking for work in an average week in 1956 was under 20 years

of age; the unemployment rate of this age group (the percent of the civilian labor force that was unemployed) was 10 percent, or about three times the rate for adult workers. Among adult workers, too, much of the unemployment could be called frictional unemployment, because it arose from voluntary job changes or the job seeking of women returning to the labor force.

Persons not in the labor force in 1956

Persons who were not in the labor force in the average week of 1956 numbered 97.6 million or 58 percent of the total population (table 1 and figure 3). This segment may be described as dependent on the productive activity of the labor force, although some members are financially independent because of their own or some other person's activity in the past. Almost one-half—47.9 million—were children under 14; a small proportion did some work but, except for the rare prodigy, were still dependent on their families or someone else. Women who were keeping house for their families—33.4 million of them—were the next largest group outside the current labor force. Young people wholly occupied with school or college work numbered 6.6 million. An almost equal number (6.4 million) were retired, voluntarily idle, temporarily ill, or out of the labor force during the slack season or for other reasons. Almost 2 million persons were unable to work because of a long-term physical or mental disability; this should be regarded as only an approximation of the number of disabled in the population because of the necessary crudeness of such a classification obtained in a general population survey.

FIGURE 3.—LABOR FORCE STATUS OF THE POPULATION OF THE UNITED STATES: 1956

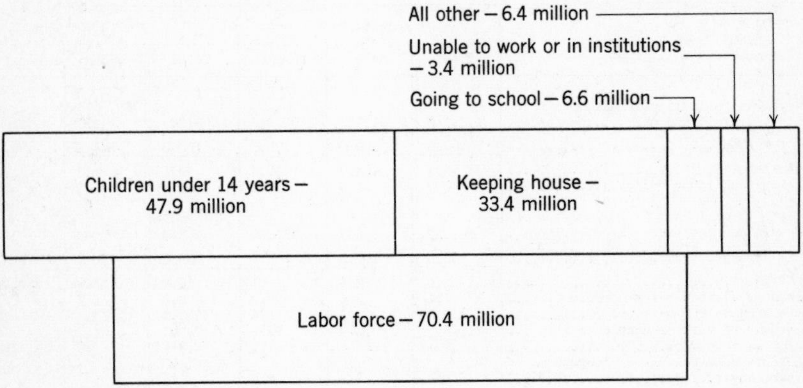

All other — 6.4 million
Unable to work or in institutions — 3.4 million
Going to school — 6.6 million

Children under 14 years — 47.9 million

Keeping house — 33.4 million

Labor force — 70.4 million

Note: Based on data in table 1.

The last group outside the labor force comprises persons in institutions (penal; homes for the aged, infirm, and needy; mental institutions; tuberculosis sanitariums; and similar places). In the structure of labor force definitions, inmates of such institutions have been classed entirely outside the labor force, although a few do perform work and receive pay for it. As a group they are not able to engage in economic activity in the free labor market and are dependent on others—their families, private charity, the State—for their support.

Although it is convenient to talk about persons in the labor force and those not in the labor force as two separate and distinct parts of the population, there is a great deal of movement from one segment to the other from time to time, as we shall see, and even at a single moment there is some uncertainty of classification for persons at the margin. In June 1947 and again in August 1955, persons reported as outside the current labor force in the Current Population Survey were asked whether or not they wanted to work for pay (or operate a business) at that time. The vast majority replied that they did not (table 6). The results are remarkably similar at the two dates for women. The increase in the proportion in the labor force (from 33.3 percent to 35.8 percent) was accompanied by a slight increase in the proportion of those not in the current labor force who would have liked to work—from 4.9 percent to 6.1 percent. At both dates, however, almost all the women who were not members of the labor force did not want to work at the time of the interview. For men, comparability between the two dates is affected by the fact that a large number of World War II veterans were temporarily not in the labor force in 1947, either because they were attending school or were postponing the return to work for other reasons. The 1955 figure of 8.8 percent who wanted to work is more consistent with normal postwar conditions.

TABLE 6.—LABOR FORCE ATTACHMENT OF THE POPULATION: 1955 AND 1947

[Current survey levels]

Labor force attachment	August 1955			June 1947		
	Total	Male	Female	Total	Male	Female
Civilian noninstitutional population 14 years old and over....thousands..	114,548	54,580	59,968	106,009	51,522	54,487
Percent...........................	100.0	100.0	100.0	100.0	100.0	100.0
Current labor force.....................	59.1	84.7	35.8	59.1	86.3	33.3
Not in current labor force...............	40.9	15.3	64.2	40.9	13.7	66.7
Not in current labor force....thous..	46,823	8,335	38,488	43,399	7,062	36,337
Percent...........................	100.0	100.0	100.0	100.0	100.0	100.0
Want to work...........................	6.5	8.8	6.1	6.7	15.8	4.9
Currently available for work...........	4.4	7.6	3.7	2.8	6.4	2.0
Not available for work.................	2.1	1.2	2.4	3.9	9.4	2.9
Do not want to work or unable to work....	93.5	91.2	93.9	93.3	84.2	95.1
Do not want to work...................	88.1	73.4	91.3	(1)	(1)	(1)
Unable to work because of long-term disability...........................	5.4	17.8	2.6	(1)	(1)	(1)

[1] Not available.

Source: Derived from U. S. Bureau of the Census, *Current Population Reports*, Series P-57, No. 158, table 5; Series P-58, No. 4, table 1; and unpublished tabulations of Current Population Survey data.

Thus a small proportion of the population outside the labor force may prefer to be gainfully employed, although they for some reason do not report themselves looking for work. But the overwhelming majority at the moment appear to be satisfied to perform some other role (home-maker, student, etc.) as dependents, or, if not satisfied, have no other choice because of age or other handicaps.[7]

Among the group outside the labor force are many potential workers, including some who say they do not want to work currently but will become available later, perhaps replacing other workers or perhaps constituting additional workers. Of the 3.3 million boys not in the labor force in an average week in 1956 because they were in school, virtually all will be in the labor force eventually. A large fraction of the 3.3 million girls in school will also work, at least temporarily. Among the group keeping house and those not in the labor force for other reasons (the retired and voluntarily idle) are also some potential workers. They include persons who will work only seasonally or occasionally when the job situation is right. In addition, there are older, semi-retired persons who often want light work but do not seek it actively; women who will take a job when they can arrange for the care of their children or other family responsi-bilities; those who will join the full-time labor force when their children are grown up or in school, whether or not their husbands are employed; and women who will enter the labor force if need arises in their families. Although for many purposes it would be useful to know their numbers, there is no provision in the present system of labor force concepts for identifying persons not in the labor force who are potential workers and may be expected to enter the working force shortly. (See Appendix C.)

Seasonal variation in the labor force

One type of movement in and out of the labor force that is fairly reg-ular and is susceptible to prediction is that associated with the seasonal expansion and contraction of the total. These labor force entries and exits reflect the agricultural planting, cultivating, and harvesting periods; the peak demands in retail trade at Easter and Christmas time; the curtail-ment of outdoor activities—construction, fishing, lumbering industries in bad-weather months; the school summer vacation period, when many teachers drop out of the labor force and large numbers of students enter to

---

[7] Reinterviews with a subsample of women not in the labor force in May 1955 for the purpose of verifying their original classification revealed that 58 percent were thoroughgoing homemakers and believed they would never work or would work only in an emergency, 22 percent were still in school or were too old or ill to work, and 20 percent planned to look for work soon or when their family re-sponsibilities lightened. The percent who thought they would not work under any circumstances or only in an emergency varied with the occupational status of the principal worker in the family and was highest at the highest occupational levels:

Occupational group of principal worker in family	*Percent of women who would never work or would work only in emergency*
Professional and managerial workers	70
Clerical and sales workers	58
Craftsmen, foremen, and kindred workers	55
Operatives, service workers, and nonfarm laborers	52

form part of the labor supply for industries having a demand for temporary workers in the summer time (agriculture, recreational activities, construction, and others). The size of the civilian labor force in each month in 1956 is presented in table 7, together with the factors that have been developed to adjust for the seasonal changes.

TABLE 7.—CIVILIAN LABOR FORCE, BY SEX, AND SEASONAL ADJUSTMENT FACTORS: 1956

[Current survey levels]

| Month | Civilian labor force (thousands) | | | Seasonal adjustment factors[1] | | | | |
| | | | | 14 years old and over | | | 14 to 19 years | |
	Total	Male	Female	Total	Male	Female	Male	Female
January....................	65,775	44,938	20,837	98.2	98.7	97.2	85.7	86.8
February...................	65,490	44,818	20,672	98.2	98.8	97.6	85.5	86.7
March......................	65,913	45,071	20,842	98.6	98.8	97.9	86.6	86.0
April......................	66,555	45,361	21,194	99.0	99.3	98.1	90.1	87.2
May........................	67,846	45,832	22,014	99.7	99.7	99.5	95.1	90.8
June.......................	69,430	47,118	22,312	101.9	102.0	101.3	125.7	118.5
July.......................	69,489	47,168	22,321	102.1	102.7	100.4	133.9	125.0
August.....................	68,947	46,876	22,071	101.9	102.4	100.8	127.6	123.2
September..................	68,069	45,697	22,372	100.8	100.1	102.4	97.2	104.2
October....................	68,082	45,550	22,532	100.6	99.5	103.1	93.4	99.7
November...................	67,732	45,508	22,224	100.3	99.5	102.3	92.4	97.7
December...................	67,029	45,135	21,894	98.8	98.6	99.3	86.9	94.1

[1] Annual average equals 100; based largely on monthly data for the period 1952 through 1956. Ratio-to-moving-average method used to compute factors. See *Current Population Reports*, Series P-50, No. 82, for detailed description of method used.

Source: Derived from U. S. Bureau of the Census, *Current Population Reports*, Series P-50, No. 72, table 6, and unpublished estimates.

In the labor force of all ages the seasonal swing ranges from a low of 98.2 in January and February to a high of 102.1 in July (annual average = 100). The pattern for the female labor force is slightly different, with a peak in October, when the activity of cotton picking is at its height. This seasonal pattern generally reflects the seasonal activity of adult workers. Teen-age workers, because they alternate labor force activity with attendance at full-time school, have a much sharper seasonal pattern. The July peak for boys is 33.9 percent above the annual average and for girls 25 percent above. At the low point in the early months of the year, the seasonal factors are about 85 percent of the average.

Year-to-year change in the labor force

The labor force normally can be expected to grow from one year to the next because of the growth of population alone; this growth in the labor force has in the past been estimated at 500,000 to 700,000 each year (at current survey levels). The actual change from year to year has varied greatly with the demand for manpower for the Armed Forces and for civilian jobs (table 8). World War II mobilization brought the labor force from 56 million in 1940 (or 56 percent of the population 14 years and over) to almost 66 million in 1944 (63 percent of the population). The increase averaged about 2.5 million a year. After the postwar demobilization, the labor force expanded sharply again by abnormally large amounts because of the flood of war veterans who had previously delayed their return to peacetime work.   Again, during the period of Korean hostilities, both the Armed Forces and civilian production facilities called on the manpower resources of the country, and a million or more persons were added both in 1950 and again in 1951.   High levels of peacetime economic activity in 1955 and 1956 were also characterized by expansions of a million or more in the number of workers and a rising proportion of the population participating in the labor force.

TABLE **8.**—PERSONS 14 YEARS OLD AND OVER IN THE LABOR FORCE: 1940 TO 1956

[Current survey levels]

Year	Annual average labor force (thousands)		Per-cent in labor force[1]	Year	Annual average labor force (thousands)		Per-cent in labor force[1]
	Number	Year-to-year change			Number	Year-to-year change	
1956....................	70,387	+1,491	59.3	1947....................	61,608	+776	57.3
1955....................	68,896	+1,077	58.7	1946....................	60,832	-4,320	57.2
1954....................	67,819	+457	58.4	1945....................	65,152	-744	61.8
1953....................	67,362	+952	58.5	1944....................	65,896	+1,506	63.1
1952....................	66,410	+578	58.7	1943....................	64,390	+4,160	62.2
1951....................	65,832	+1,233	58.8	1942....................	60,230	+2,850	58.8
1950....................	64,599	+1,028	58.4	1941....................	57,380	+1,350	56.6
1949....................	63,571	+822	58.0	1940....................	56,030	...	55.9
1948....................	62,749	+1,141	57.8				

[1] Percent of noninstitutional population 14 years old and over.

Source: Derived from U. S. Bureau of the Census, *Current Population Reports*, Series P–50, No. 61, table 1, and No. 72, tables A and B.

That the labor force will expand with military mobilization is obvious, but it is generally agreed by now that expanding job opportunities will also draw into the labor force persons who had previously remained outside because working conditions or pay scales were not sufficiently attractive. Whether the labor force contracts when job opportunities decline is not so clear.   There is some reason to think that groups with alternative activities or means of support may retire from the labor force when jobs become scarce.   Housewives may decide that staying home is preferable to working at the available jobs or continuing the search for more satisfactory jobs.   Students may devote full time to their education.   Older workers, particularly those at or near retirement age, may decide to retire. Those who no longer look for work are, therefore, not counted among the unemployed, and the labor force will shrink or fail to show its expected growth.[8]

---

[8] Whether a prolonged depression will bring additional family members into the labor force when the family head loses his job, and thus expand the total size of the labor force, was a sharp controversy during the decade of the thirties; the problem remained unsettled because of the absence of current, consistent measurements of the labor force.   See, for example, W. S. Woytinsky, *Additional Workers and the Volume of Unemployment in the Depression*, Social Science Research Council, Pamphlet Series 1, 1940; D. D. Humphrey, "Alleged 'Additional Workers' in the Measurement of Unemployment," *Journal of Political Economy*, Vol. XLVIII, No. 3, June 1940; Clarence D. Long, *The Labor Force in Wartime America*, National Bureau of Economic Research, Occasional Paper 14, 1944; Gladys L. Palmer, *The Significance of Employment Patterns in Households for Labor Market Analysis*, Industrial Research Department, University of Pennsylvania, Special Report No. 8, 1942.

Thus, although the crude size of the labor force is by no means the most sensitive index of the status of the economy, it does have some utility as an indicator which is only beginning to be understood. Many people contend that although certain population groups may voluntarily enter the labor force in response to the opportunity to work, they will not voluntarily leave it when those job opportunities disappear. They argue that such withdrawals from the current labor force in times of contracting economic activity are fictitious; such workers should be considered part of the current labor force and classified as unemployed. This is a highly controversial point, involving not only concept but measurement. Nevertheless, the relatively small year-to-year changes in the size of the labor force during the mild recessions of 1949 and 1954 suggest that the labor force is flexible in more than one direction. There is also some reason to think that from time to time labor force growth may be borrowed from the future, and that periods of sharp growth may alternate with periods when growth is slow because the most readily available recruits have already been drawn into the work force.

Economic activity during a calendar year

In addition to statistics on the labor force, another measure of economic activity of the population is provided by data on persons who work at any time during the course of the year. There is a high rate of turnover in the labor force (4 to 5 percent per month on the average) because of the permanent entrance of new workers, the entrance and exit of seasonal workers, and the retirement or death of regular workers. In addition, there is a good deal of movement in and out of the working population on the part of women who withdraw from the labor force with marriage and childbirth and return when their home responsibilities lighten. Even when they have returned, some of them tend to work intermittently and for short periods of time. Accordingly, the number who work at all during the year is considerably larger than the number in the labor force in an average week. In 1955, the civilian labor force averaged 65,847,000, but the estimated number who had done some gainful work during 1955 was 75,353,000. (This latter figure relates only to persons who were still in the civilian noninstitutional population in January 1956 and does not include persons who entered the Armed Forces or institutions, left the country, or died during the year. It also probably fails to include some persons who worked only for short periods during the year.)

It is not possible to provide satisfactory estimates of the specific groups that move in or out of the labor force during the year, because the reasons for joining or leaving the labor force are not usually known. It has been roughly estimated that approximately 1.8 million persons enter the labor force for the first time each year; the number who retire or die or, in the case of women, leave to be married, to have a child, or for other reasons may be about 100,000 smaller.[9]   These figures do not include seasonal workers.   In August 1955, the peak month, there were an estimated 700,000 workers in the civilian labor force because of seasonal demands for labor; the extent to which they join the labor force in other months of high activity, or are replaced by similar temporary workers, cannot be determined.

Approximations of the total number and the characteristics of persons who work at some time during a calendar year but do not remain in the labor force are available (table 9).   In January 1956, 10.7 million persons not in the labor force were reported to have worked at some time in 1955.   The majority of persons who move in and out of the labor force during the year are, of course, housewives—6.1 million of the 10.7 million in 1955.   Over 3 million were school and college students who work during the summer or at some time during the year, but were not doing so in January 1956.   The third major group were men who were temporarily out of the civilian labor force because it was the offseason in their industry, because they were on their way in or out of military service, or because they had retired.

TABLE 9.—PERSONS NOT IN THE LABOR FORCE IN JANUARY 1956 WHO WORKED DURING 1955, BY STATUS IN JANUARY AND SEX

[Current survey levels]

Status in January 1956	Total	Male	Female
Total not in labor force in January 1956 who worked in 1955[1]..........	10,664,000	3,202,000	7,462,000
Keeping house.........................	6,103,000	30,000	6,073,000
Going to school.......................	3,198,000	1,955,000	1,243,000
Unable to work.......................	132,000	110,000	22,000
All other.............................	1,231,000	1,107,000	124,000

[1] Persons in civilian noninstitutional population in January 1956.

Source: U. S. Bureau of the Census, *Current Population Reports*, Series P–50, No. 68, table 7.

It should not be concluded that the 75 million people who worked during the period of a year would all be available for jobs at any single point in time.   Those who have retired from the labor force because of illness or age, because they have assumed responsibilities at home, or because they have entered full-time school have become unavailable for employment, some of them permanently.   Migration from an area of job opportunities to one with few openings for women may also mean a loss from the working population.   Certain types of workers want work only during particular seasons or at particular types of jobs, such as sales jobs at Christmas time, which do not exist at other times of the year.   Some

---

[9] Estimate of Stuart H. Garfinkle of the U. S. Bureau of Labor Statistics.   The growth in the labor force from year to year is due to the growth in the population of working age, the changes in labor force participation rates, and the re-entrance of married women who had previously worked.

women can work only if others do not—for example, mothers of young children who rely on relatives to take care of their children.

Another measure of the differential turnover in the labor force, and the greater elasticity of the female labor force, may be derived from a comparison of the weekly and annual figures in table 10. The number of men who worked at some time during 1955 was 6 percent above the number in the labor force during an average week in 1955, but the number of women working at some time exceeded the weekly average by 33 percent. In the central age groups, 25 to 64 years, most men are year-round workers, and there is very little difference between the two groups. But for teen-age boys and men past their midsixties, the number working at some time during the year exceeded the average labor force in these age groups by 25 percent or more. At these ages there was considerable movement in and out of the work force during the year, reflecting in part the process of entering or retiring from the labor force; and in part, the intermittent employment of those who are still attending school or are, at the older ages, in semi-retirement. For women, those between 35 and 64 years of age are the least likely to move in and out of the labor force during the year, but even at these ages, the number working at some time exceeded the average number in the labor force by about 25 percent. The excess in the youngest and oldest age groups was two or three times as great.

Some indication of the elasticity of the labor force in various occupation and industry groups may be obtained by a comparison of the populations employed in an average week and at some time during the year.

TABLE 10.—AGE AND SEX OF THE ECONOMICALLY ACTIVE POPULATION: 1955

[Current survey levels]

Age and sex	Economically active population		Ratio of number who worked during year to number in labor force in average week
	Civilian labor force during week (average)	Worked during 1955[1]	
Total................thousands..	65,847	75,353	114.4
Percent.........................	100.0	100.0	...
Male.................................	68.4	63.2	105.7
14 to 17 years.....................	2.5	3.4	155.3
18 and 19 years....................	2.0	2.1	124.6
20 to 24 years.....................	4.9	4.7	108.9
25 to 34 years.....................	16.4	14.4	100.3
35 to 44 years.....................	16.1	14.2	100.8
45 to 54 years.....................	13.4	11.9	101.9
55 to 64 years.....................	9.3	8.4	103.3
65 years and over..................	3.8	4.1	123.1
Female...............................	31.6	36.8	133.3
14 to 17 years.....................	1.4	2.2	185.0
18 and 19 years....................	1.6	2.0	139.2
20 to 24 years.....................	3.7	4.5	137.7
25 to 34 years.....................	6.5	7.5	133.8
35 to 44 years.....................	7.3	8.1	127.2
45 to 54 years.....................	6.3	6.8	123.5
55 to 64 years.....................	3.6	4.1	128.3
65 years and over..................	1.2	1.6	152.8

[1] Persons in civilian noninstitutional population in January 1956.

Source: Derived from U. S. Bureau of the Census, *Current Population Reports*, Series P-50, No. 67, table 6, and No. 68, table 1.

Farm laborers and foremen, service workers, and sales workers all make up a larger proportion of the annual total than of the weekly average (table 11). These are also occupations in which are frequently found youthful workers and women, both likely to work intermittently. Data on class of worker and industry tell the same story: wage workers and unpaid family workers in agriculture, men working in construction, and both men and women working in trade and in private households are more heavily represented in the annual figures than in the weekly figures (table 12). On the whole, the description of the occupational and industrial attachments of the working population based on employment in an average week closely resembles that based on a much longer period.

TABLE 11.—MAJOR OCCUPATION GROUP OF EMPLOYED PERSONS, BY SEX: 1955

[Current survey levels]

Major occupation group	Total		Male		Female	
	Employed during week[1] (average)	Worked during year[2]	Employed during week[1] (average)	Worked during year[2]	Employed during week[1] (average)	Worked during year[2]
Number of employed persons........thousands..	63,193	75,353	43,290	47,624	19,904	27,729
Percent.................................	100.0	100.0	100.0	100.0	100.0	100.0
Professional, technical, and kindred workers...	9.2	9.0	8.3	8.4	11.0	10.0
Farmers and farm managers..................	6.0	5.3	8.4	7.9	0.8	0.7
Managers, officials, and proprietors, except farm...................................	10.2	8.9	12.6	11.8	5.0	3.9
Clerical and kindred workers..................	13.3	13.4	6.5	6.2	28.2	25.6
Sales workers.................................	6.3	7.0	5.7	5.7	7.7	9.3
Craftsmen, foremen, and kindred workers........	13.2	12.1	18.8	18.6	1.1	0.9
Operatives and kindred workers.................	20.2	19.4	21.3	21.4	17.8	16.2
Private household workers......................	3.1	3.8	0.1	0.1	9.6	10.2
Service workers, except private household......	8.2	8.8	6.0	6.2	12.8	13.2
Farm laborers and foremen.....................	4.5	6.8	4.0	5.2	5.5	9.5
Laborers, except farm and mine.................	5.8	5.5	8.3	8.5	0.5	0.5

[1] Major job during survey week for annual average.
[2] Longest job in 1955 for persons who worked during the year.

Source: Derived from U. S. Bureau of the Census, *Current Population Reports*, Series P-50, No. 67, table 13, and No. 68, table 3.

Uses of data on the economic activity of the population

Information on economic activity does more than describe certain characteristics of the people; it furnishes broad measures of their levels of living and of their comparative well-being. The primary purpose served by the monthly statistics on the labor force that have been compiled in the United States since 1940 has been to provide a current economic indicator. The monthly survey was initiated for that purpose, to give up-to-date information on the volume and rate of unemployment and the characteristics of persons who were jobless. Variations in the unemployment rate of different groups in the labor force have proved to be highly sensitive to changing business conditions. As a consequence, the unemployment statistics have been adopted as one of the key series for business cycle analysis. Other measures, such as the changing volume of part-time work arising from economic causes and the duration of unemployment have also shown value in interpreting economic developments.

TABLE **12.**—MAJOR INDUSTRY GROUP AND CLASS OF WORKER OF EMPLOYED PERSONS,
BY SEX: 1955

[Current survey levels]

Major industry group and class of worker	Total		Male		Female	
	Employed during week[1] (average)	Worked during year[2]	Employed during week[1] (average)	Worked during year[2]	Employed during week[1] (average)	Worked during year[2]
Number of employed persons......thousands..	63,193	75,353	43,290	47,624	19,904	27,729
Percent.................................	100.0	100.0	100.0	100.0	100.0	100.0
Agriculture.............................	10.7	12.3	12.7	13.4	6.3	10.3
Wage and salary workers.................	2.7	3.3	3.3	3.7	1.5	2.5
Self-employed workers...................	5.9	5.2	8.3	7.8	0.7	0.7
Unpaid family workers...................	2.1	3.8	1.1	1.9	4.1	7.1
Nonagricultural industries.............	89.3	87.7	87.3	86.6	93.7	89.7
Wage and salary workers.................	79.2	78.1	76.1	75.6	86.0	82.4
Forestry, fisheries, and mining.........	1.2	1.2	1.7	1.7	0.1	0.1
Construction...........................	5.2	5.0	7.4	7.7	0.4	0.4
Manufacturing.........................	26.7	24.5	28.8	27.8	22.1	19.1
Durable goods.......................	15.3	13.9	18.3	17.7	8.9	7.5
Nondurable goods....................	11.4	10.6	10.5	10.1	13.2	11.6
Transportation, communication, and other public utilities.........................	6.9	6.5	8.3	8.2	4.0	3.6
Wholesale and retail trade..............	15.2	16.4	13.6	14.0	18.6	20.5
Service industries.....................	19.4	20.4	11.4	11.8	36.9	35.2
Private households.....................	3.5	4.3	0.6	0.9	9.9	10.1
Other.................................	15.9	16.1	10.8	10.9	27.0	25.1
Public administration...................	4.6	4.1	4.9	4.4	3.9	3.5
Self-employed workers...................	9.3	8.3	11.1	10.7	5.4	4.3
Unpaid family workers...................	0.8	1.3	0.1	0.3	2.3	3.0

[1] Major job during survey week for annual average.
[2] Longest job in 1955 for persons who worked during the year.

Source: Derived from U. S. Bureau of the Census, *Current Population Reports*, Series P–50, No. 68, table 2, and unpublished tabulation of Current Population Survey data.

These measures indicating the state of health of the economy are basic-ally, of course, descriptions of the condition of people—unlike data on production, prices, sales, etc. They can show directly the immediate impact of short-run factors, such as cutbacks in government expenditures on the affected workers themselves and their families. They can also trace the effects of more gradual economic and social changes and suggest changes in levels of living from one time to another, or from place to place.

The relative number of unemployed persons in a country, a region, or an area is fairly direct evidence of the comparative economic health of the community. For an adequate appraisal, however, it is necessary to know the types of persons who make up the total. During the recent years of high employment in this country, a large proportion of the unemployed (table 4) have been young people under 20; they are jobless, not because young people need experience and cannot get jobs without it but because they have many types of jobs to choose from and are trying first one and then another. This was not true in a depression year such as 1940, when inexperience was a serious handicap and unemployment rates were very high for young people. Again, the unemployment rate of women is cur-rently sometimes higher than that of men in the same age groups. This does not mean necessarily that women are being discriminated against in hiring, but that they have been entering the labor force in rather large numbers to look for work.

Underemployment, as measured by the number of persons who have less work than they want or need because work is slack in their industry, may be a substitute for complete unemployment or may accompany or precede it. In the United States, measurement of this form of underemployment was obtained from time to time until 1955 when it was included as a regular part of the monthly survey. Although underemployment has rarely been a severe problem at the national level during the years when it has been measured, in individual labor market areas where the major industries are declining (coal and textile areas, for example), underemployment of this kind has probably been serious. The type of underemployment that characterizes some of the agricultural sectors of this country, and is common in many other less industrialized countries, is reflected not in curtailed hours of work but in meager earnings in substandard industries or subsistence returns from marginal farming or handicraft operations. This form of underemployment, as well as that in which persons work at jobs that do not utilize their maximum skills, cannot be measured from statistics on the economic activity of the population alone.

A low level of unemployment and underemployment may not necessarily indicate high living standards, if at the same time the labor force is required to work long hours a week, with little or no time off during the year for vacations or holidays. It is necessary to examine also the hours worked by the employed. The progressive reduction of the average work week in the United States may have brought greater gains in terms of health and enrichment of the average worker's life than has any other improvement in his working conditions. The increase in the practice of granting paid vacations is another and more recent gain which doubtless would not have been achieved in a less prosperous decade.

Like the reduction in the work week, the elimination of the employment of children has been an objective of social programs in most industrial countries. Statistics on the rate of employment of school-age children provide a good indicator of both the progress in extending public education and the rising of levels of living to the point where families do not need the earnings of their young members. The elimination of child labor in almost all segments of the American economy except agriculture (where it is chiefly family work) was the principal reason for excluding children under 14 years of age from the measurement of the labor force in 1940 and subsequently. Much of the employment of teen-age youth now is part-time work after school or in vacations and is, in fact, encouraged by parents and school authorities alike. But some proportion of teen-age boys and girls do leave school to enter the labor force before completing their education, either because they are needed to help support the family or because they are misfits and unable to meet the standards required at school. Thus the proportion of the teen-age population in the labor force needs to be interpreted in the light of other information on school attendance, hours worked, and type of work performed.

The ability to retire from the labor force with sufficient savings and an adequate pension upon reaching an appropriate age has long been the goal of most individuals in the labor force; the development of government social security programs for these workers has been the political expression of this common desire. The long-term trend in the labor force participation of older men has been downward in this country for many reasons (see Chapter 2) and seems to have been reinforced by recent liberalization of Social Security benefits. However, what was once thought to be a clear benefit for the individual and for society (the retirement of the senior workers was regarded as making places for younger workers) is now being questioned. The prolongation of life and the extension of the time spent in retirement have raised a whole new set of problems which many experts on the aged think could be at least partially solved by continued employment of older citizens. It is no longer clear that further declines in labor force activity of persons past 65 or 70 would be an advantage to them or to society.

The same sort of uncertainty exists with respect to the increasing employment of women, particularly married women. In this country, prior to World War II, high labor force participation rates of married women were associated generally with low incomes and the prevalence in their communities of certain low-paid occupations (e.g., domestic service, textile operatives) or a high proportion of nonwhite women. High rates tended to be found in areas where the earnings of the male workers (usually family heads) were low. The unprecedented expansion in the economic activity of married women past 35 years during the war and in most of the postwar years when incomes have been rising has been primarily in response to a persistent, strong demand for workers in clerical, sales, and service occupations. No longer is the working wife found typically in families with inadequate earnings on the part of the main breadwinner. If it is possible to generalize from this experience, it might be said that high labor force participation rates for women in a relatively urban population, and particularly for married women, may reflect an advanced stage of industrial development in the society and some degree of stringency in the labor supply. Certainly any marked reduction in the economic activity of married women in this country would be interpreted as a weakening of the overall demand for workers and would be thought to foreshadow some reductions in family living standards.

The rate of employment of mothers of young children has far greater significance in social terms than does the rate for women whose children are older or have left home. Except for a relatively few women who have strong drives toward professional or artistic careers, most mothers of young children prefer to stay at home until their children go to school. The fact that the labor force rates of nonwhite mothers of children under 5 were twice those of white mothers in 1950 is one of the indicators of difference in the economic status of the two groups.

One of the most useful of the simple indexes of the social and economic levels of a population is the occupational distribution of its employed labor force, together with the designation by class of worker. Self-employed professional workers and salaried managers have the highest average incomes in the United States, and probably the highest social standing. Population groups with a high proportion of these workers and a low proportion of laborers and operatives are in a favorable position. Or in agricultural communities, the proportion of women engaged in unpaid family work is a significant index of economic level, except in those regions where, because of local custom, women share in the farming operation, regardless of family income. In this country, women work as unpaid family workers much more frequently in the South, particularly in Negro households and in some Midwestern States, than they do in the North and West.

The higher social status associated with white-collar occupations means that changes in the proportion of any group employed in such jobs (professional and technical, managerial, clerical, and sales) are a useful measure of social progress. For example, although the movement of the nonwhite labor force out of farm and domestic-service occupations in this country was a major change during World War II years, the proportion employed in white-collar jobs is still small in comparison with the white proportion —12 percent as compared with 42 percent in 1955; in 1948, the comparable proportions were 9 percent and 39 percent. Thus, recent advances in education and the reduction in job barriers may have been great relative to the slow progress of the past, but they have not been sufficient yet to bring the occupational structure of the nonwhite labor force very close to that of white workers (table 13).

TABLE **13.**—PERCENT DISTRIBUTION OF EMPLOYED PERSONS BY MAJOR OCCUPATION GROUP, BY COLOR: ANNUAL AVERAGES, 1955 AND 1948

[Current survey levels]

Major occupation group	1955		1948	
	White	Nonwhite	White	Nonwhite
Total employed...............................	100.0	100.0	100.0	100.0
Professional, technical, and kindred workers.......	9.8	3.5	7.2	2.4
Farmers and farm managers.........................	6.0	5.0	7.8	8.5
Managers, officials, and proprietors, except farm..	11.1	2.3	11.6	2.3
Clerical and kindred workers......................	14.2	4.9	13.6	3.3
Sales workers.....................................	6.9	1.3	6.7	1.1
Craftsmen, foremen, and kindred workers............	14.1	5.2	14.6	5.3
Operatives and kindred workers....................	20.2	20.9	21.0	20.1
Private household workers.........................	1.8	14.8	1.5	15.6
Service workers, except private household..........	7.2	16.8	6.4	14.7
Farm laborers and foremen.........................	3.9	9.5	4.6	12.5
Laborers, except farm and mine....................	4.7	15.8	4.9	14.3

Note: Averages based on data for four quarterly months—January, April, July, and October.

Source: U. S. Bureau of the Census, *Current Population Reports*, Series P–50, No. 66, table 3.

Dependent population

The division of the population into the productive and the dependent segments on the basis of economic activity as defined here is certainly an unrealistic one in many ways.   A large segment of the population—namely women engaged only in their own home housework and by definition not economically active—perform functions that most families could not afford to purchase in today's labor market or could not even find persons to perform at any price, at least in some areas.   Anyone who has tried to provide paid substitutes for the mother of young children or the wife of an invalid husband can testify to this.   Similarly, householders who have to hire the services of a variety of skilled and not-so-skilled workers to do the odd jobs of carpentry, plumbing, or painting that many American husbands perform might consider that the exclusion of "work around the house" from the definition of labor force activity is also unreal.   Probably only children, old people, the disabled, the institutionalized, and the small proportion of the population in this country who want to be completely idle and can afford it can really be said to perform no useful services, and even some of the "idle" contribute voluntary services of significant value to the community.   On the other hand, many persons who do some work in the course of a year produce, in fact, very little; in 1955, 10 percent worked only 13 weeks or less and averaged less than $500.   True measures of dependency would have to evaluate the services performed and set them off against the amount of consumption of each individual, but calculations of this nature, even for broad types of workers and nonworkers, would not be feasible.   For comparison with previous dates and with other countries, the crude measure of dependency, the proportion of workers and nonworkers, must be used.

Because of the large amount of intermittent work and the movement into and out of the labor force from week to week, it is difficult to identify and measure the portion of the population of working age that is more or less permanently dependent on the economic activity of others.   When the entire calendar year is taken as a time reference, however, we can use with some assurance the data on persons who did no work at all during the year to provide this rough measure of the dependent population. During 1955, some 39.8 million persons 14 years old and over (35 percent of the total) did not do any work at all.   (This excludes persons in institutions and those who emigrated, entered the Armed Forces, or died during the year.)   Of this number, almost two-fifths were under 18 or were 65 years old and over.   In the age group 20 to 64, the great majority (57 out of 61 percent) were women (table 14).

If children under 14 years of age are added to those who did no work at all, the dependent population is estimated at 54 percent of the total civilian noninstitutional population in 1955.   With the high birth rates in recent years, the number of dependent children exceeded by more than 7 million the number of adult nonworkers (table 15).   Five years earlier, in 1950, the total dependent group was relatively the same size, but it was equally divided between adults and children.

TABLE **14.**—AGE AND SEX OF POPULATION NOT ECONOMICALLY ACTIVE: 1955

[Current survey levels]

Age and sex	Not in civilian labor force, 1955 (average)	Did not work during 1955	Age and sex	Not in civilian labor force, 1955 (average)	Did not work during 1955
Total[1]......thousands..	48,492	39,811	Female.....................	80.6	81.8
Percent.............	100.0	100.0	14 to 17 years...........	7.4	7.4
			18 and 19 years..........	2.2	1.6
Male......................	19.4	18.2	20 to 24 years...........	5.9	4.9
14 to 17 years...........	6.1	5.3	25 to 34 years...........	16.4	16.2
18 and 19 years..........	1.0	0.4	35 to 44 years...........	13.9	13.8
20 to 24 years...........	1.0	0.8	45 to 54 years...........	11.0	11.2
25 to 34 years...........	0.5	0.5	55 to 64 years...........	10.2	10.9
35 to 44 years...........	0.4	0.4	65 years and over........	13.6	15.8
45 to 54 years...........	0.7	0.6			
55 to 64 years...........	1.7	1.7			
65 years and over........	8.0	8.5			

[1] Persons in civilian noninstitutional population in an average week in 1955 or in January 1956.

Source: Derived from U. S. Bureau of the Census, *Current Population Reports*, Series P–50, No. 67, table 11, and No. 68, table 1.

How it has been possible to have record high birth rates without some reduction in the economic activity of women is the subject of discussion in subsequent chapters. But analysis of the effect on the labor force of the millions of new workers who will come of age in the near future must await study in the 1960's.

TABLE **15.**—DEPENDENCY STATUS OF THE CIVILIAN NONINSTITUTIONAL POPULATION: 1955 AND 1950

[Current survey levels]

Dependency status	1955		1950	
	Number (thousands)	Percent	Number (thousands)	Percent
Total civilian noninstitutional population[1]..	162,240	100.0	149,500	100.0
Worked during year:				
14 years old and over...........................	75,353	46.5	68,876	46.1
Full-time workers.............................	62,581	38.6	58,181	38.9
Part-time workers.............................	12,772	7.9	10,695	7.2
Did not work during year........................	86,887	53.5	80,624	53.9
14 years old and over...........................	39,811	24.5	40,294	26.9
Under 14 years..................................	47,076	29.0	40,330	27.0

[1] Population in January 1956 and January 1951.

Source: Derived from U. S. Bureau of the Census, *Current Population Reports*, Series P–50, No. 35, table A, and No. 68, table A; *1950 Census of Population*, Vol. IV, *Special Reports*, Part 2, Chapter C, Institutional Population, table 3; and unpublished estimates of the Bureau of the Census.

CHAPTER 2

TRENDS IN THE LABOR FORCE,
1890–1955

The American labor force almost tripled in size in the 65 years between 1890 and 1955, expanding at a slightly faster rate than the population of working age, that is, 14 years old and over[1] (appendix table D–1 and table 16). The average annual increase in the labor force—about 650,000 a year—has amounted to around half the average annual growth in the population of working age—1,165,000. The period of greatest expansion was the World War II decade, when the labor force showed a net growth at the average rate of 732,000 a year, or two-thirds as much as the population change. Except for war years, it was only during the prosperous decade of the twenties that the labor force grew by as much as 700,000 a year; then the average annual growth in the population of working age was at a maximum for the period studied.

TABLE 16.—PERSONS 14 YEARS OLD AND OVER IN THE LABOR FORCE, BY SEX: 1890 TO 1955

[Adjusted data—decennial census levels. In thousands]

Year	Total		Male		Female	
	Population	Labor force	Population	Labor force	Population	Labor force
1955	117,564	63,754	57,278	45,234	60,286	18,520
1950	112,354	60,617	55,312	43,930	57,042	16,687
1940	101,103	53,297	50,554	40,283	50,549	13,014
1930	89,100	47,404	45,087	37,008	44,013	10,396
1920	74,145	40,336	37,954	32,107	36,191	8,229
1900	51,441	27,640	26,416	22,641	25,025	4,999
1890	41,799	21,833	21,501	18,129	20,298	3,704
AVERAGE ANNUAL INCREASE						
1950 to 1955	+1,042	+627	+393	+261	+649	+367
1940 to 1950	+1,125	+732	+476	+365	+649	+367
1930 to 1940	+1,200	+589	+547	+327	+654	+262
1920 to 1930	+1,496	+707	+713	+490	+782	+217
1900 to 1920	+1,135	+635	+577	+473	+558	+162
1890 to 1900	+964	+581	+492	+451	+473	+130

Note: Population in continental United States, excluding Armed Forces overseas.

Source: Derived from appendix table D–1.

---

[1] The omission of children under 14 from these labor force estimates prior to 1940 is for the purpose of improving comparability with recent figures. It has the effect of understating the number of workers by several hundred thousand at the census date.

24

Comparability of data

These measures of change are, of course, only approximations. Many of the functions performed by members of the labor force in 1955 were carried out in earlier years at home by persons we would now call "non-workers"—functions such as the raising of food, the preparation of food, laundry and cleaning, caring for the ill and aged, and so forth. Because of the exclusion from the labor force of persons who perform these functions at home as part of their home housework, the change between 1890 and the present may be exaggerated. Another reason for regarding the figures as approximations is that measurement of the population engaged in some form of work for pay or in their own business or farm enterprise must be based either on decennial censuses taken under widely varying conditions or, in recent years, on sample surveys of the population.

One of the hard statistical lessons taught by the experience of the years since 1940 has been the virtual impossibility of obtaining consistent figures on the economic activity of the population with enumerations under different conditions. The Current Population Survey, operated each month by the Census Bureau, has provided estimates of the labor force status of the population since March 1940. Both the 1940 and 1950 decennial censuses of population collected information on the same subject, and it was thought that the results would serve, among many other purposes, as a benchmark or check for the sample survey. Yet the decennial census enumerators, using substantially the same questions and instructions, yielded a count of the labor force in 1950 that was several millions lower than the estimate provided by the Current Population Survey (CPS) interviewers. The same type of difference, although not so large, was found in 1940.[2] Some of the discrepancies between the 1950 Census figures on the labor force and the survey estimates for identical population groups are larger than the expected changes over one or even two decades on the basis of experience with decennial censuses.

It has been generally agreed that despite the sampling errors of the CPS estimates, the monthly sample estimates of the labor force, employment, and unemployment are more nearly accurate than the decennial census figures for 1950 (see Appendix A). This is because the survey interviewers were much more experienced than the temporary census takers, having had an average of 12 months of specialized experience in the enumeration of the labor force. For current measures of national employment and unemployment, then, there seems to be no question that the survey figures should be used, in preference to projections of decennial census data. For analysis of areas below the national level, the only data are decennial census data.

---

[2] Data on the differences between the decennial census and sample survey statistics on the labor force are presented in Appendix A.

To trace national labor force developments over time prior to 1940, the problem is somewhat different. No detailed statistics on the activity of specific population groups before 1940 exist, apart from the decennial census data and the 1937 Census of Unemployment. In the censuses before 1940, the measurement of economic activity was based on a count of gainful workers, not on the present labor force concept. The gainful-worker concept gives a somewhat higher count of the economically active population than does the labor force concept, so that direct comparisons of statistics based on the two approaches may be misleading.

Fortunately, John D. Durand has revised the decennial census statistics on the number of persons in the labor force by sex, age, and color to make them "comparable" with the 1940 Census figures adjusted to correct for some misclassifications.[3] These revisions are, of necessity, rough and uncertain, since there are no data for the years prior to 1930 on which to base estimates of the groups to be excluded from or added to the gainful-worker count. Simple adjustment ratios were used for each sex-age group, based on the relation between the number of gainful workers and the estimated number in the labor force in the specified sex-age group in 1930.

To bring this historical series up to date, the analyst has several choices: (1) He can use 1950 Census figures which provide the necessary details of classification by age, color, etc., and can be presumed to be closer to the level of enumeration of the earlier censuses. By some procedure, he can adjust the post-1950 figures to bring them to a "decennial census" level. Or (2) he can use the Current Population Survey figures for any dates since 1940 and adjust the pre-1940 statistics to bring them up to a "CPS" level. Or (3) he can compute changes since 1940 on the basis of the survey data and project earlier census data according to changes shown by the survey.

In the judgment of the writer, the first procedure is to be preferred if the major interest is the purely historical one—to measure what has happened as accurately as possible. Any adjustment of statistics is hazardous, of course, and is generally based on the assumption that differences observed at one or more points can be carried forward or backward, a dubious assumption at best. As for the problem of differences between census and survey statistics, we have two observations—one in 1940 when the difference between the survey and census labor force estimates was about 2.5 percent, and one in 1950 when the differences were over 5 percent. Whether the earlier census figures were as far from the current sample levels as the 1950 Census or as close as the 1940 Census or at some other point is obviously a question that cannot be answered. It is suggested, however, that the more useful series would be the one that has a minimum of manipulation of original data to obtain an artificial comparability.

---

[3] John D. Durand, *The Labor Force in the United States, 1890–1960*, Social Science Research Council, New York, 1948, Appendix A.

The third possible procedure appears to have merit—that is to apply rates of change since 1940 shown by the survey data to 1940 Census figures. But unfortunately the measurements of 1940–1950 developments shown by the two decennial censuses do not always agree in direction or relative amounts with those shown by the survey figures. And this is to be expected, since the population groups classified more successfully by the current sample interviewers—part-time housewives, teen-agers, older workers—vary in importance in the labor force from time to time. Consequently, it would seem that the more consistent historical series is one that makes the maximum use of decennial data.

For projections into the future, the decision must be different; interest is in where we may go from where we are now, and where we are now is measured by the current survey. Accordingly, if it is necessary to compute a long-term rate of change in the labor force activity of certain population groups for such projections, rough adjustment of earlier census figures to bring them to a current survey level may be desirable.

Estimates of the labor force by age, sex, and color from 1890 to 1955, presented in appendix table D–1, repeat those prepared by Durand for the years through 1940. Data for 1950 are decennial census data based on the tabulations of the 3⅓-percent sample, adjusted to complete count levels and to correct for the failure to report on the employment status of some persons. (See Appendix A for description of adjustment.) In the publications, all such not-reported cases were classified as not in the labor force, but for improved comparability with Durand's adjusted 1940 figures revisions were made in this instance.

Estimates for April 1955, from the Current Population Survey, have been adjusted to the so-called "decennial census level." Adjustment factors were developed from the data for April 1950, on the basis of a comparison of the civilian labor force in each age-sex-color group as measured by the decennial census and by the survey for that date.[4] Because the survey interviewers enumerate only the civilian noninstitutional population, the adjustment of differences due to differences in quality of enumeration was based on this segment of the population. To the adjusted estimates of the April 1955 civilian labor force were added figures on the Armed Forces in the continental United States, rather than the total Armed Forces, because the Armed Forces overseas were excluded from the decennial census statistics.

---

[4] The original published CPS estimates for April 1950 were based on sample figures adjusted to population totals developed from the projections of the 1940 Census figures. In the adjustment of CPS to census levels, the original age-specific civilian labor force participation *rates* were multiplied by population figures from the 1950 Census. This was done to eliminate from the measure of difference any factors that were not inherent in the enumeration process. To obtain five-year age groups for the survey estimates in 1950, some interpolation was necessary. (See Appendix A.)

Long-term developments in labor force participation

On the surface, the labor force changes are closely tied to changes in the size of the population. The proportion of the working-age population in the labor force, hereafter referred to as the "labor force participation rate," or the "labor force rate," varied only from 52.2 percent in 1890 to 54.4 percent in 1920 and 54.2 percent in 1955 (table 17). But underlying the gross changes have been many conflicting and compensating changes among various population groups, giving rise to great variation in the rates of change (appendix table D-1). The most important development has been the decline in the labor force participation of men of certain ages, which has been more than offset by the great increase in the labor force participation of women. Until 1940, the male labor force in the continental United States increased on the average each year more than the female labor force. But between 1940 and 1950 the increases were almost identical, and in the following five years the expansion of the female labor force exceeded that of the male labor force, because some men were being drawn into the Armed Forces and stationed overseas. Had the overseas forces been included in the figures in table 16, the labor force changes would have been about the same for men and women. The number of women aged 14 and over in the population, however, has exceeded the number of men since 1941, even when those in the Armed Forces abroad are included. This difference has developed because the life span of women is extending beyond that of men. Not all persons 14 years of age and over are, of course, able or willing to work, and the increase in the number of women in the oldest age groups will not necessarily affect the size of the female labor force.

TABLE 17.—LABOR FORCE PARTICIPATION RATES, BY COLOR: 1890 TO 1955

[Adjusted data—decennial census levels]

Year	All classes	White	Nonwhite
1955	54.2	54.1	55.0
1950	54.0	53.7	56.3
1940	52.7	52.1	58.1
1930	53.2	52.1	63.0
1920	54.4	53.3	64.2
1900	53.7	52.3	65.0
1890	52.2	51.0	62.4

Source: Appendix table D-1a.

Most students of the labor force are familiar with the long-run changes in the American social and economic structure that are related to labor force growth:[5] the increasing urbanization of the population which opened up employment opportunities for women but reduced the labor force par-

---

[5] Durand, *op. cit.*, Chapters 3 and 4; W. S. Woytinsky, *et al.*, *Employment and Wages in the United States*, Twentieth Century Fund, 1953, Part 3; Clarence D. Long, *The Labor Force Under Changing Income and Employment*, National Bureau of Economic Research, Princeton University Press, 1958, Chapters 7–10.

ticipation of young and old men; the long-term decline in the birth rate, permitting some married women to spend their time in paid employment instead of unpaid housework and child care; the almost complete disappearance of the spinster and the increasing proportion of married women in the population; the migration of the Negro population from Southern farms to Northern cities where they have found it possible to live and raise a family without depending on the work of every family member; the growing proportion of the population in older age groups where the proportion of workers tapers off. Other types of developments include the extension of high school and college education to larger and larger proportions of the population, made possible by rising incomes and increased government assistance. This raising of the school-leaving age has had the effect, of course, of postponing the entrance of young people into the full-time labor force. Factors that have affected particularly the employment of women include the reduction in the scheduled work week in most jobs to 40 hours, which has permitted many married women to both work and maintain their households; the vast expansion in clerical and sales jobs for which women can be employed; the introduction of mechanical devices in the home to perform household work, and the commercialization of many housekeeping functions that women have traditionally performed at home. Finally, the inauguration and extension of Social Security programs have allowed some types of persons (e.g., aging men, some mothers of young children widowed or separated from their husbands) to withdraw from the labor force.

Some of, but not all, these long-term trends were interrupted in the years after 1940. During the period of World War II and the cold war following, there has been generally full employment, accompanied for a large part of the time by an inadequate labor supply in certain ages, occupations, and industries. The institution of a peacetime military service, a new feature in American life, has affected labor force growth. Finally, there has been an unforeseen high level of birth rates. All these developments have changed many customary patterns of labor force activity.

The labor force rates for men had been slowly declining since 1900, but between 1940 and 1950 the decline leveled off (appendix table D-1). The most striking changes in the long-term patterns were an upturn in the labor force participation of the teen-age boys and a downturn for men 20 to 24 years old. (In 1950, the labor force rates of men 25 to 34 years old were temporarily depressed because an unduly large proportion of this age group was attending school or college under the war veterans' education program; by 1955 the rates were almost as high as they had been in 1940.) The labor force rates of teen-agers have been somewhat unstable in recent years, but it does appear that this age group, influenced perhaps by the number of job opportunities in the war and postwar years, has developed a new and favorable attitude toward after-school or vacation employment. On the other hand, the 20- to 24-year-olds seem to be following their older brothers, continuing in school or college to a greater extent than formerly. The rising levels of family income and the attitude toward college education as a job requirement may also be factors accounting for this change. For older men, the decade of the 1940's brought a halt in the downward trend in labor force participation, again probably because of the labor shortages during most of those years; the trend was resumed after 1950, however, and was accelerated by the liberalization of the Social Security programs in 1950 and later. This downward trend before 1940 is thought to have reflected chiefly the movement of population away from farms, although other factors, such as the speed-up of industrial production processes beyond the capacities of some older workers and shrinking fields of employment for them may have been important.

For women, the long-term trend has been toward increasing employment outside the home in all age groups except for teen-agers whose pattern of labor force activity has varied. The war and postwar years greatly stimulated this increase in the age groups from 35 to 65 years, when most married women no longer have young children at home. After 1940, there were no increases for women from 20 to 35 years, however, and even some slight decreases. These are, of course, the ages during which women marry and bear children; the proportion of women under 35 who have been preoccupied with their families has exceeded all previous expectations. There is reason to think that the absence of the younger age groups from the labor market may account in large part for the especially sharp increase in the utilization of older women in the current labor force.

Because of their numbers, the economic activity of white persons has determined the pattern of the total (table 18 and figure 4). The nonwhite population has had quite different labor force histories, however. Traditionally, white men and women have had lower overall labor force participation rates than nonwhite men and women. Because of their disadvantaged position in the labor market and because only low-paying jobs are generally available to them, Negro families have had to rely on more than one worker to meet the family needs. Living on farms as many did, family members were expected to and did work along with family heads; this was more common among nonwhite than white families. The gaps between white and nonwhite rates were narrowing for men as the nonwhite men began to live in greater proportions in urban areas and work in nonfarm occupations. By 1940, the overall rates of labor force participation of the two groups were the same, but nonwhite rates were below white rates in the age groups between 25 and 55. In 1950, the differences were even larger, although it might have been supposed that the greater assimilation of the nonwhite minority into the labor force patterns of the majority as a result of the manpower pressures of the war years would have made for greater similarity. Demographic and other factors that might have accounted for the 1940–1950 changes will be examined in greater detail in

Chapter 3, without, however, providing a full explanation of the white-nonwhite differences. The fact that there was a continued downward drift of nonwhite labor force rates between 1950 and 1955 suggests that there may be basic differences in values or in attitudes toward work on the part of white and nonwhite men that remain even when some other differences —health, education, and place of residence—are reduced.

TABLE 18.—LABOR FORCE PARTICIPATION RATES, BY AGE, COLOR, AND SEX: 1890 TO 1955

[Adjusted data—decennial census levels]

Age, color, and sex	1955	1950	1940	1930	1920	1900	1890
WHITE							
Male, 14 years old and over......	79.5	79.7	79.7	81.7	84.3	85.4	84.0
14 to 19 years.......................	38.0	39.5	34.1	38.2	50.0	60.1	48.2
20 to 24 years.......................	84.5	82.7	88.4	88.5	89.7	90.5	90.6
25 to 34 years.......................	95.6	93.5	96.2	96.1	96.4	95.0	96.0
35 to 44 years.......................	95.7	95.7	95.8	95.7	95.4	94.5	95.9
45 to 54 years.......................	94.1	92.9	93.0	93.8	93.3	92.6	93.7
55 to 64 years.......................	85.7	84.1	84.5	86.2	86.0	85.6	88.6
65 years and over....................	35.4	41.3	41.6	53.0	54.1	61.7	67.0
Female, 14 years old and over....	30.0	28.4	24.5	21.8	20.7	17.2	15.8
14 to 19 years.......................	21.5	23.6	18.7	21.9	27.5	23.8	22.3
20 to 24 years.......................	43.1	44.1	45.8	41.4	36.7	29.4	27.9
25 to 34 years.......................	31.0	30.5	31.8	24.9	21.5	16.8	14.5
35 to 44 years.......................	36.4	33.7	25.2	19.1	16.5	12.2	9.9
45 to 54 years.......................	37.7	32.0	20.8	17.3	15.4	11.3	9.8
55 to 64 years.......................	28.0	23.1	15.7	13.8	12.6	10.2	9.3
65 years and over....................	9.5	7.7	5.5	6.5	6.1	6.7	6.0
NONWHITE							
Male, 14 years old and over......	74.3	76.8	80.0	85.8	87.5	88.5	86.7
14 to 19 years.......................	37.4	43.6	46.2	55.4	62.7	74.8	61.7
20 to 24 years.......................	76.4	81.1	88.6	91.9	91.6	91.3	92.9
25 to 34 years.......................	88.9	86.7	92.1	95.1	95.1	93.6	95.8
35 to 44 years.......................	90.4	91.1	91.8	95.0	95.4	94.2	96.1
45 to 54 years.......................	86.0	88.9	89.4	94.2	94.7	93.9	95.3
55 to 64 years.......................	78.7	80.3	85.5	90.0	90.8	91.0	93.4
65 years and over....................	35.4	43.3	49.1	68.0	73.5	77.3	81.8
Female, 14 years old and over....	37.3	37.1	37.3	40.4	40.6	41.2	37.7
14 to 19 years.......................	18.1	18.4	21.6	29.9	34.8	45.4	38.3
20 to 24 years.......................	42.1	39.7	44.2	44.7	43.1	45.4	46.5
25 to 34 years.......................	45.6	44.4	45.8	44.6	42.7	39.9	36.2
35 to 44 years.......................	50.8	48.6	45.0	45.0	43.5	39.2	35.4
45 to 54 years.......................	44.6	43.6	39.6	44.0	44.9	39.7	36.4
55 to 64 years.......................	27.6	31.4	30.4	37.9	39.5	38.2	34.9
65 years and over....................	5.7	10.8	12.3	20.3	24.1	25.0	23.4

Source: Appendix table D–1a.

Nonwhite women, unlike nonwhite men, have maintained about the same overall labor force rate through the years, with declines for the oldest and youngest ages balancing the increases for the other age groups. In fact, of the four classes of the population, that of nonwhite women is the only one not showing a marked change in the proportion in the labor force in the last 65 years; by contrast, the labor force rate of white women doubled between 1890 and 1955, and in the age groups 35 to 54 quadrupled. The World War II decade, which brought about some extraordinary changes for white women, had only mild effects on the labor force rates of nonwhite women. Younger nonwhite women (under 35) showed a drop in labor

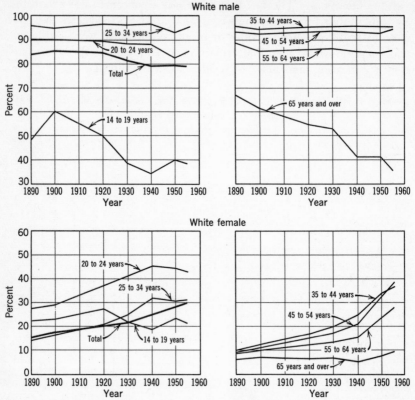

FIGURE 4.—LABOR FORCE PARTICIPATION RATES

Note: Based on data in table 18.

force rates or maintained about the same level as in the previous 20 years. Slight increases were recorded for women aged 35 to 54, although not as great as those for white women. Between 1950 and 1955 comparative stability was also maintained in the rates for nonwhite women.

Comparisons of the labor force figures for 1955 with those of earlier years should be made with caution because of the lack of similarity in the method of collecting the underlying data. It is safe to say, however, that the general picture they give is correct in outline if not in detail. The 1955 labor force was much older than the 1890 labor force and had lost some of its preponderantly male character (table 19 and figure 5). The median age had risen from 32.3 years to 39.4 years, and the percent 45 years old and over from 24.5 to 36.7. Men constituted 83 percent of the total in 1890, but 71 percent in 1955. The sex ratio doubled in the 65 years. For every 100 men in the labor force there were 20 working women in 1890 and 41 in 1955. The change in the sex ratio was much more striking for white than for nonwhite workers: For white women it

BY AGE, COLOR, AND SEX: 1890 TO 1955

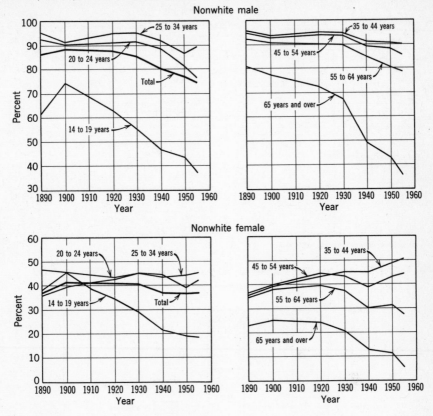

rose from 17.6 per 100 men in 1890 to 39.5 per 100 men in 1955; for nonwhite women, from 42.5 to 54.7.

The shift in the age composition of the labor force was more powerful for women than for men, and somewhat greater for white than for non-white women. In 1890, the median age of women in the labor force was under 25 years of age, the median for men 33.6 years. In 1955, the median age of the two was almost identical—38.5 years for women as compared with 39.7 years for men. White working women were, on the average, older than nonwhite women (38.9 vs. 36.2 years) in 1955 but not in 1890, or even in 1940.

The expansion in the female labor force could not have taken place without a radical change in the customs and attitudes of married women, who constituted two-thirds of the female population of working age in 1950; their proportion in 1890 was 55 percent. But single women also were in the labor force in much greater proportions in 1950, especially those aged 25 or older (table 20).

TABLE **19.**—COMPOSITION OF THE LABOR FORCE: 1955, 1940, AND 1890

[Adjusted data—decennial census levels]

Color and sex of the labor force	1955	1940	1890	Age, color, and sex of the labor force	1955	1940	1890
COLOR AND SEX				AGE DISTRIBUTION			
Total...............	100.0	100.0	100.0	Total................	100.0	100.0	100.0
Male....................	71.0	75.6	83.0	14 to 19 years...........	6.3	7.5	13.6
White................	64.4	68.5	73.7	20 to 24 years...........	9.7	14.5	17.3
Nonwhite.............	6.6	7.1	9.3	25 to 34 years...........	23.8	25.7	26.3
Female.................	29.0	24.4	17.0	35 to 44 years...........	23.5	21.1	18.3
White................	25.5	21.0	13.0	45 to 54 years...........	19.3	17.0	12.7
Nonwhite.............	3.5	3.4	4.0	55 to 64 years...........	12.7	10.2	7.5
				65 years and over........	4.7	4.0	4.3
SEX RATIO--FEMALES PER 100 MALES				MEDIAN AGE (Years)			
				Total................	39.4	36.1	32.3
Total...............	40.9	32.3	20.4	Male......................	39.7	37.8	33.6
White..................	39.5	30.6	17.6	White.................	39.9	38.0	33.8
Nonwhite...............	54.7	48.7	42.5	Nonwhite..............	37.7	35.4	31.9
				Female....................	38.5	31.7	24.6
				White.................	38.9	31.5	24.3
				Nonwhite..............	36.2	33.2	27.1

Source: Derived from appendix table D-1.

FIGURE **5.**—PERCENT DISTRIBUTION OF THE LABOR FORCE, BY AGE: 1955 AND 1890

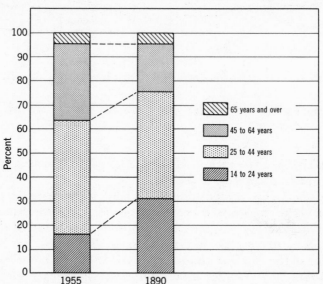

Note: Based on data in table 19.

In 1890, less than half the unmarried women in all age groups except 25 to 34 years were in the labor force; in 1950, the proportions in all age groups except the youngest and oldest were well over half, and approached four-fifths in some groups. Many of the same factors accounting for the increased employment of married women were also operative for women who were not married. But, in addition, it is probable that the opening up of opportunities for higher education for women has been an important influence in the greater propensity of single women to work for their living.   This has been reinforced by the disappearance of the three-generation household, which has meant that adult single women have no satisfying role to play in the periphery of their own families.

TABLE **20.**—MARITAL STATUS OF WOMEN IN THE LABOR FORCE, AND LABOR FORCE PARTICIPATION RATES BY MARITAL STATUS AND AGE: 1950 AND 1890

[Adjusted data—decennial census levels]

Age	1950				1890			
	Total	Single	Married	Widowed or divorced	Total	Single	Married	Widowed or divorced
Number of women in labor force..........thousands..	16,687	5,317	8,705	2,665	3,704	2,566	500	638
Percent...................	100.0	31.8	52.2	16.0	100.0	69.3	13.5	17.2
LABOR FORCE PARTICIPATION RATES								
Total, 14 years and over...	29.3	46.3	23.0	32.7	18.2	36.9	4.5	28.6
14 to 24 years.................	32.9	35.8	26.2	63.1	27.0	33.6	6.4	54.7
25 to 34 years.................	32.0	79.1	23.7	69.2	16.8	53.4	4.7	53.6
35 to 44 years.................	35.2	75.7	28.0	70.4	12.7	46.1	4.4	48.4
45 to 54 years.................	33.1	70.7	24.4	57.8	12.5	39.6	3.8	35.9
55 to 64 years.................	23.6	57.2	14.2	35.9	11.4	30.9	2.9	23.4
65 years and over.............	7.9	19.7	4.9	7.7	7.6	16.5	2.1	10.0

Source: Derived from *1950 Census of Population*, Vol. IV, *Special Reports*, Part I, Chapter A, Employment and Personal Characteristics, table 10 and appendix table D–1; John D. Durand, *The Labor Force in the United States, 1890–1960*, Social Science Research Council, New York, 1948, table A–7.

The *rate* of increase in the labor force participation of married women, however, is much greater than that of single women, or that of women who are widowed or divorced.   Overall, their labor force rate increased from 4.5 percent in 1890 to 23.0 percent in 1950, and the changes in most age groups were about the same order of magnitude.   As a consequence both of the increased tendency of married women to work outside the home and of the rising proportion of married women in the population, they constituted 52.2 percent of the 1950 female labor force, as compared with 13.5 percent in 1890.

Changes in occupational composition

Changes in the occupational composition of the labor force help to explain some of the developments in the totals.   At the beginning of this century, just under two-fifths of the working population[6] was engaged in farming and about the same proportion in manual occupations (craftsmen, operatives, and nonfarm laborers) (appendix table D–2 and figure 6).   Less than one-fifth had white-collar jobs (professional, semiprofessional, managerial, clerical, and sales jobs).   By 1950, the structure of employment had changed radically, and principally because of the decline in farming occupations.   Only about one person in ten in the 1950 labor force was a

---

[6] Gainful workers, including children 10 to 14 years.

FIGURE 6.—PERCENT DISTRIBUTION OF WORKERS, BY MAJOR OCCUPATION GROUP AND SEX: 1950 AND 1900

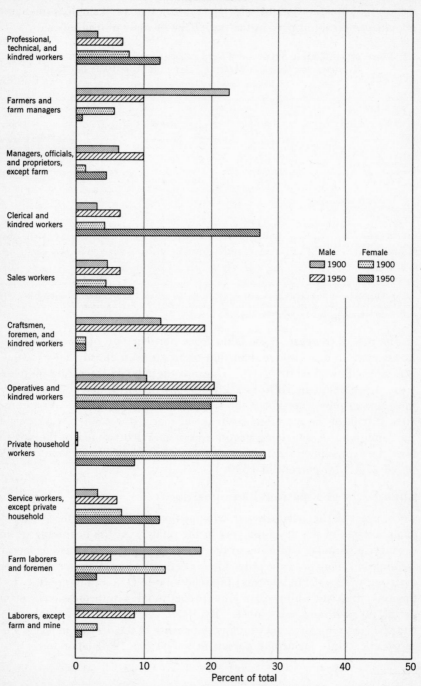

Note: Based on data in appendix table D-2.

farmer or a farm laborer. The manual occupations had grown in importance, particularly the semiskilled operatives, but the biggest relative change was for white-collar workers. They had increased in number until they constituted almost two-fifths of the labor force in the middle of the century.

The growth in white-collar jobs, particularly clerical jobs, is an important reason for the vast increase in employment of women. But it is not simply the increase in numbers but the change in type of jobs that is significant. In 1900 there were less than a million clerical workers, one-fourth of them women. Their jobs were as agents, bookkeepers and accountants, clerks and copyists, messengers, and stenographers and typists. This last was the largest group for women but was not much larger than that of bookkeepers and accountants. In 1950, the number of clerks and similar workers had reached above 7 million, of whom 62 percent were women. The largest component groups were bookkeepers (three-quarters of whom were women), stenographers and typists (almost all women), and general clerks (one-half of whom were women). General clerks consisted of many different kinds of workers but chiefly they were record keepers and handlers of records of all kinds, not office machine operators. Thus, it is the advent of the era of paper work that probably set the stage for the real breakthrough for women and their emergence from domesticity as an exclusive role. With the opening of millions of relatively pleasant office jobs, the traditional and not-so-pleasant domestic service field has been almost abandoned; 50 years ago it drew almost 30 percent of the working women.

For men, the shifts to professional and technical, managerial, craftsmen, and operative jobs were the most noteworthy changes in the 50-year period. Although the evidence of job descriptions alone is not conclusive, it does suggest that the present industrialized labor force is a more skilled one, and certainly a better-educated one, than that at the turn of the century.

A crude measure of the extent to which the changes in employment in a specific occupation group are caused by real changes in the occupational structure of total employment can be obtained by standardizing the 1950 labor force on the 1900 occupational distribution (table 21).

The major part of the increase in the number of men in the professional, clerical, operative, and service occupations could be attributed to the more-than-proportionate expansion of such jobs in the economy. In the other occupations that increased, the increase was about equally due to the growth of the labor force and the shifting occupational composition of employment.

Changes in the occupational structure of employment accounted for the greater part of the increase in women in managerial, clerical, sales, and service jobs (except private households). The outstanding change, as was indicated above, was that of clerical workers; if the 1900 occupational distribution of women had not altered, the net increase in clerical workers would have been only about 400,000 instead of more than 4 million. There was almost no "shift" to skilled industrial jobs (craftsmen) and a net shift away from operative and laborer jobs. Overall, there was no increase in private household workers, although if the structure of employment had not changed, there would have been an increase of 3 million or so.

Because of the importance of teaching and nursing jobs for women, a greater proportion of women than of men has been reported in professional work at each decennial year. Eight percent of the women who worked in 1900 were classified as professional or technical, 3 percent of the men; in 1950 the comparable figures were 12 and 7 percent (appendix table D–2). Data in table 21 also suggest that many new types of professional jobs developed for men in the 50-year period, but that for women the greater part of the increase in professional workers was due simply to the growth of the work force.

TABLE **21.**—CHANGE IN NUMBER OF WORKERS IN MAJOR OCCUPATION GROUPS, 1900 TO 1950, AND ESTIMATES OF COMPONENTS OF CHANGE, BY SEX

[Decennial census levels. In thousands]

Major occupation group	Male			Female		
	Change, 1900 to 1950	Change due to--		Change, 1900 to 1950	Change due to--	
		Change in number of workers	Change in occupational structure		Change in number of workers	Change in occupational structure
Professional, technical, and kindred wkrs...	+2,274	+636	+1,638	+1,573	+909	+664
Farmers and farm managers..................	-1,196	+4,332	-5,528	-191	+651	-842
Managers, officials, and proprietors, exc. farm....................................	+2,834	+1,289	+1,545	+622	+161	+461
Clerical and kindred workers...............	+2,065	+528	+1,537	+4,290	+444	+3,846
Sales workers.............................	+1,636	+857	+779	+1,190	+476	+714
Craftsmen, foremen, and kindred workers.....	+5,112	+2,373	+2,739	+176	+159	+17
Operatives and kindred workers.............	+6,287	+1,952	+4,335	+2,026	+2,637	-611
Private household workers..................	+27	+42	-15	-68	+3,192	-3,260
Service workers, exc. private household.....	+1,880	+546	+1,334	+1,714	+752	+962
Farm laborers and foremen..................	-2,332	+3,520	-5,852	-215	+1,457	-1,672
Laborers, except farm and mine.............	+257	+2,768	-2,511	+8	+288	-280

Note: Components of change estimated by standardizing 1950 on 1900 occupational distribution, assuming difference between 1900 and 1950 standardized is difference due to change in number of workers, and attributing remainder of net change to change in occupational structure. This procedure is an oversimplification since it assumes no interaction between number of workers and their occupational structure, but more refined measures are not warranted because of the crudity of basic data.

Source: Based on appendix table D–2.

Summary

At the opening of this century, the typical American worker was a man under 25, probably operating his own farm or working as a farm hand for someone else. If he lived in the city, he was probably an unskilled laborer. He had begun his working life in his early teens and could be expected to work for almost the rest of his life—his life expectancy (at birth) was not even 50 years.[7]   By the middle of the century, the typical working man had become either a skilled or a semiskilled industrial worker. He was between 25 and 35 years of age and had started to work only at the end of his high school years.   His life expectancy (at birth) was at least 65 years, and he could look forward to 5 or 6 years of retirement, with a pension from the Federal Government and perhaps one from his employer.

In the same period the typical American woman had changed from a rural housewife to a city dweller.   In 1900, she would be working for her living only if she had the misfortune to be unmarried or widowed, and provided she was young enough to find a job.   She might be either a domestic servant or a textile or needle trades worker.   Except for the very few educated and talented women, marriage was earnestly to be desired as the only possible escape from inevitable economic and social poverty.

At the middle of the century, marriage was still the goal of the American woman, and was achieved by all but a few.   But no longer was it also an escape route from dreary, ill-paid work as a servant or a factory hand. Typically, in the 1950's, American girls seek jobs on leaving school, marry shortly thereafter, and continue working until they start having children, when they retire for a period of years.   While they are in the labor force at the beginning of their working lives, they are probably doing clerical or secretarial work in an office or selling in a retail store.   It is probable that after they send their last child off to school they will return to the labor force,[8] voluntarily and with enthusiasm, not to pursue a career for which they have been prepared by school and college but to supplement the family income at whatever kind of work is both available and agreeable.

Both long-run and recent changes in the patterns of labor force activity are dominated by the increase in employment of women outside the home. Over and over again in this study, attention will be turned to the effects of this expansion, particularly as manifested in the 1940–1950 decade.

A hundred years ago (November 1856) these words appeared in *The Economist*:

> No one who has any knowledge of society can deny the existence of a large number of unoccupied ladies, a class quite distinct from the domestically useful or the contentedly trifling, a throng of fretting, unsatisfied minds—ready to work, but finding no field—ready to sacrifice themselves, but seeing no shrine on which to lay the offering.   Is there no means of turning all this wasted power to account?[9]

---

[7] Stuart Garfinkle, "Changes in Working Life of Men, 1900 to 2000," *Monthly Labor Review*, U. S. Department of Labor, Vol. 78, No. 3, March 1955, table 1.

[8] The modal age group of working women in 1955 was 35 to 44 years; in 1900, 14 to 24 years.

[9] *The Economist*, Vol. CLXXXI, No. 5910, London, December 1, 1956, p. 773.

Their author wanted to turn this wasted womanpower to account in voluntary good works. American women, whose powers have been turned to account so thoroughly in the past 65 years, have for the most part succeeded in drawing pay for that part of their daily work performed outside the home. Whether it has brought peace to their "fretting, unsatisfied minds" is beyond the scope of this study. It seems clear, however, that the labor supply in the United States would never have been sufficient to allow for expanding industrial production and services, rising living standards, and the extension of high school education to all classes of the population if women had remained "unoccupied ladies."

CHAPTER 3

CHANGING PATTERNS OF LABOR FORCE
PARTICIPATION, 1940–1950

Factors of change

In the search for explanations of changing labor force patterns, the analyst soon realizes that the factors determining labor force activity are far more elusive than it has been traditional to think. It is true that there is a solid body of data indicating that the tendency to work varies with age, with marital status and family responsibilities, with color, with residence (farm or nonfarm), with education, with national origin, with family income. The variations are, of course, greater for women than for men. Most men cannot choose whether or not they will earn their own and their family's living. There is a brief period of choice when they are young whether to continue their education or get a job, and at the other end of the age scale, whether to retire or go on working, if in good health. Unmarried women, and some widows and divorcees, have the same need to earn a living as do men, although they probably have not grown up facing this need as inevitable in the same way as do their brothers. With married women, though economic pressure may still be the prime determinant, there are many other considerations that are taken into account when the decision whether or not to look for a job is made. Urgent need for added income to meet current living costs may not seem a compelling reason to certain women to leave their children in someone else's care. On the other hand, the fact that their husband's incomes are ample to supply every need may be no reason for other women, particularly those with professional training, to limit their activities to homemaking and community or social life.

The census taker is ill-equipped, and the decennial census itself is an unsuitable vehicle, for the collection of data that would adequately measure the underlying reasons for labor force activity. The Current Population Survey during the years of its operation has uncovered many new facts about labor force behavior, but it too has been limited by its very nature to only a superficial examination of motivations. The simple question "Were you looking for work?" elicits from the housewife a wide variety of replies, indicating complete lack of interest, interest but inability to take a job because of household or family duties, interest but only in certain types of work or at unattainable wage scales, or actually vigorous

41

efforts to find a job.   Frequently a housewife reports inability to consider doing work outside the home because of ill health, lack of training, the state of the weather, failure to find work in the past, and finally, that provocative reason, "My husband doesn't want me to work."   Needless to say, these reasons change from time to time as the attitude of the woman or her situation changes.   These changes may occur from day to day or week to week, or they may occur only as fundamental changes in her family responsibilities or economic status or basic outlook take place.

Decennial census data obviously can shed little light on motivations, but they permit an examination of the net effects of these pushes and pulls into the labor market.   By isolating and controlling the impact of purely demographic factors such as age, color, marital status, and farm residence, the analyst is able to measure the effect of all other factors combined— the complex of economic, psychological, and social factors that determine propensity to work.   The next step is to examine the behavior of different segments of the population in different types of areas to see not only what has actually happened but what may be the underlying causes.

Previous research in this field has pointed to the conclusion that so far as the available data show, the "propensity" factor has almost always been dominant in the explanation of changes in the labor force activity of various groups in the population.[1]   This means that after the effect of the changing age distribution of the population, its increasing urbanization, the rising marriage rate, and changes in fertility were taken account of, there still had to be other factors to explain the change from one date to another.

As Chapter 2 has shown, the enormous changes in many phases of American life associated with the war and postwar eras led to certain interruptions in the historical trends.   The long-run slow decline in the labor force activity of white men was halted and the increase among white women stepped up.   The major factor in the case of white women was the rising "propensity" to work outside the home.   Nonwhite men continued to show a downtrend, with the shift from farm to nonfarm areas assuming greater importance than in the period 1920–1940 as a factor of change.   Nonwhite women, on the other hand, showed almost no change, overall, as the factors that tended to reduce labor force participation were offset by large urban migration which tended to increase labor force participation by women.

A brief summary of the measures is shown in table 22.   The method for analyzing factors of change is that developed by Edwin D. Goldfield of the Bureau of the Census and used by Durand[2] to evaluate changes during the period 1920–1940.

---

[1] S. L. Wolfbein and A. J. Jaffe, "Demographic Factors in Labor Force Growth," *The American Sociological Review*, Vol. 11, No. 4, August 1946.   John D. Durand, *The Labor Force in the United States, 1890–1960*, Social Science Research Council, New York, 1948.

[2] Durand, *op. cit.*, Appendix B.   The method used is that of multiple standardization with allocation of interactions.

TABLE **22.**—FACTORS OF CHANGE IN PERCENT OF LABOR FORCE MEMBERS AMONG MALES AND
FEMALES 14 YEARS OLD AND OVER, BY COLOR: 1940–1950 AND 1920–1940

Factors of change	Male		Female	
	White	Nonwhite	White	Nonwhite
1940 TO 1950[1]				
Change in percent in labor force..........	+0.20	-3.40	+3.60	-0.50
Due to change in:				
Age.......................................	+0.65	+0.50	-0.61	+0.03
Farm residence............................	-0.55	-1.60	+0.89	+2.14
Marital status............................	...	...	-2.81	-0.96
All other factors.........................	+0.10	-2.30	+6.13	-1.71
1920 TO 1940[2]				
Change in percent in labor force..........	-3.4	-6.8	+4.0	-3.1
Due to change in:				
Age.......................................	-0.2	-0.8	-0.6	-0.5
Farm residence............................	-0.2	-0.5	+1.3	+2.7
Marital status and family characteristics...	...	...	-0.6	+1.1
All other factors.........................	-2.9	-5.5	+3.9	-6.4

[1] Computations based on unadjusted data derived from 3⅓-percent sample in 1950 and 5-percent sample in 1940.

[2] Data for whites relate to native white. Marital status and family characteristics refer to changes in distribution of women by marital status and in percentage of married women (husband present) having one or more children under 10 years old.

Source: Derived from *1950 Census of Population*, Vol. IV, *Special Reports*, Part 1, Chapter A, Employment and Personal Characteristics, table 10; *1940 Census of Population, Employment and Personal Characteristics*, table 7; John D. Durand, *The Labor Force in the United States, 1890–1960*, Social Science Research Council, New York, 1948, table 10.

Summary of demographic changes, 1940–1950

As a basis for examining in greater detail the changing patterns of labor force participation, a brief review of the purely demographic changes that took place during the decade might be helpful.

Age. The *working* age population, that is, persons 14 years of age and above, was a substantially older group in 1950 (table 23). The median age was 38.6 years in 1950 and 36.4 in 1940. Of great importance was the decline in the number of persons in the labor force entrance age groups (14–24 years) because of the low birth rate in the 1930's. Although the total population of all ages increased from 131.7 to 150.7 million, the number between 14 and 25 years of age dropped from 26.3 million in 1940 to 24.2 million in 1950.

Farm residence.[3] World War II had as one of its major demographic effects the speeding up of the long-run decline in the farm population. Vast shifts of population brought labor supply from farms into areas where demand for war workers very often carried over to the postwar years (table 24). As farm residence tends to restrict the labor force participation of women and enlarges that of men, changes in the farm population are significant for labor force developments.

---

[3] Throughout this volume, the terms farm and nonfarm residence refer to the rural-farm population on the one hand and the combined urban and rural-nonfarm population on the other. Because of the change in urban definition in 1950, it is not possible to compare labor force data for 1940 and 1950 for urban and rural residents. The rural-farm population, however, has substantially the same definition at both dates.

TABLE **23.**—Age Composition of the Working Age Population, by Sex: 1950 and 1940

Age and sex	1950	1940	Percent distribution	
			1950	1940
BOTH SEXES				
Total, 14 years and over.................	112,354,034	101,102,924	100.0	100.0
14 to 19 years...............................	12,755,795	14,739,253	11.4	14.6
20 to 24 years...............................	11,481,828	11,587,835	10.2	11.5
25 to 44 years...............................	45,209,626	39,672,246	40.2	39.2
45 to 64 years...............................	30,637,248	26,084,276	27.3	25.8
65 years and over............................	12,269,537	9,019,314	10.9	8.9
Median age based on single years of age........	38.6	36.4	...	...
MALE				
Total, 14 years and over.................	55,311,617	50,553,748	100.0	100.0
14 to 19 years...............................	6,400,838	7,398,269	11.6	14.6
20 to 24 years...............................	5,606,293	5,692,392	10.1	11.3
25 to 44 years...............................	22,184,614	19,685,768	40.1	39.0
45 to 64 years...............................	15,322,898	13,371,199	27.7	26.4
65 years and over............................	5,796,974	4,406,120	10.5	8.7
Median age based on single years of age........	38.5	36.7	...	...
FEMALE				
Total, 14 years and over.................	57,042,417	50,549,176	100.0	100.0
14 to 19 years...............................	6,354,957	7,340,984	11.1	14.5
20 to 24 years...............................	5,875,535	5,895,443	10.3	11.7
25 to 44 years...............................	23,025,012	19,986,478	40.5	39.6
45 to 64 years...............................	15,314,350	12,713,077	26.8	25.1
65 years and over............................	6,472,563	4,613,194	11.3	9.1
Median age based on single years of age........	38.6	36.1	...	...

Source: Derived from *1950 Census of Population*, Vol. II, *Characteristics of the Population*, Part 1, U. S. Summary, table 38, and Vol. IV, *Special Reports*, Part 1, Chapter A, Employment and Personal Characteristics, table 1; *1940 Census of Population*, Vol. IV, *Characteristics by Age*, Part 1, U. S. Summary, table 24, and *Employment and Personal Characteristics*, table 1.

TABLE **24.**—Farm Residence of the Working Age Population, by Color and Sex: 1950 and 1940

Farm residence and sex	All classes		White		Nonwhite	
	1950	1940	1950	1940	1950	1940
Total, 14 years and over..	112,354,034	101,102,924	101,333,125	91,428,165	11,020,909	9,674,759
Rural farm.......................	15,884,356	21,356,501	13,868,602	18,308,535	2,015,754	3,047,966
Urban and rural nonfarm.........	96,469,678	79,746,423	87,464,523	73,119,630	9,005,155	6,626,793
Male, 14 years and over.....	55,311,617	50,553,748	49,979,010	45,823,031	5,332,607	4,730,717
Rural farm.......................	8,399,488	11,417,635	7,376,637	9,850,902	1,022,851	1,566,733
Urban and rural nonfarm.........	46,912,129	39,136,113	42,602,373	35,972,129	4,309,756	3,163,984
Female, 14 years and over...	57,042,417	50,549,176	51,354,115	45,605,134	5,688,302	4,944,042
Rural farm.......................	7,484,868	9,938,866	6,491,965	8,457,633	992,903	1,481,233
Urban and rural nonfarm.........	49,557,549	40,610,310	44,862,150	37,147,501	4,695,399	3,462,809
PERCENT DISTRIBUTION						
Total, 14 years and over..	100.0	100.0	100.0	100.0	100.0	100.0
Rural farm.......................	14.1	21.1	13.7	20.0	18.3	31.5
Urban and rural nonfarm.........	85.9	78.9	86.3	80.0	81.7	68.5
Male, 14 years and over.....	100.0	100.0	100.0	100.0	100.0	100.0
Rural farm.......................	15.2	22.6	14.8	21.5	19.2	33.1
Urban and rural nonfarm.........	84.8	77.4	85.2	78.5	80.8	66.9
Female, 14 years and over...	100.0	100.0	100.0	100.0	100.0	100.0
Rural farm.......................	13.1	19.7	12.6	18.5	17.5	30.0
Urban and rural nonfarm.........	86.9	80.3	87.4	81.5	82.5	70.0

Source: Derived from *1950 Census of Population*, Vol. II, *Characteristics of the Population*, Part 1, U. S. Summary, table 38; *1940 Census of Population*, Vol. IV, *Characteristics by Age*, Part 1, U. S. Summary, tables 2 and 6.

Marital status. Another well-known result of World War II was the marriage boom that more than made up for the marriages that had been deferred during the war, as well as those that had not taken place during the years of the Great Depression (table 25). Also, as the fashion for early marriages began to take hold, the median age at first marriage dropped by about 1.2 years for women and about 1.5 years for men during the decade. This increase in early marriages may be an example of a demographic development which was determined in part by changing labor force propensities, i.e., the willingness of young women, particularly the brides of World War II veterans, to continue in the labor force while their husbands attended school or made their adjustment to the civilian life. Their younger sisters have followed suit in the 1950's.

TABLE **25.**—MARITAL STATUS OF THE WORKING AGE POPULATION BY SEX, AND PERCENT MARRIED BY AGE AND SEX: 1950 AND 1940

Marital status and age	Male		Female	
	1950	1940	1950	1940
MARITAL STATUS				
Total, 14 years and over...........	[1]55,311,617	50,553,748	[1]57,042,417	50,549,176
Single.................................	14,587,222	17,593,379	11,406,362	13,935,866
Married................................	37,345,785	30,192,334	37,537,397	30,090,488
Spouse present.......................	35,431,034	28,657,820	35,531,513	28,516,937
Spouse absent........................	1,914,751	1,534,514	2,005,884	1,573,551
Widowed................................	2,293,309	2,143,612	6,727,213	5,700,202
Divorced...............................	1,085,301	624,423	1,371,445	822,620
Percent Distribution				
Total, 14 years and over...........	100.0	100.0	100.0	100.0
Single.................................	26.4	34.8	20.0	27.6
Married................................	67.5	59.8	65.8	59.5
Spouse present.......................	64.0	56.8	62.3	56.4
Spouse absent........................	3.5	3.0	3.5	3.1
Widowed................................	4.1	4.2	11.8	11.3
Divorced...............................	2.0	1.2	2.4	1.6
AGE (Percent of each age group married)				
14 to 19 years........................	2.7	1.4	14.0	9.8
20 to 24 years........................	39.9	27.4	65.6	51.3
25 to 29 years........................	74.2	62.7	83.3	74.1
30 to 34 years........................	84.3	77.2	86.2	80.4
35 to 39 years........................	86.8	81.6	85.5	81.5
40 to 44 years........................	87.1	83.2	83.1	80.6
45 to 49 years........................	86.2	83.6	79.8	78.3
50 to 54 years........................	85.0	81.9	75.0	73.3
55 to 59 years........................	83.1	79.9	69.1	67.2
60 to 64 years........................	79.3	76.7	60.1	58.0
65 years and over....................	65.7	63.8	35.7	34.3

[1] Data from 20-percent sample adjusted to complete-count total for persons 14 years and over.

Source: Derived from *1950 Census of Population*, Vol. II, *Characteristics of the Population*, Part 1, U. S. Summary, tables 102 and 106.

Fertility. The rise in the birth rate during the 1940's, like the low birth rate in the 1930's, has had profound effects on the size and composition of the adult female labor force. The number of mothers of young children in the population had increased by over 50 percent between 1940 and 1950; the rise was greater for white than for nonwhite women (table 26).

TABLE **26.**—MARRIED, WIDOWED, AND DIVORCED WOMEN BY AGE, COLOR, AND PRESENCE OF YOUNG CHILDREN: 1950 AND 1940

Age and color	1950			1940		
	Total women	With children under 5		Total women	With children under 5	
		Number	Percent		Number	Percent
WHITE						
Total, 15 to 49 years......	26,538,930	10,269,810	38.7	21,662,100	6,722,220	31.0
15 to 19 years.................	783,780	327,180	41.7	604,160	241,560	40.0
20 to 24 years.................	3,570,780	2,198,310	61.6	2,698,060	1,460,820	54.1
25 to 29 years.................	4,894,650	3,137,160	64.1	3,836,500	1,976,500	51.5
30 to 34 years.................	4,790,670	2,397,420	50.0	3,928,520	1,541,380	39.2
35 to 39 years.................	4,623,060	1,469,130	31.8	3,749,900	930,840	24.8
40 to 44 years.................	4,180,980	619,500	14.8	3,519,720	440,220	12.5
45 to 49 years.................	3,695,010	121,110	3.3	3,325,240	130,900	3.9
NONWHITE						
Total, 15 to 49 years......	3,284,970	1,027,290	31.3	2,733,900	722,600	26.4
15 to 19 years.................	141,030	78,660	55.8	130,460	63,440	48.6
20 to 24 years.................	488,700	283,080	57.9	417,520	194,920	46.7
25 to 29 years.................	602,040	264,540	43.9	505,640	178,120	35.2
30 to 34 years.................	564,030	181,650	32.2	466,560	120,180	25.8
35 to 39 years.................	578,130	134,730	23.3	487,940	96,260	19.7
40 to 44 years.................	485,910	61,890	12.7	393,680	48,860	12.4
45 to 49 years.................	425,130	22,740	5.3	332,100	20,820	6.3

Source: Derived from *1950 Census of Population*, Vol. IV, *Special Reports*, Part 5, Chapter C, Fertility, tables 46 and 47; *1940 Census of Population, Fertility for States and Large Cities*, tables 1 and 5.

Household relationships. Persons responsible for the maintenance of a home may have quite a different attitude toward employment than those who live in the homes of relatives. The decrease in the proportion of the working age population living in the households of parents or other relatives is another development of the decade, reflecting the generally increasing prosperity of the period. The program of mortgages for war veterans on moderate terms also made the establishment of their own homes easier for young couples (table 27).

School enrollment. Attendance at school, not a strictly demographic factor, was on the rise before 1940, but the increase received great impetus from the veterans' education program. Because school enrollment has an inhibiting effect on labor force activity, or at least full-time activity, it is important in connection with the study of changing labor force behavior. Between 1940 and 1950, the enrollment rate of white boys 14 to 24 years increased from 39.9 percent to 45.6 percent; nonwhite boys from 31.4 percent to 39.0 percent (table 28). The enrollment rate of white girls, on the other hand, remained at about 37 percent and the rate for nonwhite girls almost caught up to the rate for white girls.

Labor force participation and age, residence, and marital status

The broad changes in labor force activity by age between 1940 and 1950 have been indicated in Chapter 2 against the background of historical trends. The more detailed examination must be made on the basis of data for which there are no satisfactory historical series—cross-classification of labor force activity by color, residence, marital status, etc.

TABLE **27.**—Persons 14 Years Old and Over, by Relationship to Head of Household
and Sex: 1950 and 1940

Relationship to head and sex	1950[1]	1940	Percent distribution	
			1950	1940
Total, 14 years old and over...........	112,354,034	101,102,924	100.0	100.0
Head of household...........................	42,711,392	34,948,666	37.8	34.6
Wife of head...............................	33,240,981	26,570,502	29.8	26.3
Other relatives of head.....................	27,285,922	31,345,668	24.3	31.0
Not relative of head........................	3,769,364	5,160,080	3.4	5.1
In quasi-household..........................	5,346,375	3,078,008	4.7	3.0
Male, 14 years old and over..............	55,311,617	50,553,748	100.0	100.0
Head of household...........................	36,329,576	29,679,718	65.7	58.8
Wife of head...............................	...	...	...	...
Other relatives of head.....................	13,567,118	16,146,053	24.5	31.9
Not relative of head........................	2,020,849	2,796,227	3.7	5.5
In quasi-household..........................	3,394,074	1,931,750	6.1	3.8
Female, 14 years old and over............	57,042,417	50,549,176	100.0	100.0
Head of household...........................	6,381,816	5,268,948	11.2	10.4
Wife of head...............................	33,240,981	26,570,502	58.2	52.5
Other relatives of head.....................	13,718,804	15,199,615	24.1	30.1
Not relative of head........................	1,748,515	2,363,853	3.1	4.7
In quasi-household..........................	1,952,301	1,146,258	3.4	2.3

[1] Data from 20-percent sample adjusted to complete-count total for persons 14 years and over.

Source: Derived from *1950 Census of Population*, Vol. II, *Characteristics of the Population*, Part 1, U. S. Summary, tables 107 and 108; *1940 Census of Population*, Vol. IV, *Characteristics by Age*, Part 1, U. S. Summary, tables 1, 11, and 12.

TABLE **28.**—Percent of the Population 14 to 24 Years Old Enrolled in School,
by Age, Color, and Sex: 1950 and 1940

Age and sex	White		Nonwhite	
	1950	1940	1950	1940
Total, 14 to 24 years old............	41.7	38.4	37.0	31.5
14 and 15 years.............................	93.6	91.0	89.0	82.4
16 and 17 years.............................	75.9	70.6	64.3	53.9
18 years....................................	40.8	37.7	32.3	26.2
19 and 20 years.............................	22.0	17.4	16.0	11.5
21 to 24 years..............................	12.2	5.3	8.3	2.7
Male, 14 to 24 years old..............	45.6	39.9	39.0	31.4
14 and 15 years.............................	93.7	90.9	88.5	80.4
16 and 17 years.............................	75.7	70.3	63.7	51.3
18 years....................................	43.7	39.7	32.4	25.1
19 and 20 years.............................	25.4	19.7	16.9	11.8
21 to 24 years..............................	18.7	7.0	11.6	3.0
Female, 14 to 24 years old............	37.8	37.0	35.2	31.7
14 and 15 years.............................	93.6	91.2	89.4	84.3
16 and 17 years.............................	76.2	70.9	64.9	56.4
18 years....................................	37.9	35.7	32.3	27.1
19 and 20 years.............................	18.7	15.1	15.3	11.2
21 to 24 years..............................	6.0	3.7	5.5	2.4

Source: Derived from *1950 Census of Population*, Vol. II, *Characteristics of the Population*, Part 1, U. S. Summary, table 110.

The stability in the relative size and composition of the white male labor force between 1940 and 1950 is in contrast with the preceding 20 years when the propensity to work decreased (table 22). This stability extended to almost every age group in both the farm and nonfarm population (table 29 and figure 7), except for high-school-age boys, whose labor force activity increased, and college-age men, whose activity decreased.

TABLE **29.**—LABOR FORCE PARTICIPATION RATES, BY RESIDENCE, AGE, COLOR, AND SEX: 1950 AND 1940

[Decennial census levels]

Age and sex	Total				Urban and rural nonfarm				Rural farm			
	White		Nonwhite		White		Nonwhite		White		Nonwhite	
	1950	1940	1950	1940	1950	1940	1950	1940	1950	1940	1950	1940
Male, 14 years old and over.....	79.2	79.0	76.6	80.0	78.6	78.4	75.0	78.4	82.9	80.8	83.3	83.2
14 to 19 years........	38.9	33.3	43.6	45.8	36.6	30.1	36.3	38.6	47.7	42.1	59.8	54.9
14 to 17 years.....	24.8	17.1	31.8	32.6	21.6	13.0	22.8	23.8	35.7	27.8	50.9	43.4
18 and 19 years.....	66.9	65.0	69.1	73.1	64.6	62.7	64.2	68.2	77.4	71.7	81.3	79.7
20 to 24 years........	82.1	88.0	80.4	88.5	80.5	87.4	77.9	86.6	92.6	90.1	91.7	91.7
25 to 29 years........	91.1	95.1	84.4	92.1	90.5	95.0	82.8	91.1	95.5	95.6	93.8	94.2
30 to 34 years........	94.6	95.7	88.2	92.7	94.3	95.6	87.0	91.8	96.8	96.1	95.7	95.0
35 to 39 years........	95.2	95.4	90.2	92.9	94.9	95.2	89.1	91.9	97.0	96.2	96.4	95.8
40 to 44 years........	94.8	94.3	91.1	91.7	94.5	93.9	90.0	90.6	96.8	95.9	96.6	95.3
45 to 49 years........	93.6	93.1	89.9	90.6	93.2	92.6	88.7	88.8	96.2	95.5	96.1	95.4
50 to 54 years........	90.9	91.1	86.5	88.9	90.4	90.3	84.9	86.2	94.0	94.4	94.8	94.8
55 to 59 years........	87.1	87.9	83.2	87.7	86.2	86.4	80.6	84.1	91.8	92.8	93.5	94.4
60 to 64 years........	79.7	78.9	76.0	80.5	78.2	76.0	72.5	74.4	87.3	87.8	88.6	90.5
65 to 69 years........	59.8	59.0	58.4	64.3	56.4	53.5	50.9	52.0	76.8	75.3	80.7	82.8
70 to 74 years........	38.5	38.0	40.7	43.7	34.0	31.6	32.3	28.9	61.6	58.1	65.0	65.6
75 years and over.....	18.4	17.8	22.3	23.5	15.2	13.7	16.1	13.8	35.6	31.1	40.4	38.5
Female, 14 years old and over.....	28.1	24.5	37.1	37.6	30.0	27.6	40.2	43.8	15.1	10.7	22.1	23.2
14 to 19 years........	23.2	18.5	18.3	21.7	25.4	21.2	18.6	22.9	13.0	10.3	17.4	19.9
14 to 17 years.....	11.4	7.1	11.9	14.1	12.3	7.5	10.6	11.5	7.8	5.8	15.1	16.3
18 and 19 years.....	45.4	40.6	31.3	36.7	48.1	46.1	33.9	42.0	27.6	20.6	23.0	27.7
20 to 24 years........	43.4	45.7	39.5	44.9	45.6	50.5	42.1	52.6	24.3	22.6	26.1	28.2
25 to 29 years........	31.3	34.2	42.4	46.1	33.0	38.0	45.3	53.6	17.3	13.9	24.7	25.2
30 to 34 years........	29.2	29.1	46.5	46.2	30.8	32.6	49.8	53.5	16.9	11.0	25.8	23.7
35 to 39 years........	32.0	26.1	48.5	45.7	34.1	29.5	52.6	52.7	17.5	9.3	25.4	24.2
40 to 44 years........	35.0	24.0	48.4	44.3	37.5	27.4	52.4	51.1	18.5	8.5	26.5	24.2
45 to 49 years........	33.6	21.9	45.3	41.8	36.1	25.0	48.9	48.0	17.2	8.2	25.9	25.8
50 to 54 years........	29.8	19.8	41.3	37.6	32.1	22.6	44.3	43.1	15.0	7.9	26.2	25.3
55 to 59 years........	25.2	17.4	34.1	33.6	27.2	19.6	36.6	37.7	12.7	8.1	22.6	24.7
60 to 64 years........	20.1	13.9	27.9	27.8	21.7	15.5	30.0	30.8	10.1	7.1	18.4	21.3
65 to 69 years........	12.7	8.8	16.2	18.5	13.5	9.3	17.1	18.8	7.4	6.1	12.6	18.0
70 to 74 years........	6.3	4.8	8.2	9.5	6.4	4.9	8.0	8.9	5.0	4.3	9.0	10.9
75 years and over.....	2.5	2.1	3.8	4.9	2.5	2.0	3.9	4.4	2.4	2.8	3.6	5.9

Source: Derived from *1950 Census of Population*, Vol. IV, *Special Reports*, Part 1, Chapter A, Employment and Personal Characteristics, table 1; *1940 Census of Population, Employment and Personal Characteristics*, table 1.

Nonwhite men, as we have seen, continued to show a downward drift in labor force activity. Overall, the drop in labor force participation was consistent with the change between 1920 and 1940 (table 22). A substantial part of the change in the decade of the forties can be traced to the migration away from farms and the increase in school enrollment. The combined effect of the off-farm movement and increased school enrollment cannot be examined directly because of the absence of data for 1940. However, if the 1950 rates are standardized for 1940 age, residence, and school enrollment, the importance of these factors may be seen:

Percent of nonwhite male population in labor force

1940... 80.0
1950... 76.6
1950 standardized for 1940 farm-nonfarm residence and school
  enrollment...................................... 79.1

These figures indicate that the drop in labor force participation of non-white men between 1940 and 1950 would have been much smaller (0.9 percentage points instead of 3.4) if they had not left the farms in such large numbers or displayed such interest in remaining in school or going on to college.

The excess of white rates over nonwhite rates in 1950 was found among nonfarm residents in every age group except for boys under 18 and men 75 or more; in almost every age group, too, the excess was larger than in 1940 because of the substantial decline for nonwhites.   For farm residents, the differences between white and nonwhite men tended to be somewhat smaller in 1950 than in 1940, as white rates rose a little and nonwhite rates fell; both classes showed higher rates in 1950 for teen-agers, a large proportion of whom are unpaid family workers, a difficult type of worker to enumerate consistently from one part of the country to another, or one census to another.

Examination of the changes in labor force participation rates for white and nonwhite men in nonfarm households seems to suggest that the improvement in economic conditions over the decade affected the two groups quite differently.   White boys in the teen-age groups showed a marked increase in labor force activity (from 30.1 to 36.6 percent), but nonwhite boys showed a slight drop (38.6 to 36.3 percent).   It is no longer a sign of poverty at home for teen-agers to have some kind of job after school or on Saturdays, and many white boys held them.   But for nonwhite boys, the opportunity to stay in school was not so common in the past, and rising family incomes may have been reflected in some reduction in employment activity and continuation in school.   It is possible that the same sort of consideration may have led older nonwhite workers to retire from the labor force more easily than they did a decade earlier.

Why labor force rates for adult white men in nonfarm households should be consistently higher than for nonwhite men in 1950, and by larger amounts than in 1940, is something of a puzzle.   The difference may be due to differences in attitude toward work, differences in health, differences in actual labor market behavior, or in quality of enumerators' reporting or respondents' reporting.   Census data throw no light on differential attitudes.   They do show that a larger proportion of nonwhite men than of white men in each age group in nonfarm households were in institutions or reported as unable to work in 1950; but this was also true in 1940, and the differences were of about the same order of magnitude. As for labor market behavior, generally speaking, the average white man has a firmer attachment to the labor force than does the average nonwhite man.   He is less likely to be unemployed; he is more likely to be a salaried, white-collar worker or a year-round factory employee.   His conditions of employment are more stable.   The Negro, on the other hand, may be a casual or odd-job worker, or a seasonal worker in the building or outdoor trades where work is generally irregular.   With restricted em-

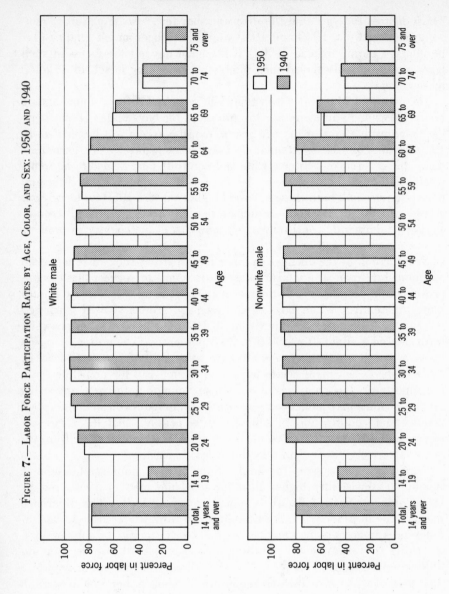

FIGURE 7.—LABOR FORCE PARTICIPATION RATES BY AGE, COLOR, AND SEX: 1950 AND 1940

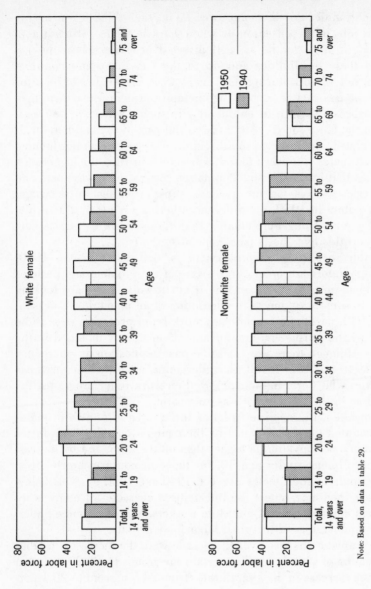

Note: Based on data in table 29.

ployment opportunities and less education, he may not think it worthwhile to seek other jobs in the offseason or when work is slack. Often a non-union worker, he may not be so well directed or protected in the job market. All these possibilities add up to the fact that some nonwhite men who are not at work during the census week either do not look for work or may be less easy to identify as unemployed than white men; they may be described to the census enumerator in such a way as to be classified as not in the labor force. Any bias on the part of the enumerator, it may be speculated, would be in the direction of reporting as not looking for work adult males who were found at home or drifting about between jobs. The fact that in the Current Population Survey, where the performance of interviewers was, on the average, superior to that of decennial census enumerators in 1950, the differences between white and nonwhite male labor force reporting were smaller than those shown by census data tends to support this hypothesis (see Appendix A).

It is possible that when unemployment is high, as it was in 1940, decennial enumerators are much more aware of the problem and perhaps more likely to assume that a Negro who is not at work is perhaps looking for work or, in some way, meets the definition of an unemployed person. Further, in 1940, persons on emergency work relief programs were to be so identified by the census enumerator and automatically included in the labor force. Although there was a sizable misclassification of emergency workers in 1940 and as a result an undercount, nevertheless for those nonwhite males who were, in fact, reported on work relief programs, the classification as in the labor force was automatic.

To sum up, then, the decline in labor force rates of nonwhite males could be accounted for in large part by their migration away from farms where labor force participation is higher than off the farm, and by increasing school enrollment, under age 30, for those in nonfarm households. The drop for nonfarm adult males between 1940 and 1950 to levels below those for white men may reflect the intermittent character of many types of employment characteristic of nonwhite workers, as well as some under-reporting by enumerators of marginal labor force activity.

The most dramatic changes over the decade were the increases in labor force participation of white women in certain age groups (table 29). In ten years' time, the increase in the overall rate (from 24.5 percent to 28.1 percent) was almost as great as in the previous 20 years. As table 22 indicates, the rate would have gone up even more if it had not been for the increase in marriage and the changing age composition of the population. The deficit of young women in the population in the age groups 18 to 24, where labor force participation is at its maximum for white women, meant that the overall rate would have been lower, on this account alone, if other increases had not taken place. Moreover, there was some decline in the rate of labor force participation in these ages.

From a 1940 pattern of labor force participation that reached a peak (48 percent) at 20 and 21 years and declined steadily thereafter, the whole picture of white female labor force participation changed radically. By 1950, the two-phase working life had emerged. The first phase included the years of leaving school, with a peak at age 19 or 20 when about 48 percent were in the labor force. After the marriage age the rate dropped off sharply until the early thirties, when it reached about 28 percent. The second phase involved the return to the labor force of many of, but by no means all, the women who had once held paid jobs. The second and lower peak (36 percent) was reached in the early forties.

By age, the changes between 1940 and 1950 were unprecedented, after age 40. Increases of 10 or more percentage points were recorded for the age groups 40 to 44, 45 to 49, and 50 to 54; even beyond these ages, the increases were almost as great.

Again, the contrast with nonwhite persons is extremely interesting. Labor force activity of nonwhite women, particularly their propensity to take paid employment, decreased, as in earlier decades, but by no means at the rate estimated for the period 1920–1940. During that time, according to Durand's estimates in table 22, the labor force participation rate of nonwhite women would have dropped by 6.4 percentage points had other demographic factors been equal. In the 1940–1950 decade, the "propensity" drop was only 1.71 percentage points. For farm residents, the net changes between 1940 and 1950 were relatively small or nonexistent in most age groups; for nonfarm residents, there were sharp decreases in the age groups under 35, but virtually no changes thereafter (table 29).

These data suggest that nonwhite women who remained on farms had about the same tendency to be in the labor force as they had a decade earlier. Approximately one in four was employed in some capacity in the spring months of the year, up until age 60.

For nonfarm residents, the reduction in labor force activity of women under 35 was somewhat sharper for nonwhite women than for white women. A larger proportion of both were married and living with their husbands in 1950 than in 1940, but the explanation lies elsewhere. The labor force participation rates themselves were moving in different directions, for married and other women (table 30 and figure 8). Single white women in the ages under 45 were in the labor force in about the same proportions in 1950 as in 1940; those over 45 showed some increase. Single nonwhite women, however, showed very sharp declines until about age 55. Married women, living with their husbands in nonfarm households, the population group which was numerically most important, showed substantial rises in labor force rates at all ages for white women, but not for nonwhite women. Under 30 years of age, the 1950 rates for nonwhite women were lower than the 1940 rates for the most part, and in the middle age groups, where there were some increases, the gains tended to be small. There seemed to be no evidence that nonwhite women withdrew from the labor force and returned after age 35, as there was for white women.

TABLE 30.—LABOR FORCE PARTICIPATION RATES OF WOMEN, BY RESIDENCE, MARITAL STATUS, AGE, AND COLOR: 1950 AND 1940

[Decennial census levels]

| Marital status and age | Total | | | | Urban and rural nonfarm | | | | Rural farm | | | |
| | White | | Nonwhite | | White | | Nonwhite | | White | | Nonwhite | |
	1950	1940	1950	1940	1950	1940	1950	1940	1950	1940	1950	1940
SINGLE												
Total, 14 years old and over.....	47.5	45.9	36.1	41.9	51.0	51.1	39.6	48.0	23.0	21.9	23.8	28.7
14 to 19 years........	23.5	19.4	17.8	21.7	25.7	22.0	17.8	22.5	13.3	11.1	17.9	20.1
14 to 17 years......	11.3	7.1	11.4	13.8	12.1	7.5	9.9	12.0	7.8	5.9	15.1	16.4
18 and 19 years.....	54.5	48.3	36.7	43.4	57.2	53.8	39.8	48.7	35.9	26.4	27.4	33.6
20 to 24 years........	75.5	73.8	56.7	65.1	77.3	78.9	60.5	72.4	56.3	45.2	39.0	46.0
25 to 29 years........	81.7	80.1	66.2	73.9	84.1	84.5	69.4	79.4	51.3	47.1	43.3	51.0
30 to 34 years........	79.0	78.2	67.9	73.3	81.7	83.0	70.8	78.1	46.8	41.8	42.9	49.7
35 to 44 years........	76.5	73.6	65.8	71.1	79.3	78.5	68.6	75.1	42.8	34.7	43.0	49.3
45 to 54 years........	71.5	63.5	57.3	62.6	74.4	67.7	61.2	66.2	36.1	28.5	27.8	47.0
55 to 64 years........	57.6	47.2	44.0	46.8	60.6	50.4	46.1	49.6	22.7	22.5	29.7	36.6
65 to 74 years........	27.1	20.9	23.8	26.9	28.1	21.9	25.9	28.1	14.0	12.7	10.3	23.3
75 years and over.....	6.9	6.8	8.7	13.8	7.0	6.6	9.0	17.7	5.7	8.2	6.1	4.0
MARRIED, HUSBAND PRESENT												
Total, 14 years old and over.....	20.7	12.5	31.8	27.3	22.0	14.6	35.2	33.7	12.6	4.3	18.0	15.4
14 to 19 years........	19.8	7.7	16.5	17.2	21.9	9.6	17.8	19.7	9.7	3.4	13.2	14.2
14 to 17 years......	11.4	4.1	14.7	13.2	12.9	4.7	15.4	15.1	5.7	3.0	13.0	12.1
18 and 19 years.....	22.4	8.7	17.3	18.6	24.5	10.8	18.7	21.3	11.2	3.5	13.2	15.2
20 to 24 years........	26.0	16.2	26.0	25.7	27.8	19.0	27.9	31.5	12.1	5.1	16.6	16.0
25 to 29 years........	21.1	17.1	32.1	31.1	22.1	19.5	34.7	37.8	12.8	5.6	18.0	16.8
30 to 34 years........	21.0	16.3	37.9	31.8	22.0	18.5	41.2	38.5	14.0	5.7	21.5	16.3
35 to 44 years........	25.3	13.8	38.7	30.5	26.9	16.0	43.1	37.1	15.8	5.0	19.9	15.9
45 to 54 years........	22.2	10.1	32.9	25.5	23.8	11.9	36.5	31.5	13.6	3.9	19.6	15.4
55 to 64 years........	12.6	6.4	22.3	19.3	13.3	7.6	25.0	23.4	9.2	2.8	15.1	13.7
65 to 74 years........	4.7	2.7	10.8	10.7	4.8	3.0	11.5	12.9	4.5	1.6	9.0	8.1
75 years and over.....	1.5	1.1	3.4	4.7	1.6	1.2	3.4	4.6	1.4	0.7	3.2	4.8
OTHER MARITAL STATUS												
Total, 14 years old and over.....	33.2	30.2	47.1	53.2	34.5	31.6	48.7	55.8	17.9	20.5	33.6	41.5
14 to 19 years........	37.8	31.0	35.0	43.2	40.2	34.4	37.7	45.8	23.6	18.0	23.9	37.4
14 to 17 years......	26.0	17.4	26.6	36.5	27.2	19.8	28.7	36.9	20.5	10.5	18.7	35.9
18 and 19 years.....	44.0	36.5	39.3	46.3	46.7	39.9	42.2	49.4	25.8	22.0	26.9	38.3
20 to 24 years........	56.6	54.7	49.1	62.5	59.0	58.5	51.3	66.6	31.0	32.2	33.0	46.8
25 to 29 years........	59.8	61.5	58.1	69.9	61.1	64.3	59.5	72.8	39.3	38.4	44.1	53.2
30 to 34 years........	61.9	64.5	63.7	72.2	63.1	66.8	64.8	74.5	41.1	41.2	48.4	56.1
35 to 44 years........	65.2	59.3	67.1	70.1	66.7	61.2	67.9	71.7	39.1	39.8	57.1	59.5
45 to 54 years........	55.6	44.1	58.3	59.4	57.0	45.3	58.9	60.3	34.2	33.9	52.1	55.3
55 to 64 years........	35.4	25.2	38.9	41.3	36.5	25.5	39.6	41.5	20.3	22.7	33.5	40.6
65 to 74 years........	11.5	7.5	13.9	16.7	11.8	7.8	14.0	15.2	8.5	9.6	13.5	20.8
75 years and over.....	2.1	1.8	3.5	4.5	2.1	1.6	3.5	3.7	2.4	2.8	3.6	6.1

Source: Derived from *1950 Census of Population*, Vol. IV, *Special Reports*, Part 1, Chapter A, Employment and Personal Characteristics, table 10; *1940 Census of Population, Employment and Personal Characteristics*, table 7.

Nonwhite women who were widowed, divorced, or living apart from their husbands were relatively much more common than white women in similar circumstances (28.4 percent of the 14-and-over age group in 1950 as compared with 16.5 percent for white women). Nonwhite women of these types had considerably lower labor force rates in 1950 than in 1940 in almost all age groups, whereas among white women in some age groups, particularly from 45 to 64, labor force participation increased substantially. As a result, there was not much difference in the labor force activity of the two groups, white and nonwhite, in 1950, except at ages 18 to 24.

In summary, the changes in labor force participation patterns for white and nonwhite women present a complex picture. There is some reason to think that where other sources of support were available—such as a husband's earnings, or pensions or other types of Social Security payments for needy and dependent persons—nonwhite women tended to reduce their labor force activity, particularly in the age groups where young children at home are a determinant factor. White women had apparently other motivations, for the group with husbands to support them presumably almost doubled their rate of labor force participation, and in some age groups actually did so (18 to 19 years, 45 to 54, and 55 to 64). Even those who were widowed or divorced were more likely to be in the labor force in 1950 than in 1940. Despite these changes, the labor force rates of nonwhite women who were married or had ever been married were still well above those for white women in 1950.

One of the labor force developments that cannot easily be explained is the different pattern for white and nonwhite women who were not married. In 1940, the rates for white single women in nonfarm households were slightly above those for nonwhite women, and the ten-year period brought some small increases for white women. But for nonwhite women there were substantial declines in almost all age groups, so that, by 1950, 51 percent of the white single women living in nonfarm homes, and about 40 percent of the nonwhite, were in the labor force. In view of the differences in income between white and nonwhite families, it is not easy to see why nonwhite women who are not married should be less likely to be in the labor force than white women, or why their rates would decline during a decade of expanding job opportunities. Disability and institutionalization were slightly more common among nonwhite than white single women in 1940, but not in 1950 (table 31).

TABLE 31.—PERCENT OF SINGLE FEMALE POPULATION UNABLE TO WORK OR IN INSTITUTIONS, BY RESIDENCE AND COLOR: 1950 AND 1940

[Decennial census levels]

Color	1950			1940		
	Total	Urban and rural nonfarm	Rural farm	Total	Urban and rural nonfarm	Rural farm
White..........................	4.4	4.7	2.6	4.4	4.6	3.4
Nonwhite.......................	4.0	4.7	2.0	4.7	5.5	2.8

Source: Derived from *1950 Census of Population*, Vol. IV, *Special Reports*, Part 1, Chapter A, Employment and Personal Characteristics, table 10; *1940 Census of Population, Employment and Personal Characteristics*, table 7, and *Persons Not in the Labor Force*, table 5.

FIGURE **8.**—URBAN AND RURAL-NONFARM RESIDENTS—PERCENT OF WOMEN IN LABOR
FORCE BY MARITAL STATUS, AGE, AND COLOR: 1950 AND 1940

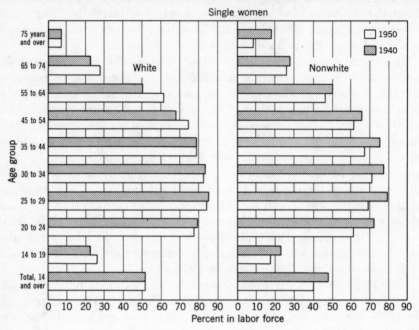

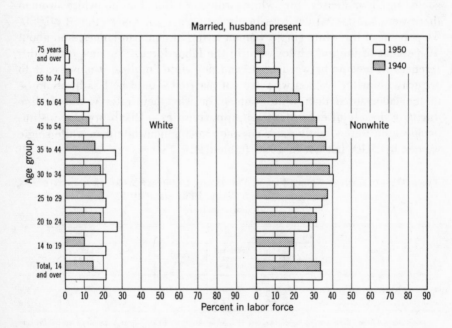

FIGURE **8.**—URBAN AND RURAL-NONFARM RESIDENTS—PERCENT OF WOMEN IN LABOR FORCE BY MARITAL STATUS, AGE, AND COLOR: 1950 AND 1940—Cont.

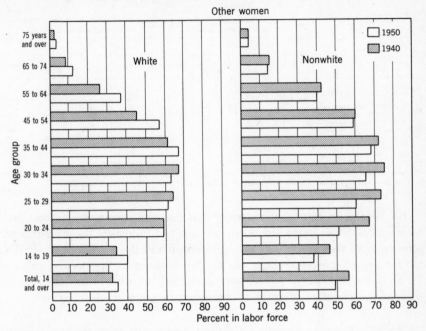

Note: Based on data in table 30.

It is true that common-law marriages are relatively more frequent among nonwhite women than among white, and that some nonwhite women reported as single were actually married and receiving some support. Illegitimate births, too, are more frequent in the nonwhite population. The need to stay at home and care for children might be another reason for the difference in labor force participation. Further, a larger proportion of nonwhite single women than of white live in households of persons to whom they are not related and who may not have accurate information on their employment status. Where no information was reported on the census schedule, the person was classified as not in the labor force. Finally, it has been suggested that nonwhite single women, like some nonwhite men, may prefer not to work rather than take the jobs open to them; with more adequate family incomes they have found this choice possible.

Effect of fertility changes

Mothers of young children (under 5) in native white families were only rarely in the labor force in 1940 (6.5 percent), but in Negro families one in five mothers of children under 5 was working or seeking work outside the home (table 32). The rate for white women *without* children under 5 years of age was, of course, much higher (24.2 percent), but that for Negro women was still almost twice as high (45.9 percent).

TABLE **32.**—LABOR FORCE PARTICIPATION RATES FOR EVER-MARRIED WOMEN WITH AND
WITHOUT CHILDREN UNDER 5 YEARS OLD, BY AGE AND COLOR: 1950 AND 1940

[Decennial census levels]

Age of woman	With children under 5				Without children under 5			
	1950		1940		1950		1940	
	White	Non-white	Native white	Negro	White	Non-white	Native white	Negro
Total, 15 to 49 years...	11.1	20.9	6.5	19.9	35.7	50.2	24.2	45.9
15 to 19 years..............	9.0	15.2	3.9	15.1	31.3	28.0	13.3	26.2
20 to 24 years..............	12.4	19.1	6.8	18.6	52.0	46.8	31.9	44.2
25 to 29 years..............	11.1	21.1	7.2	19.9	44.2	52.6	32.9	49.7
30 to 34 years..............	10.4	21.9	6.5	20.2	35.8	55.4	28.3	49.6
35 to 39 years..............	10.3	23.3	5.6	23.0	34.7	53.4	23.5	48.3
40 to 44 years..............	11.3	25.4	5.2	21.0	33.2	49.7	19.8	44.9
45 to 49 years..............	12.6	26.0	4.9	25.6	29.3	45.6	17.4	41.6

Source: Derived from *1950 Census of Population*, Vol. IV, *Special Reports*, Part 5, Chapter C, Fertility, tables 46 and 47; *1940 Census of Population*, *Women by Number of Children Under 5 Years Old*, tables 37 and 38.

By 1950, the gap between white and nonwhite women who had ever been married had narrowed; white women had increased their labor force activity, both those with very young children and those without (table 33), but for nonwhite women there was not much change. Spectacular gains of 10 or more percentage points were recorded for white women under 50 without preschool children in all age groups except 30 to 34 years.

TABLE **33.**—EXCESS OF NONWHITE LABOR FORCE PARTICIPATION RATES FOR EVER-MARRIED
WOMEN WITH AND WITHOUT CHILDREN UNDER 5 YEARS OLD: 1950 AND 1940

[Decennial census levels]

Age of woman	With children under 5		Without children under 5	
	1950	1940	1950	1940
Total, 15 to 49 years old............	9.8	13.4	14.5	21.7
15 to 19 years........................	6.2	11.2	-3.3	12.9
20 to 24 years........................	6.7	11.8	-5.2	12.3
25 to 29 years........................	10.0	12.7	8.4	16.8
30 to 34 years........................	11.5	13.7	19.6	21.3
35 to 39 years........................	13.0	17.4	18.7	24.8
40 to 44 years........................	14.1	15.8	16.5	25.1
45 to 49 years........................	13.4	20.7	16.3	24.2

Source: Based on table 32.

The contrast between the stability of rates for nonwhite women and the increase in the rates for white women was most marked at the younger ages. By 1950, the labor force rates of white women under 25 years of age without young children were actually higher than for nonwhite women (table 33), and at age 25 to 29 years the difference had narrowed from 16.8 percentage points in 1940 to 8.4 percentage points in 1950. (These are only approximate measures of change because of the difference in coverage: all white women who had ever been married in 1950 and native white women in 1940; all nonwhite women in 1950 and Negro women in 1940.)

Part of the explanation may lie in the changing proportion of women who did not have children of any age (table 34). In 1950, all but a small fraction of the white women under 25 who did not have preschool children had no other children to keep them at home; among nonwhite women, the proportion who were childless was considerably smaller. In 1940, the differences were not so great, although in the same direction. Changing patterns of fertility, however, do not always account for labor force changes. The increase in the proportion of women over 25 without small children who were completely childless was much greater for nonwhite than for white women, yet the sharp rise in labor force rates occurred among the white women, not the nonwhite.

TABLE **34.**—PERCENT OF EVER-MARRIED WOMEN WITHOUT CHILDREN UNDER 5 WHO HAD NEVER HAD ANY CHILDREN, BY AGE AND COLOR: 1950 AND 1940

Age of woman	1950		1940	
	White	Nonwhite	Native white	Negro
Total, 15 to 49 years..............	35.1	43.8	29.4	32.9
15 to 19 years............................	95.1	86.1	65.6	58.8
20 to 24 years............................	88.4	68.1	67.6	52.9
25 to 29 years............................	55.9	52.8	48.8	40.8
30 to 34 years............................	31.6	44.5	30.1	33.0
35 to 39 years............................	25.7	41.6	20.5	28.2
40 to 44 years............................	22.2	33.9	15.9	23.2
45 to 49 years............................	20.2	29.7	14.5	19.9

Source: Derived from *1950 Census of Population*, Vol. IV, *Special Reports*, Part 5, Chapter C, Fertility, tables 2 and 35; *1940 Census of Population, Women by Number of Children Under 5 Years Old*, tables 1 and 2, and *Women by Number of Children Ever Born*, tables 1 and 3.

Data are not available for 1950 to evaluate the effect of children of different ages on the labor force participation of their mothers. However, approximations can be obtained by comparing women who had never had a child, those with children under 5, and those who had had children but had none under 5. This last group approximates those with older children only, although it, of course, includes some women whose children had died (table 35).

Table 35 shows the relative importance of marriage alone, and of marriage and childbearing, in affecting labor force participation for white and nonwhite women. On the basis of the rates for single women, it can be seen that for white women marriage by itself has a deterrent effect on employment of women outside the home but that the effect is not nearly so great as that of having children in the home under school age or even older. In short, fertility rates have a greater effect on the size of the female labor force than do marriage rates alone.

The typical white woman under 45 has been married once, is still living with her husband, and has one or more children. Until she is in her early thirties, she has at least one child under 5 years of age; thereafter her children are in the school-age group. As a group, the labor force participation of white women in their first marriage decreases from a peak at age

20 to 24 to a low point at 30 to 34 years and then increases again. This pattern for the group reflects its changing composition from predominantly women with no children to predominantly women with children under 5 years of age and, finally, with children over 5 years. Within each class, labor force participation decreases somewhat with age or remains very low, as in the case of mothers of young children. Even women whose children are older do not show increasing labor force participation up to age 44. Thus, married women aged 40 to 44 who have had children and whose children are probably in their teens have a labor force participation rate of 24.8 percent, the same as that for women aged 25 to 29 whose children are probably just starting to school. These data suggest that it is at the time her last child enters school that a woman may re-enter the labor force, and that the probability that she will be in the labor force does not increase very much after that point, unless she loses her husband.

TABLE 35.—LABOR FORCE PARTICIPATION RATES OF WOMEN 15 TO 44 YEARS OLD, BY MARITAL STATUS, AGE, COLOR, AND NUMBER OF CHILDREN EVER BORN: 1950

[Decennial census levels]

Age and color	Total	Single	Ever married								
			Married once, husband present					All other ever married			
			Total	Total	No child ever born	One or more children ever born		Total	No child ever born	One or more children ever born	
						1 or more under 5	None under 5			1 or more under 5	None under 5
WHITE											
Total, 15 to 44 yrs..	32.4	52.1	25.8	22.1	46.3	9.5	24.9	41.5	55.8	20.8	48.2
15 to 19 years	27.1	28.1	22.0	20.2	30.1	7.2	24.9	33.3	39.2	22.9	39.0
20 to 24 years	42.8	75.5	27.6	25.6	53.2	10.3	27.8	40.2	60.4	26.9	46.8
25 to 29 years	30.6	81.7	23.0	20.0	52.5	9.6	24.8	38.2	59.4	21.7	50.1
30 to 34 years	28.2	79.0	23.1	19.3	46.4	9.2	23.9	39.7	56.7	18.3	49.0
35 to 39 years	31.2	77.0	27.0	22.5	41.8	9.1	25.6	43.4	55.8	17.3	48.8
40 to 44 years	33.9	76.2	30.0	25.0	39.3	10.2	24.8	45.2	53.5	16.5	46.9
20 to 44 years	33.3	77.5	25.9	22.2	48.0	9.6	24.9	41.7	56.8	20.8	48.2
NONWHITE											
Total, 15 to 44 yrs..	40.3	39.7	40.5	31.7	46.5	16.8	39.5	53.0	62.9	31.0	57.6
15 to 19 years	20.9	20.9	20.8	16.1	21.7	11.3	37.0	33.9	40.6	28.1	35.9
20 to 24 years	38.9	56.8	30.7	24.3	41.4	15.2	37.3	44.5	59.5	30.7	50.9
25 to 29 years	42.7	66.2	38.8	31.6	50.5	17.0	41.1	50.8	63.9	31.8	56.9
30 to 34 years	46.6	67.9	44.6	37.1	55.6	19.4	42.0	55.0	64.4	27.8	62.0
35 to 39 years	47.8	67.7	46.4	36.3	48.9	18.6	40.3	57.6	66.5	33.4	59.2
40 to 44 years	47.6	63.2	46.6	36.1	45.4	20.7	36.1	56.1	62.4	34.3	55.9
20 to 44 years	44.4	61.6	41.6	32.8	48.7	17.3	39.5	53.6	63.7	31.2	57.9

Note: Rates differ slightly from those in table 30 because based on "fertility" sample—in part a 3⅓-percent sample, in part a 2.4-percent sample.

Source: Derived from *1950 Census of Population*, Vol. IV, *Special Reports*, Part 5, Chapter C, Fertility, tables 24–27, 46, and 47, and unpublished tabulation of 1950 Census data.

Childless married women have the sharpest downtrend from 53.2 percent at 20 to 24 years to 39.3 percent at 40 to 44 years. This may reflect the rising earnings of their husbands as they reach middle age, or it may mean that as the healthier women bear children and leave the group, it consists to a greater extent of women who are less able physically to work outside the home.

In the category of all other women who have ever been married are those who have been married more than once, the separated, widowed, and divorced. Among these women are those who have lost their means of support through the death or desertion of their husbands, as well as women whose careers may have been one of the causes of an unsatisfactory marriage or may have made it possible for them to support themselves. As a group, they are much more likely to have paid jobs than are women whose first marriages are intact. For those with children, the labor force rates are about twice as high as for the average mother who is still married to her first husband. The differences are not so great, particularly at the younger ages, for women who have not had any children.

Turning to nonwhite women, we find a somewhat different picture. First, there is very little difference between single women and those without children who are no longer living with their first husbands (married again, separated, widowed, or divorced). This may somewhat confirm the hypothesis (p. 57) that some nonwhite women reported as "single" may, in fact, be living in common-law marriages or may be separated, widowed, or divorced. As in the case of white women, the presence of young preschool children is the greatest barrier to labor force participation, but the differences between women with small children and those without are not so great.

The greatest differentials between white and nonwhite women are for those with young children; in this class labor force rates of nonwhite women are about twice as high as those for white women. Whether this reflects income differentials, different standards, or different living arrangements, the available data do not show. Historically, nonwhite women have been under greater pressure to seek employment outside the home, even when their children were of preschool age, because their husbands' earnings were too low to support the family adequately or because they were separated or divorced. As they often lived with relatives, they could more easily arrange for the care of the children. There could not be the same degree of social disapproval of working mothers in nonwhite circles as in white circles. As we have seen, however, there was no increase between 1940 and 1950 in the proportion of working mothers in the nonwhite group, although the proportion in the white group did rise. Another difference between white and nonwhite women is the relation of age and labor force participation. Whereas white rates tend to decrease with age, after a peak generally at age 20 to 24, the nonwhite rates rise continuously with age or reach a peak in the thirties.

In view of the overall increase in employment of married women, it is obvious that there must have been substantial changes in the labor force participation rates of mothers of children of school age, even though the increases for mothers of young children were moderate. Exactly comparable data are not at hand, but rough estimates would indicate that perhaps 26 percent of the women married and living with their husbands with children of kindergarten or school age (5 years of age or more) were in the labor force in 1950, as compared to perhaps 12 percent in 1940.

Throughout this section we have been examining the effect of marriage and motherhood on labor force participation rates. Turning the problem around, we might ask what is the effect of the increased employment of women on the marriage rate and the size of family? Does having a job still tend to raise a barrier to marriage or to restrict the number of children a woman has if she does marry?

First, with respect to marriage. It is not necessary to be a statistician to feel confident that young women of today find little opposition to continuing their jobs after marriage and, in fact, are frequently urged to do so by their families and prospective husbands. The expansion of the labor force has occurred despite the marriage boom. The proportion of single women in the population aged 16 to 45 decreased, on an age-standardized basis, from 29.7 percent in 1940 to 22.8 percent in 1950. But the net increases in labor force participation were in age classes in which a high proportion were already married in 1940 (table 36).

TABLE 36.—PERCENT IN LABOR FORCE AND PERCENT MARRIED, FOR AGE COHORTS
OF WOMEN: 1950 AND 1940

[Decennial census levels]

Age in 1940	Percent of women in labor force			Percent of women who were married		
	1940	1950	Change, 1940 to 1950	1940	1950	Change, 1940 to 1950
20 to 24 years....................	45.6	31.0	-14.6	52.8	90.7	+37.9
25 to 29 years....................	35.5	33.8	-1.7	77.2	91.6	+14.4
30 to 34 years....................	30.9	36.4	+5.5	85.3	91.7	+6.4
35 to 39 years....................	28.3	34.8	+6.5	88.8	92.1	+3.3
40 to 44 years....................	26.0	30.8	+4.8	90.5	92.3	+1.8
45 to 49 years....................	23.7	25.9	+2.2	91.4	92.3	+0.9
50 to 54 years....................	21.2	20.6	-0.6	91.3	91.8	+0.5

Source: Derived from *1950 Census of Population*, Vol. II, *Characteristics of the Population*, Part 1, U. S. Summary, table 102, and Vol. IV, *Special Reports*, Part 1, Chapter A, Employment and Personal Characteristics, table 2.

It appears from these figures that women in their early twenties who married in such large numbers during the decade also usually gave up their jobs and left the labor force, probably with the birth of their first child. Women in their late twenties maintained practically the same labor force rate, although many of them also married during the period. The proportions of these two age cohorts that had married by 1950 were as high as the proportions reached by women 40 to 44 years old in 1940; it does not seem likely, therefore, that economic activity had acted as a barrier to marriage during this period, or that a significantly larger proportion would have married if they had not had the alternative of working. Indeed, the fact that substantial numbers continued to work after marriage may have made marriage financially possible.

In the age cohorts 30 to 34, 35 to 39, and 40 to 44 years, in which the marked increases in labor force participation took place over the decade, the proportions married were already fairly high in 1940. There were further increases in marriage, despite the net movement into the labor force.

On the question of the effect of increased employment of married women on the number of children, the available statistics permit a reliable answer only for children under 5 years of age. Apparently most mothers of preschool children prefer to stay home if they can and are encouraged by the teachings of current child psychology. It is not surprising to find that married women in the labor force in 1950 had only about one-third as many children of preschool age as did women not in the labor force (table 37). But for white women, the number per 1,000 of those ever married in the labor force increased by 50 percent over the decade; the number for women not in the labor force increased by only 29 percent.

TABLE 37.—CHILDREN UNDER 5 YEARS OLD PER 1,000 EVER-MARRIED WOMEN 15 TO 49 YEARS OLD, BY LABOR FORCE STATUS: 1950 AND 1940

[Decennial census levels]

Labor force status	White women			Nonwhite women		
	1950	1940[1]	Percent change, 1940 to 1950	1950	1940[1]	Percent change, 1940 to 1950
Labor force..........................	199	132	+50.8	233	182	+28.0
Not in labor force...................	641	496	+29.2	713	543	+31.3

[1] Data relate to native white and Negro women.

Source: Derived from *1950 Census of Population*, Vol. IV, *Special Reports*, Part 5, Chapter C, Fertility, tables 46 and 47; *1940 Census of Population, Women by Number of Children Under 5 Years Old*, tables 39 and 40.

The relation between employment outside the home and the number of children a woman has, including those of school age, can be measured only roughly for 1940 and 1950. Approximations can be obtained from information on the number of children ever born to women under, say, 40. Most of these children would be alive in 1950, and most of them would be under 18 years of age. For 1940, statistics are available on the number of children under 18 in families whose head was under 45. Table 38 shows the distributions by number of children in families with the wife in and out of the labor force at each date. Both workers and nonworkers were more likely to have a child in 1950 than in 1940, but the differential between them with respect to the proportion with children had not changed appreciably. However, for women who had one or more children, the difference had narrowed somewhat. In 1950, 57 percent of the mothers in the labor force had two or more children, as compared with 65 percent of the mothers not in the labor force; in 1940, 51 percent of the working mothers had two or more children in the family as compared with 62 percent of the mothers not in the labor force.

TABLE **38.**—PERCENT DISTRIBUTION OF MARRIED WOMEN BY NUMBER OF CHILDREN,
BY LABOR FORCE STATUS: 1950 AND 1940

[Decennial census levels]

Number of children[1]	1950		1940	
	Women 15 to 39 years old married once, spouse present		Wives of family heads under 45 years old	
	Labor force	Not in labor force	Labor force	Not in labor force
Total women..........................	100.0	100.0	100.0	100.0
No children..................................	47.6	15.3	55.2	22.9
1 or more children...........................	52.4	84.7	44.8	77.1
Total women with children..............	100.0	100.0	100.0	100.0
1 child......................................	42.6	34.6	49.0	37.6
2 children...................................	31.5	33.8	28.5	30.5
3 or more children...........................	25.9	31.6	22.5	31.9

[1] Children ever born in 1950; children under 18 in 1940.

Source: Derived from *1950 Census of Population*, Vol. IV, *Special Reports*, Part 5, Chapter C, Fertility, tables 25 and 27; *1940 Census of Population, Families—Employment Status*, table 11.

The data in the crude form suggest what is confirmed by more detailed statistics for 1950—that although women in the labor force who have ever been married have borne fewer children than those not in the labor force, those working women who have ever borne any children have had almost as many as the mothers not in the labor force (table 39). It appears that women who place a high value on the satisfaction of a career or on the income from a job may avoid or postpone motherhood, but that once a family has been started, a woman who works is almost as likely to have additional children as one who does not work. Some women who work from time to time were not in the labor force in April when the census was taken. If data were available on children ever born to women who worked at some time during the year, the differential between workers and nonworkers would be even smaller.

TABLE **39.**—FERTILITY OF WOMEN BY LABOR FORCE STATUS: 1950

[Decennial census levels]

Labor force status and color	Percent with no children ever born	Number of children ever born	
		Per 1,000 ever-married women	Per 1,000 mothers
Ever-married women 15 to 59 years, total:			
Labor force.............................	36.2	1,556	2,440
Not in labor force.......................	16.2	2,321	2,770
White:			
Labor force.............................	35.9	1,510	2,356
Not in labor force.......................	15.5	2,284	2,703
Nonwhite:			
Labor force.............................	37.7	1,806	2,901
Not in labor force.......................	23.5	2,718	3,554

Source: Derived from *1950 Census of Population*, Vol. IV, *Special Reports*, Part 5, Chapter C, Fertility, tables 24 and 26.

Labor force participation and education

One of the questions we seek to answer is to what extent is economic pressure the major reason that men and women seek paid employment? If there is a choice, will they choose leisure or the rewards of work, and are those rewards purely monetary or, in large part, such gains as diminished boredom, greater companionship, and other noneconomic advantages? Direct evidence on the relation between changing labor force participation and family income is available from the 1940 Census data but not for 1950. Educational attainment, however, is an indirect and crude index of socio-economic status, and it may be used in connection with changes in labor force activity to throw some light on the question of whether the expansion in the labor force came from the upper or lower end of the income scale.

Information on highest grade of school completed by labor force status is available for 1940 only for native white and Negro persons; for 1950, for all white and nonwhite. Comparison of changes in labor force participation rates by age and educational level should not be greatly affected by these differences. In order to compare absolute levels, the 1940 data for the total labor force were estimated from the data for native white and Negroes. The labor force had an estimated 1.5 million more men with college training in 1950 than in 1940, and correspondingly fewer men who had not finished high school (table 40). The educational levels of the female labor force also rose, but many of the additional workers had fewer than four years of high school education. Thus, although the growth of the female labor force was relatively greater at the upper levels, it was based in considerable measure too on an increase at the lower end of the scale.

TABLE **40.**—EDUCATIONAL ATTAINMENT OF PERSONS 18 TO 64 YEARS OLD IN THE LABOR FORCE: 1950 AND 1940

[Decennial census levels. In thousands]

Educational attainment	Male			Female		
	1950	1940[1]	Change, 1940 to 1950	1950	1940[1]	Change, 1940 to 1950
Total......................	39,644	37,204	+2,440	15,570	12,206	+3,364
Less than 4 years of high school...	24,999	26,525	−1,526	7,733	6,681	+1,052
4 years of high school............	8,823	6,509	+2,314	4,999	3,620	+1,379
1 year or more of college.........	5,822	4,170	+1,652	2,838	1,905	+933

[1] Based on distribution of native white and Negro.

Source: Derived from *1950 Census of Population*, Vol. IV, *Special Reports*, Part 5, Chapter B, Education, table 9; *1940 Census of Population*, Vol. IV, *Characteristics by Age*, Part 1, U. S. Summary, table 24, and *Educational Attainment by Economic Characteristics and Marital Status*, tables 17 and 18.

In general, the more education a person has, the more likely he or she is to be in the labor force, except at the ages where formal education is still unfinished and labor force activity is restricted by current school enrollment. For white men, changes in labor force participation between 1940 and 1950 were small, as we have seen, and bore little relation to level of education (table 41). Nonwhite men, whose labor force participation had decreased in all age groups, showed the greatest decreases at both ends of the educational ladder. Those with little or no schooling were less likely to be in the labor force than in 1940, but the same was true for those with high school education or better. When the comparison is restricted to the age groups whose education is generally completed (30 to 64 years), the picture is the same. The migration of Negroes from rural areas, as we have seen, has brought about a reduction in the proportion of the population in the labor force. Since educational standards were low for Negroes in rural areas (59 percent of Negro males in 1940 had completed only four years of school or less in rural-farm areas, as compared with 32 percent in nonfarm areas), many may have found it especially difficult to find regular jobs after migration; some withdrawal from the labor force would be expected on this account. This would not explain the reduction among better-educated nonwhite men, however. It is possible that barriers to the employment of Negro men in professional and other white-collar jobs were responsible. Rather than work at semiskilled or laboring jobs, they may have preferred to leave the labor force for a while. It should be noted that the marked excess of rates for white men over those for nonwhite men 30 to 64 years of age begins at the high school level and is particularly large for men who have had some college training but have not finished—the group perhaps most likely to be unable to adjust their job aspirations to their own capacities.

TABLE 41.—LABOR FORCE PARTICIPATION RATES OF MEN 18 TO 64 YEARS OLD, BY EDUCATIONAL ATTAINMENT AND COLOR: 1950 AND 1940

[Decennial census levels]

Educational attainment and color[1]	18 to 64 years old			30 to 64 years old		
	1950	1940	Change, 1940 to 1950	1950	1940	Change, 1940 to 1950
White men..........................	89.3	90.3	-1.0	91.8	92.4	-0.6
No school years completed.................	73.1	73.3	-0.2	76.1	75.7	+0.4
Elementary: 1 to 4 years.................	86.0	87.8	-1.8	86.2	87.8	-1.6
5 to 8 years.................	91.5	92.6	-1.1	91.5	92.3	-0.8
High school: 1 to 3 years.................	91.7	89.7	+2.0	94.5	94.7	-0.2
4 years.....................	93.0	92.5	+0.5	95.5	94.8	+0.7
College: 1 to 3 years.................	78.7	80.4	-1.7	94.5	94.7	-0.2
4 years or more.............	92.2	92.4	-0.2	95.9	95.8	+0.1
Nonwhite men.........................	85.3	89.5	-4.2	87.8	90.6	-2.8
No school years completed.................	80.4	85.2	-4.8	82.1	86.3	-4.2
Elementary: 1 to 4 years.................	88.6	91.5	-2.9	88.5	91.2	-2.7
5 to 8 years.................	88.6	91.3	-2.7	90.0	91.7	-1.7
High school: 1 to 3 years.................	83.7	84.6	-0.9	90.1	91.7	-1.6
4 years.....................	85.7	90.1	-4.4	90.7	93.0	-2.3
College: 1 to 3 years.................	71.4	79.2	-7.8	88.5	92.9	-4.4
4 years or more.............	87.1	92.9	-5.8	92.0	94.5	-2.5

[1] Native white and Negro in 1940.

Source: Derived from *1950 Census of Population*, Vol. IV, *Special Reports*, Part 5, Chapter B, Education, table 9; *1940 Census of Population, Educational Attainment by Economic Characteristics and Marital Status*, tables 17 and 18.

In examining the changing propensity of women at different educational levels to work outside their homes, we must take account of differential changes in marriage rates over the decade. For white women under 45, the increasing labor force participation seems generally to have been greater among those with the least education and, presumably, the lowest incomes (table 42 and figure 9). But this only reflects the fact that high school graduates and women with college training were marrying in greater proportions during the decade, and more frequently had young children to occupy them at home. (The number of children under 5 per 1,000 women ever married 35 to 44 years old in 1950 was 339 for women with some college education and 292 for other women.) Separate data for married women show small increases at all educational levels for white women 25 to 34 years, and substantial increases, again at all levels, for women in the age class 35 to 44 years. Among middle-aged and older women, however, the greatest increases were for the better educated ones.

When age cohorts are followed through the decade, the most remarkable changes are seen in the group of women who were 35 to 44 years old in 1940. Some increases in labor force participation occurred at all education levels, but they were greatest for women with the most education. These women were at an age in 1940 when they were relatively free to take jobs outside the home, and through the war years they found many opportunities for employment. This evidence that the increasing propensity for women to work is greater for better educated women suggests that perhaps the job opportunities that opened up during the decade were for better educated persons. It may also indicate that such factors as the desire to make use of earlier training and to escape from the confines of full-time housekeeping were operating here, in addition to, or in place of, purely economic incentives.

It is interesting that in 1940 the highest labor force rates for adult white women of all educational levels, whether married or not, were in the ages 25 to 34 years. (Under age 25, the picture is complicated by the fact that some women are still in school and the effect on their labor force participation rates of the level of their education cannot be determined.) In 1950, however, the highest rates were in the 35-to-44-year age group for all except high school graduates and college women, whose maximum rates were reached at 45 to 54 years.

To sum up, married white women of all educational levels showed a sharply increased propensity to be in the labor force except in the age groups where the major preoccupation of almost all women was marriage and the care of children. The greatest differences between 1950 and 1940 were for women aged 45 to 54 who had finished high school and in some cases gone on to college. Perhaps it may be assumed from this that women whose husbands were also better educated, and hence had higher incomes, were in the labor force in such large numbers in middle age, not to help pay for bread and butter items but to raise family living standards and to increase the interest of their own daily lives.

TABLE **42.**—LABOR FORCE PARTICIPATION RATES OF WOMEN 18 TO 64 YEARS OLD, BY EDUCATIONAL ATTAINMENT, AGE, AND COLOR: 1950 AND 1940

[Decennial census levels]

Year, age, and color[1]	Total	No school years completed	Elementary		High school		College	
			1 to 4 years	5 to 8 years	1 to 3 years	4 years	1 to 3 years	4 years or more
WHITE WOMEN								
Total								
Total, 18 to 64 years old:								
1950...................	32.6	14.6	20.1	25.6	30.3	38.5	38.8	50.9
1940...................	29.5	13.8	15.2	21.4	27.9	40.6	36.2	51.5
25 to 34 years:								
1950...................	30.3	13.1	20.9	24.9	27.7	31.8	35.0	44.3
1940...................	31.7	14.6	17.0	24.5	27.9	37.4	40.1	54.7
35 to 44 years:								
1950...................	33.4	16.7	24.1	29.2	32.2	35.6	38.1	49.1
1940...................	25.1	15.1	16.6	20.1	24.3	30.3	32.3	47.8
45 to 54 years:								
1950...................	31.8	18.1	22.2	26.5	31.3	37.2	42.0	55.3
1940...................	21.4	12.7	14.4	17.6	21.8	26.2	31.3	46.4
55 to 64 years:								
1950...................	22.9	12.5	14.6	19.8	24.4	28.4	34.2	48.7
1940...................	16.5	10.1	11.7	13.9	18.1	20.1	26.6	39.1
Married, Husband Present								
Total, 25 to 64 years old:								
1950...................	21.3	(2)	13.8	18.4	21.6	22.9	25.7	30.9
1940...................	12.6	(2)	8.9	10.4	12.9	15.4	16.3	22.1
25 to 34 years:								
1950...................	20.9	(2)	13.8	18.5	20.7	21.4	23.1	27.4
1940...................	16.2	(2)	10.5	13.8	15.3	18.3	19.0	25.5
35 to 44 years:								
1950...................	25.2	(2)	18.2	23.2	25.2	26.1	28.2	32.8
1940...................	13.4	(2)	11.8	11.8	13.1	15.1	15.9	21.6
45 to 64 years:								
1950...................	18.3	(2)	12.4	15.7	18.8	21.9	26.2	33.0
1940...................	8.2	(2)	6.9	7.0	8.7	9.9	12.4	17.2
NONWHITE WOMEN								
Total								
Total, 18 to 64 years old:								
1950...................	42.6	31.5	38.1	41.8	41.5	48.7	49.7	72.2
1940...................	43.4	35.7	39.8	43.2	44.5	52.4	54.8	72.7
25 to 34 years:								
1950...................	44.4	30.2	39.1	42.0	43.6	49.3	54.1	71.6
1940...................	46.8	38.6	41.8	45.3	49.0	55.0	64.1	76.2
35 to 44 years:								
1950...................	48.5	35.3	43.0	47.3	50.4	54.9	62.9	77.7
1940...................	45.7	37.9	43.3	45.7	48.2	50.3	60.7	72.5
45 to 64 years:[3]								
1950...................	39.3	31.7	35.8	40.1	41.9	44.1	50.7	66.8
1940...................	37.5	33.6	36.0	38.0	39.2	42.9	52.5	61.0
Married, Husband Present								
Total, 25 to 64 years old:								
1950...................	34.4	(2)	28.7	33.4	35.5	39.0	45.4	64.2
1940...................	27.9	(2)	24.6	27.9	30.0	33.5	41.9	55.2
25 to 34 years:								
1950...................	34.8	(2)	29.7	33.2	33.9	37.5	43.1	61.8
1940...................	30.5	(2)	27.0	29.8	31.7	35.6	45.1	55.4
35 to 44 years:								
1950...................	38.6	(2)	32.4	36.8	40.6	45.0	52.7	72.2
1940...................	29.4	(2)	26.7	29.6	30.5	32.3	40.9	58.8
45 to 64 years:								
1950...................	29.4	(2)	25.7	29.8	31.0	33.8	40.3	57.4
1940...................	22.4	(2)	20.9	22.3	23.1	29.4	36.4	50.0

[1] Native white and Negro in 1940.
[2] Included with elementary 1 to 4 years.
[3] Too few cases to permit greater age detail.

Source: Derived from *1950 Census of Population*, Vol. IV, *Special Reports*, Part 5, Chapter B, Education, table 10; *1940 Census of Population, Educational Attainment by Economic Characteristics and Marital Status*, tables 17 and 18, and *Employment and Family Characteristics of Women*, table 17.

·Figure 9.—Labor Force Participation Rates of White Married Women, Husband Present, by Educational Attainment and Age: 1950 and 1940

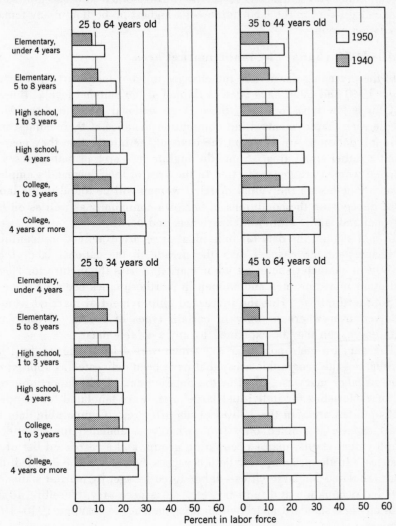

Note: Based on data in table 42.

Among nonwhite women there seems to have been a drop in labor force participation in all age and educational-level classes for single and widowed or divorced women, and some increase all along the scale for women married and living with their husbands. As in the case of white women, the changes were small for married women 25 to 34 years of age. Among married women 35 to 44 years of age, nonwhite women, like white women, showed much higher labor force rates in 1950, but here the changes were sharper for the better educated. The more substantial her education, the more likely the nonwhite woman was to have a job, at both dates. In fact, almost three-quarters of the nonwhite women who had graduated from college were in the labor force—the highest proportion of any female population group.

1940–1950 changes by labor market area

In the preceding discussion, the changes in labor force participation between 1940 and 1950 have been examined at the national level. But except for a few types of work, there is no national labor market. Most people seek employment within commuting distance of their homes, and their job decisions are made on the basis of the information they possess about a rather small area. Some do migrate in search of better jobs, but married women are generally tied to the area of their husband's employment. Whether an individual married woman will be found in the labor force depends on the conditions in her own community as well as on her personal and family attitudes, experience, and needs.

In this section, the data for individual areas are examined to determine to what extent the changes over the decade in the national labor force have been characteristic of all labor markets. Has the picture for Negro and other nonwhite men and women in Northern cities been the same as in Southern cities? Has the increased employment of married women occurred everywhere or only in certain types of cities? If there are differences, can they be explained by any available data?

The standard metropolitan areas,[4] which were defined prior to the 1950 Census, are the geographic areas that have been delineated as approximations of labor markets. Most of the detailed data on the labor force and its characteristics for individual large areas were tabulated for standard metropolitan areas in the 1950 Census program. Comparable data for 1940 can be assembled only from what was tabulated for counties— employment status, major occupation group, and a restricted list of industries. In the programs for both censuses, however, some detailed data were tabulated for large cities—labor force by age, by marital status, by detailed occupation and industry, etc. It is necessary, therefore, to use both city and standard metropolitan area statistics to examine 1940–1950 changes.

In 1950 there were 151 standard metropolitan areas of 100,000 or more population (appendix table D–3). The average (mean) labor force

---

[4] Except in New England, a standard metropolitan area is a county or group of contiguous counties which contain at least one city of 50,000 inhabitants or more. In addition to the county, or counties, containing such a city, or cities, contiguous counties are included in a standard metropolitan area if, according to certain criteria, they are essentially metropolitan in character and socially and economically integrated with the central city. In New England, towns and cities were the units used in defining standard metropolitan areas. For criteria of integration, see *1950 Census of Population*, Vol. II, *Characteristics of the Population*, Part 1, U. S. Summary, pp. 27–28.

rate in 1950 in these areas was almost unchanged from 1940 for men and increased by 2.8 percentage points for women (table 43).

For men, the rates declined or showed no change in 68 areas and rose in 83 areas, but the changes were small for the great majority. It should be noted that some of the declines are fictitious, or are overstated, because of the change in the practice of enumerating college students in the census. In 1940 students away from home attending college were listed at their parent's home, in 1950 at the college. Thus, the sharp declines in such areas as Austin, Baton Rouge, Durham, Lansing, Lexington, Madison, New Haven, and Raleigh probably reflect this procedural change.

TABLE **43.**—DISTRIBUTION OF STANDARD METROPOLITAN AREAS OF 100,000 OR MORE BY LABOR FORCE PARTICIPATION RATES OF PERSONS 14 YEARS OLD AND OVER, BY SEX: 1950 AND 1940

[Decennial census levels]

Labor force participation rate and sex	1950	1940	Labor force participation rate and sex	1950	1940
MALE			FEMALE		
All areas..................	151	151	All areas..................	151	151
66 to 67.9......................	1	...	16 to 17.9......................	...	1
68 to 69.9......................	2	1	18 to 19.9......................	1	3
70 to 71.9......................	4	1	20 to 21.9......................	...	7
72 to 73.9......................	7	4	22 to 23.9......................	4	14
74 to 75.9......................	19	13	24 to 25.9......................	5	16
76 to 77.9......................	14	29	26 to 27.9......................	11	23
78 to 79.9......................	30	45	28 to 29.9......................	24	26
80 to 81.9......................	38	41	30 to 31.9......................	27	18
82 to 83.9......................	30	14	32 to 33.9......................	38	13
84 to 85.9......................	4	2	34 to 35.9......................	19	13
86 to 87.9......................	2	1	36 to 37.9......................	10	4
			38 to 39.9......................	5	7
Mean rate....................	79.2	79.0	40 to 41.9......................	4	5
Coefficient of variation of			42 to 43.9......................	3	1
mean.......................	4.7	3.5	Mean rate....................	32.1	29.3
			Coefficient of variation of		
			mean.......................	13.1	18.5

Source: Derived from appendix table D–3.

For women, the increases were widespread, although not quite universal. Of 151 areas, 129 showed an increase between 1940 and 1950, and in 52 areas the increase was 4 percentage points or more. All the areas in which the participation rates of women declined over the decade were located in the South with the exception of Fall River, Bridgeport, and Atlantic City. The reduction in labor force participation of nonwhite women was probably a factor in these overall reductions in the Southern areas.

White women increased their labor force participation even in the South. In Southern areas, and in those outside the South where more than 5 percent of the population was nonwhite (89 areas altogether—see appendix table D–4), the average rates for both nonwhite men and women dropped (table 44), but that for white men remained substantially unchanged, and that for white women increased.

TABLE **44.**—MEAN LABOR FORCE PARTICIPATION RATES, 89 SELECTED STANDARD
METROPOLITAN AREAS, BY COLOR AND SEX: 1950 AND 1940

[Decennial census levels]

Mean and coefficient of variation	Male				Female			
	White		Nonwhite		White		Nonwhite	
	1950	1940	1950	1940	1950	1940	1950	1940
Mean labor force participation rate.	80.0	79.6	76.7	79.8	30.2	26.8	41.6	44.2
Coefficient of variation of mean....	5.4	3.6	6.9	5.3	12.9	15.7	17.5	24.4

Note: Standard metropolitan areas are those in the South and those outside the South with more than 5 percent of population nonwhite in 1950.

Source: Derived from appendix table D-4.

There were only 16 areas in which the rate of labor force participation of nonwhite men did *not* fall off: Birmingham; Chicago; Cleveland; Columbus, Ohio; Dayton; El Paso; Flint; Ft. Worth; Fresno; Greenville; Lubbock; San Francisco; Topeka; Wheeling–Steubenville; Wichita Falls; and Youngstown. By contrast, there were 58 areas in which the white male rate remained stable or rose during the decade.

In 1950, in most areas outside the South, the differential between white and nonwhite women was fairly small. White women had had some increase in labor force participation everywhere except in Columbus, Georgia, and in three resort areas where a large proportion of the population are elderly or voluntarily idle (Atlantic City, Orlando, and Tampa–St. Petersburg). For nonwhite women, the record of the decade was a fairly substantial decline in labor force activity in almost every standard metropolitan area in the South—55 out of 59. In the other regions, however, nonwhite women in most areas increased their labor force activity or showed no change. Migration to these higher income areas did not, apparently, result in a reduction in propensity to seek paid employment.

The types of areas that show the largest increases in labor force participation of all men (white and nonwhite combined) were industrial centers of the Middle West and areas with military installations: Canton, Dayton, El Paso, Flint, Fort Wayne, Fort Worth, Grand Rapids, Lorain–Elyria, Norfolk–Portsmouth, Oklahoma City, Racine, Rockford, Salt Lake City, San Diego, Tacoma, and Wichita (appendix table D–3).

Ranked by magnitude of increase, the areas in which the female rate increased by 5 or more percentage points were:

Standard metropolitan areas	Increase in female labor force rates, 1940–1950	1940 rate
Cedar Rapids	8.6	24.2
Waterloo	7.2	25.1
Topeka	7.1	27.8
Racine	6.8	22.8
Madison	6.7	29.3
Salt Lake City	6.7	22.7

| | Increase in female labor force rates, | |
Standard metropolitan areas	1940–1950	1940 rate
Stockton	6.5	22.4
Fort Wayne	6.5	26.1
Rockford	6.3	27.2
Erie	6.2	23.9
Lincoln	6.2	29.2
Columbus, Ohio	5.9	28.2
Springfield, Missouri	5.7	21.5
Kalamazoo	5.6	25.2
Lansing	5.6	25.9
Dayton	5.5	25.9
Springfield, Ohio	5.5	23.1
Phoenix	5.5	22.3
Des Moines	5.4	29.7
Syracuse	5.4	27.8
Saginaw	5.3	21.2
Flint	5.3	23.0
Terre Haute	5.3	23.8
Grand Rapids	5.3	25.0
Milwaukee	5.2	28.3
Allentown–Bethlehem–Easton	5.2	27.5
Indianapolis	5.2	29.8
Peoria	5.1	24.1
Davenport–Rock Island–Moline	5.1	24.5
Portland, Oregon	5.0	27.0

Almost all these areas, it should be noted, had below average rates in 1940 (below 29.3 percent). Consequently, if there was a demand for additional women workers it could be more readily met, perhaps, than in areas where a large proportion of the adult female population was already in the labor force. Only a few areas with rates above 30 percent in 1940 increased by more than 3 percentage points (Chicago, Greenville, Hartford, Minneapolis–St. Paul, New Britain–Bristol, Rochester).

The increase in labor force participation of married women was almost universal, in all labor markets (appendix table D–5). The only large city in which the 1950 rate was below the 1940 rate was Tampa, Florida. Data for cities of 100,000 or more must be used to trace changes for married women, since information by marital status cannot be assembled for standard metropolitan areas in 1940.

The changes were substantial, on the average, even when the city rates are standardized for age (table 45). The increase in the average (mean) labor force participation rate of married women living with their husbands was 8 percentage points. With the changes in the proportions of married women working outside their homes, there also came greater uniformity. The coefficient of variation of the mean rate was reduced from 31.5 percent in 1940 to 18.2 percent in 1950. In 1940 the rates ranged from 32.5 percent in Charlotte, North Carolina, to 8.0 percent in Scranton,

Pennsylvania. The same two cities had the highest and lowest rates in 1950—38.4 and 15.4 percent; variations among the cities between the extremes was less, however, in 1950 (appendix table D–5).

TABLE 45.—MEAN LABOR FORCE PARTICIPATION RATES OF MARRIED WOMEN, HUSBAND PRESENT, 91 CITIES OF 100,000 OR MORE: 1950 AND 1940

[Decennial census levels]

Mean and coefficient of variation	1950	1940
Unstandardized labor force rates:		
Mean...	25.7	17.8
Coefficient of variation of mean.............	18.2	31.5
Standardized rates:[1]		
Mean...	25.8	17.7
Coefficient of variation of mean.............	17.0	29.8

[1] Standardized for age using age distribution of married women in all cities of 100,000 or more in 1950 as standard.
Source: Derived from appendix table D–5.

As for all women, the greatest increases for married women tended to be in cities where the rate had been relatively low in 1940. But even in Charlotte, Fall River, New Bedford, and Washington, where 30 percent or more of the married women were in the labor force in 1940, gains of 6 or 7 points were recorded. Moreover, even by age there was substantial uniformity of increases. Only in the age group 25 to 34 did some cities show a decline rather than a rise.

In 1940, the highest labor force rates for married women in these cities were in either the 14-to-24-year or the 25-to-34-year age groups. By 1950 the pattern had changed in many areas, and married women 35 to 44 years had rates as high or higher than younger women. This shift seemed to be more characteristic of Middle Western and Western cities than of the older Eastern industrial centers.

Do any of these data throw light on the reasons for variation in the labor force participation among areas, or on differing patterns of change over the decade? For men, of course, there is a high degree of uniformity among labor markets; the coefficient of variation of the mean labor force participation rate in standard metropolitan areas in 1950 was 4.7 percent. For women, the variation was greater, although less in 1950 than in 1940. (The coefficient of variation of the mean for standard metropolitan areas was 13.1 percent in 1950 and 18.5 percent in 1940.) Prior to 1950, there was some evidence that the labor force participation rates of women tended to be higher where the average earnings of men were low, but this evidence was in some cases derived from rather limited data for a small number of large cities, and may have reflected to some extent the traditionally high rates for Negro women.[5] The 1950 data for cities and

[5] For analysis of the correlation between earnings and labor force participation, see Paul H. Douglas, *The Theory of Wages*, Macmillan Company, New York, 1934; Clarence D. Long, *The Labor Force Under Changing Income and Employment*, National Bureau of Economic Research, Princeton University Press, 1958; Nedra Bartlett Belloc, "Labor Force Participation and Employment Opportunities for

standard metropolitan areas do not generally support the theory that the propensity of women to work outside the home will be strongest in areas where the earnings of men are lowest. The coefficient of correlation of the average earnings of men in 1949 and the age-standardized labor force participation rates of women in 1950 was −0.46 in cities of 100,000; the comparable correlation coefficient of 1939 earnings and 1940 labor force rates was −0.58. There was no correlation at all between the median income of white men and the labor force rates of white women in the 151 standard metropolitan areas of 100,000 or more in 1950. Nor was there any correlation between the median income of married men who were family heads and the labor force rates of married women, spouse present, in the 77 standard metropolitan areas of 250,000 or more; or between the income of men who were family heads and the proportion of families with secondary workers, in such areas.

In 1950, as in 1940, the areas with the largest proportion of women in the labor force were those in the South, with a large percentage of Negroes; the textile, tobacco, and electrical-appliance manufacturing centers; and capital cities and trade and insurance centers where there is, typically, an abundance of white-collar jobs suitable for women. These areas were not necessarily those where average earnings for women were high. In fact, the coefficient of correlation between the median income of women who worked year round in 1949, and the percent of the female population in the year-round labor force in 1950 in standard metropolitan areas of 250,000 or more was only +0.28.[6]

Although the level of earnings, whether of men or women, in an area had little bearing on the percent of women in the labor force at a single point in time, there is some evidence that the *change* in the labor force participation of women between 1940 and 1950 was related to one or more factors reflected in the level of male earnings in 1950. In cities of 100,000 or more, there was a positive correlation (+0.55) between the change in labor force rates of women (standardized for age) and the median wage or salary income of men in 1949. This suggests that perhaps where the earnings of men were high, employers in certain activities could not find men to fill the lower paid jobs and had to turn to women. The greatest increases were recorded in cities where the labor force participation of women had been below average in 1940 and where, presumably, there was a relatively high proportion of women free to enter the labor market.

Women," *Journal of the American Statistical Association,* Vol. 45, No. 251, September 1950; and Sanford M. Dornbusch, "Correlations Between Income and Labor Force Participation by Race," *American Journal of Sociology,* Vol. LXI, No. 4, January 1956.

[6] The relationship of earnings of year-round workers and the percent in the year-round labor force was examined in order to eliminate the possible effect of part-year employment. Average earnings of women might be low in an area because a large proportion of the female population worked only part of the year.

Unfortunately, it is not possible to test the hypothesis that areas with the greatest expansion in the female labor force, 1940 to 1950, were those which also recruited large numbers of women into the labor force during World War II and which, therefore, had a large supply of women with work experience. Comparable data on labor force participation of women are not available for a war year, except for a few areas. As a substitute, the change between 1940 and 1944 in the proportion of manufacturing employees who were women (based on unpublished estimates of the Bureau of Employment Security) was examined for selected areas, in relation to the 1940–1950 change in labor force rates. The coefficient of correlation between these two measures was not high— +0.30. It is still possible, however, that wartime experience was a significant factor in the amount of expansion between 1940 and 1950 and that data covering the entire labor force would demonstrate this.

A summary picture of the 1940–1950 developments in individual labor markets shows a mixed record of small increases or decreases in the labor force participation of men, and for women increasing labor force participation in 129 out of 151 major labor markets. The decline in labor force rates of nonwhite men was almost universal, both in Southern areas and those outside the South; nonwhite women also showed decreasing labor force participation in most Southern areas, but in areas outside the South they either increased their proportion in the labor force or showed no change. White women had rising labor force participation rates in almost every area, both in the South and elsewhere.

The marked rise in the tendency of married women to work outside the home was observed in all large cities (100,000 or more) except Tampa, Florida. The proportion of married women in the labor force increased an average of 8 percentage points in these cities.

Various efforts to relate the rate of expansion in the female labor force to other characteristics of an area have, for the most part, proved unrewarding. However, there seems to be some evidence that increase in the proportion of women in the labor force was positively correlated with the level of earnings of men by area. We may hypothesize, therefore, that the availability of men for the types of jobs in which both sexes are employed may be an important factor in determining the demand for women in an area's labor force. Where higher paying jobs are plentiful for men, they may move out of or refuse the lower paid ones, which then must be filled by women.

Changes in utilization of women in the labor force

With the marked changes in the female labor force between 1940 and 1950, it is appropriate to inquire whether or not there were radical changes in this decade in the types of jobs held by women. Population statistics describing jobs consist of descriptions of occupations, the kind of work a person does, and of industries, the kind of place he performs that work. Thus, for example, clerical occupations are found in almost all industries—manufacturing, mining, construction, trade, etc.[7]

Occupation. Despite the impetus given to the employment of women during World War II, there are few examples of feminine invasions of completely masculine fields. The proportion of women in most occupations in 1950 was not far from what it had been in 1940, except for clerical, sales, and service occupations where women have traditionally been accepted (table 46). The increase in the proportion of women employed as farm laborers reflects the greater dependence of agriculture on family workers.

TABLE **46.**—WOMEN AS PERCENT OF TOTAL EMPLOYED IN MAJOR OCCUPATION GROUPS: 1950 AND 1940

[Decennial census levels]

Major occupation group	1950	1940	Major occupation group	1950	1940
Professional, technical, and kindred workers.....................	39.5	41.6	Craftsmen, foremen, and kindred workers...........................	3.0	2.2
Farmers and farm managers..........	2.7	3.0	Operatives and kindred workers......	27.1	25.3
Managers, officials, and proprietors, except farm.................	13.5	11.0	Private household workers...........	94.8	94.4
Clerical and kindred workers.......	62.3	53.9	Service workers, except private household.........................	44.6	38.4
Sales workers......................	33.9	26.1	Farm laborers and foremen...........	18.7	10.3
			Laborers, except farm and mine......	3.7	3.3

Source: Derived from *1950 Census of Population*, Vol. II, *Characteristics of the Population*, Part 1, U. S. Summary, table 125.

Appendix table D–6 shows the 1940 and 1950 proportions of females in various specific occupations in which women made up as much as 10 percent of the total employed in 1950. In professional and technical fields, women made gains as accountants, authors, and editors, and as sports instructors and entertainers, but not in most scientific fields. In the managerial field they advanced in the occupations of credit men, floor managers, and managers or proprietors of general merchandise and apparel stores and insurance and real estate firms. Among clerical occupations, the proportion of women bookkeepers, cashiers, and bill collectors rose substantially, but so did the proportion employed as messengers. In sales occupations, advertising agents, hucksters, and real estate agents were more likely to be women in 1950 than in 1940.

In the skilled occupations (craftsmen and foremen) there were relatively more women decorating windows, working as engravers, opticians, and—a

---

[7] The occupational and industrial classification used for the 1950 Census of Population differs in some respects from the classification used in 1940. The Census Bureau has revised the 1940 data to show the numbers in each occupation (or industry) on a comparable basis with 1950 (see *1950 Census of Population*, Vol. II, *Characteristics of the Population*, Part 1, U. S. Summary, tables 125 and 131; Parts 2–50, tables 74 and 80). Comparable statistics on occupation and industry by age, race, and other characteristics have not been prepared by the Census Bureau. Adjustments of 1940 or 1950 data were made by the author for the present study in order to examine some of the changes that occurred by age, and by race, on a more nearly comparable basis. The adjustments are fairly arbitrary, however, and should not be considered to have the validity of official Census Bureau revisions.

curious change—as paper hangers. (This last may reflect only the fact that, in 1950, resources were not available to edit the occupational returns with the same care as was done in 1940. In that census, returns for women in unlikely occupations were scrutinized to make reasonably sure that they were correct.) In the semiskilled occupations (operatives) women increased their importance as photographic process workers, and as operatives in the manufacture of furniture, glass and structural clay products, miscellaneous nonmetallic products, electrical machinery, aircraft and parts, meat products, some textile mills, and leather footwear; also, as operatives in transportation other than railroads and in business and repair services.

In most service occupations a substantial proportion of the total were women in 1940, but especially large increases were recorded among hospital attendants, cleaners, cooks, elevator operators, ushers, and waitresses.

With all employed women as a base, the most marked changes were in the proportion employed in clerical and private household jobs. Clerical workers rose from 21.6 percent of all employed women in 1940 to 27.8 percent; private household workers fell from 18.0 percent to 8.6 percent (table 47; see also appendix table D–6 for greater detail). Middle-aged women, who entered the labor force in such large numbers, had tradition-ally been unwelcome in some kinds of jobs—as telephone operators, secretaries, receptionists, waitresses, etc. Was there any change in this attitude or were they hired for the same kinds of jobs they had filled before?

The median age of all employed women increased from 32.3 years to 36.4 years, and the sharpest increases tended to be in the lower status occupations (table 48). The only exception was an increase of almost five years in the median age of professional and technical workers, in large part a reflection of the increase in the average age of women employed as teachers.

Looking below the major group level to types of work in which a con-siderable number of women are employed, we find that, although the median age of women employed as nurses, teachers, laundry workers, waitresses, and most other occupations increased substantially, the median for stenographers and typists, telephone operators, and miscellaneous clerical workers showed virtually no increase at all. Nevertheless, the age distribution within these latter occupations shifted somewhat, indicat-ing that there was some relaxation in the standards for jobs for which youth has been a criterion of employment. Although well over one-half the employed women were under 35 years of age in 1950 as in 1940, the proportion under 35 had decreased and the proportion 45 years and over had increased. Among stenographers and typists, for example, who are typically recruited from young workers in the female labor force, the proportion aged 45 or more rose from 8 to 15 percent; among office machine operators, from 5 to 12 percent (table 49 and figure 10; see also appendix table D–7).

TABLE **47.**—PERCENT DISTRIBUTION OF EMPLOYED WOMEN BY MAJOR OCCUPATION GROUP, BY AGE: 1950 AND 1940

[Decennial census levels]

Year and major occupation group	Total, 14 years and over	14 and 15 years	16 and 17 years	18 and 19 years	20 to 24 years	25 to 34 years	35 to 44 years	45 to 54 years	55 to 64 years	65 and over
1950										
Total employed women............	100.0	100.0	100.0	100.0	100.0	100.0	100.0	100.0	100.0	100.0
Profess'l, techn'l, & kindred wkrs..	12.6	1.8	1.7	6.8	12.7	12.3	13.5	14.2	13.7	12.7
Farmers and farm managers..........	0.8	0.7	0.2	0.1	0.1	0.3	0.7	1.1	1.8	4.0
Mgrs., offs., & propr's, exc. farm..	4.4	0.5	0.4	0.5	1.3	3.0	5.5	7.0	7.3	8.3
Clerical and kindred workers........	27.8	3.5	17.8	45.4	45.1	31.4	23.3	20.7	14.7	9.6
Sales workers......................	8.6	11.2	22.6	11.3	6.8	7.2	8.8	9.3	9.0	7.6
Craftsmen, foremen, & kindred wkrs..	1.5	0.3	0.5	0.7	1.0	1.5	1.8	1.8	1.8	1.6
Operatives and kindred workers......	19.6	2.5	13.4	15.1	16.7	22.3	22.0	19.3	18.3	14.7
Private household workers..........	8.6	40.3	16.0	5.8	4.6	6.7	8.3	9.9	13.1	20.0
Service workers, exc. priv. hshld...	12.4	12.5	17.4	10.8	9.0	11.8	12.4	13.1	16.5	17.6
Farm laborers and foremen..........	2.9	25.8	9.0	2.7	2.0	2.6	2.8	2.8	3.0	3.1
Laborers, except farm and mine......	0.8	0.9	1.0	0.8	0.7	0.9	0.9	0.8	0.8	0.8
1940										
Total employed women............	100.0	100.0	100.0	100.0	100.0	100.0	100.0	100.0	100.0	100.0
Profess'l, techn'l, & kindred wkrs..	13.6	0.4	1.3	6.7	11.9	15.8	14.8	14.4	14.0	12.3
Farmers and farm managers..........	1.4	...	0.1	0.1	0.1	0.4	1.3	3.0	5.3	10.5
Mgrs., offs., & propr's, exc. farm..	3.6	...	0.1	0.3	0.8	2.4	5.1	7.5	8.6	9.1
Clerical and kindred workers........	21.6	0.5	7.5	23.5	28.3	26.0	20.5	13.3	8.9	5.5
Sales workers......................	7.3	2.3	6.0	8.8	8.1	7.0	7.3	7.4	6.3	4.4
Craftsmen, foremen, & kindred wkrs..	1.0	0.4	0.3	0.5	0.7	1.0	1.3	1.4	1.3	1.2
Operatives and kindred workers......	18.5	0.9	15.8	19.9	20.6	19.9	18.4	16.4	13.0	10.9
Private household workers..........	18.0	37.2	41.1	23.1	15.0	14.4	17.2	20.2	25.1	29.7
Service workers, exc. priv. hshld...	11.2	3.4	9.0	10.8	10.6	10.0	11.1	13.3	14.7	13.6
Farm laborers and foremen..........	2.9	54.3	17.8	5.1	2.7	2.1	2.2	2.4	2.2	2.3
Laborers, except farm and mine......	0.9	0.6	1.0	1.2	1.2	1.0	0.8	0.7	0.6	0.5

Source: Based on appendix table D–7.

TABLE **48.**—MEDIAN AGE OF EMPLOYED WOMEN, BY MAJOR OCCUPATION GROUP: 1950 AND 1940

[Decennial census levels]

Major occupation group	Median age	
	1950	1940
Total employed women.............................	36.4	32.3
Professional, technical, and kindred workers.............	38.3	33.4
Farmers and farm managers.............................	50.6	52.1
Managers, officials, and proprietors, except farm........	44.7	44.3
Clerical and kindred workers............................	30.6	29.4
Sales workers...	37.3	31.4
Craftsmen, foremen, and kindred workers.................	39.7	36.7
Operatives and kindred workers.........................	36.7	31.0
Private household workers..............................	41.1	33.6
Service workers, except private household..............	38.7	33.8
Farm laborers and foremen.............................	36.1	26.6
Laborers, except farm and mine.........................	36.3	29.1

Source: Based on appendix table D–7.

As we have seen, in 1950 there was a "shortage" of women workers under 35 years, both because of the deficit in the population in some of the component age groups and because of the stability of the proportions in the population who were in the labor force. Women 18 to 34 years constituted 56 percent of all employed women in 1940 and 44 percent in 1950. Faced with a restricted number of women in the age group that they normally favor, employers were forced to turn to other ages for their labor supply. The process of selection is, of course, a double one: Employers make choices among applicants, and job applicants make choices among jobs, which for many women may include the choice of remaining outside the labor force, if sufficiently attractive jobs are not available.

TABLE 49.—PERCENT OF EMPLOYED WOMEN IN SPECIFIED OCCUPATION GROUPS, BY AGE: 1950 AND 1940

[Decennial census levels. "N.e.c." means not elsewhere classified]

Occupation	Under 35 years		35 to 44 years		45 years and over		Median age (years)	
	1950	1940	1950	1940	1950	1940	1950	1940
Total employed women.................	46.7	58.0	23.3	19.9	30.0	22.1	36.4	32.3
Nurses and student nurses..................	56.1	68.5	20.5	15.9	23.4	15.6	32.7	29.2
Teachers (n.e.c.)...........................	31.8	53.6	29.4	23.8	38.8	22.6	41.2	34.0
Farmers and farm managers..................	15.4	10.5	20.3	19.2	64.3	70.3	50.6	52.1
Specified managers and officials...........	24.9	28.1	26.0	26.4	49.1	45.5	44.7	43.3
Mgrs., officials, & propr's of trade establishments, exc. eat'g & drink'g places....	20.3	21.6	29.1	27.7	50.6	50.7	45.2	45.3
Managers, officials, and propr's of misc. industry and service establishments.......	23.5	24.0	27.0	29.3	49.5	46.7	44.8	43.9
Bookkeepers, cashiers, etc..................	55.5	64.7	22.8	21.3	21.7	14.0	32.9	30.8
Office machine operators...................	70.4	76.0	17.7	19.1	11.9	4.9	28.4	28.5
Stenographers, typists, and secretaries....	67.7	74.9	17.5	17.0	14.8	8.1	28.9	28.2
Telephone operators........................	59.8	64.3	19.7	23.6	20.5	12.1	30.4	31.1
Other clerical workers.....................	58.3	66.3	19.8	18.9	21.9	14.8	31.7	30.0
Other sales workers (n.e.c.)...............	45.1	61.6	24.0	19.6	30.9	18.8	37.0	30.9
Other craftsmen............................	39.2	45.6	25.1	23.4	35.7	31.0	39.3	36.9
Dressmakers and seamstresses, exc. factory.	13.7	20.4	18.7	22.7	67.6	56.9	52.1	47.5
Laundry and dry cleaning operatives........	41.5	55.8	26.7	23.6	31.8	20.6	38.2	33.1
Other specified operatives.................	46.9	58.7	25.8	21.4	27.3	19.9	36.2	32.1
Operatives (n.e.c.):								
Metal, machinery.........................	55.0	77.9	26.4	14.4	18.6	7.7	33.6	26.9
Food and kindred products................	48.2	71.8	26.3	16.6	25.5	11.6	35.7	28.5
Textile mill products....................	45.1	65.3	28.9	21.0	26.0	13.7	36.7	30.8
Apparel & other fabric. textile products..	44.5	62.6	25.8	20.5	29.7	16.9	37.1	30.8
Paper and paper products.................	49.9	67.1	24.9	18.8	25.2	14.1	35.1	29.9
Leather and leather products.............	46.6	69.5	25.5	16.0	27.9	14.5	36.3	28.0
Other manufacturing......................	51.3	72.7	24.7	15.9	24.0	11.4	34.5	27.5
Nonmanufacturing........................	43.9	56.1	25.5	21.1	30.6	22.8	37.4	32.9
Private household workers..................	36.2	53.4	22.5	19.1	41.3	27.5	41.1	33.6
Attendants, ushers, and bootblacks........	49.4	60.3	20.1	17.4	30.5	22.3	35.3	30.9
Barbers, beauticians, and manicurists.....	50.0	69.0	29.8	20.3	20.2	10.7	35.0	29.5
Charwomen and janitors.....................	17.8	18.5	22.1	27.2	60.1	54.3	48.7	46.3
Cooks, except private household............	21.7	29.2	27.9	28.1	50.4	42.7	45.1	42.4
Practical nurses and midwives.............	21.3	28.5	18.7	18.2	60.0	53.3	49.1	46.3
Service workers (n.e.c.)..................	32.8	46.7	23.6	24.0	43.6	29.3	42.3	36.4
Waitresses and bartenders.................	62.4	79.1	22.9	14.1	14.7	6.8	30.9	26.4
Farm laborers (wage) and foremen..........	52.2	62.6	20.8	17.1	27.0	20.3	34.0	29.6
Farm laborers, unpaid family workers......	45.6	69.8	23.1	14.3	31.3	15.9	36.9	25.1

Source: Derived from appendix table D-7.

Whatever the determining factors, the general effect was to increase the selection of young women, under 25 years of age, for clerical jobs, and to reduce their selection for industrial occupations (operatives and laborers) and service occupations[8] (table 50). Apparently, the abundance

---

[8] "Selection" is measured by comparing the percentage of each age group in an occupation group in 1950 with the percentage that would have obtained if the 1940 distribution of employed women by age within each occupation group had remained unchanged. It is assumed that, other things being equal, the 1950 clerical, sales, operative, etc., jobs would have been filled by the same proportions of young and middle-aged workers as in 1940; to the extent that this did not happen because of the different numbers of young and middle-aged workers employed in 1950, some selection was exercised. For example, distribution of the 1950 total employed in clerical jobs by the 1940 age patterns gives the number of clerical workers in the 20-to-24-year age group that would have been employed if

FIGURE **10.**—EMPLOYED WOMEN 35 YEARS OLD AND OVER AS PERCENT OF TOTAL WOMEN
EMPLOYED IN SELECTED OCCUPATIONS: 1950 AND 1940

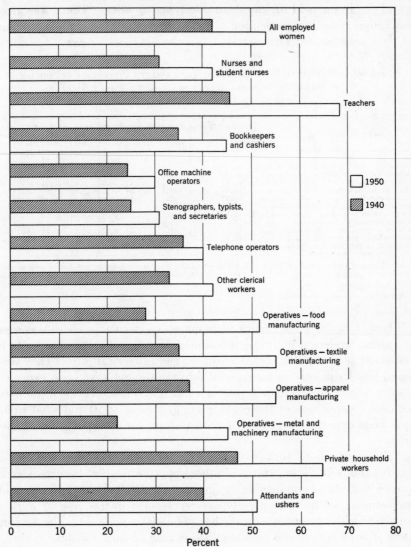

Note: Based on data in table 49.

nothing had changed but the number of different kinds of jobs. Summing the number of 20- to 24-
year-olds in each occupation group and computing a percent distribution of the total age class by
occupation indicates how the age group would have been utilized under 1940 conditions. The
differences between this distribution and the actual distribution of the age group in 1950 is some
measure of the shifts that took place because of changing age preferences of employers and changing
occupational preferences of various age groups. Thus, under 1940 conditions, the proportion of 20-
to 24-year-old workers employed in clerical jobs in 1950 would have been 35.1 percent instead of
45.1 percent; the proportion employed as operatives would have been 21.0 percent instead of 16.7
percent (see also table 47).

of white-collar jobs which did not require extensive training attracted an increasing proportion of young women and made it possible for them to avoid the lower-paid or less desirable types of work. There was also a marked increase in the selection of teen-agers for sales jobs and a reduction in their selection for farm work.

TABLE **50.**—DIFFERENCE BETWEEN ACTUAL AND EXPECTED PERCENTAGE OF AGE GROUP
IN MAJOR OCCUPATION GROUP, FOR EMPLOYED WOMEN: 1950

[Decennial census levels—actual minus expected]

Major occupation group	14 and 15 years	16 and 17 years	18 and 19 years	20 to 24 years	25 to 34 years	35 to 44 years	45 to 54 years	55 to 64 years	65 and over
Profess'l, techn'l, and kindred wkrs...	+1.4	+0.3	+0.5	+2.1	-1.9	-0.2	+0.4	-0.3	-0.6
Farmers and farm managers..............	+0.7	+0.1	+0.1	...	+0.1	...	-0.6	-1.3	-2.7
Mgrs., off'ls, and propr's, exc. farm..	+0.5	+0.2	+0.1	+0.4	+0.2	-0.6	-2.3	-4.0	-4.4
Clerical and kindred workers...........	+2.7	+6.3	+14.6	+10.0	-1.2	-3.0	+2.9	+2.2	+1.3
Sales workers..........................	+7.9	+14.2	+0.7	-2.5	-0.8	+0.3	+0.3	+0.9	+1.6
Craftsmen, foremen, and kindred wkrs...	-0.4	-0.1	-0.1	...	+0.1	-0.1	-0.4	-0.4	-0.5
Operatives and kindred workers.........	+1.3	-6.5	-6.3	-4.3	+1.9	+2.6	+1.4	+3.3	+1.3
Private household workers..............	+18.4	-7.7	-5.5	-2.4	-0.1	...	-0.1	...	+3.3
Service workers, exc. private hshld....	+7.9	+5.5	-1.3	-2.4	+1.0	+0.2	-2.2	-1.3	-0.1
Farm laborers and foremen..............	-40.7	-12.2	-2.5	-0.6	+0.6	+0.6	+0.4	+0.6	+0.5
Laborers, except farm and mine........	+0.3	-0.1	-0.3	-0.3	+0.1	+0.2	+0.2	+0.3	+0.3

Note: Expected percentage of age group in specified occupation group is computed by distributing total number of women in the occupation group in 1950 by the 1940 age distribution for that group, and calculating percent distribution within each age-class.

Source: Derived from appendix table D-7.

Changes in other age groups were not so spectacular. There was some increasing tendency, however, for women 45 years of age and older to be employed as operatives, as saleswomen, and in clerical jobs. They were found less frequently in managerial jobs than might have been expected. On the whole, however, there was not much difference between the occupational composition of these older age groups in 1950 and what would have been expected from 1940 patterns of age for the various occupation groups.

Private household work in other person's homes has never been very attractive and, with the expansion of other opportunities, has been avoided by women in the most employable age groups. In 1950, 14- and 15-year-olds and women past 65 were greatly overrepresented in this type of work as compared with expectations on the basis of 1940 experience. The development of baby sitting as a paid occupation may account for this.

One of the results of the fashion for early marriages, according to some college administrators and other persons concerned with the professional education of women, has been a dwindling interest on the part of college girls in preparing for a professional career. Although they expect to work from time to time during their married lives, it is said that they do not want to postpone marriage long enough to obtain an advanced degree or to acquire further training. A comparison of the types of jobs held by white women college graduates in 1940 and 1950 shows a small decline in the proportion in professional and technical occupations, from 74.4

percent to 70.8 percent for women 25 to 64 years of age (table 51). The difference is largely due to changes among women past 35 years of age; the proportion in professional jobs was notably smaller and the proportion in clerical and sales jobs larger than in 1940. The most recent college graduates, women 25 to 34 years, had much the same occupational distribution at both dates.

TABLE 51.—MAJOR OCCUPATION GROUP OF EMPLOYED WHITE WOMEN WITH FOUR YEARS OR MORE OF COLLEGE, BY AGE: 1950 AND 1940

[Decennial census levels]

Occupation group and age	1950		1940[1]	
	Number	Percent	Number	Percent
Total, 25 to 64 years old....................	955,050	100.0	573,540	100.0
Professional, technical, and kindred workers.......	675,990	70.8	426,500	74.4
Managers, officials, and proprietors, except farm..	42,840	4.5	22,460	3.9
Clerical and sales workers.........................	179,310	18.7	95,840	16.7
All other...	56,910	6.0	28,740	5.0
25 to 34 years old.............................	291,900	100.0	267,880	100.0
Professional, technical, and kindred workers.......	199,560	68.4	192,220	71.8
Managers, officials, and proprietors, except farm..	8,730	3.0	7,060	2.6
Clerical and sales workers.........................	70,230	24.0	58,480	21.8
All other...	13,380	4.6	10,120	3.8
35 to 44 years old.............................	305,760	100.0	163,760	100.0
Professional, technical, and kindred workers.......	219,090	71.7	127,360	77.8
Managers, officials, and proprietors, except farm..	14,340	4.7	6,900	4.2
Clerical and sales workers.........................	55,680	18.2	22,180	13.5
All other...	16,650	5.4	7,320	4.5
45 to 64 years old, total.....................	357,390	100.0	141,900	100.0
Professional, technical, and kindred workers.......	257,340	72.0	106,920	75.3
Managers, officials, and proprietors, except farm..	19,770	5.5	8,500	6.0
Clerical and sales workers.........................	53,400	15.0	15,180	10.7
All other...	26,880	7.5	11,300	8.0
45 to 54 years old...........................	239,700	100.0	97,200	100.0
Professional, technical, and kindred workers.......	173,160	72.2	74,440	76.6
Managers, officials, and proprietors, except farm..	12,900	5.4	5,580	5.7
Clerical and sales workers.........................	37,860	15.8	10,700	11.0
All other...	15,780	6.6	6,480	6.7
55 to 64 years old...........................	117,690	100.0	44,700	100.0
Professional, technical, and kindred workers.......	84,180	71.6	32,480	72.7
Managers, officials, and proprietors, except farm..	6,870	5.8	2,920	6.5
Clerical and sales workers.........................	15,540	13.2	4,480	10.0
All other...	11,100	9.4	4,820	10.8

[1] Native white in 1940.

Source: Derived from *1950 Census of Population*, Vol. IV, *Special Reports*, Part 5, Chapter B, Education, table 11; *1940 Census of Population, Educational Attainment by Economic Characteristics and Marital Status*, table 22.

Industry. The factors that affected the changing occupational structure of the employment of young and middle-aged or older women were also mirrored in the statistics on industry (table 52, figure 11, and appendix table D–8). Employment of all women in manufacturing increased from 21.4 percent to only 23.7 percent, but for women 25 and older there were rather substantial increases. Since some of the women employed in manufacturing work in clerical, sales, and laborer occupations, the increase in the proportions in manufacturing exceed the increases in craftsmen and operative jobs.

TABLE 52.—PERCENT DISTRIBUTION OF EMPLOYED WOMEN BY MAJOR INDUSTRY GROUP, BY AGE: 1950 AND 1940

[Decennial census levels]

Year and major industry group	Total, 14 years and over	14 and 15 years	16 and 17 years	18 and 19 years	20 to 24 years	25 to 34 years	35 to 44 years	45 to 54 years	55 to 64 years	65 years and over
1950										
Total...........	100.0	100.0	100.0	100.0	100.0	100.0	100.0	100.0	100.0	100.0
Agriculture, forestry, and fisheries..........	3.8	26.8	9.4	3.0	2.3	3.1	3.6	4.1	5.0	7.2
Mining..........	0.2	...	...	0.1	0.2	0.1	0.1	0.1	0.1	0.1
Construction..........	0.6	0.2	0.3	0.6	0.7	0.7	0.7	0.6	0.5	0.5
Manufacturing..........	23.7	3.1	14.0	22.5	25.9	28.6	25.1	21.0	17.1	10.9
Transportation, communication, and other public utilities..........	4.4	0.6	2.2	7.1	7.8	4.5	3.6	3.6	2.5	1.2
Wholesale and retail trade..........	23.1	18.7	39.1	27.5	21.5	22.4	23.9	22.9	21.5	18.2
Finance, insurance, and real estate..........	5.1	0.4	3.3	10.8	8.5	4.5	3.7	4.0	4.0	4.2
Business and repair services..........	1.2	0.2	0.7	1.3	1.5	1.3	1.2	1.1	0.8	0.8
Personal services..........	15.1	42.7	19.6	9.4	8.8	12.9	15.3	17.3	22.2	32.0
Entertainment and recreation services..........	0.9	2.6	3.5	1.4	1.0	0.9	0.8	0.7	0.7	0.6
Professional and related services..........	17.7	4.6	7.4	14.0	17.9	15.8	17.7	19.9	21.4	21.3
Public administration..........	4.2	0.2	0.5	2.3	3.9	5.0	4.4	4.7	4.3	2.9
1940										
Total...........	100.0	100.0	100.0	100.0	100.0	100.0	100.0	100.0	100.0	100.0
Agriculture, forestry, and fisheries..........	4.5	53.0	18.2	5.5	3.0	2.6	3.7	5.5	7.6	12.7
Mining..........	0.1	...	...	0.1	0.1	0.1	0.1	0.1	0.1	0.1
Construction..........	0.3	0.1	0.2	0.3	0.4	0.3	0.4	0.3	0.3	0.2
Manufacturing..........	21.4	2.4	16.0	24.4	26.6	24.8	20.4	15.4	10.2	6.8
Transportation, communication, and other public utilities..........	3.1	0.2	0.8	2.5	3.1	3.8	3.8	2.6	1.6	0.9
Wholesale and retail trade..........	18.7	4.7	13.2	20.6	20.3	18.7	18.7	18.6	16.1	12.3
Finance, insurance, and real estate..........	4.2	0.1	1.1	3.8	4.6	4.4	4.2	4.0	3.8	3.6
Business and repair services..........	0.7	0.1	0.3	0.8	0.8	0.8	0.8	0.6	0.5	0.4
Personal services..........	26.1	37.3	45.1	28.4	21.5	21.6	26.0	30.8	37.8	43.9
Entertainment and recreation services..........	0.8	0.5	1.0	1.1	0.9	0.8	0.7	0.6	0.5	0.4
Professional and related services..........	17.2	1.4	3.9	11.4	16.1	18.8	18.0	18.3	18.7	16.9
Public administration..........	2.8	0.1	0.2	1.1	2.4	3.2	3.4	3.3	3.0	1.9

Source: Derived from appendix table D-8.

FIGURE 11.—PERCENT OF EMPLOYED WOMEN IN MANUFACTURING AND TRADE, BY AGE: 1950 AND 1940

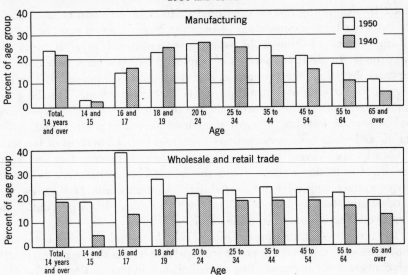

Note: Based on data in table 52.

The industries in which young women under 25 were employed, in proportions greater than would have been expected on the basis of 1940 patterns, are transportation and communication, finance, insurance and real estate, and professional and related services (table 53). They had shifted out of the personal service industries, except for 14 and 15 year olds. Girls under 20 were working in trade establishments much more frequently than would have been expected. Except for these shifts, the distribution of the various age groups among the different industry groups did not differ much from what would have been expected from 1940 patterns.

TABLE 53.—DIFFERENCE BETWEEN ACTUAL AND EXPECTED PERCENTAGE OF AGE GROUP IN MAJOR INDUSTRY GROUP, FOR EMPLOYED WOMEN: 1950

[Decennial census levels—actual minus expected]

Major industry group	14 and 15 years	16 and 17 years	18 and 19 years	20 to 24 years	25 to 34 years	35 to 44 years	45 to 54 years	55 to 64 years	65 and over
Agriculture, forestry, and fisheries...	-30.7	-9.0	-1.7	-0.2	+0.9	+0.4	-0.8	-2.0	-5.3
Mining and construction................	-0.2	-0.1	-0.1	+0.1	+0.1	-0.1	...	-0.1	...
Manufacturing..........................	-0.4	-7.0	-5.0	-2.7	+2.2	+2.6	+3.5	+4.8	+2.2
Transportation, communication, and other public utilities................	+0.2	+0.9	+3.5	+3.5	-0.7	-1.7	-0.2	...	-0.3
Wholesale and retail trade.............	+11.3	+19.7	+1.7	-2.9	-0.7	+1.1	-0.7	-0.1	+0.6
Finance, insurance, and real estate....	+0.2	+1.8	+6.1	+3.1	-0.7	-1.4	-1.0	-1.0	-0.8
Business and repair services...........	...	+0.1	...	+0.2	...	...	+0.1	...	...
Personal services......................	+15.0	-11.3	-7.3	-3.3	+0.8	+0.3	-1.1	-1.8	+2.6
Entertainment and recreation services..	+1.9	+2.1	+0.1	+1.9	-2.9	-0.6	+0.5	+0.6	+1.3
Professional and related services......	+2.7	+2.7	+2.1	+1.9	-2.9	-0.6	+0.5	+0.6	+1.3
Public administration..................	...	+0.1	+0.6	+0.4	+0.4	-0.6	-0.3	-0.5	-0.4

Note: Expected percentage of age group in specified industry group is computed by distributing total number of women in the industry group in 1950 by the 1940 age distribution for that group, and calculating percent distribution within each age-class.

Source: Derived from appendix table D-8.

Utilization of Negro women. The decrease in the labor force participation of nonwhite women in areas in the South may be better understood by examining the occupational shifts. In the country as a whole, the most striking occupational change for Negro women was the decline in importance of household work, the traditional type of work for this group. In 1940, 60 percent of employed Negro women were domestic servants; by 1950, the proportion had declined to 42 percent. The proportion in farming also dropped, from 16 to 9 percent. On the other hand, sharp gains were recorded in the proportion engaged as operatives and as service workers. Negro women employed in professional, managerial, and white-collar occupations rose from 6 to 12 percent of the total.

Clearly, these overall changes suggest some improvement in the Negro social and economic status. When the detailed occupations are examined, however, the changes are not so striking. Appendix table D–9 shows comparable statistics for any occupation which included 0.5 percent of the employed Negro women in either 1940 or 1950.

The upward shift for women from private household to other service occupations was, in effect, a transfer from private homes to commercial establishments without any upgrading or real change in type of work. The occupations that showed gains were charwomen, cooks, waitresses, and practical nurses. Similarly, in the operatives group, laundry and dry-cleaning operatives gained most in relative importance. In manufacturing, Negro women made substantial gains in the apparel and fabricated-textile industries and some gains in food processing. Professional or other white-collar occupations in which larger proportions of Negro women were employed in 1950 were trained nurses, teachers, stenographers, typists, and secretaries.

Changes by regions show a different picture. Negro women made much less occupational progress in the South than in other regions. In 1950, they were still heavily concentrated in private households and other service work and showed only small gains over the decade in the higher status industrial occupations. In 1940, about 60 percent or more of the Negro women in each region were employed in private household work. By 1950, this proportion had dropped by about 30 percentage points outside the South, but by only 13 points in the South. Substantial gains were made in the skilled and semiskilled occupations in all regions, except the South. The proportion in skilled and semiskilled occupations was only 10 percent in the South in 1950 as compared with 20 percent or more in the Northeastern and North Central Regions. The lack of job opportunities in the South in the more attractive, higher paying occupations may well have been the reason why Negro women chose to withdraw from the labor force or to remain at home when family incomes permitted a choice.

Conclusion

Demographic changes account only in small part for the changes in labor force participation that took place in the United States between 1940 and 1950. The increasing propensity of white women past 35 years of age to be in the labor force more than compensated for the losses that would have taken place because of increased family responsibilities of younger women. The fact that so many of the age classes over 35 had worked during World War II may have meant that they were more prone to look for work again as the postwar boom built up, and, perhaps more important, employers were more likely to hire them. Those younger women who were in the labor force were working in disproportionate numbers in clerical jobs, in business establishments. Jobs in manufacturing were accordingly opened up for the older women.

The increasing employment of married women was universal, in all types of labor markets, and, therefore, may reflect widespread changes in customs and attitudes brought about by the manpower shortages during World War II. However, the increase seems to have been greatest in those areas where earnings of men were highest, and presumably the demands were pressing for women to take some of the lower paid jobs that men would not fill. In general, the types of persons whose propensity to work increased most over the decade were not those who were in the lower socio-economic groups. The evidence is not yet clear, but the data analyzed give some support for the belief that, in addition to the need or desire for income, other motives for labor force activity have assumed importance in recent years.

CHAPTER 4

TRENDS IN THE PART-TIME LABOR FORCE

Some implications of trend in part-time work

Evaluation of the growth of the labor force in recent years and knowledge of the socio-economic effects of the marked increase in employment of married women and teen-agers require an examination of the nature of the commitment of these added workers to the labor force, as well as of their gross numbers. Furthermore, the extent to which part-time employment (including part-year) becomes a permanent feature of the Nation's job structure is important for many reasons. If more and more jobs can be filled with workers who are recruited for short-time periods or for less than a full work week, the supply of potential workers is indeed elastic. Married women with some, but not constant, responsibilities at home, semi-retired workers, and students who need some job income number in the millions.

It is interesting to speculate about the ultimate possibilities of the development of a labor force based in substantial measure on part-time work. The value to the economy in terms of expanding the labor supply is obvious. It is also conceivable that the task of earning a family living might be shared among several part-time workers, providing each with some measure of stimulating activity and leisure time. A quasi-leisure class might appear in this country, based not on inherited wealth, as in other older countries, but on the combined result of high productivity and short hours of work of a large segment of the population. And with leisure to be used at the age when energy and interests are still abundant, the average man might extend his education and turn his attention to other cultural activities, as leisure classes have done elsewhere.

For the immediate present, there are both advantages and disadvantages to the expansion of part-time work. For the individual who has some time free and the need or desire for additional income, a part-time job may be a great boon. Many of the multiworker families, whose joint incomes make possible the purchase of a house, a car, a television set, a washing machine, have a combination of full-time and part-time jobs.

On the debit side are the possible effects on the wage structure and the skill levels of the population. To the extent that married women, or any segments of the labor force, are seeking work of a supplementary nature to ease the family budget but not to carry the whole burden, they may become a force for depressing or dampening wage rates or salary scales because of their willingness to accept somewhat lower salaries than do regular full-time workers. Or, even if they do not enter on a job at substandard rates, they may be far more complacent about remaining at low levels than they would were they full-time wage earners.

Another possible danger is the dilution of the skills of the work force. If many jobs are geared to the intermittent type of worker, and are available to any one who has 20 hours free a week or 3 or 4 weeks free during a peak season, there may not be much incentive for the individual worker to spend time or money acquiring training or special skills. The high school girl who expects to marry upon graduation, have a family, and then perhaps pick up part-time jobs in selling or service trades as her family budget requires it may see little reason to acquire the skills she might need to hold a full-time job. Her employer, for his part, would not be likely to select her for further training or advancement so long as she remains a part-time worker.[1]

Definitions of part-time labor force

The immediate problem, however, is not to evaluate the composition of the work force but to measure it and to determine whether it is changing. Many labels have been given to those workers who do not seek to work full time the year round. Secondary workers, part-time workers, marginal workers, and intermittent workers are terms that describe all or part of the group whose only common characteristic is that they are not likely to be working full time each week of the year.[2] Some of them work full time for part of the year and then definitely withdraw from the labor force to go back to school or to take care of their home responsibilities. Others almost never work full time but want steady part-time work throughout the year. Still others may work either full or part time when suitable work is available but take no active steps, or only sporadic steps, to locate work when their jobs end; these have been sometimes called "fringe workers," presumably because they are on the outskirts of the labor force and are not clearly in or out of the labor force at all times. In this chapter, the terms "part time workers" and "part time labor force" will be used to describe those workers who do not *usually* work or seek to work full time the year round.

---

[1] For a further discussion of the advantages and disadvantages of part-time work for women, and the attitudes of trade unions and women's organizations, see "Part-Time Employment for Women with Family Responsibilities," *International Labour Review*, Vol. LXXV, No. 6, June 1957, pp. 543–553.

[2] The term "marginal workers" has often been used, notably by Jaffe and Stewart, to describe "people who combine labor force activity with some other activity, such as attending school or keeping house. These marginal workers may continue both activities simultaneously, or they may alternate and move in and out of the labor force." Because so many married women are now regularly in the labor force and also keeping house, the criterion of dual activity no longer discriminates between types of workers. Also, no matter how fully defined, the word "marginal" carries the connotation of inferior, or below standard. See A. J. Jaffe and Charles D. Stewart, *Manpower Resources and Utilization*, John Wiley & Sons, New York, 1951, p. 122.

Information on the number of hours worked during the census week by employed workers was collected in the 1940 and 1950 Censuses of Population, and in the Current Population Survey each month from 1941 on. Information on the number of weeks worked during the preceding calendar year by all persons who did any work was also collected in the decennial censuses in 1940 and 1950, and in the Current Population Survey each year from 1950 on. Reasons for part-time work during the survey week used to be recorded occasionally in the CPS, and since May 1955 they have been recorded monthly. These various indicators have suggested how the labor force might be divided into persons who work full time the year round and those who prefer to work only part time, but they have not served to identify persons who would have been working full time the year round if unemployment or temporary illness had not prevented it. The full-time labor force is larger than the number working full time the whole year. Conversely, all persons who do not work full time throughout the year are not automatically in the part-time labor force.

In 1956, for the first time, information was collected on the reasons why persons who were in the labor force at some time during 1955 did not work every week. It is thus possible, using somewhat arbitrary criteria, to divide the working population into the full-time and the part-time labor force. In the full-time labor force are persons who usually worked full time and who were in the labor force all year except for periods of illness or unpaid absence, or because they entered the labor force or retired during the year. In the part-time labor force are persons who usually worked part time or who chose to work only part of the year because of home or school responsibilities (table 54). Full-time workers in the civilian labor force all year numbered 52 million in 1955, or two-thirds of the total who did any work at all during the year. These were full-time workers who worked the year round, or who remained in the labor force the year round, even though they may have been unemployed, on layoff, or absent from work for a few weeks because of illness, strike, or unpaid vacation. They contributed 85 percent of the man-years worked. About 5 percent of the total were full-time workers who were out of the labor force for part of the year because of prolonged illness, unpaid absence, and other miscellaneous reasons.

The part-time labor force, that is, persons who work for only part of a week or part of a year because of the pressure of other activities, numbered about 20 million during 1955—about 27 percent of all workers. They provided an estimated 7 million man-years or 12 percent of the total man-years available in civilian employment. These are essentially the workers who form the labor supply for industries with sharp seasonal peaks, with schedules that do not call for full-time workers, or with other characteristics that are not attractive to full-time workers. They may also form a supplementary labor supply in occupations (such as nursing and teaching) in which the demand for workers is so great that it cannot be met by available full-time workers. Some of the jobs these workers fill may be marginal, although the persons themselves may be indistinguishable in training and skill from year-round workers who have full-time jobs. What does distinguish them is their deliberate decision that they will not make themselves available for full-time, year-round work.

TABLE 54.—TYPE OF WORKERS IN THE ANNUAL LABOR FORCE: 1955

[Current survey levels]

Type of worker	Workers		Man-years[1]	
	Number (thousands)	Percent	Number (thousands)	Percent
Total who worked in 1955................................	75,353	100.0	58,358	100.0
FULL-TIME LABOR FORCE				
Total......................................	55,218	73.3	51,380	88.1
In civilian labor force all year.........................	51,663	68.6	49,522	84.9
Worked 50 to 52 weeks at full-time jobs.....................	42,624	56.6	42,624	73.0
Worked at full-time jobs less than 50 weeks because of unemployment or layoff..	5,861	7.8	4,069	7.0
Lost 3 to 12 weeks from full-time jobs because of—				
Illness......................................	1,768	2.3	1,574	2.7
Unpaid absence...	1,410	1.9	1,255	2.2
In civilian labor force part of year.........................	3,555	4.7	1,858	3.2
Lost more than 12 weeks from full-time jobs because of—				
Illness......................................	1,261	1.7	583	1.0
Unpaid absence...	522	0.7	301	0.5
Worked at full-time jobs less than 50 weeks for miscellaneous reasons (retirement, service in Armed Forces, etc.).........	1,772	2.3	974	1.7
PART-TIME LABOR FORCE				
Total......................................	20,135	26.7	6,978	11.9
Usually worked at part-time jobs............................	12,772	16.9	4,090	7.0
Worked at full-time jobs less than 50 weeks because of home or school responsibilities..	7,363	9.8	2,888	4.9

[1] Paid vacations and other paid leaves of absence are considered weeks worked. Weeks worked by full-time workers counted as full weeks; weeks worked by persons who usually work part-time as half weeks. Man-year assumed to be 50 weeks.

Source: U. S. Bureau of the Census, *Current Population Reports*, Series P-50, No. 68, tables 1 and 11.

Most of the data on part-year or part-week workers provide only approximations to this group. In the following pages, the various types of census statistics will be examined for evidence on characteristics and trends in part-time work, although at no point do they measure exactly the concept used here.

Composition of part-time labor force

Is there evidence that the labor force has shifted in its composition to include a larger proportion of voluntary part-time workers? (The term "voluntary" is used for convenience; many, of course, would work full time if they were free to do so.) This is a question whose answer is particularly affected by quality of enumeration. Part-time and intermittent workers are frequently missed altogether by census enumerators who do not ask all the required questions necessary to identify them. Thus, what may appear to be a change in the proportion of full-time and part-time workers may in fact be only a change in the quality of enumeration.

Another problem is to distinguish between voluntary part-time work and work that is essentially a form of partial unemployment arising because work is slack and business conditions poor. The mere existence of part-time work does not prove underemployment. Part-time workers may be numerous because hours have been cut back or because labor shortages have made it impossible to recruit full-time employees or for other reasons. In connection with the Current Population Survey, a series of occasional surveys, inaugurated in 1947, and now regular questions in the monthly interview permit identification of voluntary part-time workers. These data show that, as a rule, over half of all persons who worked part time (less than 35 hours) during a given week did so of their own volition or because they were not free to accept full-time jobs (table 55). Throughout most of the postwar years the extent of voluntary part-time work has remained fairly constant at from 6.5 to 8.5 percent of the civilian labor force in a given week. In 1956, it averaged 9 percent.

TABLE 55.—PART-TIME WORKERS: 1949 TO 1956

[Current survey levels]

Date	Total persons at work during survey week (thousands)	Worked less than 35 hours		Usually worked part time, not available for full-time work		
		Number (thousands)	Percent of total at work	Number (thousands)	Percent of total at work less than 35 hours	Percent of civilian labor force
1949: May.......................	57,010	8,536	15.0	5,057	59.2	8.2
August....................	55,426	8,293	15.0	3,994	48.2	6.3
1950: May.......................	58,007	9,003	15.5	5,033	55.9	8.0
August....................	57,901	7,898	13.6	4,211	53.3	6.5
1951: May.......................	59,405	8,552	14.4	5,303	62.0	8.4
1952: May.......................	59,008	8,308	14.1	5,222	62.9	8.3
1954: May.......................	58,983	10,067	17.1	5,570	55.3	8.6
August....................	56,701	9,022	15.9	4,278	47.4	6.5
1955: May.......................	60,699	9,693	16.0	5,772	59.5	8.9
August....................	59,254	8,772	14.8	4,212	48.0	6.2
July-December average....	61,244	10,701	17.5	5,437	50.8	8.1
1956: May.......................	63,144	11,372	18.0	7,122	62.6	10.5
August....................	60,899	9,626	15.8	4,898	50.9	7.1
January-June average.....	61,520	10,973	17.8	6,113	55.7	9.1
July-December average....	62,117	11,383	18.3	5,999	52.7	8.8

Source: Derived from U. S. Bureau of the Census, *Current Population Reports*, Series P–50, No. 18, table 2; No. 28, table 2; No. 34, table 1; No. 56, table 1; No. 67, table 16; and No. 72, table 17.

Whether voluntary part-time employment increased in importance between 1940 and 1950 cannot be determined directly but perhaps may be inferred from some of the data on the characteristics of the workers themselves (table 56 and figure 12). Much of the part-time or part-year work recorded at the time of the 1940 Census was partial unemployment, rather than the kind of supplementary work discussed here. If there had been no increase in supplementary part-time work, the proportion of persons working on short schedules would be expected to decline as the economy reached full-employment levels. Despite the differences in the economic situation in 1940 and 1950, the extent of part-time employment during the census week was not very different at the two dates, except in certain age groups. It may be inferred, then, that there was a considerable extension of part-time work deliberately scheduled to attract otherwise unavailable workers, and that the expansion of certain segments of the labor force was possible because part-time workers could, in fact, be recruited. A familiar example of the type of change that has occurred is the way in which retail food stores and other establishments have extended their scheduled hours in order to meet the needs of customers who cannot shop during normal daytime hours. To staff their businesses, and to avoid extended work weeks, they have had to set up elaborate combinations of full- and part-time work schedules.

TABLE **56.**—PERSONS EMPLOYED LESS THAN 35 HOURS DURING WEEK AS PERCENT OF TOTAL AT WORK, AND OF TOTAL POPULATION: 1950 AND 1940

[Decennial census levels]

Age, color, and sex	Percent of total at work				Percent of total population			
	Total		Nonfarm residents		Total		Nonfarm residents	
	1950	1940	1950	1940	1950	1940	1950	1940
MALE								
Total, 14 years and over..	10.1	11.1	9.2	11.1	7.3	7.3	6.5	7.1
White........................	9.7	10.7	8.8	10.7	7.0	7.1	6.3	6.9
Nonwhite.....................	14.0	15.1	13.0	15.5	9.5	9.8	8.4	8.9
14 to 17 years..............	57.6	32.6	66.1	45.2	12.4	4.2	11.1	3.3
White........................	61.2	34.5	68.4	48.8	12.6	3.9	11.4	3.2
Nonwhite.....................	38.6	26.3	48.5	28.0	10.7	6.9	8.6	4.0
18 and 19 years.............	21.7	17.3	23.2	18.9	11.0	7.5	10.5	7.0
White........................	21.7	17.1	23.3	18.7	10.9	7.2	10.5	6.9
Nonwhite.....................	21.7	18.4	22.7	20.2	11.9	9.7	10.3	7.6
20 to 64 years..............	7.9	10.2	7.4	10.3	6.5	7.9	5.9	7.8
White........................	7.5	9.8	7.0	10.0	6.2	7.6	5.7	7.6
Nonwhite.....................	11.9	14.0	11.3	14.7	9.1	10.3	8.3	9.7
65 years and over...........	21.0	16.0	17.6	15.7	7.8	5.8	5.7	4.5
White........................	20.5	15.5	17.0	15.1	7.5	5.5	5.5	4.4
Nonwhite.....................	27.5	21.7	26.7	25.8	10.6	9.2	8.3	7.1
FEMALE								
Total, 14 years and over..	20.5	19.0	19.2	18.2	5.5	4.1	5.4	4.5
White........................	18.9	17.2	17.6	17.0	4.9	3.6	4.9	4.0
Nonwhite.....................	32.6	29.6	30.8	26.8	10.6	9.3	10.9	9.6
14 to 17 years..............	61.1	33.4	60.4	·30.6	5.7	1.6	5.9	1.3
White........................	61.8	30.7	60.9	30.5	5.8	1.2	6.1	1.2
Nonwhite.....................	56.6	41.1	56.0	31.4	5.4	4.4	4.5	2.5
18 and 19 years.............	18.0	20.1	17.0	19.2	7.0	5.5	7.1	5.9
White........................	16.7	18.7	16.1	18.6	6.9	5.2	7.0	5.8
Nonwhite.....................	33.6	31.8	29.4	26.6	8.4	8.2	7.8	7.1
20 to 44 years..............	17.8	17.5	16.6	16.8	5.8	5.2	5.7	5.5
White........................	16.1	16.0	15.0	15.7	5.1	4.5	5.0	5.0
Nonwhite.....................	29.1	26.9	27.5	24.5	11.5	10.3	11.7	10.7
45 to 64 years..............	22.5	21.8	21.1	21.5	6.0	3.8	6.0	4.1
White........................	20.7	19.7	19.3	19.8	5.3	3.2	5.3	3.6
Nonwhite.....................	37.6	34.6	36.6	33.5	13.2	11.0	14.0	11.9
65 years and over...........	31.4	25.4	29.9	24.9	2.2	1.4	2.1	1.4
White........................	29.1	22.0	27.6	22.1	2.0	1.1	1.9	1.1
Nonwhite.....................	52.3	45.1	52.1	46.1	4.9	5.1	5.2	5.1

Source: Derived from *1950 Census of Population*, Vol. IV, *Special Reports*, Part 1, Chapter A, Employment and Personal Characteristics, tables 1 and 13; *1940 Census of Population, Employment and Personal Characteristics*, tables 1 and 29.

The marked expansion in the early teen-age labor force, noted earlier, consisted to a large extent of part-time workers. Almost three-fifths of the 14- to 17-year-old boys at work in 1950 (58 percent) were working less than 35 hours, and one-fifth less than 15 hours; in 1940, only one-third were part-time workers, 10 percent under 15 hours. In nonfarm house-holds, two-thirds of the youngest age group were part-time workers in 1950, almost one-half in 1940. Some expansion in the part-time labor force of 18- and 19-year-olds also occurred.

Although labor force participation changed little for older men past their midsixties, there was some increase in part-time employment for this group, particularly for farm residents. For men in the prime ages, 20 to 64, the proportion working part time declined moderately from 10 percent to 8 percent.

As was true of teen-age boys, many more teen-age girls were part-time workers in 1950—61 percent as compared with 33 percent. Again, among older women, those 65 years and over, a similar, although more moderate, increase occurred in the proportion working part time; almost one-third of the women 65 and over at work in 1950 were part-time workers, but only one-quarter were in 1940. Thus, it may have been the expansion of opportunities for part-time employment that made labor force activity seem desirable and possible to a larger proportion of women in this age group.

FIGURE 12.—PART-TIME WORKERS AS PERCENT OF TOTAL NONFARM RESIDENTS AT WORK, BY AGE AND SEX: 1950 AND 1940

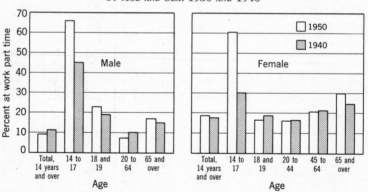

Note: Based on data in table 56.

White women in the age groups between 20 and 64 worked part time at the census date in about the same proportions in 1950 as in 1940. To a large extent, white women who were underemployed in 1940 must have been replaced in the 1950 labor force by women whose short work week was a matter of their own convenience. Some increasing tendency to part-time work appears for nonwhite women—a development that may mean that the improvement in earnings of other workers in the family may have permitted some full-time workers to retire from the labor force or to work only part time. It has been suggested that the demand for part-time jobs was strong on the part of both white and nonwhite women, and that the greater availability of part-time work brought white women into the labor force, but allowed nonwhite women in the labor force to reduce their hours of work.

At all ages, except the youngest, nonwhite women are more likely to have part-time jobs than white women because they so often find work in domestic and service occupations, which traditionally have irregular schedules. The greater proportion of part-time workers among 14- to 17-year-old white girls in 1950 reflects the fact that at this age most white children remain in school and therefore are available for part-time work only. The differences are not great, however.

Industries and occupations of part-time workers

An industry may have relatively large proportions of short-time workers during a specific week for a variety of reasons. Work may be limited because of the weather or the lack of materials to process or because it is offseason in the particular trade. Hours may also be curtailed if business activity is slack either generally or in the specific industry. Union agreements, arrived at as a part of a share-the-work program or as a means of increasing earnings, may have set a shorter-than-average week as the maximum in an industry. Certain types of activities, like some teaching or entertainment jobs, have relatively short scheduled hours, although many unreported hours may be worked. Finally, an industry may rely to a large extent on part-time workers because its conditions of employment or pay scales do not attract sufficient full-time workers but do appeal to persons for whom short hours are satisfactory.

As indicated above, the decennial census data, which are the only statistics available giving hours distributions for a detailed list of industries, do not permit distinctions between one kind of part-time worker and another. One clue to the nature of the part-time employment in a specific industry may be the relative level of unemployment in the industry at the same time. Thus, industries with a large proportion of part-time workers at the census date and a large proportion of their labor force unemployed might be assumed to be subject to partial as well as total unemployment, either of a seasonal or a cyclical nature. Those with a large proportion of part-time workers and a small proportion of their labor force wholly unemployed would fall into the group whose scheduled hours are short by agreement or custom, or whose labor supply consists to a large extent of regular part-time workers. Table 57 presents the results of such a comparison for 1950 and 1940.

In 1940, most of the industries with high rates of part-time employment at the time of the census (industries in the upper quartile) were extractive and manufacturing industries, and most of them had above average (median) unemployment rates as well. The only one with an unemployment rate of less than 5 percent was pottery manufacturing, in which 19.8 percent of the employed women worked part time but 3.8 percent were wholly unemployed. These data suggest that most of the persons working a short

TABLE **57.**—Unemployment Rates in Industries with High Proportion of Part-Time Workers, by Sex: 1950 and 1940

[Decennial census levels]

Year and industry[1]	Male		Female	
	At work — Percent under 35 hours	Experienced labor force — Percent unemployed	At work — Percent under 35 hours	Experienced labor force — Percent unemployed
1950				
Total....................................	10.1	4.8	20.5	4.4
Agriculture..............................	16.3	2.4	54.3	4.2
Forestry.................................	10.1	5.0	...	...
Fisheries................................	22.5	8.5	...	...
Coal mining..............................	32.2	5.6	...	...
Construction.............................	15.8	10.4	...	...
Logging..................................	23.8	12.2	...	...
Sawmills, planing mills, and mill work...	14.7	5.0	...	...
Pottery and related products.............	11.3	4.1	22.4	3.6
Canning & preserving fruits, vegetables, & sea foods...	10.6	16.6	33.9	25.6
Tobacco manufacturing....................	13.3	9.7	26.3	12.9
Knitting mills...........................	12.1	4.2	24.9	3.9
Dyeing and finishing textiles, except knit goods.......	13.0	4.9	...	...
Yarn, thread, and fabric mills...........	10.4	5.6	19.9	5.8
Miscellaneous textile mill products......	9.8	4.9	...	...
Printing, publishing, and allied industries.	16.8	2.9	...	...
Footwear, except rubber manufacturing....	15.8	6.5	19.5	4.9
Trucking service.........................	11.0	6.4	...	...
Water transportation.....................	19.5	15.1	...	...
Air transportation.......................	10.2	4.1	...	...
Wholesale food and related products......	...	...	19.9	8.5
Retail food stores, except dairy products.	11.6	3.7	21.5	2.9
Dairy products stores and milk retailing.	...	...	24.4	4.0
Five and ten cent stores.................	10.5	4.2	24.8	6.1
Shoe stores..............................	9.9	3.6	26.8	3.3
Gasoline service stations................	...	...	23.3	1.9
Drug stores..............................	16.9	3.4	22.0	4.5
Eating and drinking places...............	...	...	20.6	7.7
Liquor stores............................	...	...	21.3	3.0
Retail florists..........................	...	...	20.1	2.6
Jewelry stores...........................	...	...	19.5	4.2
Fuel and ice retailing...................	10.4	5.6	...	...
Miscellaneous retail stores..............	...	...	25.8	3.2
Real estate offices......................	...	...	22.8	3.8
Miscellaneous business services..........	9.8	4.7	...	...
Miscellaneous repair services............	12.4	5.0	22.6	3.8
Private households.......................	37.2	9.3	43.2	7.2
Dressmaking shops........................	...	...	54.9	4.4
Shoe repair shops........................	11.4	4.2	21.2	3.3
Miscellaneous personal services..........	...	...	24.5	2.9
Radio broadcasting and television........	11.2	4.1	...	...
Theaters and motion pictures.............	25.0	7.3	44.6	7.2
Bowling alleys, and billiard and pool parlors..........	35.8	7.7	42.9	4.1
Miscellaneous entertainment and recreation services....	26.6	10.2	42.4	7.2
Educational services, government.........	18.8	1.2	30.2	0.8
Educational services, private...........	23.3	2.2	40.0	1.4
Welfare and religious services...........	14.0	1.5	23.0	1.5
Nonprofit membership organizations.......	10.0	3.8	20.6	2.6
Miscellaneous professional and related services........	11.0	4.7	29.5	4.6
Postal service...........................	...	...	24.1	2.7
1940[2]				
Total....................................	11.1	13.7	19.0	11.1
Agriculture..............................	...	...	35.7	6.8
Fishery..................................	21.6	14.3	...	...
Coal mining..............................	53.2	20.6	...	...
Sand and gravel production...............	14.8	16.4	...	...
Stone quarrying..........................	17.4	38.0	...	...
Miscellaneous nonmetallic mining.........	17.1	12.4	...	...
Construction.............................	20.0	46.9	...	...
Beverage industries.....................	...	...	22.9	7.3

[1] Industries in highest quartile.
[2] Industry of unemployed is industry of last job for persons seeking work and usual industry for emergency workers.

TABLE **57.**—UNEMPLOYMENT RATES IN INDUSTRIES WITH HIGH PROPORTION OF PART-TIME WORKERS, BY SEX: 1950 AND 1940—Cont.

[Decennial census levels]

Year and industry[1]	Male		Female	
	At work — Percent under 35 hours	Experienced labor force — Percent unemployed	At work — Percent under 35 hours	Experienced labor force — Percent unemployed
1940[2]--Cont.				
Canning & preserving fruits, vegetables, & sea food....	14.5	25.6	32.8	31.3
Confectionery manufacturing............................	...	...	21.0	15.5
Tobacco manufacturing.................................	26.0	18.3	40.9	14.1
Cotton manufacturing..................................	21.5	8.9	33.7	7.4
Silk and rayon manufacturing..........................	15.4	16.9	26.1	13.2
Woolen and worsted manufacturing......................	23.4	19.3	38.6	15.4
Knit goods..	21.8	10.5	31.5	7.6
Dyeing and finishing textiles.........................	20.9	10.3	29.8	7.8
Carpets, rugs, and other floor coverings..............	15.4	8.3	29.9	7.0
Hats, except cloth and millinery......................	42.2	12.7	32.0	7.4
Miscellaneous textile goods...........................	...	...	23.3	8.1
Not specified textile mills...........................	...	...	22.1	13.9
Apparel and accessories...............................	14.7	15.9	22.9	27.5
Miscellaneous fabricated textile products.............	...	...	19.6	31.1
Logging...	17.4	25.9	...	...
Paperboard container manufacturing....................	...	...	14.7	10.4
Printing, publishing, and allied industries..........	14.7	8.6	...	...
Rubber products manufacturing.........................	22.4	10.4	28.6	6.8
Footwear industries, except rubber....................	29.6	14.4	34.8	8.1
Leather, tanned, curried, and finished................	18.1	14.0	...	...
Leather products, except footwear.....................	...	...	21.0	13.6
Glass and glass products..............................	15.3	11.1	...	...
Structural clay products..............................	16.6	16.2	...	...
Cut-stone and stone products..........................	15.7	19.7	...	...
Pottery and related products..........................	...	...	19.8	3.8
Blast furnaces, steel works, and rolling mills.........	26.7	13.9	...	...
Automobiles and automobile equipment manufacturing....	18.5	10.8	...	...
Trucking service......................................	14.6	17.0	...	...
Water transportation..................................	21.8	19.1	...	...
Radio broadcasting and television.....................	...	...	19.7	8.2
Limited price variety stores..........................	...	...	19.7	10.4
Miscellaneous repair services.........................	...	...	20.9	12.3
Domestic service......................................	17.2	16.6	22.7	13.1
Miscellaneous personal services.......................	...	...	20.5	12.6
Theaters and motion pictures..........................	18.8	16.4	33.1	17.3
Miscellaneous amusement and recreation services........	23.5	23.3	40.4	30.7
Educational services..................................	20.4	9.1	35.4	9.4

[1] Industries in highest quartile.

[2] Industry of unemployed is industry of last job for persons seeking work and usual industry for emergency workers.

Source: Derived from *1950 Census of Population*, Vol. II, *Characteristics of the Population*, Part 1, U. S. Summary, table 130, and Vol. IV, *Special Reports*, Part 1, Chapter D, Industrial Characteristics, table 10; *1940 Census of Population*, Vol. III, *The Labor Force*, Part 1, U. S. Summary, table 74; *Industrial Characteristics*, table 13; and *Population*, Series P–14, No. 13, table 2.

week at that time were characteristically underemployed. But in 1950, when the economy was much closer to a full-employment level, a large proportion of the industries with high percentages of part-time workers were trade and service industries and few had high unemployment rates. The censuses were taken in April, and several seasonal industries had both high unemployment and part-time work: fisheries, construction, logging, canning and preserving food, tobacco manufacturing, water transportation. Private household work and the entertainment industries also were in this class. For the others, it appears that the high rate of part-time employment in 1950 meant the extensive use of workers scheduled to work part time because they did not want or could not accept full-time work.

TABLE **58.**—PERSONS EMPLOYED LESS THAN 35 HOURS DURING WEEK AS PERCENT OF TOTAL
AT WORK, BY MAJOR INDUSTRY GROUP AND SEX: 1950 AND 1940

[Decennial census levels]

Major industry group	Male		Female	
	1950	1940	1950	1940
Total....................................	10.1	11.1	20.5	19.0
Agriculture, forestry, and fisheries..............	16.4	11.0	54.0	35.7
Mining.......................................	20.4	34.8	8.6	14.3
Construction.................................	15.8	20.0	17.6	15.4
Manufacturing................................	7.0	12.9	13.2	21.3
Transportation, communication, and other public utilities.................................	6.0	7.6	7.0	6.7
Wholesale and retail trade......................	7.7	5.8	18.5	13.4
Wholesale................................	5.0	5.0	12.2	9.9
Retail....................................	8.4	6.0	19.3	13.8
Finance, insurance, and real estate..............	6.0	4.8	10.2	8.5
Business and repair services....................	7.9	8.2	16.6	12.0
Personal services.............................	13.1	8.1	34.0	20.6
Private household.........................	37.2	17.2	43.2	22.7
Other....................................	8.1	5.3	19.4	15.1
Entertainment and recreation services..........	25.7	21.6	40.5	36.1
Professional and related services...............	12.4	11.8	22.3	23.4
Public administration........................	4.2	4.4	9.5	6.4

Source: Derived from *1950 Census of Population*, Vol. IV, *Special Reports*, Part 1, Chapter D, Industrial Characteristics, table 10; *1940 Census of Population, Industrial Characteristics*, table 13.

Table 58 summarizes the extent of part-time work in the major industry groups at both dates (see also figure 13). It shows a sharp drop in mining, construction, and manufacturing, but an increase in agriculture, trade, and many of the service industries, particularly for women. Thus, the stability in the percent working part time conceals a marked drop in part-time work in the basic industries that were depressed in 1940, and an increase where work schedules are generally more flexible, and wage rates are relatively low, for the most part. It is in these low-paying jobs that many women and young untrained workers tend to find their job opportunities. Specific industries employing 100,000 or more women in 1950 with extreme increases in the percent of women working part time are:

	1950	1940
Agriculture...................................	54.3	35.7
Retail food stores............................	21.5	14.7
Five- and ten-cent stores.....................	24.8	19.7
Apparel and accessories stores....................	18.0	14.4
Drug stores..................................	22.0	11.2
Eating and drinking places....................	20.6	14.3
Miscellaneous retail stores......................	25.8	17.2
Real estate offices...........................	22.8	16.8
Private households............................	43.2	22.7
Hotels and lodging places.....................	15.0	9.7
Medical and other health services................	10.3	7.0

In terms of occupations, for women, the big increases in proportion of part-time workers took place among librarians, professional and student nurses, real estate agents, sales workers (not elsewhere classified), private

FIGURE **13.**—PART-TIME WORKERS AS PERCENT OF TOTAL AT WORK, BY MAJOR INDUSTRY GROUP AND SEX: 1950 AND 1940

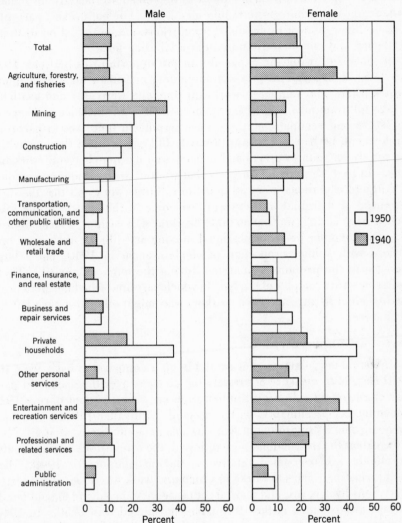

Note: Based on data in table 58.

household workers, beauticians, cooks (except private household), house-keepers, waitresses, and farm laborers. The proportion of teachers employed part time dropped, both for men and women, although in this occupation the proportion of women who were married doubled over the decade. In the teaching profession, 35 hours a week is not always a good index of full-time work, and the changes may not be meaningful. Occupations in which male workers were employed part time to a greater extent in 1950 than in 1940 are messengers, newsboys, filling station attendants, private household workers, janitors and porters, waiters and bartenders, and farmers and farm laborers. In addition to using more part-time help in 1950, farmers had to depend more heavily on female workers, most of whom were family members. For both sexes, part-time work declined in most professional occupations, the industrial occupations (craftsmen and operatives), and nonfarm laboring jobs.

In short, following the expansion in job opportunities between 1940 and 1950 it appears that, except for a few industries and occupations, most workers who wanted to work full time and were able and available to take full-time jobs could have them in 1950. In the sales and service industries and occupations, there were significant increases in part-time employment, perhaps because with nearly full employment these activities had to rely on young workers and persons who did not choose to work full time. In part, this change suggests that workers with a moderate amount of skill and experience were attracted to full-time work and that the inexperienced or marginal workers were welcome in the less desirable jobs, such as baby sitting, waiting on table, working as a cashier, a farm laborer, etc. On the other hand, professional nursing and library work were professions with a high proportion of single women in 1940, but a large increase in the proportion married during the ten-year period. These professions are examples of the type in which part-time schedules were probably essential to attract needed workers who might otherwise have left the labor force.

Part-year employment

Unfortunately, data are not available on a comparable basis from the 1940 Census to measure accurately the changes over the decade in part-year employment. In 1940, information on weeks worked during 1939 was collected, presumably, on the basis of "equivalent full time weeks." There is some reason to doubt that this was done uniformly, if at all. But to the extent the instructions were followed, the proportions working under six months are overstated relative to the distribution for 1949, when the information relates to weeks in which *any* work was done. In the basic tabulations by age, sex, and marital status, self-employed and unpaid family workers are excluded in the 1940 tables but included in 1950. In 1940, emergency workers, who typically had little work during 1939, were generally omitted from the tables; or, if included, their weeks on emergency work programs were counted as weeks worked. Thus, the inclusion of the self-employed in 1950 would overstate year-round workers and the inclusion of unpaid family workers and the unemployed would overstate the part-year workers, relative to 1940. What the net effect of these differences is cannot be determined.

It is possible to compare wage and salary workers at both dates, and by industry, on the arbitrary assumption that had emergency workers been included in 1939 with the data in terms of weeks rather than equivalent full-time weeks, the distributions would look about the same as those available. For men, year-round work increased substantially—from 59.6 to 66.0 percent—and in every industry group except trade and some of the service industries (table 59). Industry here is the industry of the jobs held at the time of the census or, for unemployed workers, the last job. For women, the overall proportion working year round did not change, but there were marked increases in manufacturing and educational services.

TABLE 59.—PERCENT DISTRIBUTION OF WAGE AND SALARY WORKERS BY NUMBER OF MONTHS WORKED, BY MAJOR INDUSTRY GROUP AND SEX: 1949 AND 1939

[Decennial census levels]

Major industry group of current job and sex	Months worked in 1949				Months worked in 1939			
	Total wage and salary workers, 1950	Under 6	6 to 11	12	Total wage and salary workers, 1940[1]	Under 6	6 to 11	12
Male...........................	100.0	11.2	22.8	66.0	100.0	10.2	30.3	59.6
Agriculture.......................	100.0	21.2	26.8	51.9	100.0	15.2	39.1	45.8
Forestry and fisheries...............	100.0	20.1	31.9	48.0	100.0	12.4	41.3	46.2
Mining...........................	100.0	20.8	40.7	38.4	100.0	15.8	54.8	29.4
Construction......................	100.0	17.2	37.1	45.7	100.0	19.1	50.9	29.9
Manufacturing....................	100.0	8.5	24.4	67.1	100.0	9.0	33.4	57.6
Transportation, communication, and other public utilities............	100.0	7.4	19.1	73.5	100.0	6.6	22.7	70.7
Wholesale and retail trade..........	100.0	10.9	16.9	72.3	100.0	8.7	20.2	71.1
Wholesale trade.................	100.0	7.4	15.2	77.5	100.0	5.9	17.3	76.8
Retail trade....................	100.0	12.1	17.5	70.4	100.0	9.5	21.1	69.5
Finance, insurance, and real estate..	100.0	6.6	11.3	82.1	100.0	4.0	10.4	85.6
Business and repair services........	100.0	10.0	18.5	71.5	100.0	9.8	24.9	65.3
Personal services.................	100.0	16.2	20.1	63.8	100.0	9.8	22.3	67.9
Private household..............	100.0	26.9	23.1	50.0	100.0	12.4	24.7	62.9
Other.........................	100.0	13.0	19.2	67.8	100.0	8.5	21.1	70.3
Entertainment & recreation services..	100.0	21.2	22.3	56.5	100.0	17.2	32.1	50.8
Professional services..............	100.0	9.5	22.1	68.4	100.0	5.4	31.2	63.4
Educational....................	100.0	10.4	31.7	57.8	100.0	5.6	49.1	45.3
Other.........................	100.0	8.6	13.3	78.0	100.0	5.3	12.8	81.9
Public administration..............	100.0	5.0	10.7	84.3	100.0	4.5	12.0	83.5
Industry not reported..............	100.0	34.4	28.3	37.3	100.0	25.7	33.3	41.0
Female.........................	100.0	19.3	24.9	55.8	100.0	14.2	31.5	54.3
Agriculture.......................	100.0	50.0	24.0	25.9	100.0	37.9	40.9	21.1
Forestry and fisheries...............	100.0	33.8	17.9	48.3	100.0	16.7	30.4	52.9
Mining...........................	100.0	10.2	15.8	74.0	100.0	10.7	21.2	68.1
Construction......................	100.0	15.5	19.1	65.4	100.0	13.4	23.3	63.3
Manufacturing....................	100.0	17.9	27.8	54.4	100.0	14.5	40.7	44.7
Transportation, communication, and other public utilities............	100.0	9.6	13.8	76.6	100.0	6.5	13.0	80.6
Wholesale and retail trade..........	100.0	22.6	20.9	56.5	100.0	17.0	24.0	59.0
Wholesale trade.................	100.0	16.9	18.2	64.9	100.0	13.4	21.8	64.9
Retail trade....................	100.0	23.4	21.3	55.3	100.0	17.4	24.2	58.3
Finance, insurance, and real estate..	100.0	11.6	12.8	75.6	100.0	6.5	11.0	82.5
Business and repair services........	100.0	17.1	17.2	65.7	100.0	12.9	20.6	66.5
Personal services.................	100.0	25.7	23.0	51.2	100.0	16.9	25.6	57.4
Private household..............	100.0	29.2	22.9	47.9	100.0	18.1	25.5	56.4
Other.........................	100.0	19.2	23.4	57.4	100.0	12.8	25.9	61.3
Entertainment & recreation services..	100.0	27.3	22.1	50.6	100.0	21.2	28.3	50.5
Professional services..............	100.0	15.4	37.7	46.9	100.0	9.1	48.5	42.4
Educational....................	100.0	13.4	56.6	29.9	100.0	7.6	68.7	23.6
Other.........................	100.0	17.3	19.0	63.7	100.0	11.1	20.8	68.1
Public administration..............	100.0	11.3	12.5	76.1	100.0	6.9	13.1	80.0
Industry not reported..............	100.0	39.6	22.9	37.5	100.0	20.1	22.8	57.1

[1] Excludes emergency workers.

Source: Derived from *1950 Census of Population*, Vol. IV, *Special Reports*, Part 1, Chapter D, Industrial Characteristics, table 13; *1940 Census of Population*, Vol. III, *The Labor Force*, Part 1, U. S. Summary, table 89.

Part-year employment—less than six months—became more prevalent for men in agriculture, forestry and fisheries, mining, retail trade, and almost all the service industries. For women, the increases were generally more substantial and more widespread. By 1949, one-fifth or more of the women working in agriculture, forestry and fisheries, retail trade, private households, and entertainment and recreation services worked less than half the year. Overall, the proportion was about 20 percent in 1949 as compared with 14 percent in 1939.

For analysis of trends in part-time employment by age and marital status, it is necessary to turn to the Current Population Survey from 1950 on. Data are available from this source to provide a somewhat more refined classification of part-time workers than was possible from decennial census data. Persons who worked at any time during the year are divided into those usually working full time or part time, and the number of weeks worked by each during the year is recorded. This information is obtained annually. The closest approximation to part-time work force as defined in this chapter—those not working (or seeking to work) full time the year round—is the sum of persons who usually work part time and those working full time for 26 weeks or less. In addition to some persons who entered or left the civilian labor force during the year, a small proportion of the latter group may have consisted of persons who had prolonged periods of unemployment during the year and who would have been working full time if work had been available. Data for 1955 suggest that the great majority of those who worked for 26 weeks or less did so for reasons that did not imply unemployment during the remainder of the year, however. For consistency with already published data, the two groups are referred to as "part time and intermittent workers."

In the period 1950 to 1955, an average of 7.5 million men and 11 million women usually worked part time or worked only for short periods during the year. These were years of strong demand for labor, first during the Korean hostilities and then again after the brief recession in 1954. The number of these part-time and intermittent workers decreased from 18,700,000 in 1950 to 17,078,000 in 1953, but by 1955 it had risen to almost 20,800,000; their proportion of the total who worked during the year was 27.1 percent in 1950, 24.2 percent in 1953, and 27.5 percent in 1955. About one-third of the 6.5 million increase in the annual work force between 1950 and 1955 consisted of these workers.

Men who work part time or intermittently tend to be young workers, although a sizable proportion, about one-fifth, are 55 years or more (table 60). The proportion under 20 years of age increased from 34.4 percent in 1950 to 41.0 percent in 1955. Women in this category are more evenly distributed by age and did not change in age composition over the period.

In some age groups, part-time and intermittent workers made up the large majority of all workers at both dates—those under 20 and women 65 and over (table 61). In the central age groups for men, full-time year-round work is the norm; less than 10 percent were part-time or intermittent workers. But for women, the proportion was close to 40 percent, except for the youngest and oldest age groups. This means that about two out of five adult women who work at some time during the year are available for work only part of the year or part of the week.

TABLE **60.**—PART-TIME AND INTERMITTENT WORKERS, BY AGE AND SEX: 1955 AND 1950

[Current survey levels]

Age and sex	Part-time and intermittent workers		Part-time workers		Intermittent workers	
	1955	1950	1955	1950	1955	1950
MALE						
Number who worked during year....	8,141,000	8,120,000	4,810,000	4,484,000	3,331,000	3,636,000
Percent......................	100.0	100.0	100.0	100.0	100.0	100.0
14 to 17 years......................	28.5	23.7	36.8	32.9	16.5	12.1
18 and 19 years.....................	12.5	10.7	11.0	8.2	14.5	13.9
20 to 24 years......................	12.6	13.8	7.3	9.1	20.4	19.7
25 to 34 years......................	9.1	12.2	6.2	9.0	13.3	16.1
35 to 44 years......................	6.3	9.4	5.3	7.5	7.8	11.8
45 to 54 years......................	8.0	9.1	7.6	8.8	8.5	9.4
55 to 64 years......................	8.9	10.3	8.7	10.4	9.2	10.3
65 years and over...................	14.1	10.7	17.1	14.0	9.7	6.7
FEMALE						
Number who worked during year....	12,636,000	10,588,000	7,962,000	6,211,000	4,674,000	4,377,000
Percent......................	100.0	100.0	100.0	100.0	100.0	100.0
14 to 17 years......................	12.5	12.1	14.3	13.8	9.5	9.5
18 and 19 years.....................	7.5	7.1	4.6	4.7	12.3	10.5
20 to 24 years......................	11.5	11.4	6.6	7.1	19.7	17.6
25 to 34 years......................	19.1	22.2	15.9	18.8	24.6	27.0
35 to 44 years......................	19.5	19.5	21.7	21.3	15.6	16.9
45 to 54 years......................	15.0	14.8	18.2	17.2	9.4	11.3
55 to 64 years......................	9.6	8.9	11.3	11.5	6.7	5.3
65 years and over...................	5.5	4.1	7.3	5.5	2.2	2.0

Source: Derived from U. S. Bureau of the Census, *Current Population Reports*, Series P–50, No. 35, table A, and No. 68, table A; and unpublished tabulations.

Between 1950 and 1955, there were some changes in the tendency of certain age groups to work part time, although no change in the overall proportion. Larger proportions of the young workers and of men 65 and over were in this category in 1955 than in 1950, but these increases were offset by decreases in other age groups.

Women were more likely to be regular part-time workers than to work intermittently during the year, except in the age groups 18 to 24 years when marriage or childbirth tend to lead to complete withdrawals from the labor force rather than to part-time work. Attendance at school or college also prevents year-round work for some in these age groups. Between 1950 and 1955 some increases took place in the overall proportion of women usually working part time—from 26.6 percent to 28.7 percent —but only a small part of this increase was due solely to the increase in the number of middle-aged or married women in the annual work force.

On the contrary, married women, as well as widowed and divorced women, were working full time the year round more frequently in 1955 than in 1950 (table 62 and figure 14), particularly those in the middle age groups. At both dates, however, the proportion usually working part time was the same, but the group working intermittently for a half a year or less declined slightly between 1950 and 1955. Regular part-time work was somewhat more frequent in 1955 among single girls (teen-agers for the most part).

TABLE **61.**—PART-TIME AND INTERMITTENT WORKERS AS PERCENT OF TOTAL WHO WORKED DURING YEAR, BY AGE AND SEX: 1955 AND 1950

[Current survey levels]

Age and sex	Part-time and intermittent workers		Part-time workers		Intermittent workers	
	1955	1950	1955	1950	1955	1950
MALE						
Total who worked during year...	17.1	17.8	10.1	9.8	7.0	8.0
14 to 17 years....................	91.5	87.0	69.8	67.0	21.7	20.0
18 and 19 years....................	62.7	57.5	32.8	24.2	29.9	33.3
20 to 24 years....................	29.4	24.5	9.9	8.9	19.5	15.6
25 to 34 years....................	6.9	9.3	2.8	3.9	4.1	5.4
35 to 44 years....................	4.8	7.8	2.4	3.4	2.4	4.4
45 to 54 years....................	7.1	9.0	4.0	4.8	3.1	4.2
55 to 64 years....................	11.5	13.9	6.7	7.7	4.8	6.2
65 years and over..................	36.8	32.6	26.4	23.5	10.4	9.1
FEMALE						
Total who worked during year...	45.6	45.3	28.7	26.6	16.9	18.7
14 to 17 years....................	95.1	91.9	68.5	61.8	26.6	30.1
18 and 19 years....................	62.5	57.9	24.5	22.6	38.0	35.3
20 to 24 years....................	43.1	35.8	15.6	13.0	27.5	22.8
25 to 34 years....................	42.4	44.3	22.1	22.0	20.3	22.3
35 to 44 years....................	40.1	40.8	28.2	26.2	11.9	14.6
45 to 54 years....................	36.8	39.4	28.3	26.9	8.5	12.5
55 to 64 years....................	39.4	42.6	29.2	32.3	10.2	10.3
65 years and over..................	57.9	59.5	49.1	47.5	8.8	12.0

Source: U. S. Bureau of the Census, *Current Population Reports*, Series P–50, No. 35, table 1, and No. 68, table 1.

TABLE **62.**—PERCENT DISTRIBUTION OF WOMEN BY LENGTH OF WORK EXPERIENCE DURING THE YEAR, BY MARITAL STATUS: 1955 AND 1950

[Current survey levels]

Year and work experience	Total	Single	Married, husband present	All other
1955				
Total women who worked during year.......	100.0	100.0	100.0	100.0
Year-round full-time workers....................	37.9	43.2	32.5	47.0
Worked at full-time jobs 27 to 49 weeks........	16.5	12.9	17.4	19.1
Worked part-time or intermittently.............	45.6	43.8	50.1	33.9
Part time..................................	28.7	26.8	31.7	22.0
Intermittently...............................	16.9	17.0	18.4	11.9
1950				
Total women who worked during year.......	100.0	100.0	100.0	100.0
Year-round full-time workers....................	36.8	45.2	29.9	44.3
Worked at full-time jobs 27 to 49 weeks........	17.9	15.6	18.6	19.4
Worked part time or intermittently.............	45.3	39.2	51.6	36.5
Part time..................................	26.6	22.0	30.5	22.5
Intermittently...............................	18.7	17.2	21.1	14.0

Source: Derived from U. S. Bureau of the Census, *Current Population Reports*, Series P–50, No. 35, table 5, and No. 68, table 6.

FIGURE 14.—PERCENT DISTRIBUTION OF WOMEN, BY LENGTH OF WORK EXPERIENCE DURING THE YEAR AND MARITAL STATUS: 1955 AND 1950

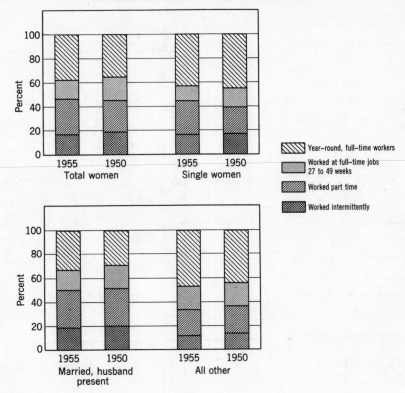

Note: Based on data in table 62.

In terms of their contribution to the labor supply of the industry, part-time and intermittent workers were a very substantial part of the work force—one-third or more—in agriculture, trade, and service industries in both 1950 and 1955 (table 63), on the basis of their longest job during the year. In construction and nondurable goods manufacturing, as many as one-fifth of the workers were employed only part time or as few as 26 weeks during the year. Agriculture and trade increased their use of these workers between 1950 and 1955.

Men and boys in the part-time labor force were employed in about the same proportions in the various industry groups in 1955 as in 1950. Women who worked only part time made up a larger part of the annual work force in trade, 29.2 percent in 1955 as compared with 25.1 percent in 1950; and in agriculture the proportion was 66.0 percent as compared with 60.1 percent. Government offices (including the postal service) were also apparently increasing their utilization of women who worked only part time.

TABLE **63.**—PART-TIME AND INTERMITTENT WORKERS AS PERCENT OF TOTAL EMPLOYED, BY MAJOR INDUSTRY GROUP AND SEX: 1955 AND 1950

[Current survey levels]

Major industry group of longest job and sex	Part-time and intermittent workers		Part-time workers		Intermittent workers	
	1955	1950	1955	1950	1955	1950
BOTH SEXES						
Total who worked during year.........	27.5	27.1	16.9	15.5	10.6	11.6
Agriculture.........................	45.1	42.0	34.7	29.4	10.4	12.6
Nonagricultural industries...............	25.2	24.9	14.5	13.4	10.7	11.5
Wage and salary workers................	25.4	24.8	14.0	12.5	11.4	12.3
Forestry, fisheries, and mining......	13.3	15.2	4.0	5.0	9.3	10.2
Construction.........................	20.6	25.9	7.9	10.3	12.7	15.6
Manufacturing.......................	15.2	17.7	5.6	5.5	9.6	12.2
Durable goods....................	11.1	14.1	2.9	2.8	8.2	11.3
Nondurable goods.................	20.5	21.4	9.2	8.3	11.3	13.1
Transportation, communication, and other public utilities..............	12.3	10.3	4.7	3.9	7.6	6.4
Wholesale and retail trade...........	36.0	32.4	20.8	17.5	15.2	14.9
Service industries....................	37.1	35.9	24.5	23.7	12.6	12.2
Public administration................	14.3	15.1	7.2	4.9	7.1	10.2
Self-employed workers..................	16.6	19.6	12.4	15.3	4.2	4.3
Unpaid family workers..................	65.2	64.3	61.1	55.5	4.1	8.8
MALE						
Total who worked during year.........	17.1	17.9	10.1	9.9	7.0	8.0
Agriculture.........................	27.6	26.5	20.9	18.2	6.7	8.3
Nonagricultural industries...............	15.5	16.3	8.5	8.4	7.0	7.9
Wage and salary workers................	15.6	16.5	8.1	7.9	7.5	8.6
Forestry, fisheries, and mining......	13.0	14.7	4.2	5.1	8.8	9.6
Construction.........................	20.5	25.3	7.9	10.0	12.6	15.3
Manufacturing.......................	10.5	12.3	4.6	4.2	5.9	8.1
Durable goods....................	8.5	10.7	2.5	2.5	6.0	8.2
Nondurable goods.................	13.9	14.4	8.1	6.6	5.8	7.8
Transportation, communication, and other public utilities..............	9.0	8.3	3.8	3.2	5.2	5.1
Wholesale and retail trade...........	22.4	20.5	13.7	12.0	8.7	8.5
Service industries....................	24.3	24.6	15.8	16.4	8.5	8.2
Public administration................	9.1	10.3	3.7	3.4	5.4	6.9
Self-employed workers..................	11.7	13.4	8.1	9.8	3.6	3.6
Unpaid family workers..................	(1)	82.9	(1)	73.5	(1)	9.4
FEMALE						
Total who worked during year.........	45.5	45.3	28.7	26.6	16.8	18.7
Agriculture.........................	84.5	84.6	66.0	60.1	18.5	24.5
Nonagricultural industries...............	41.2	40.6	24.5	22.6	16.7	18.0
Wage and salary workers................	40.5	39.7	22.8	20.5	17.7	19.1
Forestry, fisheries, and mining......	(1)	(1)	(1)	(1)	(1)	(1)
Construction.........................	(1)	(1)	(1)	(1)	(1)	(1)
Manufacturing.......................	26.8	30.4	8.2	8.4	18.6	22.0
Durable goods....................	21.5	27.5	4.4	4.0	17.1	23.5
Nondurable goods.................	30.4	32.0	10.8	10.8	19.6	21.2
Transportation, communication, and other public utilities..............	24.7	20.8	7.6	7.4	17.1	13.4
Wholesale and retail trade...........	52.0	48.7	29.2	25.1	22.8	23.6
Service industries....................	44.6	43.6	29.6	28.6	15.0	15.0
Public administration................	25.4	26.4	14.7	8.3	10.7	18.1
Self-employed workers..................	37.6	44.4	31.0	37.3	6.6	7.1
Unpaid family workers..................	61.3	61.3	58.6	52.6	2.7	8.7

[1] Percent not shown where base is less than 200,000 in 1955 or less than 100,000 in 1950.

Source: Unpublished tabulations of Current Population Survey data.

Conclusion

About one-fourth of the annual labor force consists of persons who usually work part time or who are not available for year-round work because of housekeeping responsibilities or attendance at school. There is no evidence that the relative importance of this group has changed very much during the years since 1950, except perhaps in the sharp labor force expansion between 1955 and 1956. It seems likely that in the decade from 1940 to 1950 there were substantial increases in the amount of voluntary part-time work on a weekly or annual basis in agriculture, retail trade, and some of the service industries (personal services, entertainment and recreation, educational work), but the total number of such workers cannot be determined from available statistics. Part-time work that was largely a form of partial unemployment decreased in mining, construction, and most types of manufacturing.

The expansion of the teen-age labor force has been to a large extent associated with increases in part-time employment. This may have been true for married women or women in the middle and older years during the decade of the 1940's, but these women have been showing a greater degree of attachment to the labor force in recent years, with a slowly rising proportion becoming regular, full-time workers.

The part-time labor force is largely utilized to fill jobs that require little skill, responsibility, or training and that rank rather low in status and wage rates—gas station attendants, newsboys, messengers, private household workers, waiters and waitresses, general sales workers, and the like. On the basis of census statistics alone there is not much reason to believe that "that interesting part time job" which is the goal of so many better educated married women has become a very common feature of the present labor market.

C H A P T E R 5

FAMILY EMPLOYMENT PATTERNS

Uses of family employment statistics

In the preceding chapters, most of the discussion has been in terms of the behavior of individuals as members of the labor force. For many purposes, however, it is desirable to know how labor force members are distributed in families and how these patterns are changing over time. Many important economic decisions are made on a family basis— decisions on major purchases such as a house or an automobile, for example—and take into account the present or prospective income of the family group, not of the family head alone. It is probable that labor market decisions also have a family base, particularly in the case of workers who are not the heads of families, and are affected by and, in turn, affect the family's aspirations for a different level of living. The traditional ideal for the average American husband was to support his wife in suitable style and to give his children more advantages than he had had in his youth. In this ideal, probably no reliance was placed on the earnings of a second family member. Yet it is the families with more than one earner that dominate numerically the upper income groups in the United States today. About 60 percent of the families with incomes of $10,000 or more in 1955 had two or more earners, and in 27 percent, the wife of the family head was in the paid labor force.

Knowledge of the family status of labor force members, therefore, and of the employment status of family members will shed light on the flexibility of the labor force, the structure of consumer units, and the capacity of existing demand for goods and services to expand or contract. The purchasing power of a family or a community may be expected to have greater stability when secondary workers (workers other than family heads or principal earners) are employed, provided they are not employed in the same industry as the family head. The distribution of unemployment, as well as of employment, in families is important to know since families are the units that social agencies have to deal with; not too much information, particularly for individual areas, is available on this problem. The whole question of the economic security of the family should be examined in terms of the composition, worker resources, and needs of families at different stages of the family life cycle.

The increasing importance of secondary workers, particularly wives of family heads, may have impact in rather subtle ways that are not yet possible to measure. It has been suggested that worker mobility will decrease if two job changes, not one, are involved in a change of residence. Perhaps husbands and wives, both of whom are professional or managerial workers, would be more restricted in their choice of place of residence than would those with other occupational attachments. On the other hand, employers of secondary workers have been known to deplore their excessive mobility; married women whose husbands change jobs and move to another community usually expect and are expected to leave their own jobs too.

In times of full or nearly full employment such as has characterized the United States for the past 15 years, the difficult problem of the unemployed family head whose wife is employed has not been commonly met as it was in depression years, except in a few individual depressed areas. Declining industries there have thrown men out of work, and new industries have created jobs for their wives but not for them. The picture of the unemployed husband engaged in housework while his wife is working at a paid job would probably still arouse the indignation and pity of all but the most hardened feminist. It is doubtless safe to predict that a widespread and continuing period of unemployment would threaten what now seems to be the fairly firm establishment of a married woman's right to work.

Analysis of family employment patterns can be made only with statistics derived from population censuses and surveys. The 1940 Decennial Census program included a large body of data relating individual labor force activity to family characteristics. This segment of the 1950 program was not completed. Hence, in this chapter, it is necessary to patch together what information is at hand, much of it from the Current Population Survey, which is not strictly comparable with data from the decennial censuses. The 1940–1950 changes are measured on the basis of data for households and household members related to the head, because family definitions differ at the two dates and the labor force data for families are not comparable. (See *1950 Census of Population*, Vol. II, *Characteristics of the Population*, Part 1, U. S. Summary, pp. 43 and 44.)

Number of workers in the family

Although vast changes have taken place in the labor force in recent years, in some respects the overall structure was about the same in 1950 as in 1940. At both dates, only about 40 percent of the labor force were in families where there was no other worker or were single individuals maintaining a household (table 64). About 30 percent of the labor force were secondary workers, that is, wives or children of household heads or other relatives. The proportion who were wives had risen; the proportion who were adult relatives of household heads had declined.

TABLE **64.**—PRINCIPAL AND SECONDARY WORKERS BY NUMBER OF PERSONS IN THE LABOR FORCE IN THEIR FAMILIES: 1950 AND 1940

[Decennial census levels]

Number of persons in the labor force in the family	1950			1940		
	Total labor force	In primary families, or primary individuals		Total labor force	In primary families, or primary individuals	
		Principal workers	Secondary workers		Principal workers	Secondary workers
Number......................	60,053,968	...	...	52,966,280	...	...
Percent......................	100.0	...	...	100.0	...	...
In primary families, or primary individuals[1]......................	91.4	62.7	28.7	89.5	59.7	29.8
1 person in labor force...........	41.5	41.5	...	38.9	38.9	...
2 persons in labor force.........	32.8	16.4	16.4	28.8	14.4	14.4
3 persons in labor force.........	10.9	3.6	7.3	13.3	4.4	8.9
4 or more in labor force.........	6.2	1.2	5.0	8.5	2.0	6.5
Secondary family members and secondary individuals[2]............	8.6	...	...	10.5	...	...

[1] Primary family is one that contains the head of a household among its members; a primary individual is a head of a household living without relatives in the household. Primary families together with primary individuals are substantially the same as families under the 1940 definition.

[2] Secondary family is a family that does not contain a household head among its members; secondary individuals are persons who do not maintain households, and who are not living with any relatives.

Source: Derived from *1950 Census of Population*, Vol. IV, *Special Reports*, Part 1, Chapter A, Employment and Personal Characteristics, tables 6 and 7, and Part 2, Chapter A, General Characteristics of Families, tables A and 26; *1940 Census of Population, Families—Employment Status*, table II.

Over the decade there was a slight increase in the proportion of two-worker families and a slight decrease in three-or-more-worker families (table 65). The average (mean) number of related workers per household was slightly lower in 1950 than in 1940—1.3 as compared with 1.4 workers. During the depression years of 1940 and earlier, many married couples and other persons were forced to move in to share the living quarters of their relatives. The decline in the proportion of many-worker families reflects the separation of some of these doubled-up groups into their own homes. The number of household members 14 years old and over related to the head, excluding his wife, decreased by 4.3 million between 1940 and 1950.[1]

The effect of these changes appears more clearly in table 66. In 1950, 58 percent of the labor force consisted of heads of households; in 1940, 54.6 percent. Wives of heads constituted 11.7 percent in 1950 but only 6.2 percent in 1940. A marked decrease occurred in the proportion of labor force members who were otherwise related to the head of the household in which they lived: 28.7 percent in 1940, 21.7 percent in 1950. Most of this last group were still single. At both dates, in the neighborhood of 10 percent of the labor force were persons who were not living in the homes of their relatives and who were presumably more or less independent of their families (except for college students away from home in 1950, still receiving parental support).

[1] Paul C. Glick, *American Families*, John Wiley & Sons, New York, 1957. See pp. 10–23 for detailed discussion of changes in household composition.

TABLE **65.**—PERCENT DISTRIBUTION OF HOUSEHOLDS BY NUMBER OF RELATED MEMBERS IN THE LABOR FORCE: 1950 AND 1940

[Decennial census levels]

Related household members in labor force	1950		1940	
	All households	Husband-wife households	All households	Husband-wife households
All households..........................	100.0	100.0	100.0	100.0
None in labor force......................	12.1	6.2	9.8	4.6
1 or more in labor force..................	87.9	93.8	90.2	95.4
Households with 1 or more members in labor force...........................	100.0	100.0	100.0	100.0
1 in labor force..........................	66.2	64.9	65.1	64.9
2 in labor force..........................	26.1	27.4	24.1	24.5
3 in labor force..........................	5.8	5.8	7.5	7.3
4 or more in labor force..................	1.9	1.9	3.3	3.3

Source: Derived from *1950 Census of Population*, Vol. IV, *Special Reports*, Part 2, Chapter A, General Characteristics of Families, table E.

TABLE **66.**—PERSONS IN THE LABOR FORCE BY RELATIONSHIP TO HEAD OF HOUSEHOLD: 1950 AND 1940

[Decennial census levels]

Relationship to head of household	1950		1940	
	Number	Percent	Number	Percent
Total labor force......................	59,670,540	100.0	52,966,280	100.0
Head of household............................	34,574,870	58.0	28,918,380	54.6
Male....................................	31,793,450	53.3	26,794,540	50.6
Female..................................	2,781,420	4.7	2,123,840	4.0
Wife of head.................................	6,982,920	11.7	3,292,140	6.2
Other relative of head.......................	12,968,530	21.7	15,188,460	28.7
Not relative of head or not in private household..................................	5,144,220	8.6	5,567,300	10.5
Male....................................	3,275,910	5.5	3,303,720	6.2
Female..................................	1,868,310	3.1	2,263,580	4.3
Mean number of related workers per household.	1.3	...	1.4	...

Source: Derived from *1950 Census of Population*, Vol. IV, *Special Reports*, Part 1, Chapter A, Employment and Personal Characteristics, table 6; *1940 Census of Population, Employment and Personal Characteristics*, table 9.

Family members in the labor force other than the family head numbered about 20 million in 1950 and 18.5 million in 1940. As might be expected, their composition had changed considerably (table 67). There were relatively twice as many wives of household heads among the secondary workers in 1950 (35 percent versus 17.8 percent) and a sharp decrease in the proportion of male workers, from 53.4 to 40.3 percent.

Census inquiries on family income have never extended to the point of determining what proportion of a person's income is actually contributed to the family of which he is a part. High-school-age workers typically contribute little to the family funds, and the same is probably true of elderly relatives, 65 years and over. It could be assumed that the most substantial and permanent types of secondary workers in a family are the wife and, in addition, those adult members (25 to 64 years old) who are not currently married and likely to set up their own households. On this assumption, the secondary workers in families in 1950 were to a much greater extent important contributors to the family budget than in 1940. About 11.5 million or 57.7 percent of the 1950 total and 8.6 million or 46.6 percent of the 1940 total could be so classified. All the increase was due to the gain among wives; other adult members decreased both in number and in proportion of total.

TABLE 67.—SECONDARY WORKERS IN HOUSEHOLDS RELATED TO THE HEAD, BY RELATIONSHIP, MARITAL STATUS, AGE, AND SEX: 1950 AND 1940

[Decennial census levels]

Relationship, marital status, and age	1950			1940		
	Total	Male	Female	Total	Male	Female
All secondary workers related to household head..........	19,951,450	8,048,140	11,903,310	18,480,600	9,860,540	8,620,060
Wife of head.........................	6,982,920	...	6,982,920	3,292,140	...	3,292,140
Other relative.......................	12,968,530	8,048,140	4,920,390	15,188,460	9,860,540	5,327,920
14 to 17 years....................	1,446,780	1,015,530	431,250	1,200,520	870,820	329,700
18 years and over.................	11,521,750	7,032,610	4,489,140	13,987,940	8,989,720	4,998,220
Married, spouse present........	1,965,310	1,462,810	502,500	1,714,680	1,370,240	344,440
All other.....................	9,556,440	5,569,800	3,986,640	12,273,260	7,619,480	4,653,780
18 to 24 years....................	5,389,440	3,356,430	2,033,010	7,269,900	4,694,560	2,575,340
Married, spouse present........	547,290	363,300	183,990	429,000	317,100	111,900
All other.....................	4,842,150	2,993,130	1,849,020	6,840,900	4,377,460	2,463,440
25 to 64 years....................	5,901,550	3,526,000	2,375,550	6,573,380	4,187,380	2,386,000
Married, spouse present........	1,378,120	1,063,600	314,520	1,257,840	1,026,880	230,960
All other.....................	4,523,430	2,462,400	2,061,030	5,315,540	3,160,500	2,155,040
65 years and over.................	230,760	150,180	80,580	144,660	107,780	36,880
Married, spouse present........	39,900	35,910	3,990	27,840	26,260	1,580
All other.....................	190,860	114,270	76,590	116,820	81,520	35,300
PERCENT DISTRIBUTION						
All secondary workers related to household head..........	100.0	40.3	59.7	100.0	53.4	46.6
Wife of head.........................	35.0	...	35.0	17.8	...	17.8
Other relative.......................	65.0	40.3	24.7	82.2	53.4	28.8
14 to 17 years....................	7.3	5.1	2.2	6.5	4.7	1.8
18 years and over.................	57.7	35.2	22.5	75.7	48.7	27.0
Married, spouse present........	9.8	7.3	2.5	9.3	7.5	1.8
All other.....................	47.9	27.9	20.0	66.4	41.2	25.2
18 to 24 years....................	27.0	16.8	10.2	39.3	25.4	13.9
Married, spouse present........	2.7	1.8	0.9	2.3	1.7	0.6
All other.....................	24.3	15.0	9.3	37.0	23.7	13.3
25 to 64 years....................	29.6	17.7	11.9	35.6	22.7	12.9
Married, spouse present........	6.9	5.3	1.6	6.8	5.6	1.2
All other.....................	22.7	12.3	10.3	28.8	17.1	11.7
65 years and over.................	1.2	0.8	0.4	0.8	0.6	0.2
Married, spouse present........	0.2	0.2	...	0.2	0.2	...
All other.....................	1.0	0.6	0.4	0.6	0.4	0.2

Source: Derived from *1950 Census of Population*, Vol. IV, *Special Reports*, Part 1, Chapter A, Employment and Personal Characteristics, table 6; *1940 Census of Population, Employment and Personal Characteristics*, table 3.

The marked rise over the decade in average (median) family wage or salary income from $1,319 in 1939 to $3,194 in 1949 (for husband-wife families) has generally been attributed to rising pay rates and greater regularity of employment, together with an increase in the number of earners in the average family. By far the most important factor was the increase in average annual earnings, however. The average number of family members in the labor force, as we have seen, changed very little between 1940 and 1950, but the proportion of family members who were unemployed dropped from 14.5 percent in 1940 to 4.7 percent in 1950 (based on the percent of related members in the household in the labor force who were unemployed). The decline in unemployment is also reflected in the moderate increase in the proportion of families with more than one person drawing wage or salary income; 28 percent of all nonfarm primary families in 1939 and 35 percent in 1951 had more than one person with earnings (table 68).

TABLE **68.**—PERCENT DISTRIBUTION OF NONFARM PRIMARY FAMILIES, BY NUMBER OF WAGE OR SALARY EARNERS: 1951 AND 1939

Number of earners	1951 (current survey level)	1939 (decennial census level)
Total nonfarm primary families[1].	100.0	100.0
No earners.	13.6	17.3
1 earner.	51.0	54.8
2 earners.	28.3	20.8
3 earners or more.	7.1	7.1

[1] Two-or-more-person families headed by the head of a household.

Source: Derived from *1940 Census of Population, Family Wage or Salary Income in 1939*, table 4, and unpublished tabulation of Current Population Survey data.

During the labor force expansion of the fifties, the proportion of families with more than one earner continued to rise. Comparable data for primary families are not available, but data for all families show that, by 1955, 43.1 percent had two or more earners as compared with 39.1 percent in 1951.

Regularity of employment of secondary workers

Most family heads are year-round, full-time workers, but other family members tend to work only part of the year, or on a part-time basis, if they work at all (table 69). Male relatives of the family head who were of working age in 1956 (14 years old and over) had generally worked at some time during the preceding year: 73.2 percent had done some work, but only 27.7 percent were year-round workers on a full-time basis. As for women, wives were less likely to have worked than daughters or other female relatives, but the proportions who were regular workers were not far different. In 1955, 13.1 percent of the wives of family heads and 18.3 percent of the daughters or other women in the family worked full time every week.

For married women, in general, the major reason for not working the full year is, of course, the need or desire to stay at home to take care of other obligations; 77.2 percent of the married women (spouse present) who worked during 1955, but were not year-round full-time workers, gave this as their reason for their irregular or part-time employment, as compared with 15.4 percent who mentioned unemployment or layoffs.[2] For

---

[2] See *Current Population Reports*, Series P–50, No. 68, table 10.

single women and girls, school or college attendance was the most common reason for part-time work (61.0 percent); unemployment was a factor for 22.1 percent.

TABLE 69.—PERCENT DISTRIBUTION OF PERSONS BY WORK STATUS IN 1955, BY FAMILY STATUS IN MARCH 1956 AND SEX

[Current survey levels]

Family status and sex	Total	Year-round full-time workers	Other workers	Non-workers
Total, 14 years and over..............	100.0	37.0	28.4	34.6
In families...................................	100.0	37.3	27.7	35.0
Head..	100.0	66.6	21.5	11.8
Married, spouse present.....................	100.0	71.5	21.0	7.4
Other status...............................	100.0	34.4	24.7	40.9
Wife of head..............................	100.0	13.1	27.4	59.5
Other relative.............................	100.0	23.0	38.7	38.3
Unrelated individuals..........................	100.0	38.7	28.4	32.9
Male, 14 years and over.................	100.0	58.6	28.2	13.2
In families...................................	100.0	60.3	27.1	12.6
Head..	100.0	70.9	21.1	8.0
Married, spouse present.....................	100.0	71.5	21.0	7.4
Other status...............................	100.0	54.6	22.6	22.8
Wife of head..............................	...	...	...	...
Other relative.............................	100.0	27.7	45.5	26.8
Unrelated individuals..........................	100.0	44.0	33.8	22.1
Female, 14 years and over..............	100.0	17.4	28.6	54.0
In families...................................	100.0	15.5	28.3	56.3
Head..	100.0	27.6	25.4	47.0
Married, spouse present.....................	...	...	...	...
Other status...............................	100.0	27.6	25.4	47.0
Wife of head..............................	100.0	13.1	27.4	59.5
Other relative.............................	100.0	18.3	31.8	49.8
Unrelated individuals..........................	100.0	35.0	24.6	40.4

Source: Unpublished tabulations of Current Population Survey data.

For single men and boys, most of whom are not the principal earners in a family, school or college attendance prevented regular full-time employment in 1955 for 55.4 percent, unemployment for 34.9 percent, and other reasons, such as military service, for 20.9 percent. Some persons, of course, have more than one reason for not regularly working full time throughout the year.

Incomes of secondary workers

Secondary workers, on the average, have much lower incomes than does the family head, and they do not seem to have maintained their share in generally rising money incomes since 1950 (table 70). To some extent, this is because they are typically part-year or part-time workers, as we have seen. But even those who were regular workers had average incomes still well below the average for family heads.

The median incomes of families with and without supplementary earners may be seen in table 71. In 1955, the one-earner family averaged $4,069, the two-earner family $5,250, and families with three or more earners $6,496. Thus, although the average family substantially improves its income when a second or third member takes a paid job, it by no means doubles or triples its income; rather, the order of magnitude of increase in money income (before taxes) is 25 or 30 percent. Stated another way, the importance of the secondary earner is shown by the fact that the majority of families with incomes of more than $500 a month have two or more earners. The extent to which the upper income families in the United States have become multiearner families may be seen in table 72 and figure 15.

TABLE 70.—MEDIAN INCOME OF RELATED FAMILY MEMBERS: 1955 AND 1950

[Current survey levels]

Relationship to head	1955	1950	Percent change, 1950 to 1955	Year-round full-time workers, 1955
Head of family--male, married, wife present..	$3,924	$2,994	+31.1	$4,403
Wife of head...................................	1,095	926	+18.3	2,699
Relative of head:				
Male....................................	1,138	1,172	-2.9	3,167
Female.................................	875	926	-5.5	2,685

Source: Derived from U. S. Bureau of the Census, *Current Population Reports*, Series P–60, No. 9, table 19, and No. 23, table 4.

TABLE 71.—MEDIAN FAMILY INCOME BY NUMBER OF EARNERS: 1948 TO 1955

[Current survey levels]

Number of earners	1955	1951	1950	1948
All families..........................	$4,421	$3,709	$3,319	$3,187
No earners.................................	1,294	921	923	953
1 earner...................................	4,069	3,401	3,128	2,900
2 earners..................................	5,250	4,459	3,913	3,774
3 earners or more..........................	6,496	6,120	5,268	5,209

Source: U. S. Bureau of the Census, *Current Population Reports*, Series P–60, No. 6, table 7; No. 9, table 8; No. 12, table 6; and No. 24, table 7.

TABLE 72.—PERCENT OF FAMILIES WITH TWO OR MORE EARNERS, BY INCOME LEVEL: 1955, 1953, AND 1950

[Current survey levels]

Income level	1955	1953	1950
Total families......................	43.1	42.0	39.2
Under $1,000.............................	21.3	18.4	19.6
$1,000 to $1,999.........................	25.9	25.7	29.3
$2,000 to $2,999.........................	33.4	32.0	30.0
$3,000 to $3,999.........................	33.1	30.6	35.0
$4,000 to $4,999.........................	39.2	38.5	48.4
$5,000 to $5,999.........................	44.9	50.1	59.2
$6,000 to $6,999.........................	60.4	61.1	65.3
$7,000 and over..........................	66.9	68.6	57.2
$7,000 to $9,999.....................	69.5	71.0	66.3
$10,000 and over.....................	61.5	63.2	41.2

Source: Derived from unpublished tabulations of Current Population Survey data.

FIGURE **15.**—PERCENT OF FAMILIES WITH TWO OR MORE EARNERS, BY INCOME LEVEL: 1955 AND 1950

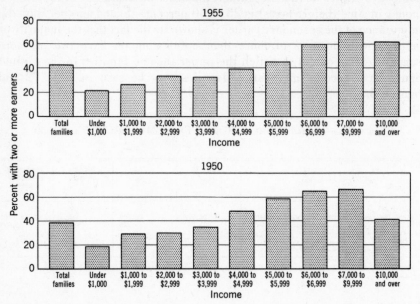

Note: Based on data in table 72.

Whether or not multiworker families are typically better off economically than are single-worker families cannot be determined from their average incomes alone. Size and composition of family must be taken into account as well as the added costs of working. The most recent data on the number of earners by size of family and income are for 1948; they show that at that time multiworker families had higher average incomes in every size of family class (table 73). In the larger families, per capita incomes would have been extremely low if additional persons had not taken paid jobs; as it was, about one-half of the families with five or more persons had more than one earner.

TABLE **73.**—MEDIAN FAMILY INCOME BY NUMBER OF EARNERS AND SIZE OF FAMILY: 1948

[Current survey levels]

Size of family	Total families	Families having specified number of earners			
		None	1	2	3 or more
Total..........................	$3,187	$953	$2,900	$3,774	$5,209
2 persons...........................	2,659	911	2,491	3,673	...
3 persons...........................	3,250	1,007	2,961	3,853	4,689
4 persons...........................	3,468	1,103	3,184	3,962	5,343
5 persons...........................	3,527	(1)	3,081	3,868	5,417
6 persons or more..................	3,369	(1)	2,821	3,453	5,204

[1] Median not shown where there were fewer than 100 cases in sample reporting on income.

Source: U. S. Bureau of the Census, *Current Population Reports*, Series P–60, No. 6, table 7.

What proportion of the added income is net income for the family is unknown. Workers usually have higher expenses than do nonworkers—expenses for clothing, transportation, meals away from home, and, of course, income taxes. When the housewife takes a paid job, she may no longer have time to do all of her own housework or may need to pay someone to substitute for her in supervising her children. Moreover, secondary workers do not always contribute their full earnings to the family purse. The problem of measurement of relative economic status of single- and multiworker families is further complicated by the fact that consumption standards do not remain fixed but may change as gross income changes. Measurement of psychological gains is an even more formidable task. Who is to say that the housewife, whose entire earnings are spent on her own appearance and on paying someone else to scrub her floors and iron her husband's shirts, has not improved her lot?

TABLE 74.—HUSBAND-WIFE FAMILIES BY AGE OF HEAD AND NUMBER OF WORKERS: APRIL 1955

[Current survey levels]

Workers in husband-wife families	Total husband-wife families	Age of head (years)			
		14 to 24	25 to 44	45 to 64	65 and over
Percent with 1 or more workers........	93.9	98.0	99.4	96.6	60.2
Head the only worker.....................	54.0	64.4	65.0	46.2	27.4
Head and other workers..................	36.7	30.5	33.8	47.6	16.8
Other workers only......................	3.2	3.1	0.6	2.8	16.0
Percent with workers other than head..	39.9	33.6	34.4	50.4	32.8
Wife the only other worker...............	22.9	29.7	24.8	23.3	10.8
Wife and other relatives.................	4.9	1.4	3.4	8.1	3.2
Other relatives only.....................	12.1	2.5	6.2	19.0	18.8

Source: Estimates derived from U. S. Bureau of the Census, *Current Population Reports*, Series P–50, No. 62, table 7, and Series P–20, No. 67, table 5.

Family income depends both on the development of the earning power of the head and on the availability of secondary earners. In the majority of husband-wife families (two-thirds), there is no other worker in addition to the head until he is past 45 years of age (table 74). Prior to that time, the cost of rearing a family devolves on the head alone; and probably the burden is greatest in the years just before the last child leaves home. (The average husband, it is estimated, is about 50 years old and the wife about 48 years old when the last child marries.[3]) Median family income, however, reaches a peak when the head is between 45 and 54 years of age (table 75), and when other members in addition to the head are most likely to be in the labor force; 50 percent of the husband-wife families, it is estimated, have some other member in the labor force in addition to the head when the head is between 45 and 64 years of age. To the extent that these other members are adult children (in about one-half of the

---

[3] Glick, *op. cit.*, p. 68.

families with supplementary workers, the additional workers are persons other than the wife), their earnings may not add very much to income available for family expenses, but they will certainly cover some of the items (clothing, recreation, etc.) that have hitherto had to come out of the head's pay check. As already indicated, it is debatable whether added income earned by secondary workers results in a net improvement of family economic status. But it would be hard to convince an American father that he would be better off in any way if his adult children remained wholly dependent on him.

TABLE 75.—MEDIAN FAMILY INCOME BY AGE OF FAMILY HEAD: 1955

[Current survey levels]

Age of head	Median family income	Age of head	Median family income
Total...........................	$4,421	45 to 54 years......................	$5,088
14 to 24 years......................	3,319	55 to 64 years......................	4,375
25 to 34 years......................	4,495	65 years and over...................	2,326
35 to 44 years......................	4,917		

Source: U. S. Bureau of the Census, *Current Population Reports*, Series P–60, No. 24, table 4.

Occupations of secondary workers

Secondary workers, as might be expected, tend to work in occupations which are suitable for young or moderately skilled workers, or which attract the labor force that is available only for part-time work. The proportion of secondary workers in an occupation is, therefore, a clue to the flexibility, if not the quality, of its labor supply. Three-fifths of the persons employed in clerical jobs or as farm laborers were secondary workers in March 1956 and about one-half of those in sales and service occupations (table 76). Data from the 1950 Census show quite similar proportions for all secondary workers. They also show that for men, secondary workers are a small minority of the employed in all occupations except in the age group under 35 years, where they constitute two-fifths or more of clerical, sales, and service workers and farm and nonfarm laborers (table 77). For women, of course, the great majority of the employed in all age-occupation groups, with few exceptions, were secondary workers. However, most women employed at age 65 or older are not secondary workers but widowed family heads or individuals living alone, without other relatives. In the major occupation groups at the top and bottom of the scale —professional and technical workers and service workers—secondary workers accounted for only 60 percent of all employed women. Even now, married women are less likely to be found in professional jobs requiring long periods of education and full-time work. For other reasons, service jobs are to some extent shunned by women who have the choice of remaining at home as a housewife; widowed and divorced women heading their own households, or living as lodgers or servants, tend to be over-represented in this level of job.

TABLE 76.—MAJOR OCCUPATION GROUP OF EMPLOYED SECONDARY WORKERS: 1956 AND 1950

Major occupation group	1956 (current survey level)		1950 (decennial census level)					
			Both sexes		Male		Female	
	Both sexes	Percent of total employed in occupation	Number	Percent of total employed in occupation	Number	Percent of total employed in occupation	Number	Percent of total employed in occupation
Total......................	22,031,000	34.9	18,859,350	33.8	7,343,790	18.4	11,515,560	73.2
Professional, technical, and kindred workers..............	1,852,000	29.8	1,474,530	30.4	303,360	10.4	1,171,170	60.2
Farmers and farm managers.....	395,000	11.1	447,660	10.4	395,520	9.5	52,140	43.8
Managers, officials, and proprietors, exc. farm........	1,027,000	16.2	804,690	16.4	328,950	7.8	475,740	70.7
Clerical and kindred workers..	5,401,000	61.9	4,051,650	59.0	644,970	24.9	3,406,680	79.7
Sales workers.................	1,954,000	47.3	1,667,610	42.8	580,230	22.6	1,087,380	82.2
Craftsmen, foremen, and kindred workers.................	970,000	11.8	1,146,870	14.9	967,560	13.0	179,310	75.8
Operatives and kindred wkrs...	4,485,000	34.8	4,069,740	36.8	1,673,130	20.8	2,396,610	79.4
Service workers, incl. private household....................	3,571,000	48.7	2,443,050	42.8	437,970	18.1	2,005,080	61.2
Farm laborers and foremen.....	1,235,000	63.4	1,466,910	60.7	1,038,750	53.2	428,160	92.5
Laborers, exc. farm and mine..	1,141,000	30.7	948,660	28.1	853,140	26.3	95,520	77.7
Occupation not reported.......	...	...	337,980	48.1	120,210	28.6	217,770	77.4

Source: Derived from U. S. Bureau of the Census, *Current Population Reports*, Series P-60, No. 23, table 5; No. 24, table 8; and unpublished tabulations; *1950 Census of Population*, Vol. IV, *Special Reports*, Part 1, Chapter B, Occupational Characteristics, table 1, and Part 2, Chapter A, General Characteristics of Families, table 19.

TABLE 77.—SECONDARY WORKERS AS PERCENT OF TOTAL EMPLOYED IN EACH AGE-OCCUPATION GROUP, BY SEX: 1950

[Decennial census levels]

Major occupation group and sex	Total, 14 years and over	Under 35 years	35 to 44 years	45 to 64 years	65 years and over
MALE					
Total employed secondary workers.............	18.4	36.4	8.9	5.0	6.8
Professional, technical, and kindred workers......	10.4	19.9	5.6	2.8	4.6
Farmers and farm managers........................	9.5	23.3	7.3	3.8	3.1
Managers, officials, and proprietors, exc. farm...	7.8	19.2	6.0	3.1	5.5
Clerical and kindred workers......................	24.9	42.8	12.2	6.4	6.9
Sales workers.....................................	22.6	41.4	9.0	4.6	6.8
Craftsmen, foremen, and kindred workers...........	13.0	26.4	7.3	4.5	6.0
Operatives and kindred workers....................	20.8	35.5	9.5	5.6	7.0
Service workers...................................	18.1	40.1	9.9	6.1	9.6
Farm laborers and foremen.........................	53.2	71.9	23.0	15.0	21.4
Laborers, except farm and mine....................	26.3	46.6	12.7	7.3	8.6
Occupation not reported...........................	28.6	48.7	15.5	9.1	12.0
FEMALE					
Total employed secondary workers.............	73.2	83.4	75.1	58.3	34.3
Professional, technical, and kindred workers......	60.2	64.4	68.4	50.8	26.2
Farmers and farm managers........................	43.8	72.6	53.4	36.6	24.1
Managers, officials, and proprietors, exc. farm...	70.7	85.9	77.5	63.3	35.8
Clerical and kindred workers......................	79.7	87.4	76.6	59.5	33.9
Sales workers.....................................	82.2	91.2	85.1	69.1	45.8
Craftsmen, foremen, and kindred workers...........	75.8	85.0	76.9	65.7	48.0
Operatives and kindred workers....................	79.4	89.0	80.6	64.6	40.1
Service workers...................................	61.2	74.8	64.9	47.9	28.0
Farm laborers and foremen.........................	92.5	95.5	93.3	88.9	73.8
Laborers, except farm and mine....................	77.7	87.4	77.1	62.4	59.3
Occupation not reported...........................	77.4	86.6	80.7	68.5	43.6

Source: Derived from *1950 Census of Population*, Vol. IV, *Special Reports*, Part 1, Chapter B, Occupational Characteristics, table 6, and General Characteristics of Families, tables 19 and 27.

According to recent evidence on the occupation of husbands and wives, the concentration of secondary workers in clerical occupations is characteristic of wives of men in all nonfarm occupation groups down to craftsmen (table 78). Although wives of professional and technical men are frequently professional or technical workers themselves (31.9 percent), they are still more likely to be clerical workers (39.4 percent). Even wives of craftsmen were concentrated in clerical jobs (31.3 percent). Employed wives of operatives, service workers, and nonfarm laborers were more apt to be operatives or service workers themselves than clerical workers, but the proportions doing clerical work were not negligible.

TABLE 78.—OCCUPATION OF WIFE, BY OCCUPATION OF HUSBAND: MARCH 1956

[Current survey levels]

Major occupation group of wife	Total[1]	Major occupation group of husband								
		Profess'l, techn'l, and kindred workers	Farmers & farm mgrs., laborers, & foremen	Managers, officials, & prop's, exc. farm	Clerical and kindred workers	Sales workers	Craftsmen, foremen, and kindred workers	Operatives and kindred workers	Service workers, incl. priv. hshld.	Laborers, except farm and mine
Number of employed wives thousands..	9,739	796	921	1,392	657	595	1,816	2,134	639	668
Percent......................	100.0	100.0	100.0	100.0	100.0	100.0	100.0	100.0	100.0	100.0
Profess'l, techn'l, & kindred wkrs..	10.5	31.9	8.5	9.4	12.2	13.3	10.0	6.6	5.5	2.4
Farmers and farm managers, laborers, and foremen....................	6.2	0.8	57.1	0.6	0.5	...	0.7	1.5	...	1.5
Mgrs., off'ls, & propr's, exc. farm.	5.5	4.1	2.4	17.2	2.9	9.7	3.4	3.0	4.2	2.2
Clerical and kindred workers........	28.1	39.4	6.0	36.1	43.2	44.9	31.3	20.9	24.1	13.9
Sales workers......................	9.6	7.9	2.7	16.9	11.3	14.1	10.0	9.8	4.9	3.3
Craftsmen, foremen, & kindred wkrs..	1.5	0.4	0.5	1.8	1.1	1.2	2.1	1.4	1.1	1.9
Operatives and kindred workers......	19.0	8.9	9.8	8.5	15.2	5.9	24.1	32.1	18.8	28.6
Private household workers...........	6.4	1.0	6.3	0.4	2.7	2.7	5.2	8.2	14.2	23.2
Service workers, exc. priv. hshld...	12.6	5.3	6.5	8.6	11.0	7.9	12.7	16.1	27.2	19.9
Laborers, except farm and mine......	0.5	0.3	0.2	0.5	...	0.3	0.5	0.5	...	3.0

[1] Total includes wives of members of the Armed Forces living off post or with their families on post, who are not shown separately.

Source: Derived from U. S. Bureau of the Census, *Current Population Reports*, Series P–50, No. 73, table 10.

Contributions of the working wife

In March 1956, there were 10.5 million working couples in which both husband and wife were in the labor force—27.4 percent of all married couples in which both members were living in the same household. This proportion has been rising steadily ever since annual statistics were developed; 19.5 percent were working couples in 1947. Most working wives put in a full work week when they are employed, but over the course of a year only a minority work full time the year round. About three-quarters of the working wives worked full time (35 hours or more) during the survey week in March 1956—those under 45 years as well as those 45 years and over. But during the preceding year, 1955, only one-third of those who did any work in addition to housework (about 40 percent of the total) worked full time the year round. One-third usually worked part time, and one-third worked at full-time jobs only part of the year.

In general, a married woman is more likely to be in the labor force if her husband's income is low, but her likelihood of being a full-time worker in any given week does not seem to depend directly on his income (table 79 and figure 16). Full-time work the year around was more frequent at the higher income levels than at the lower, however, probably reflecting the fact that, at the age when married women are most likely to be free to take regular jobs, their husbands are likely to be at their peak earning power.

TABLE 79.—PERCENT OF WIVES IN LABOR FORCE, PERCENT OF EMPLOYED WIVES WORKING FULL TIME DURING SURVEY WEEK, AND PERCENT WORKING FULL TIME YEAR ROUND, BY INCOME OF HUSBAND

[Current survey levels]

Income of husband in 1955	Percent of wives in labor force, March 1955	Percent of employed wives who worked full time during survey week, March 1956	Percent of wives employed during 1955 who worked full time year round
Total..........................	29.0	75.1	32.5
Under $1,000....................	28.8	68.2	24.6
$1,000 to $1,999................	30.3	74.6	25.1
$2,000 to $2,999................	34.0	74.9	28.8
$3,000 to $3,999................	30.8	76.9	35.9
$4,000 to $4,999................	30.5	79.2	35.4
$5,000 to $5,999................	26.7	77.3	36.2
$6,000 to $6,999................	24.9	74.7	37.1
$7,000 to $9,999................	20.7	68.7	31.3
$10,000 and over................	12.0	59.1	([1])

[1] Percent not shown where base is less than 200,000.

Source: Derived from U. S. Bureau of the Census, *Current Population Reports*, Series P–50, No. 73, tables H, 9, and 12.

At the lowest end of the money income scales are farmers, Negro workers, and workers who have suffered unemployment, who have just begun their labor force careers, or who are retiring. Women whose husbands are in these categories are themselves likely to be unable to work regularly at full-time jobs. Year-round work for women on a full-time basis is infrequent in agriculture and in the service jobs in which many Negroes are found. Further, wives of unemployed workers also tend to have a higher unemployment rate themselves and thus may be less likely to work the year around.

Some indication of the effect of a wife's work may be seen in the difference in median income of husband-wife families. The median in 1955 for families with the wife of the head in the paid labor force was $5,622, or $1,296 more than the median for families without a working wife ($4,326). It would be incorrect to assume that all the difference was due to the wife's earnings. As table 74 shows, the greatest proportion of couples with the wife in the labor force is found when the husband is middle-aged and probably earning more than at any other time in his life.

FIGURE **16.**—PERCENT OF WIVES IN LABOR FORCE, PERCENT OF EMPLOYED WIVES WORKING FULL TIME DURING SURVEY WEEK, AND PERCENT WORKING FULL TIME YEAR ROUND, BY INCOME OF HUSBAND: 1956

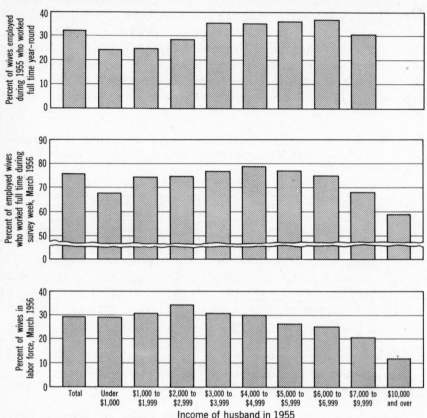

Note: Based on data in table 79.

Nevertheless, repeated observations have shown that up to the top income classes, the higher the family income, the greater the proportion of families with the wife in the labor force. In 1956, the proportion ran from 10.5 percent for families with incomes under $1,000 to 44.1 percent for those with incomes of $7,000 to $9,999 (table 80). Thereafter it dropped off sharply. Five years earlier the pattern was the same, but the proportion of families in which the wife worked at a paid job was considerably smaller in the upper income classes.

It would be interesting to know the social as well as the economic level of families in which the wife is in the labor force. The only clue to this from census statistics is suggested by data on the occupation of the husband. Table 81 shows the percent of married men in each major occupation group whose wives were in the labor force in 1956.

TABLE **80.**—PERCENT OF FAMILIES WITH WIFE IN PAID LABOR FORCE, BY FAMILY INCOME IN PRECEDING YEAR: 1956 AND 1951

[Current survey levels]

Family income of husband-wife families in preceding year	Percent with wife in paid labor force		Family income of husband-wife families in preceding year	Percent with wife in paid labor force	
	1956	1951		1956	1951
Total.....................	25.9	22.8	$4,000 to $4,999..............	22.4	26.7
			$5,000 to $5,999..............	25.7	33.8
Under $1,000...............	10.5	13.2	$6,000 to $6,999..............	36.3	37.3
$1,000 to $1,999............	15.4	18.5	$7,000 to $9,999..............	44.1	28.4
$2,000 to $2,999............	20.1	18.2	$10,000 and over..............	28.9	14.2
$3,000 to $3,999............	21.1	21.3			

Source: U. S. Bureau of the Census, *Current Population Reports*, Series P–60, No. 9, table D, and derived from unpublished tabulations of Current Population Survey data.

Women whose husbands are self-employed professional workers (lawyers, physicians, architects, engineers, etc.), the occupations with the highest average incomes, are least likely to be in the labor force. Only 19.4 percent were working wives. At the other extreme, wives of service workers, many of whom are Negro and hold low-paid jobs as cooks, janitors, porters, and waiters, were most likely to be in the labor force: 37.7 percent in 1956. In between these two extremes there was a good deal of similarity among occupations of different kinds. Wives of nonfarm proprietors, clerical and sales workers, operatives and nonfarm laborers all had about the same labor force rates—about 32 percent—although the median incomes for these occupation groups differed considerably. Women whose husbands are the aristocrats of industrial workers, the skilled craftsmen, had a labor force rate as low as that of wives of salaried professional workers, although the average income of that white-collar occupation was higher.

TABLE **81.**—LABOR FORCE PARTICIPATION RATES OF MARRIED WOMEN, BY MAJOR OCCUPATION GROUP OF EMPLOYED HUSBAND, 1956, AND MEDIAN INCOME OF ALL EMPLOYED MEN IN 1955

[Current survey levels]

Major occupation group of husband in March 1956	Percent of wives in labor force, March 1956	Median income of all men in occupation group in 1955	Major occupation group of husband in March 1956	Percent of wives in labor force, March 1956	Median income of all men in occupation group in 1955
Total employed............	29.9	$3,797	Clerical and sales workers.....	33.1	$4,126
			Clerical and kindred wkrs....	34.0	3,950
Professional, technical, and kindred workers..............	26.0	5,429	Sales workers.................	32.2	4,472
Self-employed workers.......	19.4	8,338	Craftsmen, foremen, and kindred workers.....................	27.4	4,423
Salaried workers...........	27.4	5,269	Operatives and kindred wkrs....	32.1	3,695
Farmers and farm managers.....	28.2	1,283	Service workers, incl. private household....................	37.7	3,036
Managers, officials, and proprietors, exc. farm..........	29.4	5,228	Farm laborers and foremen......	26.2	1,039
Self-employed workers.......	32.4	4,532	Laborers, exc. farm and mine...	31.8	2,599
Salaried workers...........	25.7	5,712			

Source: U. S. Bureau of the Census, *Current Population Reports*, Series P–50, No. 73, table 10, and Series P–60, No. 23, table 5.

The possibility that "attitudinal" factors have some influence in determining whether a married woman will work is also suggested by an earlier study which provided data on both occupation and income of husband. In the lowest income group (under $3,000), wives of professional and managerial men were most likely to be in the labor force in April 1952; the rate for wives of professional men dropped as their incomes rose. Wives of craftsmen had somewhat lower rates and at the top income class had the lowest rates of all (table 82).

TABLE **82.**—PERCENT OF WIVES IN THE LABOR FORCE IN APRIL 1952, BY MAJOR OCCUPATION
GROUP AND INCOME OF HUSBAND: 1951

[Current survey levels]

Major occupation group of husband in April 1952	Income of husband in 1951			
	Under $3,000	$3,000 to $3,999	$4,000 to $4,999	$5,000 and over
Professional, technical, and kindred workers........	40	30	25	18
Farmers and farm managers..........................	22	(¹)	(¹)	(¹)
Managers, officials, and proprietors, except farm..	41	24	28	21
Clerical, sales, and kindred workers...............	32	31	32	18
Craftsmen, foremen, and kindred workers............	30	25	23	14
Operatives and kindred workers.....................	32	26	25	22
Service workers, including private household.......	34	30	(¹)	(¹)
Farm laborers and foremen..........................	18	(¹)	(¹)	(¹)
Laborers, except farm and mine....................	26	29	(¹)	(¹)

¹ Fewer than 100 cases in sample reporting on income.

Source: U. S. Bureau of the Census, *Current Population Reports*, Series P–60, No. 12, table F.

Available data suggest that a married woman's decision to enter the labor force is influenced more by whether or not she has young children than it is by the amount of her husband's income or by his occupation (table 83). In 1956, only 15.5 percent of the married women 20 to 44 years of age with children under 6 were in the labor force, as compared with 39.1 percent of those with children of school age (6 to 17) and 58.6 percent of those with no children. The range of labor force participation of all wives 20 to 44 years old from highest to lowest income class of husband was only from 18.2 to 35.0 percent. Only one-fifth of the mothers of young children whose husbands had less than $3,000 income were in the labor force as compared with almost three-fifths of the women with no children whose husbands had at least $5,000.

According to table 83, there was little change between 1951 and 1956 in the proportion of mothers of young children who were in the labor force at any income level. But the labor force participation rate of mothers of older children increased from 33.1 to 39.1 percent, and the increase appears to be somewhat more marked at the upper end of the income scale. This is also clearly seen in the data for wives 20 to 44 years (figure 17) and for wives of all ages. The number of working wives of men in the lower income groups has increased some over the five-year period, but in the brackets of $4,000 a year and above, the increases have been about 10 percentage points—remarkable changes for such a time period. The trend between 1951 and 1956 is consistent with the findings of Chapter 3 that the sharpest changes between 1940 and 1950 were for married women past 35 years of age whose children are no longer young and whose husbands are at or near peak earning capacity (table 84).

TABLE **83.**—LABOR FORCE PARTICIPATION RATES OF WIVES BY PRESENCE OF CHILDREN, BY INCOME OF HUSBAND: 1956 AND 1951

[Current survey levels]

Survey date and income of husband	All wives	Wives 20 to 44 years			
		Total	No children under 18	With children under 18	
				None under 6 years	Some under 6 years
MARCH 1956					
Total	29.0	30.3	58.6	39.1	15.5
Under $1,000	28.8	35.0	(¹)	50.2	20.0
$1,000 to $1,999	30.3	38.1	59.0	54.6	22.4
$2,000 to $2,999	34.0	36.6	60.6	47.1	20.0
$3,000 to $3,999	30.8	30.4	61.0	39.0	16.7
$4,000 to $4,999	30.5	29.6	62.6	38.5	15.8
$5,000 to $5,999	26.7	26.7	56.5	39.3	11.2
$6,000 to $6,999	24.9	24.0	(¹)	35.9	11.1
$7,000 and over	17.6	18.2	(¹)	24.3	8.5
APRIL 1951					
Total	25.2	27.9	52.9	33.1	14.4
Under $1,000	28.1	37.2	55.2	42.8	20.7
$1,000 to $1,999	29.2	35.2	55.4	42.1	20.8
$2,000 to $2,999	28.3	32.2	59.1	41.3	15.5
$3,000 to $3,999	26.5	28.6	52.9	35.4	15.1
$4,000 to $4,999	20.9	22.0	51.3	27.2	8.8
$5,000 to $5,999	15.9	14.8	29.3	18.1	7.3
$6,000 to $6,999	15.2	14.8	(¹)	(¹)	9.4
$7,000 and over	9.5	7.7	(¹)	(¹)	5.2

¹ Percent not shown where base is less than 200,000.

Source: U. S. Bureau of the Census, *Current Population Reports*, Series P–50, No. 73, table 9.

FIGURE **17.**—LABOR FORCE PARTICIPATION RATES OF WIVES 20 TO 44 YEARS OLD, BY INCOME OF HUSBAND: 1956 AND 1951

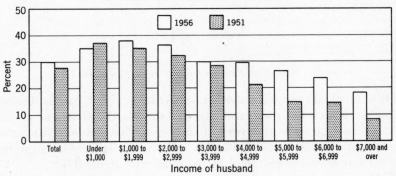

Note: Based on data in table 83.

TABLE **84.**—LABOR FORCE PARTICIPATION RATES OF MARRIED WOMEN 20 YEARS OLD
AND OVER LIVING WITH THEIR HUSBANDS, BY AGE: 1956 AND 1951

[Current survey levels]

Age of woman	March 1956	April 1951
Total married women, husband present.....	29.1	25.4
20 to 24 years....................................	30.9	29.1
25 to 34 years....................................	26.3	25.6
35 to 44 years....................................	34.3	30.5
45 to 64 years....................................	31.5	23.7
45 to 54 years............................	26.5	...
55 to 64 years............................	23.5	...
65 years and over................................	7.8	6.5

Source: Derived from U. S. Bureau of the Census, *Current Population Reports*, Series P–50, No. 39, table 2; and No. 73, table 2.

The majority of working mothers work a full week, just as do the majority of all women (table 85). Over the period of a year, however, the proportion who can and do work regularly every week is considerably smaller for mothers of preschool children than for other married women (table 86). Only 13.2 percent of the working mothers with children under 6 worked full time the year around in 1955. The proportion for mothers of school-age children was more than twice as great (30.5 percent). Women with no children under 18 years at home, including both the recently married and those whose children had grown up, were, of course, most likely to be regular full-time workers (43.9 percent in 1955). Data for the year 1950 show that the picture was about the same then, except that the proportion of year-round, full-time workers was smaller for women without young children.

TABLE **85.**—FULL- AND PART-TIME EMPLOYMENT OF MARRIED WOMEN, HUSBAND PRESENT,
BY PRESENCE AND AGE OF OWN CHILDREN: MARCH 1956

[Current survey levels]

Employment status of married women, husband present	Total	No children under 18	With children under 18	
			None under 6 years	Some under 6 years
Number........................thousands..	10,675	5,492	3,270	1,913
Percent.............................	100.0	100.0	100.0	100.0
Employed full time........................	75.9	80.4	72.7	68.4
Employed part time........................	24.1	19.6	27.3	31.6

Source: U. S. Bureau of the Census, *Current Population Reports*, Series P–50, No. 73, table E.

How much do working mothers contribute to the family income? Available data on this point are limited to the year 1950, and as we have seen, average incomes of wives of family heads have increased by about 20 percent since that time (table 70). However, the general magnitude of the contribution is indicated by the 1950 data (table 87).

Table 87 shows that despite the fact that most of these women could or did work only part of the year, their gross incomes formed a substantial part of the total received by the family. It appears that the average working mother may have augmented her husband's income by one-third or one-half. In 1950, this meant that without his wife's earnings, the typical father would have had just under $3,000 (before taxes) to support his family. Because of his wife's employment, his family had another thousand dollars or more. Again, it should be emphasized that these are gross figures and take no account of the added expenses that may have been incurred because the wife was employed outside the home.

TABLE 86.—WORK EXPERIENCE IN 1955 AND 1950 OF MARRIED WOMEN, HUSBAND PRESENT, BY PRESENCE AND AGE OF OWN CHILDREN

[Current survey levels]

Work experience of married women, husband present, and year	Total	No children under 18	With children under 18	
			None under 6 years	Some under 6 years
1955				
Worked during year.........thousands..	15,510	7,273	4,410	3,827
Percent.............................	100.0	100.0	100.0	100.0
Full time.................................	68.3	73.1	62.0	61.7
50 to 52 weeks.........................	32.5	43.9	30.5	13.2
27 to 49 weeks.........................	17.4	17.3	14.9	15.4
1 to 26 weeks..........................	18.4	11.9	16.6	33.1
Part time................................	31.7	26.9	38.0	38.3
1950				
Worked during year: Percent..........	100.0	100.0	100.0	100.0
Full time.................................	69.5	76.1	64.3	61.1
50 to 52 weeks.........................	29.9	40.3	25.4	12.3
27 to 49 weeks.........................	18.6	20.2	18.1	15.1
1 to 26 week⋅	21.1	15.6	20.8	33.7
Part time................................	30.5	23.9	35.7	38.9

Source: U. S. Bureau of the Census, *Current Population Reports*, Series P–50, No. 73, table J.

TABLE 87.—MEDIAN INCOME IN 1950 OF MARRIED WOMEN IN PAID LABOR FORCE IN APRIL 1951, AND OF THEIR HUSBANDS, BY PRESENCE AND AGE OF OWN CHILDREN

[Current survey levels]

Presence of children in 1951	Median income in 1950	
	Wives	Husbands
All married women, husband present................	$1,484	$2,712
Married women 20 to 44 years old, husband present......	1,530	2,828
No children under 18 years.........................	1,797	2,737
With children under 18 years:		
None under 6 years................................	1,392	2,950
Some under 6 years................................	935	2,826

Source: Derived from unpublished tabulations of Current Population Survey data.

Incidence of unemployment among family members

Unemployment was about one-third as severe in 1950 as in 1940, but its impact on different types of family members varied in about the same way at both dates. Whether in depression or almost full employment, a family (household) head is less likely to be unemployed than any other person in the family, except his wife (table 88). In part, this is because, in times of depression, jobless persons often moved in with their relatives and would be expected to show a higher unemployment rate than that of the family head. Also, family heads were sometimes given preference in employment during the depression years. In comparatively good times, there is still some doubling up of unemployed workers with employed relatives, so that again the unemployment rate of the relatives would be expected to exceed that of the head. When jobs are more abundant, persons who do not maintain their own households may feel freer to leave one job and look for another, thus risking some period of unemployment in the interim.

TABLE **88.**—UNEMPLOYMENT RATES BY RELATIONSHIP TO HEAD OF HOUSEHOLD AND AGE: 1950 AND 1940

[Decennial census levels]

Year and relationship to head of household	Total, 14 years and over	14 to 24 years	25 to 44 years	45 to 64 years	65 years and over
1950					
Head.......................................	3.4	4.2	3.0	3.8	4.4
Male...................................	3.3	4.0	2.8	3.7	4.5
Female.................................	4.9	6.2	5.4	4.6	3.9
Wife of head..............................	3.4	4.7	3.4	2.9	2.8
Other relative of head....................	8.6	10.0	7.2	7.1	5.8
Male...................................	10.0	11.1	8.7	9.4	6.5
Female.................................	6.5	8.2	4.8	4.5	4.6
1940					
Head.......................................	11.4	14.2	10.4	12.6	9.1
Male...................................	11.1	14.2	10.1	12.4	9.2
Female.................................	14.9	14.6	15.7	15.2	7.6
Wife of head..............................	6.3	6.4	5.6	8.1	6.3
Other relative of head....................	22.4	27.3	15.8	18.7	13.5
Male...................................	23.8	27.6	18.4	22.3	14.3
Female.................................	19.7	26.5	11.1	13.1	11.0

Note: Unemployment rate is percent of civilian labor force unemployed in 1950; percent of total labor force in 1940.

Source: Derived from *1950 Census of Population*, Vol. IV, *Special Reports*, Part 1, Chapter A, Employment and Personal Characteristics, table 7; *1940 Census of Population, Employment and Personal Characteristics*, table 19.

Women who were heads of households had higher unemployment rates than men who were household heads in both 1940 and 1950 in all age groups except the oldest. These women tend to be widowed or divorced and very often do not have sufficient or recent work experience; they therefore find it difficult to locate jobs.

Evidence on the changing age composition of the labor force has seemed to suggest that the labor force participation of secondary family members is somewhat less directly correlated with need for added income than it used to be. However, at any given time, it may still be true that second members in the family are more likely to look for jobs if the head is unemployed. Data for March 1956, when the overall unemployment rate was 4.3 percent and the unemployment rate of family heads was only 2.9 percent, show that families with an unemployed head had the highest proportion of other members in the labor force—48.3 percent (table 89). The other labor force members in families with unemployed heads were also more likely to be unemployed themselves. However, only 14.3 percent of the families with more than one worker whose head was out of work had no other family member employed, full time or part time, in 1956. Contrast this proportion in a period of full employment with the comparable one in 1940, when unemployment was at depression levels; at that time, 30.8 percent of the husband-wife families with more than one worker whose head was unemployed had no other employed worker in the family.

TABLE **89.**—EMPLOYMENT STATUS OF FAMILY HEADS AND EMPLOYMENT STATUS OF RELATED PERSONS: MARCH 1956

[Current survey levels]

Employment status of related persons in husband-wife families	Total	Employment status of family head					
		Labor force					Not in labor force
		Total	Employed			Unemployed	
			Full time	Part time			
Number........................thousands..	37,200	33,873	31,963	967	943		3,329
Percent...................................	100.0	100.0	100.0	100.0	100.0		100.0
1 or more related persons in labor force....	41.0	41.6	41.2	46.6	48.3		35.1
Wife in labor force......................	29.0	30.3	29.8	29.7	37.1		18.5
Wife not in labor force; other related persons in labor force....................	12.0	11.3	11.4	16.9	11.2		16.6
No related persons in labor force...........	59.0	58.4	58.8	53.4	51.7		64.9
1 or more related persons in labor force....	100.0	100.0	100.0	100.0	100.0		100.0
1 or more employed full time...............	73.6	73.1	73.5	61.4	74.1		79.0
None full time; 1 or more part time.......	21.9	22.5	22.6	30.6	11.6		14.5
None employed; 1 or more unemployed.......	4.5	4.4	3.9	8.0	14.3		6.5

Source: U. S. Bureau of the Census, *Current Population Reports*, Series P-50, No. 73, table 7.

Conclusion

The number of women in the labor force who are wives of household or family heads increased substantially between 1940 and 1950—and therefore the number of family groups with two workers. But the proportion with more than two workers declined as it became possible for other related family members to find and support their own separate living quarters.

As Chapter 4 suggested, most secondary workers—that is, wives and relatives of family heads—work irregularly or only part of the year and, accordingly, have incomes considerably below the average for family heads. Even those who were regular full-time workers have lower paid jobs than did the family head, on the average.

The majority of families with incomes of more than $500 a month in 1955 had two or more earners. A married woman is more likely to be in the labor force when her husband's income is low, but whether or not she works full time at any given moment does not seem to depend on his income. Full-time work the year round is more frequent at the higher income levels than at the lower, probably because a wife is free to take a regular job when her husband is close to the age of his maximum earnings.

It is still generally true that as husbands' incomes rise, the proportion of wives in the labor force falls, but over the past five years the most substantial increases in the proportion of working wives have been at the income classes above the average. Once again we find evidence that points toward the conclusion that the recent labor force expansion has come from the segments of the population whose need for food, clothing, and shelter may not be the primary factor determining the labor force participation of secondary workers.

CHAPTER 6

PROJECTIONS OF THE LABOR FORCE TO 1975[1]

Recent developments affecting the labor force

A decade ago, the maker of labor force projections generally followed the procedure of devising some measure of the "normal" rates of growth and extending this into the future, after allowing for temporary deviations caused by the wartime disruptions. It was believed that there was a normal rate that could be calculated on the basis of average changes during a base period long enough to reflect both prosperity and depression (for example, 1920 to 1940). Furthermore, the normal rates were calculated on the basis of the behavior of age cohorts. The labor force rate of women aged 25 to 29, for example, at the beginning of a five-year period could be expected to change at the same average rate, over the five-year period, as it had in the past for this age group. This procedure assumed that the labor force percentage in an age group had a stable relationship to the percentages of the same group grown five years older. The effect of the long period of full employment after the war, the persistently high marriage and birth rates, and continuation of military service for young men has been to raise doubts about the earlier thinking. Labor force changes have not followed the pattern of prewar normals. For example, the labor force rates of younger women are much lower and those of middle-aged women much higher than would have been considered reasonable ten years ago. At present, there is no generally accepted concept of the normal labor force which takes into account war and postwar experience.

As we have seen in the earlier chapters, one of the key factors in labor force developments in recent years has been the shortage of young workers. The low birth rate of the 1930's has meant comparatively small numbers entering the working age population in the years between 1945 and 1955. At slightly higher ages, the factor of increased school and college enrollment has limited the size of the labor force of young men, and the continued high proportion of young women marrying and having children has affected the female labor force. The postwar fashion for early marriages and the almost universal emphasis on a satisfactory family life as a prime objective for both young men and young women were probably unpredictable.

---

[1] This chapter is based on material, some of which has appeared in *Current Population Reports*, Series P–50, No. 69, prepared by the present author.

With the strong demand for labor during most of the 1950's, based in part on the defense program, middle-aged and older women free to take jobs outside the home were the only substantial source of additional workers. In all probability, if they had not been available and if traditional attitudes about the suitability of both married and middle-aged women for many jobs had not broken down, the high levels of employment of the 1950's could never have been achieved.   The unprecedented rise in the employment of these women is indicated by the fact that, by 1955, the labor force participation rates of women past 45 years of age had reached levels not generally expected to be achieved until 1960 or 1970.

We may also speculate about other causes.   Women past 35 years of age in the middle of the decade of the 1950's had been an important part of the manpower resources during World War II.   For those who left the labor force after the war to become full-time housewives again, and in some cases to raise the family that had been postponed during the depression and war years, the return to a paid job was not hard after their children were old enough to be in school most of the day.   The incentives to do so seem to be on the increase.   There is a rising proportion of families who are buying their own homes (50 percent of the Nation's occupied dwelling units were owner occupied in 1950; 55 percent in 1956) and becoming customers for the kitchen equipment, furniture, and other household goods they see displayed temptingly on their television screens.   The purchase of an automobile, by now essential for most families, is frequently made possible by an additional salary in the family to help finance the payments. A survey conducted by the Bureau of the Census in 1956 for the Board of Governors of the Federal Reserve Systems showed that "in every income class, families in which the wife is an additional worker have the highest frequency of new or used car purchase, use auto credit to a greater extent, and have nonmortgage debt more often than families in which there is only one wage earner."[2]

For those older women whose children were following the fashion of their generation, going on to college or marrying and having children at an early age (or continuing higher education and independent family life), there were perhaps compelling reasons for adding to the total family income.   Furthermore, the younger generation's need for financial assistance is sometimes matched by the need of the oldest generation.   Support of aging and ailing parents is frequently a reason for a middle-aged woman to seek a paid job, in these years when the elderly population, too, has been growing fast.   And as the needs for additional income have multiplied, great advances have been made in the most recent past in lightening and speeding up the job of housework so that women can carry a paid job as well, without exhaustion; frozen or precooked dishes, prepared mixes, and

[2] Board of Governors of the Federal Reserve System, *Consumer Installment Credit*, "Growth and Import," Part I, Vol. 2, p. 184.

automatic appliances make it far easier for the working wife to keep her family well fed and clean.

The decade of the 1940's had seen increases in labor force participation even for younger married women, both those with little children and those who had no children or whose children were of school age (see Chapter 3). The labor force rates for women with children under 5 rose from 7.7 to 11.9 percent and for those without children from 28.6 percent to 39.3 percent. In the years since 1950, the Current Population Survey data show some leveling off in the rates for women under 45 who have no little children, but further increases for mothers of young children, particularly women in the 20 to 24 year age group for which the population shortage has continued (table 90). Even though the majority of married women under 45 with no preschool children have children of school age, they are more than twice as likely to be in the labor force than are mothers of young children. Thus, the future birth rate is probably the most important determinant of the number of women in the labor force under 45 years of age, assuming that this differential persists. Although in the first half of the decade of the 1950's the differential has narrowed somewhat, it is highly unlikely that it will disappear in the foreseeable future.

TABLE 90.—LABOR FORCE PARTICIPATION RATES OF MARRIED, WIDOWED, AND DIVORCED WOMEN, BY AGE AND PRESENCE OF CHILDREN: APRIL 1955 AND 1951

[Current survey levels]

Age of married, widowed, and divorced women	Total		With children under 6		No children under 6	
	1955	1951	1955	1951	1955	1951
Total, 14 years and over...........	30.6	28.4	18.2	15.8	35.2	33.2
14 to 44 years.......................	33.2	31.5	18.1	15.8	48.2	46.5
14 to 19 years.....................	22.8	21.0	10.4	12.3	31.8	28.4
20 to 24 years.....................	32.8	30.8	19.8	14.6	63.3	60.3
25 to 34 years.....................	29.6	29.0	17.9	15.9	51.8	50.5
35 to 44 years.....................	37.9	35.3	18.2	16.9	45.3	42.7
45 to 54 years.......................	39.9	35.4	25.5	19.2	40.3	35.8
55 to 64 years.......................	29.4	25.2	(¹)	(¹)	29.5	25.2
65 years and over...................	9.5	8.2	(¹)	(¹)	9.5	8.2

¹ Percent not shown where base is less than 100,000.

Source: Derived from U. S. Bureau of the Census, *Current Population Reports*, Series P–50, No. 39, table 4, and unpublished tabulation of Current Population Survey data.

Assumptions underlying labor force projections

As in other types of projections, such as projections of the total population or of the number of households, it is customary to assume that developments of the past will continue into the future, either at the same rate or at some specified variation of the rate. The population projections, for example, start with varying assumptions about the future birth rate, based on what has happened in the recent past. Projections of households and families have their starting point in the recent changes in the proportion of the population that is single. In the present labor force projections, the proportion of each sex-age group that will be in the labor force is projected on the basis of both recent and long-run rates of change, and these proportions are multiplied by the population that will, presumably, be found in each age group at future dates. In none of the population households or labor force projections is there an assumption of normality.

Ideally, any labor force projection should take into account, in addition to the size and composition of the population, the specific level of economic activity and the structure of demand for workers at future dates. The extent to which women enter the labor force, for example, will depend in part on the types of jobs that will need to be filled. A world in which all clerical work is performed by high-speed automatic computers will have many fewer jobs for women with only a high school education, unless other opportunities develop. In this chapter, however, no such ideal projection technique has been attempted. Instead, it has been assumed that the labor force at future dates will be largely determined by the size of the population at those dates and the trends in labor force participation that may be expected for specific age groups, taking account, explicitly or implicitly, of developments in marriage and birth rates and the tendency to continue in school or to retire. A common assumption underlying both population and labor force projections is that high employment will continue through 1975, and that there will be no large-scale war or other catastrophe.

Four different projections are presented here, in order to illustrate the effect of four possible assumptions and to permit the user to select from a range of possibilities. It should not be inferred that the actual maximum and minimum labor force are included in the range shown, for, under other assumptions about changing labor force participation in specific age groups, it is possible to raise or lower substantially the total numbers in the labor force.

In addition to the continuation of high employment, several other developments are basic to these projections. The first is that school and college enrollment will continue to increase, both in absolute numbers and in proportion of the age groups affected. This will have the effect of holding down expansion of labor force activity, particularly for men aged 18 to 24 years. Although many young men who attend college hold part-time jobs during the college year and full-time jobs in the summer, their average labor force rate is lower than that for persons who have already left school permanently and entered the full-time labor force. Secondly, marriage and birth rates will continue at high levels, and this will restrict the labor force participation of young women 18 to 35 years of age. Thirdly, the long-term downward trend in the employment of men past 65 will continue. This decline has been greatly accelerated in the years between 1950 and 1955, with the extension of Social Security coverage, but the extent to which the *rate* of decrease recorded will slacken is a question.

The present projections provide statistics on an *annual average* basis, whereas census data and previous projections have been for April of each year; for that reason alone, the projections in this report would be at a higher level, for the annual average is about 1.5 percent above April. A detailed explanation of the method of constructing each projection is presented in Appendix B. They may be briefly described as follows.

The various labor force projections have as their starting point the average labor force participation rates for men and women in specific age groups for 1955 (the average of 12 monthly observations), as obtained from the Current Population Survey. These rates relate to the total labor force including the Armed Forces (both in the continental United States and overseas) and the total population in each age group, including the population in institutions. The projected rates are multiplied by the Series A population projections for each age group (as published in *Current Population Reports*, Series P–25, No. 123) to obtain the projected number in the labor force.

Labor force Projection I is a revision of the earlier estimates published in 1952, in *Current Population Reports*, Series P–50, No. 42; the average annual rates of change in labor force participation rates based on data for 1920 and the average of April 1954, 1955, and 1956 were projected into the future. (The earlier projection had used the average of 1949, 1950, and 1951 as the terminal point for the computation of rates of change.) It is, essentially, a projection of experience over a 35-year span and may be regarded as the extrapolation of the long-run trend at *high employment* levels. Projection II is based on an extrapolation of the rates of change that have taken place in the recent past—1950 to 1955. This also was a period of generally high employment, modified somewhat by the 1953–1954 recession, and in a sense could be considered an average of prosperity and mild recession—a condition of the economy that will continue, it has been assumed. Some adjustment has been made for the unusual build-up of the male labor force during the Korean hostilities, and no further cutbacks in defense production on Armed Forces strength have been assumed. Projection IV is simply an extension of 1955 rates; it serves as a kind of measuring stick, to show what would happen if there were no changes in labor force participation but only changes in the composition of the population.

Projection III is based on the assumption that the factors that have affected labor force participation of young people in the recent past—extension of school and college enrollment, early marriage, and high fertility—will continue to be operative through 1975. Other age groups, however, will resume the 1920–1955 rates of change because there will no longer be a severe shortage of persons at the ages when entrance into the full-time labor force is customary. Between 1955 and 1960, the population aged 18 to 24 years will increase by an average amount of about 225,000 a year, as compared with an annual average decrease of almost 200,000 between 1950 and 1955. By 1965 to 1970, the increase of the population in these entrance ages will reach a peak of over 900,000 a year, and the gain will still exceed 400,000 a year in the period 1970–

1975. With such a potential influx of young people into the labor force, the demand for older workers, particularly women, may be sharply reduced, but it is not likely that the long-run upward trend in labor force participation of older women will be reversed, if employment remains generally high. Specifically, Projection III assumes a continuation of 1950–1955 rates of change in labor force participation rates for men aged 14 to 24 years and for women aged 14 to 34 years. In other age groups, Projection III assumes a continuation of the long-run rates of change that underlie Projection I.

Comparison of Projections I to IV, 1975

Under these assumptions, the labor force would rise from 68.9 million persons in 1955 to a level of 93.7 million in 1975 according to Projection II, 93.4 million according to Projection I, 91.4 million with Projection III, and 89.8 million with Projection IV. These levels imply increases ranging from 30 to 36 percent in a 20-year period. The number of men in the labor force in 1975 would be at a maximum for these projections if there were no further change in labor force participation rates (Projection IV); the projected 1975 male labor force ranges from 62.2 million with Projection IV to 60.1 million with Projections II and III, as compared with 48.0 million in 1955. For women, the range is relatively much greater. The maximum labor force projected is 33.6 million, assuming a continuation of 1950 to 1955 rates of change (Projection II); the minimum is 27.6 million under the assumption of Projection IV. Thus, the increase in the male labor force might range from 25 to 30 percent and the increase for the female labor force from 33 to 61 percent. The variations in labor force rates and in the size of the labor force in 1975 under the present four projections are shown in table 91 and figure 18. (See also appendix tables B–1 to B–4.) Because some of the changes in specific age groups offset each other, it is necessary to look beyond the totals to see the full range of the projections. (In the following discussion, Projection III rates are not cited separately, for they are identical with either Projection I or Projection II rates.)

In general, it can be said that not too much variation should be expected in the rates of participation in the labor force of adult men. The long-run trend has been stable or slightly downward in almost all adult age groups. The period 1950–1955 saw slight increases in the rates of labor force participation of adult men, perhaps as a reflection of the general stringency of the labor supply. Workers who were on the margin of employability because of health or temperament may have been considered acceptable when others were not available. In view of the long-term trend, continuation of an increase in rates for the age groups 35 to 64 seems unlikely, but the possibility cannot be ignored in the light of recent experience.

The age group 65 and over has been showing declining rates of labor force activity in almost every decade, and this decline appears to gather

TABLE **91.**—ANNUAL AVERAGE TOTAL LABOR FORCE AND LABOR FORCE PARTICIPATION RATES, BY AGE AND SEX: 1950, 1955, AND PROJECTED FOR 1975

[Current survey levels]

Age and sex	1950 (actual)	1955 (actual)	1975[1]			
			Projection I	Projection II	Projection III	Projection IV
ANNUAL AVERAGE TOTAL LABOR FORCE (thousands)						
Total, 14 years and over............	65,128	68,899	93,385	93,705	91,397	89,782
Male................................	46,413	48,040	60,856	60,104	60,090	62,231
14 to 19 years.....................	3,407	3,378	4,994	4,638	4,638	5,694
20 to 24 years.....................	5,074	4,832	8,663	8,253	8,253	8,741
25 to 34 years.....................	11,149	11,462	15,079	15,220	15,079	15,064
35 to 44 years.....................	10,274	10,835	10,729	10,873	10,729	10,718
45 to 54 years.....................	8,201	8,879	10,766	10,934	10,766	10,709
55 to 64 years.....................	5,729	6,129	7,923	8,292	7,923	7,960
65 years and over..................	2,579	2,525	2,702	1,894	2,702	3,345
Female..............................	18,715	20,859	32,529	33,601	31,307	27,551
14 to 19 years.....................	1,988	1,987	3,079	2,993	2,993	3,329
20 to 24 years.....................	2,685	2,458	4,995	4,413	4,413	4,357
25 to 34 years.....................	4,126	4,266	6,580	6,026	6,026	5,362
35 to 44 years.....................	4,239	4,814	5,755	5,666	5,755	4,609
45 to 54 years.....................	3,279	4,160	6,410	7,558	6,410	5,232
55 to 64 years.....................	1,790	2,394	4,346	5,336	4,346	3,430
65 years and over..................	608	780	1,364	1,609	1,364	1,232
ANNUAL AVERAGE LABOR FORCE PARTICIPATION RATES						
Total, 14 years and over............	57.6	58.0	58.8	59.0	57.5	56.5
Male................................	83.1	82.3	78.9	77.9	77.9	80.7
14 to 19 years.....................	52.5	49.0	43.4	40.3	40.3	49.5
20 to 24 years.....................	88.0	89.5	88.7	84.5	84.5	89.5
25 to 34 years.....................	94.9	96.5	96.6	97.5	96.6	96.5
35 to 44 years.....................	96.4	96.9	97.0	98.3	97.0	96.9
45 to 54 years.....................	94.4	95.1	95.6	97.1	95.6	95.1
55 to 64 years.....................	85.3	86.4	86.0	90.0	86.0	86.4
65 years and over..................	44.4	38.5	31.1	21.8	31.1	38.5
Female..............................	32.7	34.5	39.8	41.1	38.3	33.7
14 to 19 years.....................	31.3	29.7	27.9	27.1	27.1	30.2
20 to 24 years.....................	45.9	45.8	52.5	46.4	46.4	45.8
25 to 34 years.....................	33.9	34.8	42.7	39.1	39.1	34.8
35 to 44 years.....................	38.9	41.4	51.7	50.9	51.7	41.4
45 to 54 years.....................	37.6	43.5	53.3	62.8	53.3	43.5
55 to 64 years.....................	26.7	32.2	40.8	50.1	40.8	32.2
65 years and over..................	9.4	10.3	11.4	13.4	11.4	10.3

[1] Projection I: Projection of average annual rates of change in labor force participation rates between 1920 and average of April 1954, 1955, and 1956.

Projection II: Projection of average annual rates of change between 1950 (adjusted) and 1955.

Projection III: Use of Projection II rates for men 14 to 24 years and women 14 to 34 years, use of Projection I rates for other groups.

Projection IV: Continuation of 1955 labor force rates to 1975.

Source: Based on appendix tables B–1 to B–4 and unpublished estimates.

some momentum with each extension of Social Security coverage or liberalization of benefits. The various projections for this age group show extremely wide variations in 1975, from 38.5 percent assuming no change in the current rate (Projection IV), to 31.1 percent assuming the long-run trend will continue (Projection I), down to 21.8 percent assuming that the recent rate of change will continue to 1975 (Projection II).[3] At the other

[3] About 1950, rates in the neighborhood of 30 percent for men in this age group were recorded in a few other industrialized countries: Austria, Czechoslovakia, Great Britain, Australia, and New Zealand. In Belgium, the Federal Republic of Germany, and Hawaii, the rates were close to 25 percent, the minimum reached in any industrialized country. See "Age Structure and the Labour Supply" by Ulla Olin and Edith G. Adams, *Proceedings of the World Population Conference, 1954*, United Nations Publication, XIII.8 (Vol. III), 1955.

end of the age range, there is a difference of only a few percentage points between Projection I and II rates for the age groups 14 to 19 years and 20 to 24 years: 43.4 percent versus 40.3 percent for boys 14 to 19 years, and 88.7 versus 84.5 percent for men 20 to 24 years. Both are, of course, below Projection IV rates, since they both reflect the assumption that school and college enrollment rates will continue to rise.

For women, the projections for the youngest (14 to 19) and oldest (65 and over) age groups show little variation at 1975. For the 20-to-24-year age group there is a marked difference in the results of Projections

FIGURE 18.—LABOR FORCE BY AGE AND SEX: 1950, 1955, AND PROJECTED FOR 1975

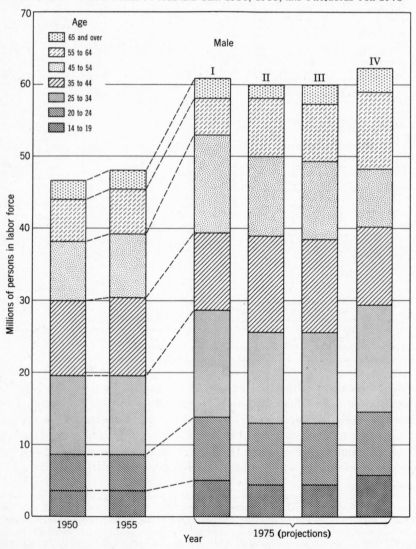

I and II: Projection II, reflecting recent changes, allows for almost no increase in rate between 1955 and 1975, whereas Projection I shows an increase of 6 or 7 percentage points, in line with long-term trends. Both projections indicate rising rates for the next older age group, women 25 to 34 years of age; again the Projection II rate is below the Projection I rate in 1975 (39.1 percent versus 42.7 percent).

For women 35 to 44 years of age, there is no difference between long-run and short-run rates of change. Both Projections I and II give a rate of about 51 percent in 1975 compared with 41 percent in 1955, and even greater increases would not be improbable. Fertility experts seem to detect a decline in the age at which women regard their families as complete. This would mean that in the average family, children will be in full-time school, and their mothers will be ready to re-enter the labor force in greater numbers at about age 35, when age barriers are operative in only a few occupations, at least at the present time. Higher proportions in this age group (35 to 44 years) will have had a college education and will be anxious to make use of it. The return to the labor force for this age group, therefore, may tend more frequently to be on a full-time, permanent basis, rather than for occasional supplementary income. These incentives would, of course, extend into the next age group too—the 45-to-54-year group.

FIGURE **18.**—LABOR FORCE BY AGE AND SEX: 1950, 1955, AND PROJECTED FOR 1975—Cont.

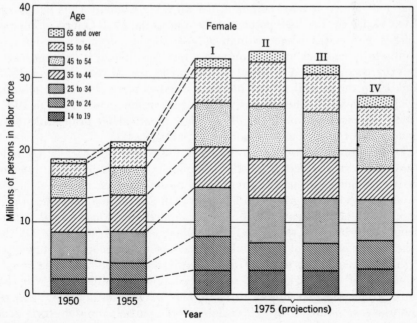

Note: Based on data in table 91.

It is among middle-aged women that the projected rates of labor force participation show the greatest variation and are the most difficult to evaluate. Projection II rates for women 45 to 54 and 55 to 64 years old are 10 points above Projection I rates and almost 20 points above Projection IV (or 1955) rates. The extent of increase in the participation of women 55 to 64 years old, particularly, may depend somewhat on the availability of younger workers. The recent sharp changes, as has been suggested earlier, seem to be associated with shortages of young workers. Another factor has perhaps been the growing realization of the problems of prolonged retirement on limited incomes. Women in this age group have been entering the labor force perhaps to supplement a husband's pension. A third factor, which, with the aging of the population, will become more important is the increasing proportion of the age group over 55 who are living alone as heads of households; this development will give added incentive to older women to find jobs that will enable them to continue in independence as long as possible.

If the rates of change in the labor force participation of married, widowed, and divorced women that took place between 1950 and 1955 were to continue into the future, about one-half of these women between 35 and 64 years of age would be in the labor force in 1975 (table 92, figure 19, and appendix table B–5). For women aged 45 to 54 years, the proportion would reach three-fifths, and almost as much for women who were married and living with their husbands. Even in cities such as Washington, D. C., or New Bedford, Massachusetts, where the employment of married women is most common, the rates for women in the age group 45 to 54 did not reach 60 percent at the time of the 1950 Census of Population; a national average as high as this implies dramatic changes in community customs and job opportunities. Although it may represent an extreme assumption to postulate that during the 20 years between 1955 and 1975 the annual rate of increase in labor force activity of middle-aged women will be the same as we have seen in the 5 years 1950 to 1955, some increases will undoubtedly occur. Most earlier projections have understated rather than overstated such increases.

If the number of women in the labor force over 35 years of age is to reach the levels projected for 1975, the labor force participation rates of married women will have to continue on upward, for the number of single women in those age groups will be less than 2.5 million, or about 5 percent of the population over 35. Their contributions to the total female labor force over 35 will therefore be small—about 6 percent. On the other hand, because of the population wave of young people, starting after 1955 and increasing until 1975, the projected number of young, single women aged 18 to 24 will be relatively large: 3.2 million in 1960, 4.0 million in 1965, 4.6 million in 1970, and 4.7 million in 1975. During the five-year period 1950–1955, labor force participation of single girls in these age groups leveled off, however, perhaps because of some increase in junior or senior college enrollment. (Data are not available by marital status and school enrollment to test this hypothesis.) Accordingly, the projected number of single women aged 18 to 24 years in the labor force will not rise as sharply as the population in this age group, but it might reach 3.2 million in 1975 as compared with 2.1 million in 1955.

TABLE **92.**—LABOR FORCE PARTICIPATION RATES OF MARRIED, WIDOWED, AND DIVORCED WOMEN, BY AGE: 1950, 1955, AND PROJECTED FOR 1975

[Current survey levels]

Marital status and age	Annual average total labor force (thousands)			Annual average labor force participation rates		
	1950[1] (esti-mated)	1955 (actual)	1975[2] (pro-jected)	1950[1] (esti-mated)	1955 (actual)	1975[2] (pro-jected)
Married, widowed, and divorced.......	12,731	15,272	27,004	27.7	31.0	40.7
14 to 19 years.............................	253	249	469	26.3	26.7	25.4
20 to 24 years.............................	1,248	1,237	2,573	31.2	32.8	36.6
25 to 34 years.............................	2,997	3,291	5,073	27.6	29.8	36.1
35 to 44 years.............................	3,507	4,159	5,333	35.1	38.6	50.2
45 to 54 years.............................	2,746	3,630	7,153	34.1	40.9	62.5
55 to 64 years.............................	1,484	2,067	4,974	23.9	29.8	49.1
65 years and over.........................	496	639	1,429	8.3	9.2	12.7
Married, husband present..............	9,060	10,813	19,282	25.0	28.5	40.9
14 to 19 years.............................	219	194	348	25.2	24.7	22.8
20 to 24 years.............................	1,106	1,009	1,861	30.0	30.1	30.5
25 to 34 years.............................	2,483	2,652	4,096	24.9	26.5	32.6
35 to 44 years.............................	2,695	3,241	4,345	30.7	34.4	47.3
45 to 54 years.............................	1,810	2,539	5,323	28.0	35.4	58.1
55 to 64 years.............................	605	1,008	2,998	14.4	21.6	44.8
65 years and over.........................	142	170	311	6.4	6.6	7.4

[1] Annual average estimated on basis of data for March 1950.

[2] Projection of average annual rates of change in labor force participation rates from 1950 to 1955.

Source: Based on appendix table B–5 and unpublished estimates.

To summarize, then, the developments that seem probable under a high employment assumption:

Marriage and birth rates. These will continue high, perhaps as high as during the first part of the five-year period 1950–1955. As a result young women, 18 to 34 years of age, will probably be to some extent immobilized outside the labor force, and although increases in labor force activity of married women may occur, in line with the general, long-term rise, no sharp upswings seem indicated for these ages.

School and college enrollment. Estimates of the Census Bureau show a 1950–1955 increase of 1 million (from 9.1 million to 10.2 million) in school enrollment of young people aged 14 to 24 years. This represents a rise from 39.5 percent of the population in those ages to 46.0 percent. There is still room for increases in the proportion attending school, even at the high-school-age level; in fact, 1956 data showed a further rise (table 93). Young women of college age (18 to 24 years) showed only small increases in enrollment rates during the period, but the increases were notable for young men.

FIGURE **19.**—LABOR FORCE PARTICIPATION RATES OF MARRIED WOMEN, HUSBAND PRESENT,
BY AGE: 1950, 1955, AND PROJECTED FOR 1975

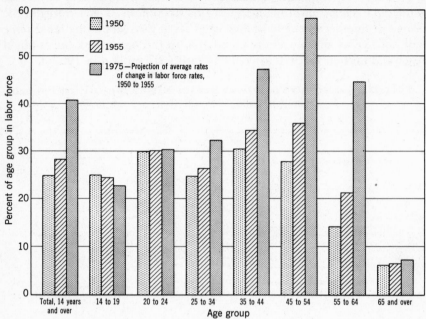

Note: Based on data in table 92.

To what extent the college enrollment rates will continue to increase is a subject of speculation among experts. It is reasonable to believe that they will rise somewhat if family incomes remain relatively high and the social and economic value placed on education does not diminish. This assumes, of course, that educational facilities will expand to meet the growing demand for college training.

TABLE **93.**—PERCENT OF THE POPULATION 14 TO 24 YEARS OLD ENROLLED IN SCHOOL,
BY AGE AND SEX: 1956, 1955, AND 1950

Age	Total			Male			Female		
	1956	1955	1950	1956	1955	1950	1956	1955	1950
14 to 17 years............	88.2	86.9	83.3	89.1	88.6	84.3	87.3	85.2	82.2
18 and 19 years...........	35.4	31.5	29.4	45.1	42.5	35.2	27.4	22.5	24.3
20 to 24 years............	12.8	11.1	9.0	20.6	18.1	14.2	6.8	6.1	4.6

Source: U. S. Bureau of the Census, *Current Population Reports,* Series P–20, No. 74, table 1.

Retirement rate. The long-run decline in labor force participation of men 65 years or older was accelerated during the five-year period 1950–1955 by the two major revisions in Social Security coverage during that period. More recently, there appears to have been a halt in the rapid decline shown during those five years, but it is not likely that there will be an upward swing such as occurred during World War II.   Not only is retirement somewhat more attractive with higher benefits, but the increased employment rate of younger family members, particularly women, may relieve some of the financial burden that hitherto fell on men past 65. Further, for men who have retired, job opportunities for selling or other part-time work may not be so abundant because of the competition from women in the middle age brackets.

Women aged 65 and over, in contrast to men, have shown small increases in labor force activity, despite the expansion of Social Security coverage. As a large proportion of women in the next younger age group return to or remain in the labor force, it is not unlikely that this will carry over past age 65.   Whether the 1956 law permitting women to retire at age 62 and draw Social Security benefits will reverse the recent trend may not be seen for some time.

Characteristics of the projected labor force

The general effects of the changes in age composition of the population and of the varying assumptions about labor force activity in the future may be seen in table 94.

TABLE **94.**—PERCENT DISTRIBUTION OF ANNUAL AVERAGE LABOR FORCE, BY AGE AND SEX: 1950, 1955, AND PROJECTED FOR 1965 AND 1975

Year and projection	Total, 14 years and over			Under 45 years		45 years and over	
	Both sexes	Male	Female	Male	Female	Male	Female
1950	100.0	71.3	28.7	45.9	20.0	25.4	8.7
1955	100.0	69.7	30.3	44.3	19.6	25.4	10.7
1965: Projection I	100.0	66.9	33.1	41.9	20.6	25.0	12.5
II	100.0	66.1	33.9	41.4	19.9	24.7	14.0
III	100.0	67.1	32.9	41.8	20.3	25.3	12.6
IV	100.0	69.2	30.8	43.3	19.4	25.9	11.4
1975: Projection I	100.0	65.2	34.8	42.3	21.8	22.9	13.0
II	100.0	64.1	35.9	41.6	20.4	22.5	15.5
III	100.0	65.7	34.3	42.3	21.0	23.4	13.3
IV	100.0	69.3	30.7	44.8	19.7	24.5	11.0

Source: Based on table 91 and appendix tables B–1 to B–4.

Assuming the projected changes in labor force participation rates, we find the outstanding development of the 20-year period would be the increasing relative number of women past their middle forties—from 10.7 percent of the labor force in 1955 to between 13.0 and 15.5 percent in 1975. The proportion of the labor force members who were men would drop 4 or 5 percentage points, equally divided between under 45 years and 45 years old and over.   The implications of these changes from the standpoint of productivity and other qualitative aspects of the labor force are beyond the scope of this study.

The increase in the number of married women in the labor force from 51.8 percent of the total women in the labor force in 1955 to a possible 57.4 percent in 1975 (Projection II) also would have some bearing on the character of the labor force.   Hitherto married women have tended to have higher turnover rates than other workers, in part because they may not have placed the same emphasis on stability of employment.

The number of working mothers may also be expected to rise (table 95).   In 1955, it is estimated that 24 percent of the married, widowed, and divorced women under 45 in the labor force had one or more children under 5.   This proportion might rise to at least 35 percent[4] in 1975 if the number of children under 5 in the population increases to the maximum level projected (assuming a continuation of 1954–1955 fertility levels, see Series AA projection in *Current Population Reports,* Series P–25, No. 123).

TABLE **95.**—MARRIED, WIDOWED, AND DIVORCED WOMEN UNDER 45 YEARS OLD IN THE LABOR
FORCE WITH CHILDREN UNDER 5 YEARS OLD: 1955 TO 1975

[Current survey week]

Year	Total	With children under 5	
		Number	Percent
1955 (actual)..............................	8,936,000	[1]2,147,000	24.0
PROJECTED[2]			
Assuming 1954-1955 fertility level continues to 1975:			
1960.....................................	9,758,000	2,970,000	30.4
1965.....................................	10,605,000	3,319,000	31.3
1970.....................................	11,772,000	3,882,000	33.0
1975.....................................	13,448,000	4,699,000	34.9
Assuming 1950-1953 fertility level continues to 1975:			
1960.....................................	9,758,000	2,408,000	24.7
1965.....................................	10,605,000	2,769,000	26.1
1970.....................................	11,772,000	3,236,000	27.5
1975.....................................	13,448,000	3,858,000	28.7

[1] Estimated on basis of data for women with children under 6.
[2] Projection based on average annual change in labor force participation rates between 1950 and 1955; see Appendix B.
Source: Derived from appendix table B–5 and unpublished estimates.

The projected decline in the labor force participation rate of men past 65 years of age means that the actual number of workers in the oldest age group would change very little over the next two decades.   The number of retired persons who are dependent on pensions and their savings, or the help of their families or the State will, therefore, grow larger and larger, as the number reaching 65 increases and the expectation of life lengthens.   Projection I assumes that 16.6 million men and women past 65 will be outside the labor force in 1975, and Projection II, 17.2 million; in 1955 there were 10.8 million.   At present, relatively few persons past 65 who are no longer employed have enough retirement income to meet their needs adequately.   Although most of them get along by drawing on savings or by depending on the help of their families, as many as one-fifth of the older population require old-age assistance.   Equally serious as the economic needs may be the psychological and social needs that the

[4] See Appendix B for description of estimation procedures.

possession of a job seems to fill in the life of most American men, and some American women, particularly those who no longer have a family to occupy them. Perhaps recognition of these problems will set in motion legal and social forces to maintain as active members of the labor force a larger proportion of the age group than these projections imply.[5]

Clearly the most important point to be noted is the timing and volume of the large changes in the labor force that will occur because of the changing structure of the population and the assumed changes in labor force rates. Table 96 illustrates these changes, on the basis of Projections I and II. Between 1955 and 1960, it will be the workers past 35 years of age who will dominate labor force growth; those 35 to 64 years will increase by over 700,000 to 800,000 a year, on the average. But in the following five-year period the influx of over half a million young workers a year (aged 14 to 24 years) will tax training, placement, and managerial skills. At the same time there will be almost no net increases in the age group 25 to 44, the age span which constitutes the training period for many leadership positions. The older group 45 to 64 years of age will increase by more than about half a million a year. When 1965 is reached, a new era in manpower will begin. On the average, almost 1 million workers a year between the ages of 20 and 35 will be added to the current labor supply until 1975. For the individual worker seeking to find the best possible job as a start for his career, the decade 1965–1975 may be a hard one, however, because of the large number of competitors at the lower end of the ladder.

TABLE **96.**—PROJECTIONS I AND II—AVERAGE ANNUAL CHANGES IN THE LABOR FORCE,
BY AGE: 1955 TO 1975

[Current survey levels. In thousands]

Projection and age	1955 to 1960	1960 to 1965	1965 to 1970	1970 to 1975
PROJECTION I				
Total, 14 years and over............	+858	+1,198	+1,410	+1,432
14 to 19 years.............................	+170	+326	+110	-65
20 to 24 years.............................	+91	+319	+560	+304
25 to 34 years.............................	-132	+2	+417	+898
35 to 44 years.............................	+223	+92	-150	+3
45 to 54 years.............................	+314	+227	+207	+80
55 to 64 years.............................	+149	+196	+236	+169
65 years and over.........................	+43	+36	+30	+43
PROJECTION II				
Total, 14 years and over............	+895	+1,214	+1,432	+1,420
14 to 19 years.............................	+137	+296	+93	-73
20 to 24 years.............................	+65	+284	+491	+235
25 to 34 years.............................	-150	-16	+402	+867
35 to 44 years.............................	+228	+95	-149	+5
45 to 54 years.............................	+390	+293	+277	+130
55 to 64 years.............................	+216	+259	+310	+236
65 years and over.........................	+9	+3	+8	+20

Source: Based on appendix tables B–1 and B–2.

[5] For a detailed discussion of the problems of the older population in retirement, see Henry D. Sheldon, *The Older Population in the United States,* John Wiley & Sons, New York, 1958.

BIBLIOGRAPHY

Altman, R., *Availability for Work*, Harvard University Press, Cambridge, 1950.

Bancroft, G., and E. H. Welch, "Recent Experience With Problems of Labor Force Measurement," *Journal of the American Statistical Association*, Vol. 41, September 1946.

Beasley, R. B., *Labor-Force Participation, Its Significance to Labor Market Analysis*, U. S. Department of Labor, Bureau of Employment Security, 1952.

Bell, D., "The Great Back-to-Work Movement," *Fortune*, Vol. 54, July 1956.

Belloc, N. B., "Labor Force Participation and Employment Opportunities for Women," *Journal of the American Statistical Association*, Vol. 45, September 1950.

Board of Governors, Federal Reserve System, *Consumer Installment Credit*, Part I, Vol. 2, "Growth and Import," 1957.

Census of Partial Employment, Unemployment, and Occupations: 1937, Vol. IV, *The Enumerative Check Census*, 1938.

Colm, G., *The American Economy in 1960*, National Planning Association, Planning Pamphlets, No. 81, Washington, 1952.

Dornbusch, S. M., "Correlations Between Income and Labor Force Participation by Race," *American Journal of Sociology*, Vol. LXI, January 1956.

———, and D. M. Heer, "The Evaluation of Work by Females, 1940–1950," *American Journal of Sociology*, Vol. LXIII, July 1957.

Douglas, P. H., *The Theory of Wages*, MacMillan Company, New York, 1934.

Ducoff, L. J., and M. J. Hagood, *Labor Force Definition and Measurement*, Social Science Research Council, New York, 1947.

Durand, J. D., *The Labor Force in the United States, 1890–1960*, Social Science Research Council, New York, 1948.

Eaton, E. I., "The Effect of Changes in Working Life on Expenditure Patterns," *Proceedings of Seventh Annual Meeting of Industrial Relations Research Association*, Publication No. 14, 1955.

Eckler, A. R., *et al.*, "Concepts Employed in Labor Force Measurement and Uses of Labor Force Data," *Journal of the American Statistical Association*, Vol. 50, September 1955.

Edwards, A. M., *Comparative Occupation Statistics for the United States, 1870 to 1940*, U. S. Bureau of the Census, 1943.

Employment and Unemployment Statistics, Report prepared for the Eighth International Conference of Labour Statisticians, International Labour Office, Geneva, 1954.

Eskin, L., "Sources of Wartime Labor Supply in the United States," *Monthly Labor Review*, Vol. 59, August 1944.

Garfinkle, S., "Changes in Working Life of Men, 1900–2000," *Monthly Labor Review*, Vol. 78, March 1955.

Ginzberg, E., *The Negro Potential*, Columbia University Press, New York, 1956.

Glick, P. C., *American Families*, John Wiley and Sons, New York, 1957.

Goldstein, H., "Recent Trends in and Outlook for College Enrollments," *Monthly Labor Review*, Vol. 79, March 1956.

Hauser, P. M., "The Labor Force and Gainful Workers—Concept, Measurement, and Comparability," *American Journal of Sociology*, Vol. LIV, January 1949.

———, "The Labor Force as a Field of Interest for the Sociologist," *American Sociological Review*, Vol. 16, August 1951.

————, "Mobility in Labor Force Participation," in *Labor Mobility and Economic Opportunity*, Social Science Research Council, John Wiley and Sons, New York, 1954.

Hill, J. A., *Women in Gainful Occupations, 1870 to 1920*, U. S. Bureau of the Census, Monograph IX, 1929.

Hitch, T. K., "Meaning and Measurement of 'Full' or 'Maximum' Employment," *Review of Economics and Statistics*, Vol. XXXIII, February 1951.

Hooks, J. M., *Women's Occupations Through Seven Decades*, Women's Bureau Bulletin, No. 218, 1951.

Humphrey, D. D., "Alleged 'Additional Workers' in the Measurement of Unemployment," *Journal of Political Economy*, Vol. XLVIII, June 1940.

Interim Report of the Review of Concepts Subcommittee to the Committee on Labor Supply, Employment and Unemployment Statistics, *Hearings before the Subcommittee on Economic Statistics of the Joint Committee on the Economic Report*, 84th Congress, November 7 and 8, 1955.

International Labour Review, "Employment of Married Women and Mothers of Families," Vol. LXIII, June 1951.

————, "The Employment of Older Women," Vol. LXXII, July 1955.

————, "Part-Time Employment for Women with Family Responsibilities," Vol. LXXV, June 1957.

————, "The World's Working Population: Its Distribution by Status and Occupation," Vol. LXXIV, August 1956.

————, "The World's Working Population: Its Industrial Distribution," Vol. LXXIII, May 1956.

————, "The World's Working Population: Some Demographic Aspects," Vol. LXXIII, February 1956.

Jaffe, A. J., "Trends in the Participation of Women in the Working Force," with comments by S. Cooper and S. Lebergott, *Monthly Labor Review*, Vol. 79, May 1956.

————, and C. D. Stewart, *Manpower Resources and Utilization*, John Wiley and Sons, New York, 1951.

Kaplan, D. L., and M. C. Casey, *Occupational Trends in the United States: 1900 to 1950*, U. S. Bureau of the Census Working Paper No. 5, 1958.

Kiser, C. V., "Changes in Fertility by Socio-Economic Status During 1940–1950," *The Milbank Memorial Fund Quarterly*, Vol. XXXIII, October 1955.

Kuvin, L., "Revised Estimates of Employment and Unemployment," *Conference Board Bulletin*, National Industrial Conference Board, Vol. XII, July 1938.

Kyrk, H., *The Family in the American Economy*, University of Chicago Press, Chicago, 1953.

Lebergott, S., "Measuring Unemployment," *Review of Economics and Statistics*, Vol. XXXVI, November 1954.

Long, C. D., "Impact of Effective Demand on the Labor Supply," *American Economic Review*, Vol. XLIII, May 1953.

————, *The Labor Force in War and Transition, Four Countries*, National Bureau of Economic Research, Occasional Paper 36, 1952.

————, *The Labor Force in Wartime America*, National Bureau of Economic Research, Occasional Paper 14, March 1944.

————, *The Labor Force under Changing Income and Employment*, National Bureau of Economic Research, Princeton University Press, Princeton, 1958.

Manpower in the United States: Problems and Policies, edited by W. Haber, *et al.*, Industrial Relations Research Association Series, Harper and Brothers, New York, 1954.

Mansfield, E., "Community Size, Region, Labor Force and Income 1950," *Review of Economics and Statistics*, Vol. XXXVII, November 1955.

————, "Some Notes on City Income Levels," *Review of Economics and Statistics*, Vol. XXXVIII, November 1956.

Measurement of Underemployment, Report prepared for Ninth International Conference of Labour Statisticians, International Labour Office, Geneva, 1957.

Miller, F. S., "Household Employment in the United States," *International Labour Review*, Vol. LXVI, October 1952.

Miller, H. P., *Income of the American People*, John Wiley and Sons, New York, 1955.

Moore, G. H., "Analyzing Business Cycles," *The American Statistician*, Vol. 8, April-May 1954.

Moore, W. E., "Persistent Problems of Labor Force Analysis," *Population Index*, Vol. 17, April 1951.

Muntz, E. E., "Women's Changing Role in the United States Employment Market," *International Labour Review*, Vol. LXXIV, November 1956.

Myrdal, A., and V. Klein, *Women's Two Roles—Home and Work*, Rutledge and Kegan Paul, London, 1956.

National Manpower Council, *Womanpower*, Columbia University Press, New York, 1957.

Nourse, E. G., "Ideal and Working Concepts of Full Employment," Proceedings of Sixty-Ninth Annual Meeting of the American Economic Association, *American Economic Review*, Vol. XLVII, May 1957.

Olin, U., and E. G. Adams, "Age Structure and the Labour Supply," *Proceedings of the World Population Conference, 1954*, United Nations Publication, XIII.8 (Vol. III), 1955.

Palmer, G. L., *Labor Mobility in Six Cities*, Social Science Research Council, New York, 1954.

———, *The Significance of Employment Patterns in Households for Labor Market Analysis*, University of Pennsylvania, Industrial Research Department, Special Report No. 8, 1942.

———, and A. Ratner, *Industrial and Occupational Trends in National Employment 1910-1940, 1910-1948*, University of Pennsylvania, Industrial Research Department, Research Report No. 11, 1949.

Parnes, H. S., *A Study in the Dynamics of Local Labor Force Expansion*, Ohio State University, Columbus, 1951.

Pidgeon, M.-E., *Women Workers and Their Dependents*, Women's Bureau Bulletin, No. 239, 1952.

Rees, A., *et al.*, *The Measurement and Behaviour of Unemployment*, National Bureau of Economic Research, Princeton University Press, Princeton, 1957.

Sheldon, H. D., *The Older Population in the United States*, John Wiley and Sons, New York, 1958.

Shiskin, J., and H. Eisenpress, "Seasonal Adjustments by Electronic Computer Methods," *Journal of the American Statistical Association*, Vol. 52, December 1957.

Shister, J., *Economics of the Labor Market*, J. B. Lippincott, Philadelphia, 1956.

Sierra-Berdecia, F., and A. J. Jaffe, "The Concept and Measurement of Underemployment," *Monthly Labor Review*, Vol. 78, March 1955.

Smuts, R., *Working Women in Large Cities*, National Manpower Council, unpublished manuscript.

Stewart, C. D., "Manpower Implications of Changing Patterns of Working Life," *Proceedings of Seventh Annual Meeting of Industrial Relations Research Association*, Publication No. 14, 1955.

———, "The Shifting Patterns in the Available Labor Force in the United States," *Proceedings of Fifth Annual Meeting of Industrial Relations Research Association*, Publication No. 10, 1953.

———, "A Shorter Workweek as a Factor in Economic Growth," *Monthly Labor Review*, Vol. 79, February 1956.

———, "Uses of Unemployment Statistics in Economic Policy," *Monthly Labor Review*, Vol. 78, March 1955.

Stigler, G. J., *Domestic Servants in the United States 1900-1940*, National Bureau of Economic Research, Occasional Paper 24, 1946.

Tietze, C., and P. Lauriat, "Age at Marriage and Educational Attainment in the United States," *Population Studies*, Vol. IX, November 1955.

United Nations, *Application of International Standards to Census Data on the Economi-cally Active Population*, Population Studies, No. 9, 1951.

———, *The Determinants and Consequences of Population Trends*, Population Studies, No. 17, 1953.

———, *Population Census Methods*, Population Studies, No. 4, November 1949.

U. S. Congress, Joint Committee on the Economic Report, "Potential Growth of the United States During the Next Decade," 83d Congress, 1954.

U. S. Department of Commerce, Bureau of the Census, *1940 Census of Population*, Vol. II, *Characteristics of the Population*, Parts 1-7.

———, Vol. III, *The Labor Force*, Parts 1-5.

———, Vol. IV, *Characteristics by Age*, Parts 1-4.

———, *The Labor Force (Sample Statistics)*,
Employment and Personal Characteristics.
Characteristics of Persons Not in the Labor Force.
Employment and Family Characteristics of Women.
Wage or Salary Income in 1939.
Industrial Characteristics.
Occupational Characteristics.
Usual Occupation.

———, *Differential Fertility 1940 and 1910*,
Fertility for States and Large Cities.
Women by Number of Children Ever Born.
Women by Number of Children under 5 Years Old.

———, *Educational Attainment by Economic Characteristics and Marital Status.*

———, *Estimates of Labor Force, Employment, and Unemployment in the United States, 1940 and 1930.*

———, *Families,*
Employment Status.
Family Wage or Salary Income in 1939.

———, *U. S. Census of Population, 1950*, Vol. II, *Characteristics of the Population*, Parts 1-50.

———, Vol. IV, *Special Reports,*
Part 1, Chapter A, Employment and Personal Characteristics.
Part 1, Chapter B, Occupational Characteristics.
Part 1, Chapter C, Occupation by Industry.
Part 1, Chapter D, Industrial Characteristics.
Part 2, Chapter A, General Characteristics of Families.
Part 2, Chapter C, Institutional Population.
Part 5, Chapter B, Education.
Part 5, Chapter C, Fertility.

———, *Population*, "All Experienced Persons in the Labor Force by Occupation and In-dustry for the United States: 1940," Series P-14, No. 13.

———, *Population—Special Reports*, "Normal Growth of the Labor Force in the United States: 1940 to 1950," Series P-44, No. 12.

———, *Current Population Reports*, Series P-50,
Annual Report on the Labor Force, Nos. 2, 13, 19, 31, 40, 45, 59, 67, 72.
Educational Attainment of Workers, Nos. 14, 49.
Employment of White and Nonwhite Persons: 1955, No. 66.
Illustrative Statistics on Labor Force, Employment, and Unemployment, from the Current Population Survey of the Bureau of the Census, No. 61.
Job Mobility of Workers in 1955, No. 70.
Labor Force Projections to 1975, Nos. 42, 69.
Marital Status and Family Characteristics of Workers, Nos. 5, 11, 22, 29, 39, 44, 50, 62, 73, 76.

Multiple Jobholding, Nos. 30, 74.

Part-Time Workers, Nos. 3, 7, 12, 17, 18, 21, 25, 26, 28, 33, 34, 46, 52, 53, 55–57, 60, 63.

School Enrollment of Workers, Nos. 14, 23, 32, 41, 47, 51, 58, 64, 71.

Seasonal Variations in the Labor Force, Employment, and Unemployment, No. 82.

Women Past Thirty-Five in the Labor Force: 1947 to 1956, No. 75.

Work Experience in (calendar year), Nos. 8, 15, 24, 35, 43, 48, 54, 68, 77.

Work Experience of the Labor Reserve: March 1951, No. 38.

———, *Current Population Reports*, "Monthly Report on the Labor Force," Series P–57.

———, *Current Population Reports*, Series P–60,

Income of Families, Nos. 1, 2, 3, 5, 6, 7, 9, 12, 15, 20, 24.

Income of Persons, Nos. 2, 3, 5, 6, 7, 9, 11, 14, 16, 19, 23.

———, *Current Population Reports*, Series P–20,

Fertility, Nos. 8, 18, 27, 46.

Marital Status and Family Status, Nos. 10, 23, 53.

Projections of the Number of Households and Families to 1975, No. 69.

———, *Current Population Reports*, "Concepts and Methods Used in the Current Labor Force Statistics Prepared by the Bureau of the Census," Series P–23, No. 2, and "Expansion of the Current Population Survey Sample: 1956," Series P–23, No. 3.

———, *Current Population Reports*, "Revised Projections of the Population of the United States, by Age and Sex: 1960 to 1975," Series P–25, No. 123.

———, *Unemployment, Employment, and the Labor Force: A List of Recent Methodological Studies*, April 1956, (Mimeo.).

U. S. Department of Labor, *Changes in Women's Occupations, 1940–1950*, Women's Bureau Bulletin, No. 253, 1954.

———, *Part-Time Jobs for Women*, Women's Bureau Bulletin, No. 238, 1951.

———, *Tables of Working Life: Length of Working Life for Men*, Bureau of Labor Statistics Bulletin, No. 1001, 1950.

———, *Tables of Working Life for Women*, Bureau of Labor Statistics Bulletin, No. 1204, 1957.

Webb, J. N., "Concepts Used in Unemployment Surveys," *Journal of the American Statistical Association*, Vol. 34, March 1939.

Wells, J. A., "Labor Turnover of Women Factory Workers, 1950–1955," *Monthly Labor Review*, Vol. 78, August 1955.

Wolfbein, S. L., "The Changing Geography of American Industry," *Monthly Labor Review*, Vol. 77, July 1954.

———, "The Changing Length of Working Life," *Proceedings of Seventh Annual Meeting of Industrial Relations Research Association*, Publication No. 14, 1955.

———, and A. J. Jaffe, "Demographic Factors in Labor Force Growth," *American Sociological Review*, Vol. 11, August 1946.

Wool, H., "Long-Term Projections of the Labor Force," in *Studies in Income and Wealth*, Vol. 16, National Bureau of Economic Research, Princeton University Press, Princeton, 1954.

Woolsey, T. D., *Estimates of Disabling Illness Prevalence in the United States*, Federal Security Agency, Public Health Monograph No. 4, 1953.

Woytinsky, W. S., *Additional Workers and the Volume of Unemployment in the Depression*, Social Science Research Council, Pamphlet Series 1, 1940.

———, "Income Cycle in the Life of Families and Individuals," *Social Security Bulletin*, Vol. 6, June 1943.

———, *et al.*, *Employment and Wages in the United States*, Twentieth Century Fund, New York, 1953.

APPENDIX A

QUALITY OF CENSUS LABOR FORCE DATA
AND METHODS OF ADJUSTMENT

Internal consistency of 1950 Census data

On the basis of internal evidence alone, the national data on the labor force from the 1950 Census of Population could be rated as fairly satisfactory, with a few major exceptions. The percentage of the population that did not report on employment status was low (1.1 percent), as was the percentage of the employed without information on hours worked (2.6 percent), occupation (1.3 percent), and industry (1.5 percent) (table A–1). The percentage for whom work experience in 1949 was left blank was larger, almost 7 percent, or about the same proportion as had no report on income in 1949. The questions on both work experience and income were asked of only one in five persons 14 years of age and over and were neighboring questions on the 1950 Census schedule; almost two-thirds of the persons for whom the information on either item was omitted had no reports on both items.

Because of the comparatively low level of unemployment, few enumerators had much practice recording information on the experience of the unemployed, and the rather complicated design of the enumeration schedule further increased the difficulty. A description of the occupation of the last job of the unemployed was omitted in about one-fifth of the cases. The not-reported rate, however, was much higher for young workers than for adults, which suggests that many of those for whom no job description was reported had, in fact, never worked. Enumerators were instructed to enter "never worked" for such persons, but if they failed to do so, the blanks in the occupation and industry sections were coded as "not reported"; one-fifth of the unemployed without occupation reports were under 20 years of age, whereas only one-tenth of those reporting were in this age class. The question on duration of unemployment, to be asked of a sample of only one in five unemployed, was overlooked so many times that the results were not tabulated.

The total count of unemployed workers was more nearly complete than the reports on their job experience. It did fall short of the estimate obtained from the Current Population Survey (see later) and for some types of analysis may be seriously inadequate. However, the detailed information provided by the census for population groups and geographic areas that cannot be measured by the current sample is still useful. Analysis of unemployment rates by industry, occupation, and geographic areas, undertaken in connection with the present study, gave results that seemed quite consistent with other data on employment and unemployment. For example, all the standard metropolitan areas with census unemployment rates in the upper quintile that were classified by the Bureau of Employment Security at the time of the census were classified as areas of substantial or very substantial labor surplus (coded D or E). In the low quintile, only three were coded D or E in March, and these had ceased to be problem areas by May. Industries with high unemployment rates according to the census (forestry, construction, lumber and logging, automobile manufacturing, shipbuilding, manufacturing of railroad equipment, food processing, some apparel industries, and tobacco manufacturing) were also at relatively low levels of activity according to other sources. For comparisons among areas or from one area to another over time, the census data, even though incomplete, are still valuable, in the writer's opinion.

TABLE **A–1.**—Not-Reported Rates in 1950 Census for Specified Labor Force Categories

Labor force category	Total	Male	Female
Employment status of persons 14 years old and over......................................	1.1	1.1	1.1
EMPLOYED PERSONS			
Hours worked in census week....................	2.6	2.4	3.2
Occupation of current job......................	1.3	1.1	1.8
Industry of current job.......................	1.5	1.3	2.1
UNEMPLOYED PERSONS			
Occupation of last job........................	20.4	19.7	22.3
14 to 19 years old............................	34.6	34.2	35.4
20 to 24 years old............................	22.2	22.3	22.0
25 years old and over.........................	17.4	16.8	19.1
Industry of last job..........................	25.2	24.5	27.1
WORK EXPERIENCE IN 1949			
Total......................................	6.8	6.8	6.8
Labor force...................................	4.6	4.7	4.5
Not in labor force............................	9.3	14.9	7.6

Source: Derived from *1950 Census of Population*, Vol. II, *Characteristics of the Population*, Part 1, U. S. Summary, tables 123, 126, and 130; Vol. IV, *Special Reports*, Part 1, Chapter A, Employment and Personal Characteristics, tables 4 and 13; and Chapter B, Occupational Characteristics, tables 4 and 6.

In connection with the general quality of the labor force data, another problem arose in the selection of the 20-percent sample by the enumerators. For some reason that it has never been possible to determine, there was a small bias in the sample of white heads of households and of the white male population 14 years old and over. The count of the male labor force from 100-percent tabulations is 462,000 (or about 1 percent) above the count obtained from the 20-percent tabulations, and 436,000 greater than the count from the 3⅓-percent sample tabulations (a subsample of the 20-percent sample). For the female labor force, there was no such bias; the sample estimates are within about 50,000 of the complete count total (table A–2).

TABLE **A-2.**—COMPARISON OF COMPLETE COUNT AND SAMPLE DATA ON EMPLOYMENT STATUS, BY SEX: 1950

Employment status and sex	Complete count	20 percent	3 1/3 percent	Percent distribution			Ratio of complete count to--	
				Complete count	20 percent	3 1/3 percent	20 percent	3 1/3 percent
MALE								
Total, 14 years and over..	55,311,617	54,601,105	54,610,050	100.0	100.0	100.0	101.3	101.3
Labor force.....................	43,553,386	43,091,000	43,117,500	78.7	78.9	79.0	101.1	101.0
Civilian labor force...........	42,598,767	42,126,325	42,147,060	77.0	77.1	77.2	101.1	101.1
Employed....................	40,519,462	40,037,490	40,062,870	73.3	73.3	73.4	101.2	101.1
Unemployed..................	2,079,305	2,088,835	2,084,190	3.8	3.8	3.8	99.5	99.8
Not in labor force.............	11,758,231	11,510,105	11,492,550	21.3	21.1	21.0	102.2	102.3
Keeping house...............	286,139	265,475	262,800	0.5	0.5	0.5	107.8	108.9
Unable to work..............	2,753,711	2,747,915	2,756,670	5.0	5.0	5.0	100.2	99.9
Inmates of institutions.....	878,905	873,060	869,700	1.6	1.6	1.6	100.7	101.1
Other and not reported......	7,839,476	7,623,655	7,603,380	14.2	14.0	13.9	102.8	103.1
FEMALE								
Total, 14 years and over..	57,042,417	57,102,295	57,083,190	100.0	100.0	100.0	99.9	99.9
Labor force.....................	16,500,582	16,551,990	16,553,040	28.9	29.0	29.0	99.7	99.7
Civilian labor force...........	16,472,888	16,519,690	16,521,960	28.9	28.9	28.9	99.7	99.7
Employed....................	15,719,987	15,750,660	15,753,000	27.6	27.6	27.6	99.8	99.8
Unemployed..................	752,901	769,030	768,960	1.3	1.3	1.3	97.9	97.9
Not in labor force.............	40,541,835	40,550,305	40,530,150	71.1	71.0	71.0	100.0	100.0
Keeping house...............	31,894,294	32,072,440	32,073,180	55.9	56.2	56.2	99.4	99.4
Unable to work..............	1,811,927	1,872,030	1,866,750	3.2	3.3	3.3	96.8	97.1
Inmates of institutions.....	565,231	563,760	564,120	1.0	1.0	1.0	100.3	100.2
Other and not reported......	6,270,383	6,042,075	6,026,100	11.0	10.6	10.6	103.8	104.1

Source: Derived from *1950 Census of Population*, Vol. IV, *Special Reports*, Part 1, Chapter A, Employment and Personal Characteristics, table E.

The employment status of the population by sex, color, and residence was tabulated on a complete count basis only for persons 14 years old and over as a total; other cross-tabulations by personal characteristics (age, marital status, relationship, etc.) were made on the basis of the 20-percent or 3⅓-percent samples. Thus, statistics on the labor force by age will not add to the complete count total, unless adjustments are made. As far as it is possible to tell, the relationships within the complete count and sample data are about the same; for example, the percent of the male population in the labor force is 78.7 according to the complete count, 78.9 according to the 20-percent sample, and 79.0 according to the 3⅓-percent sample.

In order to provide improved 1950 Census figures on the labor force by age, sex, and color that had a minimum of sampling error and bias and some correction for the effect of failure to report labor force status, the following adjustments were made for the historical series in table D-1 of this study.

1. *Distribution of not-reported cases.* All persons for whom labor force status was not reported in 1950 were originally classed as not in the labor force and combined with "all other" persons not in the labor force in the tables in Volume II of the 1950 Census of Population. The number for whom labor force status was not reported was available by age, sex, color, residence, and marital status from tabulations of the 3⅓-percent sample.

The percent of the "not reported" group that might be in the labor force was estimated on the basis of the percent reported for the comparable age-sex-color-residence-marital status groups. Adjustment ratios were computed for the original sample data.

2. *Adjustment of complete count totals.* The complete counts of persons in the labor force by color, residence, and sex were adjusted upward by the percentages obtained in step 1.

3. *These adjusted totals* based on 100-percent data were then distributed by age according to the adjusted distributions obtained in step 1.

4. *Corresponding adjustments* were made for persons not in the labor force. The combination of the figures for the adjusted labor force and not in labor force by age does not agree exactly with the complete count figures on the population by age, but the differences are not large enough to affect the labor force participation rates.

The original and adjusted labor force figures are shown in table A–3. The combined adjustments added about 800,000 to the male labor force as estimated from the 3⅓-percent sample and about 130,000 to the female labor force. The ratio adjustment of the sample data to complete count totals has the effect of reducing the sampling variability of the original estimates. The adjustment for the not-reported cases also improves the data because some of the persons for whom information was not available were undoubtedly in the labor force. Whether the true number is greater or smaller than the adjustment is, of course, unknown, but some indication is provided by the census-CPS matching study to be described.

Most of the analysis of the 1950 Census data in this study is concerned with labor force participation rates rather than with absolute numbers. As the age-specific labor force rates are not greatly affected by this adjustment, it was not thought necessary to carry them beyond the totals by age, color, and residence.

Apart from sampling and incomplete reporting, there were other aspects of the decennial census enumeration that gave rise to problems in the labor force data. Chief among these was the classification of persons as not in the labor force who were, in fact, employed or looking for work, but who either reported themselves as housewives, students, retired, etc., or were not asked the prescribed questions by the enumerators. (See section on "Comparison of 1950 census and Current Population Survey data," p. 157.) This failure to identify workers, many of whom were part-time or intermittent workers, was reflected both in the count of the labor force and in the statistics on hours worked during the census week and weeks worked during the year 1949. In the distribution of employed persons by the number of hours worked, the proportion working only a small number of hours is certainly understated. The number of persons who worked at all during 1949 is also probably understated, as is

TABLE A-3.—LABOR FORCE BY AGE, COLOR, RESIDENCE, AND SEX: 1950

[Decennial census levels. Original data are based on 3⅓-percent sample; adjusted to complete-count totals after correction for failure to report employment status. See pp. 153-154]

Age and sex	All classes		White						Nonwhite					
	Original	Adjusted	Urban		Rural nonfarm		Rural farm		Urban		Rural nonfarm		Rural farm	
			Original	Adjusted	Original	Adjusted	Original	Adjusted	Original	Adjusted	Original	Adjusted	Original	Adjusted
Male, 14 yrs. and over...	43,117,500	43,929,687	25,442,880	25,911,908	7,559,340	7,792,108	6,056,880	6,128,628	2,587,710	2,619,397	616,200	626,343	854,490	851,303
14 to 17 years	1,099,530	1,143,110	441,900	461,861	193,170	204,159	299,820	309,345	52,110	53,763	27,900	28,857	84,630	85,125
18 and 19 years	1,443,120	1,476,644	692,700	708,626	321,810	333,397	263,040	267,218	75,450	76,840	34,170	34,773	55,950	55,790
20 to 24 years	4,537,140	4,630,386	2,558,190	2,609,043	907,320	935,973	589,470	596,407	289,320	294,229	90,900	92,959	101,940	101,775
25 to 34 years	10,552,680	10,748,614	6,441,270	6,556,272	1,974,120	2,033,152	1,150,170	1,162,652	686,790	694,852	145,740	147,918	154,590	153,768
25 to 29 years	5,333,940	5,432,086	3,187,080	3,244,859	1,005,870	1,035,910	590,460	596,705	332,820	337,227	67,410	68,168	72,720	72,327
30 to 34 years	5,218,740	5,316,528	3,254,190	3,311,413	968,250	997,242	559,710	565,947	353,970	357,625	78,330	79,750	81,870	81,441
35 to 44 years	9,836,490	10,007,939	5,890,530	5,992,621	1,729,320	1,778,708	1,262,400	1,274,667	659,490	666,477	133,290	134,991	161,460	160,475
35 to 39 years	5,165,070	5,257,735	3,086,100	3,140,346	931,320	958,732	644,070	650,531	350,250	354,297	70,530	71,455	82,800	82,374
40 to 44 years	4,671,420	4,750,204	2,804,430	2,852,275	798,000	819,976	618,330	624,136	309,240	312,180	62,760	63,536	78,660	78,101
45 to 54 years	7,813,320	7,947,675	4,770,120	4,853,203	1,221,120	1,256,598	1,101,720	1,112,234	493,170	497,952	97,800	99,051	129,390	128,637
45 to 49 years	4,162,380	4,235,908	2,515,650	2,561,468	668,560	687,918	578,060	583,610	275,700	278,333	53,640	54,269	70,770	70,310
50 to 54 years	3,650,940	3,711,767	2,254,470	2,291,735	552,560	568,680	523,660	528,624	217,470	219,619	44,160	44,782	58,620	58,327
55 to 64 years	5,462,010	5,556,333	3,368,130	3,425,181	832,530	857,581	869,040	878,092	242,790	245,534	55,620	56,530	93,900	93,415
55 to 59 years	3,103,410	3,155,681	1,920,120	1,952,223	469,050	482,790	478,410	483,182	149,340	150,772	32,190	32,626	54,300	54,088
60 to 64 years	2,358,600	2,400,652	1,448,010	1,472,958	363,480	374,791	390,630	394,910	93,450	94,762	23,430	23,904	39,600	39,327
65 years and over	2,373,210	2,418,986	1,280,040	1,305,101	379,950	392,540	521,220	528,013	88,590	89,750	30,780	31,264	72,630	72,318
Female, 14 yrs. and over.	16,553,040	16,686,840	11,220,780	11,339,284	2,238,060	2,249,306	984,240	987,378	1,626,000	1,634,092	265,230	260,830	218,730	215,950
14 to 17 years	476,430	490,049	274,260	283,853	82,260	84,827	56,730	57,458	28,980	29,683	10,980	11,052	23,220	23,176
18 and 19 years	964,620	973,418	676,440	684,261	134,520	135,727	71,730	71,360	54,930	55,360	12,120	12,029	14,880	14,681
20 to 24 years	2,520,840	2,554,009	1,792,110	1,810,532	324,540	326,404	128,820	140,950	212,310	213,865	33,000	32,586	30,060	29,672
25 to 34 years	3,867,300	3,893,164	2,574,510	2,600,898	507,060	508,865	203,340	200,745	470,640	472,734	65,790	64,637	45,960	45,285
25 to 29 years	2,047,470	2,061,812	1,388,910	1,402,756	260,190	261,375	100,350	99,107	239,940	241,377	33,990	33,436	24,090	23,761
30 to 34 years	1,819,830	1,831,352	1,185,600	1,198,142	246,870	247,490	102,990	101,638	230,700	231,357	31,800	31,201	21,870	21,524
35 to 44 years	3,798,720	3,819,599	2,494,590	2,517,712	524,070	525,385	225,120	221,981	444,240	445,818	65,880	64,516	44,820	44,187
35 to 39 years	1,934,040	1,944,436	1,247,160	1,258,634	269,940	270,613	114,030	112,384	243,690	244,661	35,220	34,510	24,000	23,634
40 to 44 years	1,864,680	1,875,163	1,247,430	1,259,078	254,130	254,772	111,090	109,597	200,550	201,157	30,660	30,006	20,820	20,553
45 to 54 years	2,858,730	2,874,920	1,951,440	1,969,029	380,130	381,478	168,930	166,657	277,380	278,359	46,230	45,306	34,620	34,091
45 to 49 years	1,587,510	1,596,660	1,069,920	1,079,773	215,430	216,109	94,110	92,833	163,560	164,257	26,010	25,543	18,480	18,145
50 to 54 years	1,271,220	1,278,260	881,520	889,256	164,700	165,369	74,820	73,824	113,820	114,102	20,220	19,763	16,140	15,946
55 to 64 years	1,557,300	1,568,080	1,107,420	1,118,750	211,530	212,215	94,380	93,249	105,060	105,575	21,720	21,340	17,190	16,951
55 to 59 years	935,130	941,078	661,800	668,264	127,200	127,554	57,360	56,669	65,940	66,107	12,360	12,165	10,470	10,319
60 to 64 years	622,170	627,002	445,620	450,486	84,330	84,661	37,020	36,580	39,120	39,468	9,360	9,175	6,720	6,632
65 years and over	509,100	513,601	350,010	354,249	73,950	74,405	35,190	34,978	32,460	32,698	9,510	9,364	7,980	7,907

Source: Original data from 1950 Census of Population, Vol. IV, Special Reports, Part 1, Chapter A, Employment and Personal Characteristics, table 1; adjusted data derived from the same report, table 10, and from Vol. II, Characteristics of the Population, Part 1, U. S. Summary, table 50.

the proportion of those who reported work experience but who did only a small amount of work. Failure to remember brief spells of employment was probably an important reason for underenumeration of the annual work force. Decennial statistics on the numbers and characteristics of persons in occupations and industries in which part-time or occasional workers tend to work in large proportions (farm workers, sales workers, and service workers, particularly private household workers) are also affected by the failure to obtain a more nearly complete count of such persons with the labor force questions that preceded.

A full description of the 1950 Census questions and definitions used, and an appraisal of the quality of other items, may be found in the text of the various census reports, in particular, *U. S. Census of Population: 1950,* Vol. II, *Characteristics of the Population,* Part 1, U. S. Summary, and Vol. IV, *Special Reports,* Part 1, Chapter A, Employment and Personal Characteristics.

Comparability of 1950 Census and earlier census data

The data on the labor force for 1940 and 1950 are not exactly comparable with the statistics for gainful workers from earlier censuses. "Gainful workers" were persons reported as having a gainful occupation, that is, an occupation in which they earned money or a money equivalent, or in which they assisted in the production of marketable goods, regardless of whether they were working or seeking work at the time of the census. A person was not considered to have had a gainful occupation if his activity was of a limited extent. Certain classes of persons, such as retired workers, some inmates of institutions, recently incapacitated workers, and seasonal workers neither working nor seeking work at the time of the census, were frequently included among gainful workers; but, in general, such persons are not included in the labor force. The labor force, however, does include new workers, seeking work at the time of the census, and these were not reported as gainful workers.

The Census Bureau has published statistics for 1930, based on the gainful worker concept, that have been adjusted for comparability with the 1940 statistics based on the labor force concept.[1] On the basis of the adjustment factors computed for 1930, Durand has made adjustments of earlier census data—1890, 1900, and 1920—and has constructed a series of estimates of the labor force from 1890 to 1940, by sex, age, color, and nativity that are presumably comparable, in a rough fashion, from one date to another.[2] The 1940 data in his series are also adjustments of the original census data, to correct for misclassification of public emergency workers and for the omission of employment status entries; some of these adjustments had been published earlier in the report just referred to.

---

[1] See *1940 Census of Population, Estimates of Labor Force, Employment, and Unemployment in the United States, 1940 and 1930.*

[2] See John D. Durand, *The Labor Force in the United States, 1890–1960,* Appendix A.

In order to extend the series to 1950 in this study, the 1950 data adjusted to complete count totals, including estimates for persons whose employment status was not reported, have been used. When the more detailed analysis of 1940–1950 changes is made, the unadjusted, and for the most part, published statistics have been used at the national level, because it was believed that further adjustments would not have changed the relationships shown. Data for individual areas have not been adjusted at all, except that, for 1940, the estimated number of persons in the Armed Forces has been subtracted from the employed group, in order to arrive at the number of employed civilians, comparable with 1950.

Comparison of 1950 Census and Current Population Survey data

Despite the fact that population censuses in this country are carried out by field workers who are frequently part-time and intermittent workers themselves, they characteristically give an undercount of such workers. Census enumerators apparently expect most men to be working, women to be keeping house, and teen-agers to be in school; and it is presumably not always easy to ask the required set of questions to establish whether or not they are in fact in the labor force. As a result, whenever comparable data have been available for the same date collected by a more highly skilled staff, they have shown a larger number of teen-agers and married women working, and more unemployed persons. In 1940, the Work Projects Administration sample survey in 41 counties, the origin of the Current Population Survey, was conducted at the same time as the decennial census, and with substantially the same questions and instructions. The survey estimate of unemployment was 17 percent higher than the census count. In 1950, the published Current Population Survey estimate of the civilian labor force was 5 percent higher than the census count and the unemployment estimate 24 percent higher. Even the reinterviews currently conducted by the supervisory staff in the Current Population Survey as part of a quality control program tend to give a slightly higher count of the labor force, although the original interviewers are comparatively well trained.

In addition to the disparity in the experience of the field workers, other factors affect the comparability of the published statistics on the labor force from the 1950 Census and the Current Population Survey.

1. *Date of enumeration.* The decennial census relates to the population in the United States on April 1, but the labor force information was collected for the week prior to the enumerator's visit. About 70 percent of the population was enumerated by April 18 and 90 percent by the first of May. However, for only about one-quarter was the reference week for labor force activity the same as the CPS reference week—April 2 to 8. It is estimated that about 35 percent of the census returns refer to a week prior to the CPS week and about 40 percent refer to a week later than the CPS week. The possible spread is from the calendar week ending March 25 to the calendar week ending July 4.

During these weeks employment was rising, both in agriculture and in nonagricultural pursuits; unemployment was falling, at least until early June when students on vacation started to look for jobs. Theoretically, persons enumerated prior to the CPS week of enumeration would be less likely to be in the labor force than those enumerated at the same time as the CPS, and their unemployment rate would be higher; the opposite would be true for persons enumerated after the CPS for April was completed. The census enumeration was completed much later in rural areas than in urban, however, so that the group of persons enumerated later than the CPS week would be more heavily weighted with rural residents and would have a higher proportion engaged in agriculture, for example.

2. *Population controls.* The current survey sample estimates for 1950 were adjusted to independent estimates of the civilian noninstitutional population, by age and sex. (Separate adjustments were made for male veterans of World War II and all other males in the sample.) These independent estimates were prepared by projecting the total population as measured in the 1940 Census, taking account of births, deaths, estimated immigration, and emigration. From the total were subtracted an estimate of the institutional population, based on 1940 data, and an estimate of the Armed Forces, based largely on official figures from the various services.

The total population, the institutional population, and the Armed Forces, according to the 1950 Census of Population, all differed slightly in number and age composition from the projected data used to estimate the population controls for the sample. These differences alone would cause the two published measures of the labor force to differ. Also, the census data on the total labor force include members of the Armed Forces stationed in the continental United States, but not those stationed abroad. In the Current Population Survey publications, the total Armed Forces, including those overseas, are customarily added to the sample estimates to provide data on the total labor force.

3. *Sampling variability.* The Current Population Survey estimates in 1950 were based on a sample of about 23,000 interviewed households located in 68 sample areas, comprising 125 counties and independent cities and the District of Columbia. They would be expected to differ from a complete count or from any other sample of the population enumerated under the same conditions because of sampling variability alone. Many of the major estimates differ from comparable figures from the complete census count or from the 20-percent or 3⅓-percent census samples by more than could be expected solely on the basis of sampling variability, however.

Some of the sources of difference between the two sets of labor force estimates for April 1950 can be eliminated by reweighting the original CPS estimates to population controls based on 1950 Census data and adjusting the census sample data to the same complete count totals. Table

A–4 presents the original CPS estimates of the civilian labor force, by age and sex, as published, and similar census data, based on the 20-percent sample; it also shows the CPS estimates reweighted by age, sex, and color to the 1950 Census population controls as compared with 20-percent sample data from the decennial census adjusted to the complete count. The reweighted CPS estimates are slightly closer to the census figures adjusted to the complete totals in the case of males, but the opposite is true in the case of females. On the basis of the adjusted CPS figures, which are more comparable with the census figures, it can be seen that the labor force status of men between the ages of 25 and 64 and of women aged 18 to 24 is most likely to be reported consistently by two sets of enumerators. In the age groups for which enumerators tend to assume other activities for the respondent—school attendance, keeping house—and do not inquire fully about labor force activity, the differences are much greater. Respondents, too, may assume that their part-time or casual work is not to be reported in a decennial census.

TABLE **A–4.**—COMPARISON OF CENSUS AND CURRENT POPULATION SURVEY DATA ON THE LABOR FORCE, BY AGE AND SEX: 1950

Age and sex	Original civilian labor force			Adjusted civilian labor force[1]		
	Census as published (20 percent)	April CPS as published	Ratio of census to CPS	Census adjusted to complete count	April CPS adjusted to 1950 population controls	Ratio of census to CPS
Male, 14 years and over.....	42,126,325	44,120,000	95.4812	42,598,767	44,409,169	95.9233
14 to 19 years.................	2,306,915	2,795,000	82.5372	2,331,611	2,869,797	81.2465
14 to 17 years.................	1,064,370	1,429,000	74.4836	1,075,579	1,463,929	73.4721
18 and 19 years...............	1,242,545	1,366,000	90.9623	1,256,032	1,405,868	89.3421
20 to 24 years.................	4,244,615	4,678,000	90.7357	4,291,570	4,547,870	94.3644
25 to 34 years.................	10,243,225	10,499,000	97.5638	10,358,081	10,617,154	97.5599
35 to 44 years.................	9,731,525	9,820,000	99.0990	9,840,340	10,058,929	97.8269
45 to 54 years.................	7,778,755	8,126,000	95.7267	7,866,205	8,105,748	97.0448
55 to 64 years.................	5,444,785	5,743,000	94.8073	5,507,375	5,606,634	98.2296
65 years and over.............	2,376,505	2,459,000	96.6452	2,403,585	2,603,037	92.3378
Female, 14 years and over...	16,519,690	18,063,000	91.4560	16,472,888	18,114,218	90.9390
14 to 19 years.................	1,437,045	1,677,000	85.6914	1,433,299	1,687,048	84.9590
14 to 17 years.................	474,345	694,000	68.3494	472,980	692,754	68.2753
18 and 19 years...............	962,700	983,000	97.9349	960,319	994,294	96.5830
20 to 24 years.................	2,528,530	2,598,000	97.3260	2,521,757	2,599,838	96.9967
25 to 34 years.................	3,856,255	4,044,000	95.3574	3,844,561	4,092,552	93.9404
35 to 44 years.................	3,785,795	4,055,000	93.3612	3,774,483	4,121,621	91.5776
45 to 54 years.................	2,853,735	3,245,000	87.9425	2,845,724	3,195,224	89.0618
55 to 64 years.................	1,550,985	1,868,000	83.0292	1,547,038	1,806,578	85.6336
65 years and over.............	507,345	576,000	88.0807	506,026	611,357	82.7710

[1] Census data from the 20-percent sample adjusted by color and sex to complete-count totals without correction for not-reported employment status; CPS age-specific civilian labor force rates multiplied by 1950 Census population controls by age and color.

Source: Census data derived from *1950 Census of Population*, Vol. II, *Characteristics of the Population*, Part 1, U. S. Summary, tables 50, 118, and 119; CPS data from *Current Population Reports*, Series P–57, No. 94, table 6. Population controls for adjusted CPS data from *1950 Census of Population*, Vol. II, *Characteristics of the Population*, tables 38, 50, 118, and 119, and Vol. IV, *Special Reports*, Part 2, Chapter C, Institutional Population, table 3.

The major area of difference is in the classification of persons as unemployed. The adjusted census count of unemployed male workers was 79 percent of the CPS estimate, the count of unemployed female workers 84 percent (table A–5). The differences by age seem to be erratic and may be

TABLE A-5.—COMPARISON OF CENSUS AND CURRENT POPULATION SURVEY DATA ON EMPLOYMENT AND UNEMPLOYMENT, BY AGE AND SEX: 1950

Age and sex	Total			Employed						Unemployed		
				Agriculture			Nonagricultural industries					
	Census complete count[1]	April CPS adjusted to 1950 population controls[2]	Ratio of census to CPS	Census complete count[1]	April CPS adjusted to 1950 population controls[2]	Ratio of census to CPS	Census complete count[1]	April CPS adjusted to 1950 population controls[2]	Ratio of census to CPS	Census adjusted to complete count[2]	April CPS adjusted to 1950 population controls[2]	Ratio of census to CPS
Male, 14 years and over	40,510,176	41,770,426	96.9829	6,291,657	6,330,784	99.3820	34,218,519	35,439,642	96.5544	2,079,305	2,638,743	78.7991
14 to 19 years	1,995,497	2,536,061	78.6849	643,648	836,334	76.9606	1,351,849	1,699,727	79.5333	249,806	333,736	74.8514
14 to 17 years	903,872	1,302,067	69.4182	378,972	529,637	71.5532	524,900	772,430	67.9544	109,623	161,862	67.7262
18 and 19 years	1,091,625	1,233,994	88.4627	264,676	306,697	86.2989	826,949	927,297	89.1784	140,183	171,874	81.5615
20 to 24 years	3,916,492	4,139,553	94.6115	576,805	526,923	109.4667	3,339,687	3,612,630	92.4448	337,926	408,317	82.7607
25 to 34 years	9,894,823	10,062,029	98.3382	1,161,876	1,062,727	109.3297	8,732,947	8,999,302	97.0403	447,294	555,125	80.5754
35 to 44 years	9,534,991	9,628,710	99.0267	1,235,962	1,156,470	106.8737	8,299,029	8,472,240	97.9555	350,444	430,219	81.4571
45 to 54 years	7,605,784	7,690,785	98.8948	1,094,237	1,093,269	100.0885	6,511,547	6,597,516	98.6969	315,613	414,963	76.0581
55 to 64 years	5,278,894	5,241,514	100.7132	936,454	960,635	97.4828	4,342,440	4,280,879	101.4380	262,711	365,120	71.9520
65 years and over	2,283,695	2,471,774	92.3909	642,675	694,426	92.5477	1,641,020	1,777,348	92.3297	115,511	131,263	87.9997
Female, 14 years and over	15,715,164	17,222,558	91.2476	584,144	925,015	63.1497	15,131,020	16,297,543	92.8423	752,901	891,660	84.4381
14 to 19 years	1,272,088	1,562,433	81.4171	75,276	69,128	108.8936	1,196,812	1,493,305	80.1452	137,128	124,615	110.0413
14 to 17 years	395,995	631,863	62.6710	49,568	49,910	99.3148	346,427	581,953	59.5283	60,372	60,891	99.1477
18 and 19 years	876,093	930,570	94.1458	25,708	19,218	133.7704	850,385	911,352	93.3103	76,756	63,724	120.4507
20 to 24 years	2,382,464	2,439,725	97.6530	52,536	67,047	78.3570	2,329,928	2,372,678	98.1982	132,026	160,113	82.4580
25 to 34 years	3,682,450	3,896,271	94.5122	111,707	145,693	76.6729	3,570,743	3,750,578	95.2051	168,280	196,281	85.7342
35 to 44 years	3,659,820	3,939,725	92.8953	129,332	208,317	62.0842	3,530,488	3,731,408	94.6154	135,884	181,896	74.7042
45 to 54 years	2,752,650	3,060,325	89.9463	110,132	205,794	53.5157	2,642,518	2,854,531	92.5728	101,892	134,899	75.5321
55 to 64 years	1,490,272	1,735,011	85.8941	72,387	154,739	46.7801	1,417,885	1,580,272	89.7241	59,721	71,567	83.4477
65 years and over	475,420	589,068	80.7072	32,774	74,297	44.1121	442,646	514,771	85.9889	17,970	22,289	80.6227

[1] Sum of census data on employed and unemployed differs slightly from civilian labor force total in table A-4, because data for employed by age were available on complete count basis and are not based on adjusted 20-percent sample.

[2] Census data from the 20-percent sample adjusted to complete-count totals without correction for not-reported employment status; CPS adjusted labor force in table A-4 distributed by employment status within age groups on basis of original distribution.

Source: Census data on employed derived from 1950 Census of Population, Vol. II, Characteristics of the Population, Part 1, U. S. Summary, table 132; data for unemployed derived from tables 50, 118, and 119. CPS data derived from same source as table A-4.

due in part to the sampling variability of the current survey estimates. There does not seem to be any real reason why decennial and CPS enumerators would give the most consistent results for men 65 years and over or for girls 14 to 19 years of age—both age classes in which the status of being unemployed is not always clear and unequivocal.

The census count of male workers employed in agriculture is almost identical with the CPS estimate, but this is in large part because some of the census returns refer to a later period, when agricultural employment was closer to the seasonal peak. Except in the younger age groups, the census count and the CPS estimates for male workers in nonagricultural industries are very close. For female workers, the disparities are generally much greater.

Results of the census-CPS matching project

Because it was anticipated that the current survey estimates would differ from the 1950 Census counts, a matching project was planned in advance of the census. Procedures were set up for transcribing the census reports for the members of all households in the sample for the Current Population Survey in April 1950. Tabulations were then made of the employment status, occupation, industry, class of worker, and other characteristics as reported by the census and by the CPS enumerators. (A check of the coverage of population and dwelling units by the two groups was also conducted.) This project served as the only check on the employment status statistics of the census; the Post-Enumeration Survey, which provided so much information on other aspects of the census, did not include employment status questions because of the lapse of time between the census date and the Post-Enumeration Survey.

Not all households in the CPS sample could be matched with census records because families moved out of the sample dwelling units prior to the visit of the census taker, because addresses were not sufficiently precise in one set of records or the other, and for a variety of other reasons. Records for persons living in quasi-households were not matched. Altogether, records for 51,123 persons were matched. Some 1,154 persons interviewed in CPS could not be found in census records, and 1,304 reported by the census enumerator as resident in CPS households could not be found in CPS records. Unmarried college students away from home were listed at their home addresses in the CPS but at their college addresses in the census; 287 of the unmatched persons were in this group. Their exclusion from the tabulations of the matched sample accounts in part for the differences between the estimates from this sample and from the complete census count on the one hand, or the estimates from the full CPS sample on the other (see table A–6).

The results of the census-CPS matching study can be used in two ways: (1) Comparison of the gross and net differences between the two sets of data will indicate some of the sources of difference between decennial census and current survey measures of the same population groups and will provide some basis for interpreting the seriousness of the discrepancies. Because there were differences in both directions—some of the persons classified as unemployed by the census were returned as not in the labor force by the CPS, for example—it is impossible to say that one set of data was right and the other wrong. Differences in timing and in the identity of respondents also preclude such a judgment. On balance, however, the evidence seems to point to a better enumeration on the part of the CPS interviewers. Census Bureau experience has shown that a trained interviewer will make fewer assumptions and will tend to classify more persons as members of the labor force than will a novice enumerator. Hence, if the first interviewer classifies a person as unemployed and the second as keeping house, the presumption is that the first interviewer is more likely to be right. However, if the first reports her as employed and the second unemployed, there is no basis for judgment, without a third interview or some other validation.

TABLE A-6.—PERCENT DISTRIBUTION OF THE POPULATION BY EMPLOYMENT STATUS AS MEASURED BY 1950 CENSUS, CURRENT POPULATION SURVEY, AND CENSUS-CPS MATCHING STUDY, BY SEX

Employment status and sex	Employment status according to census enumerators			Employment status according to CPS enumerators			
	Census complete count	Census-CPS match		April CPS as published	Adjusted to 1950 population controls	Census-CPS match	
		Total sample	Enumerated in same week			Total sample	Enumerated in same week
MALE							
Total, 14 years and over....	100.0	100.0	100.0	100.0	100.0	100.0	100.0
Labor force........................	79.7	81.2	81.3	83.3	83.0	83.7	84.3
Not in labor force.................	20.3	18.8	18.7	16.7	17.0	16.3	15.7
Labor force....................	100.0	100.0	100.0	100.0	100.0	100.0	100.0
Employed:							
Agriculture.....................	14.8	14.4	13.9	14.2	14.3	15.1	14.9
Nonagricultural industries......	80.3	80.9	81.1	79.8	79.8	79.2	78.7
Unemployed......................	4.9	4.7	5.0	6.0	5.9	5.7	6.4
FEMALE							
Total, 14 years and over....	100.0	100.0	100.0	100.0	100.0	100.0	100.0
Labor force........................	29.2	29.1	29.0	32.1	32.1	31.6	31.7
Not in labor force.................	70.8	70.9	71.0	67.9	67.9	68.4	68.3
Labor force....................	100.0	100.0	100.0	100.0	100.0	100.0	100.0
Employed:							
Agriculture.....................	3.5	3.1	2.7	5.1	5.1	5.5	5.6
Nonagricultural industries......	91.9	92.6	92.7	90.0	90.0	89.6	88.7
Unemployed......................	4.6	4.3	4.6	4.9	4.9	4.9	5.7

Source: Derived from *1950 Census of Population*, Vol. II, *Characteristics of the Population*, Part 1, U. S. Summary, tables 50 and 55; U. S. Bureau of the Census, *Current Population Reports*, Series P-57, No. 94, table 6; and unpublished tabulations from census-CPS matching study.

(2) A second use of the matching study is to provide a basis for examining variability in response, by limiting the analysis to reports for persons enumerated in both the census and the survey during the same week. Here the factor of time reference is controlled, and the remaining

differences presumably reflect differences in enumerator performance, differences in responses, or both. Only about one-fourth of the matched sample had a common reference week, so that national estimates constructed from this group, particularly for some of the smaller categories, have relatively high sampling error. Too much reliance cannot be placed on these data for interpretation of the differences between the published or adjusted census and CPS data.

In connection with the first use—to interpret 1950 Census-CPS differences—it is important to know how well the census and CPS returns from the matched sample represent the full census or the full CPS. With respect to the major employment status categories, the full matched sample closely resembles the complete census in the case of females but has a somewhat higher proportion of males in the labor force than does the census, in part because of the omission of some college students away from home (table A–6). The estimates from the matched sample are also much like the full CPS, except that the proportion of the labor force employed in agriculture is higher in the matched sample. (The exclusion of persons in quasi-households from the matching study would be expected to result in a lower estimate of nonagricultural workers.) Differences between the matched sample enumerated in the same week and the census or the CPS are somewhat greater.

Comparisons of the census and the CPS reports for the full sample of 51,000 identical individuals (weighted to U. S. totals by age, sex, and color) are shown in tables A–7 and A–8. With respect to labor force status (in the labor force or not in the labor force), decennial and CPS enumerators classified about 92 percent of the persons in the matched sample the same way, although there were many differences within these two major classes. An estimated 2,447,000 males outside the labor force according to census enumerators were in the labor force according to the CPS; conversely, 1,106,000 males were not in the labor force according to the CPS, but were in the labor force according to the census (table A–8). These classes were even larger in the case of females: 3,069,000 in the labor force according to the CPS but not the census, 1,650,000 in the labor force according to the census but not the CPS.

The larger part of the group classified as labor force members in one enumeration but not in the other were employed in nonagricultural industries:

Persons in the labor force in one enumeration but not the other

	Male		Female	
Employment status	Labor force in census	Labor force in CPS	Labor force in census	Labor force in CPS
Employed in agriculture....	229,000	643,000	227,000	700,000
Employed in nonagricultural industries.............	606,000	1,192,000	1,097,000	1,936,000
Unemployed.............	271,000	612,000	326,000	433,000

TABLE A-7.—EMPLOYMENT STATUS OF CIVILIAN NONINSTITUTIONAL POPULATION, BASED ON REPORTS FOR IDENTICAL PERSONS ENUMERATED BY CENSUS AND CURRENT POPULATION SURVEY ENUMERATORS, BY SEX: 1950

[In thousands]

Employment status according to CPS enumerators	Population 14 years old and over	Employment status according to census enumerators									Not reported
		Civilian labor force					Not in labor force				
		Total	Employed			Unemployed	Total	Keeping house	Unable to work	Other	
			Total	Agriculture	Nonagricultural industries						
MALE											
Total...........	53,477	43,442	41,385	6,269	35,116	2,057	10,035	167	2,546	6,743	579
Civilian labor force...........	44,783	42,336	40,550	6,040	34,510	1,786	2,447	63	411	1,604	369
Employed...........	42,232	40,397	39,882	5,980	33,902	515	1,835	47	324	1,133	331
Agriculture...........	6,749	6,106	6,023	5,654	369	83	643	15	116	397	115
Nonagricultural industries...........	35,483	34,291	33,859	326	33,533	432	1,192	32	208	736	216
Unemployed...........	2,551	1,939	668	60	608	1,271	612	16	87	471	38
Not in labor force...........	8,694	1,106	835	229	606	271	7,588	104	2,135	5,139	210
Keeping house...........	106	19	15	5	10	4	87	24	36	25	2
Unable to work...........	1,580	162	113	28	85	49	1,418	17	990	399	12
Other...........	7,008	925	707	196	511	218	6,083	63	1,109	4,715	196
FEMALE											
Total...........	56,446	16,414	15,715	517	15,198	699	40,032	32,758	1,557	4,762	955
Civilian labor force...........	17,833	14,764	14,391	290	14,101	373	3,069	2,234	97	526	212
Employed...........	16,959	14,323	14,212	288	13,924	111	2,636	1,920	80	436	200
Agriculture...........	975	275	275	251	24	...	700	607	12	71	10
Nonagricultural industries...........	15,984	14,048	13,937	37	13,900	111	1,936	1,313	68	365	190
Unemployed...........	874	441	179	2	177	262	433	314	17	90	12
Not in labor force...........	38,613	1,650	1,324	227	1,097	326	36,963	30,524	1,460	4,236	743
Keeping house...........	33,774	1,396	1,143	200	943	253	32,378	30,074	861	888	555
Unable to work...........	781	8	2		6	...	773	191	479	91	12
Other...........	4,058	246	173	25	148	73	3,812	259	120	3,257	176

Source: Derived from unpublished tabulations from census-CPS matching study.

TABLE A-8.—COMPARISON OF ESTIMATES OF EMPLOYMENT STATUS BASED ON REPORTS FOR IDENTICAL PERSONS ENUMERATED BY CENSUS AND CURRENT POPULATION SURVEY ENUMERATORS, BY SEX: 1950

[In thousands]

Employment status and sex	Civilian labor force			Employed — Total			Employed — Agriculture			Employed — Nonagricultural industries			Unemployed		
	Census	CPS	Difference	Census	CPS	Difference	Census	CPS	Difference	Census	CPS	Difference	Census	CPS	Difference
MALE															
Total............	43,442	44,783	-1,341	41,385	42,232	-847	6,269	6,749	-480	35,116	35,483	-367	2,057	2,551	-494
Status in Opposite Enumeration															
Civilian labor force.......	42,336	42,336	...	40,550	40,397	+153	6,040	6,106	-66	34,510	34,291	+219	1,786	1,939	-153
Employed............	40,397	40,550	-153	39,882	39,882	...	5,980	6,023	-43	33,902	33,859	+43	515	668	-153
Agriculture.........	6,106	6,040	+66	6,023	5,980	+43	5,654	5,654	...	369	326	+43	83	60	+23
Nonagricultural industries..	34,291	34,510	-219	33,859	33,902	-43	326	369	-43	33,533	33,533	...	432	608	-176
Unemployed..........	1,939	1,786	+153	668	515	+153	60	83	-23	608	432	+176	1,271	1,271	...
Not in labor force.........	1,106	2,447	-1,341	835	1,835	-1,000	229	643	-414	606	1,192	-586	271	612	-341
Keeping house........	19	63	-44	15	47	-32	5	15	-10	10	32	-22	4	16	-12
Unable to work.......	162	411	-249	113	324	-211	28	116	-88	85	208	-123	49	87	-38
All other...........	925	1,604	-679	707	1,133	-426	196	397	-201	511	736	-225	218	471	-253
Not reported........	...	369	-369	...	331	-331	...	115	-115	...	216	-216	...	38	-38
FEMALE															
Total............	16,414	17,833	-1,419	15,715	16,959	-1,244	517	975	-458	15,198	15,984	-786	699	874	-175
Status in Opposite Enumeration															
Civilian labor force.......	14,764	14,764	...	14,391	14,323	+68	290	275	+15	14,101	14,048	+53	373	441	-68
Employed............	14,323	14,391	-68	14,212	14,212	...	288	275	+13	13,924	13,937	-13	111	179	-68
Agriculture.........	275	290	-15	275	288	-13	251	251	...	37	24	+13	...	2	-2
Nonagricultural industries..	14,048	14,101	-53	13,937	13,924	+13	37	24	+13	13,900	13,900	...	111	177	-66
Unemployed..........	441	373	+68	179	111	+68	2	...	+2	177	111	+66	262	262	...
Not in labor force.........	1,650	3,069	-1,419	1,324	2,636	-1,312	227	700	-473	1,097	1,936	-839	326	433	-107
Keeping house........	1,396	2,234	-838	1,143	1,920	-777	200	607	-407	943	1,313	-370	253	314	-61
Unable to work.......	8	97	-89	8	80	-72	2	12	-10	6	68	-62	...	17	-17
All other...........	246	526	-280	173	436	-263	25	71	-46	148	365	-217	73	90	-17
Not reported........	...	212	-212	...	200	-200	...	10	-10	...	190	-190	...	12	-12

Source: Based on table A-7.

In general, the types of employed workers who were most likely to be classified as nonworkers in the opposite enumeration were self-employed workers and unpaid family workers. Self-employed workers include some who conduct small businesses from their homes; their activity is sometimes so limited that it is often disregarded in labor force surveys. Unpaid family workers are always difficult to enumerate consistently because so much of the work they perform is considered part of their household chores and not work in a family enterprise. Persons who worked only a few hours during the week constituted a third major source of disagreement among women, but among men they were not so numerous as full-time workers who were classified as not in the labor force in the opposite enumeration (table A–9). It should be remembered that some of these differences may have represented real changes in status.

TABLE **A–9.**—CHARACTERISTICS OF PERSONS EMPLOYED IN ONE ENUMERATION AND NOT IN THE LABOR FORCE IN THE OTHER, BASED ON REPORTS FOR IDENTICAL PERSONS ENUMERATED BY CENSUS AND CURRENT POPULATION SURVEY ENUMERATORS, BY SEX: 1950

[In thousands]

Age, class of worker, and major industry group	Male			Female		
	Employed in census, not in labor force in CPS	Employed in CPS, not in labor force in census	Difference	Employed in census, not in labor force in CPS	Employed in CPS, not in labor force in census	Difference
AGE						
Total.....................	835	1,835	–1,000	1,324	2,636	–1,312
14 to 17 years..................	181	502	–321	100	278	–178
18 to 24 years..................	116	258	–142	186	281	–95
25 to 44 years..................	103	407	–304	497	1,058	–561
45 to 64 years..................	207	389	–182	448	810	–362
65 years and over..............	228	279	–51	93	209	–116
CLASS OF WORKER						
Total.....................	835	1,835	–1,000	1,324	2,636	–1,312
Wage and salary workers........	442	936	–494	818	1,323	–505
At work:						
1 to 14 hours..............	84	275	–191	161	452	–291
15 to 34 hours.............	120	223	–103	194	347	–153
35 hours or more..........	172	431	–259	348	513	–165
Hours not reported.........	66	7	+59	115	11	+104
With a job but not at work.....	118	125	–7	172	109	+63
Self-employed workers..........	209	519	–310	158	566	–408
Unpaid family workers..........	66	255	–189	176	638	–462
MAJOR INDUSTRY GROUP						
Total.....................	835	1,835	–1,000	1,324	2,636	–1,312
Agriculture.....................	229	643	–414	227	700	–473
Construction....................	95	144	–49	6	14	–8
Manufacturing...................	95	250	–155	118	216	–98
Transportation, communication, and other public utilities....	37	78	–41	21	17	+4
Wholesale and retail trade.....	108	312	–204	310	541	–231
Service industries.............	175	339	–164	464	1,091	–627
All other industries..........	10	60	–50	41	52	–11
Industry not reported..........	86	9	+77	137	5	+132

Source: Unpublished tabulations from census-CPS matching study.

Part-time and intermittent workers are most commonly found in agriculture, trade, and the service industries, and these were the industries in which workers were concentrated who were reported as not in the labor force in the opposite enumeration. Again, some of these differences may have represented real changes in status (table A–9). Much of the net difference for males arose from the greater tendency of CPS interviewers to classify teen-age boys as employed, particularly in agriculture. For females, the differences were more heavily concentrated in the age groups 25 to 64 years.

Turning to the unemployed group, we find that most of the difference between the two sets of data stems from the classification of persons as not in the labor force in one enumeration who were classified as unemployed in the other (table A–8). A fairly large number of persons in nonagricultural employment, scattered through all industries, were reported as unemployed in the opposite enumeration. However, about three-quarters of the net difference between the census and CPS measures of unemployment can be attributed to the greater tendency of CPS enumerators to identify persons as unemployed who were reported as nonworkers by the census. There is some evidence that teen-age and elderly persons were more likely than other age groups to be classified inconsistently from one enumeration to another.

The classification "unable to work" was supposed to be given to persons who could not work because of a long-term physical or mental illness or disability. No check questions were included on either the census or the current survey schedule to verify this status. In fact, if the enumerator was told that an individual was unable to work, he was instructed in both enumerations to omit the remaining questions on employment status, occupation, and industry. It was assumed that this approach would give only a rough measure of the disabled group, but the difference between the census and CPS figures was larger than anticipated. From the matched sample, 4.1 million persons were classified as unable to work according to census enumerators and 2.4 million according to the CPS. Table A–10 shows that about one-fifth of the net difference was due to the classification of persons by one or the other group of enumerators as in the labor force. The hypothesis has been advanced that the census enumerators were confused about the two categories "unable to work" and "unemployed," but the matched sample does not confirm this. Most of the differences arise from the use of different nonworker classifications—"keeping house" in the case of women and "other" nonworkers in the case of men.

All persons for whom employment status was not reported in the census were classified as not in the labor force, although some of them were probably employed or unemployed. In the matched sample, 64 percent of the males and 22 percent of the females for whom there was no report on employment status in the census were reported as in the labor force by the CPS enumerators. These estimates are not inconsistent with those developed independently by the author, which were based on the assumption that the not-reported cases had the same labor force rates as persons in comparable age-sex-color-residence-marital status groups.

TABLE **A-10.**—STATUS IN OPPOSITE ENUMERATION OF PERSONS REPORTED AS UNABLE TO WORK, BASED ON REPORTS FOR IDENTICAL PERSONS ENUMERATED BY CENSUS AND CURRENT POPULATION SURVEY ENUMERATORS, BY SEX: 1950

[In thousands]

Employment status	Male			Female		
	Unable to work		Differ-ence	Unable to work		Differ-ence
	Census	CPS		Census	CPS	
Total........................	2,546	1,580	+966	1,557	781	+776
Status in Opposite Enumeration						
Civilian labor force...............	411	162	+249	97	8	+89
Employed......................	324	113	+211	80	8	+72
Agriculture....................	116	28	+88	12	2	+10
Nonagricultural industries......	208	85	+123	68	6	+62
Unemployed.....................	87	49	+38	17	...	+17
Not in labor force.................	2,135	1,418	+717	1,460	773	+687
Keeping house..................	36	17	+19	861	191	+670
Unable to work.................	990	990	...	479	479	...
Other..........................	1,109	399	+710	120	91	+29
Not reported...................	...	12	-12	...	12	-12

Source: Based on table A-7.

As indicated in Chapter 3, the differences between the labor force participation rates of white and nonwhite men were greater in the census statistics than in the CPS, and the excess of rates for whites over those for nonwhites as shown by the census in some age groups did not appear in the current survey data (table A-11). From the matching study, the rates for identical persons in specific age groups show somewhat greater disparity in the case of nonwhite men than of white men:

	White		*Nonwhite*	
Age	*Census*	*CPS*	*Census*	*CPS*
14 to 17 years........................	25.6	33.6	37.6	46.1
18 to 24 years........................	83.2	85.9	81.9	89.6
25 to 44 years........................	95.5	97.1	91.0	94.3
45 to 64 years........................	90.3	92.0	88.3	93.1
65 years and over....................	44.4	46.0	43.7	43.9

The net difference in the white male labor force, estimated from the matched sample, was 1,100,000 or 2.3 percent of the white male population 14 years and older; for nonwhite males, the net difference was 235,000 or 4.6 percent of the population 14 and over. The sample data for nonwhite males are too unreliable to pinpoint with assurance the sources of difference between the two enumerations, particularly by age, but there is some indication that a substantial part may have arisen because the CPS enumerators tended to identify persons as unemployed whom the census enumerators called not in the labor force.

Employment status estimates from the matched sample based on reports for persons enumerated in the same week in the census and the current sample survey indicate gross and net differences of much the same character as those based on the full sample (tables A-12 and A-13). Approximately the same proportion (93 percent) were classified consistently as far as labor force status is concerned—in the labor force or not in the labor force—in the two enumerations based on the same week. Classification of persons as employed in one enumeration and as unemployed in the other may have been a somewhat larger factor in the difference in the estimates of male unemployment than was the case using the full matched sample.

TABLE A–11.—MALES IN CIVILIAN LABOR FORCE AS PERCENT OF CIVILIAN NONINSTITUTIONAL POPULATION, BY AGE AND COLOR: CENSUS AND CURRENT POPULATION SURVEY, 1950

Age	Census		April 1950 CPS	
	White	Nonwhite	White	Nonwhite
Total..........................	80.0	78.6	83.3	83.4
14 to 17 years.....................	24.3	32.1	33.1	40.9
18 to 24 years.....................	77.2	79.0	82.3	87.7
25 to 44 years.....................	94.8	91.2	96.9	94.1
25 to 34 years.................	93.6	89.5	95.9	91.7
35 to 44 years.................	96.1	93.0	98.0	96.8
45 to 64 years.................	90.0	87.5	91.7	92.9
45 to 54 years.................	93.7	90.7	95.9	97.9
55 to 64 years.................	85.3	82.2	86.5	84.5
65 years and over.................	42.5	45.3	46.0	46.6

Source: Derived from *1950 Census of Population*, Vol. IV, *Special Reports*, Part 1, Chapter A, Employment and Personal Characteristics, table 4, and unpublished tabulations of Current Population Survey data.

On the basis of the writer's experience, one of the most difficult parts of any labor force survey based on household interviews is the reporting of occupation of persons in the labor force. The kind of work a person does can be described in many different ways and, unlike many other population characteristics, a person's occupation may have no single, *correct* report. The census or survey enumerator has a few rules to follow, but for the great majority of cases he must rely on what he is told by the respondent, who frequently is not the worker himself but his wife, his mother, or his landlady. The distinctions in coding between proprietors and certain craftsmen who operate their own businesses, between managers and salesmen, between craftsmen and operatives, between operatives and laborers can hinge on the presence or absence of a phrase in the job description entered on the schedule. Comparison of the occupational returns for persons enumerated in the same week and employed both according to the census and the CPS enumerators shows that for women, who are concentrated in relatively few occupations, 90 percent were in the same major group in both enumerations. For men, however, only 77 percent were in the same major group. The greatest discrepancies in the job descriptions of men were in the professional, managerial, clerical, and farm laborer groups. The most common differences were the reporting of "census professional workers" as managerial or clerical workers by CPS; the reporting of "CPS managerial workers" as salesmen, craftsmen, or operatives by the census; and the reporting of "CPS clerical workers" as professional workers by the census (table A–14). On balance, relative to CPS enumerators, census enumerators tended to upgrade male clerical

TABLE A–12.—EMPLOYMENT STATUS OF CIVILIAN NONINSTITUTIONAL POPULATION, BASED ON REPORTS FOR IDENTICAL PERSONS ENUMERATED IN *SAME WEEK* BY CENSUS AND CURRENT POPULATION SURVEY ENUMERATORS, BY SEX: 1950

[In thousands]

Employment status according to CPS enumerators	Population 14 years old and over	Employment status according to census enumerators									
		Civilian labor force					Not in labor force				
		Total	Employed			Unemployed	Total	Keeping house	Unable to work	Other	Not reported
			Total	Agriculture	Nonagricultural industries						
MALE											
Total..............	53,477	43,478	41,289	6,046	35,243	2,189	9,999	107	2,606	6,712	574
Civilian labor force......	45,055	42,513	40,585	5,900	34,685	1,928	2,542	60	500	1,554	428
Employed...........	42,185	40,317	39,911	5,870	34,041	406	1,868	52	335	1,085	396
Agriculture.........	6,708	5,947	5,900	5,489	411	47	761	22	78	508	153
Nonagricultural industries...	35,477	34,370	34,011	381	33,630	359	1,107	30	257	577	243
Unemployed........	2,870	2,196	674	30	644	1,522	674	8	165	469	32
Not in labor force......	8,422	965	704	146	558	261	7,457	47	2,106	5,158	146
Keeping house......	113	31	15	...	15	16	82	16	44	22	...
Unable to work......	1,539	178	115	37	78	63	1,361	...	934	427	...
Other..............	6,770	756	574	109	465	182	6,014	31	1,128	4,709	146
FEMALE											
Total..............	56,446	16,384	15,629	441	15,188	755	40,062	32,927	1,457	4,635	1,043
Civilian labor force......	17,920	14,972	14,568	243	14,325	404	2,948	2,173	94	468	213
Employed...........	16,905	14,450	14,420	243	14,177	30	2,455	1,800	62	387	206
Agriculture.........	1,005	247	247	206	41	...	758	634	...	98	26
Nonagricultural industries...	15,900	14,203	14,173	37	14,136	30	1,697	1,166	62	289	180
Unemployed........	1,015	522	148	...	148	374	493	373	32	81	7
Not in labor force......	38,526	1,412	1,061	198	863	351	37,114	30,754	1,363	4,167	830
Keeping house......	33,887	1,175	921	183	738	254	32,712	30,320	816	900	676
Unable to work......	742	...	...	...	...	...	742	220	419	89	14
Other..............	3,897	237	140	15	125	97	3,660	214	128	3,178	140

Source: Unpublished tabulations from census-CPS matching study.

TABLE A–13.—COMPARISON OF ESTIMATES OF EMPLOYMENT STATUS BASED ON REPORTS FOR IDENTICAL PERSONS ENUMERATED IN *SAME WEEK* BY CENSUS AND CURRENT POPULATION SURVEY ENUMERATORS, BY SEX: 1950

[In thousands]

Employment status and sex	Civilian labor force			Employed									Unemployed		
				Total			Agriculture			Nonagricultural industries					
	Census	CPS	Difference	Census	CPS	Difference	Census	CPS	Difference	Census	CPS	Difference	Census	CPS	Difference
MALE															
Total................	43,478	45,055	-1,577	41,289	42,185	-896	6,046	6,708	-662	35,243	35,477	-234	2,189	2,870	-681
Status in Opposite Enumeration															
Civilian labor force......	42,513	42,513	...	40,585	40,317	+268	5,900	5,947	-47	34,685	34,370	+315	1,928	2,196	-268
Employed............	40,317	40,585	-268	39,911	39,911	...	5,870	5,900	-30	34,041	34,011	+30	406	674	-268
Agriculture........	5,947	5,900	+47	5,900	5,870	+30	5,489	5,489	...	411	381	+30	47	30	+17
Nonagricultural industries..	34,370	34,685	-315	34,011	34,041	-30	381	411	-30	33,630	33,630	...	359	644	-285
Unemployed......	2,196	1,928	+268	674	406	-268	30	47	-17	644	359	+285	1,522	1,522	...
Not in labor force......	965	2,542	-1,577	704	1,868	-1,164	146	761	-615	558	1,107	-549	261	674	-413
Keeping house......	31	60	-29	15	52	-37	...	22	-22	15	30	-15	16	8	+8
Unable to work......	178	500	-322	115	335	-220	37	78	-41	78	257	-179	63	165	-102
All other............	756	1,554	-798	574	1,085	-511	109	508	-399	465	577	-112	182	469	-287
Not reported......	...	428	-428	...	396	-396	...	153	-153	...	243	-243	...	32	-32
FEMALE															
Total................	16,384	17,920	-1,536	15,629	16,905	-1,276	441	1,005	-564	15,188	15,900	-712	755	1,015	-260
Status in Opposite Enumeration															
Civilian labor force......	14,972	14,972	...	14,568	14,450	+118	243	247	-4	14,325	14,203	+122	404	522	-118
Employed............	14,450	14,568	-118	14,420	14,420	...	243	247	-4	14,177	14,173	+4	30	148	-118
Agriculture........	247	243	+4	247	243	+4	206	206	...	41	37	+4	...	...	...
Nonagricultural industries..	14,203	14,325	-122	14,173	14,177	-4	37	41	-4	14,136	14,136	...	30	148	-118
Unemployed......	522	404	+118	148	30	+118	...	...	...	148	30	+118	374	374	...
Not in labor force......	1,412	2,948	-1,536	1,061	2,455	-1,394	198	758	-560	863	1,697	-834	351	493	-142
Keeping house......	1,175	2,173	-998	921	1,800	-879	183	634	-451	738	1,166	-428	254	373	-119
Unable to work......	...	94	-94	...	62	-62	...	...	...	...	62	-62	...	32	-32
All other............	237	468	-231	140	387	-247	15	98	-83	125	289	-164	97	81	+16
Not reported......	...	213	-213	...	206	-206	...	26	-26	...	180	-180	...	7	-7

Source: Based on table A–12.

TABLE A–14.—MAJOR OCCUPATION GROUP OF EMPLOYED PERSONS, BASED ON REPORTS FOR IDENTICAL PERSONS INTERVIEWED IN *SAME WEEK* BY CENSUS AND CURRENT POPULATION SURVEY ENUMERATORS, AND CLASSIFIED AS EMPLOYED BY BOTH, BY SEX: 1950

[In thousands]

Major occupation group according to CPS enumerators	Total	Major occupation group according to census enumerators										
		Profes-sional, techn'l, and kindred workers	Farmers and farm managers	Managers, offi-cials, and pro-prietors, exc. farm	Clerical and kindred workers	Sales workers	Crafts-men, foremen, and kindred workers	Opera-tives and kindred workers	Service workers, incl. private house-hold	Farm laborers and foremen	Laborers, exc. farm and mine	Occupa-tion not re-ported
MALE												
Total employed in both census and CPS	39,911	2,821	4,186	4,766	2,619	2,380	7,393	8,371	2,437	1,611	2,911	416
Professional, technical, and kindred workers	2,453	2,157	...	109	39	8	78	23	...	...	8	31
Farmers and farm managers	4,284	...	3,767	23	8	8	31	39	...	330	47	31
Managers, officials, and proprietors, exc. farm	5,575	150	17	3,990	164	296	413	228	132	10	72	103
Clerical and kindred workers	2,831	296	8	125	2,040	78	39	100	55	...	75	15
Sales workers	2,277	31	24	148	101	1,802	23	62	...	8	23	55
Craftsmen, foremen, and kindred workers	7,086	109	85	164	62	23	5,559	709	36	33	257	49
Operatives and kindred workers	8,504	31	23	111	117	101	869	6,518	26	72	581	55
Service workers, incl. private household	2,605	31	...	39	...	23	101	106	2,149	8	132	16
Farm laborers and foremen	1,499	...	228	16	...	...	20	26	...	1,083	73	53
Laborers, exc. farm and mine	2,727	...	27	41	80	41	252	544	39	67	1,628	8
Occupation not reported	70	16	7	...	8	...	8	16	...	...	15	...
FEMALE												
Total employed in both census and CPS	14,420	1,595	73	463	4,525	1,409	230	2,671	3,108	163	65	118
Professional, technical, and kindred workers	1,523	1,445	...	8	29	15	8	...	10	...	...	8
Farmers and farm managers	64	...	41	...	...	...	...	...	...	23	...	...
Managers, officials, and proprietors, exc. farm	637	23	...	346	77	92	8	8	61	...	...	22
Clerical and kindred workers	4,505	92	...	38	4,212	92	15	...	25	...	...	31
Sales workers	1,396	...	...	23	115	1,179	8	15	48	...	...	8
Craftsmen, foremen, and kindred workers	193	...	...	15	...	...	107	71	...	...	...	...
Operatives and kindred workers	2,746	8	...	...	61	15	77	2,512	18	...	47	8
Service workers, incl. private household	3,148	17	9	33	31	16	7	41	2,926	27	...	41
Farm laborers and foremen	156	10	23	...	...	...	...	...	10	113	...	...
Laborers, exc. farm and mine	42	...	...	...	...	...	...	24	...	...	18	...
Occupation not reported	10	...	...	...	...	...	...	...	10	...	...	...

Source: Unpublished tabulations from census-CPS matching study.

workers to professional and downgrade managerial workers and proprietors to salesmen and craftsmen.

In summary, the net difference of 3.5 million between the census count and the adjusted CPS estimate of the civilian labor force is the result of many gross differences in classification, reflecting both changes in status between the two visits and incorrect reports in one or the other enumeration. The census-CPS matching study shows that for the great majority of the population—92 percent—the census and CPS enumerators reported consistently on labor force status, that is, whether or not a person was in the labor force. This occurred even though the experience, terms of employment, and many other operating conditions under which the two sets of enumerators worked were vastly different. Where there was disagreement, it was not always in the same direction. But when the two sets of reports for identical persons are balanced, the CPS interviewers were found to have uncovered more evidence of labor force activity among self-employed workers, unpaid family workers, and wage and salary workers working less than full time. These were employed chiefly in agriculture, retail trade, and service industries. Most of the shortage of unemployed workers in the census data as compared to the CPS reports was among persons classified as nonworkers by the census enumerators, although about one-quarter of the difference was the result of classifying persons as employed rather than unemployed.

Adjustment of CPS data to decennial census levels

In order to extend the historical series to a date in the midfifties, ratios were computed to adjust the 1955 estimates from the Current Population Survey to a decennial level. These ratios are based on the differences observed in 1950 and assume, of course, that differences of the same relative magnitude, and in the same direction, would persist through time. This assumption was made for lack of a better one. Actually, with the improvements in the training and control of the current survey interviewers that have been inaugurated since 1950, the differences might be even greater. The greater importance of married women workers whose attachments to the labor force are somewhat more tenuous than those of men would also probably enhance the difficulties of consistent enumeration and lead to wider disparities than in 1950.

The adjustment ratios have been computed separately for white and nonwhite men and women, in five-year age groups, although the relative sampling error of the data for the smaller groups may be extreme. Moreover, the CPS data were not tabulated by five-year age groups in 1950, so that interpolation was necessary. It is believed that the major categories by age and color are sufficiently useful to justify the detailed computation of the adjustment.

Civilian labor force participation rates by age, color, and sex were computed from the CPS data for April 1950 and multiplied by the 1950

Census civilian noninstitutional population in the appropriate age-sex-color groups. These estimates were compared with comparable figures from the 1950 Census, corrected for persons not reporting on employment status, and adjusted to complete count totals. Adjustment factors were computed to bring the CPS data on the 1950 population base to the census level. These factors were then applied to the CPS civilian labor force figures for April 1955 by age, color, and sex. Estimates of the Armed Forces in the continental United States were added to obtain data for the total labor force on a basis comparable with the 1950 Census. Labor force participation rates were computed, using the total, rather than the institutional, population as a base.

The adjustment ratios are shown in table A–15. It should be emphasized that the best estimates of the 1955 labor force are the unadjusted data from the Current Population Survey, and the best estimates of change from 1950 to 1955 are also those derived from comparisons of CPS data for the two dates. The "decennial census level" data for 1955 should be used only in connection with decennial data to measure changes for periods for which current survey data are not available.

TABLE **A–15.**—FACTORS USED TO ADJUST CURRENT POPULATION SURVEY ESTIMATES OF CIVILIAN LABOR FORCE TO CENSUS BASE, BY AGE, COLOR, AND SEX

Age	Male		Female	
	White	Nonwhite	White	Nonwhite
14 to 19 years	.8395353	.8473370	.8705514	.8649815
20 to 24 years	.9554664	.9155120	.9842688	.9442864
25 to 34 years	.9834515	.9811598	.9606533	.8891573
25 to 29 years	.9833747	.9865078	.9730059	.8902389
30 to 34 years	.9835290	.9754847	.9469576	.8880240
35 to 44 years	.9873142	.9679609	.9201480	.9576134
35 to 39 years	.9843413	.9725586	.9014078	.9559219
40 to 44 years	.9906013	.9628783	.9398971	.9596557
45 to 54 years	.9828355	.9291690	.9042906	.8626566
45 to 49 years	.9853857	.9341671	.9234867	.8819369
50 to 54 years	.9799706	.9230067	.8817389	.8372548
55 to 64 years	.9908743	.9750548	.8766064	.7834673
55 to 59 years	.9902742	.9600751	.8707266	.7806722
60 to 64 years	.9916557	.9984813	.8855219	.7879877
65 years and over	.9263914	.9487351	.8618752	.6805633

Source: Derived from table A–3 and unpublished tabulations of Current Population Survey data.

Sampling variability

Most of the data presented in this study are based on samples, rather than on complete counts of the population. Information on the sample design and estimates of the sampling variability of 20-percent data from the 1950 Census of Population may be found in *1950 Census of Population*, Vol. II, *Characteristics of the Population*, Part 1, U. S. Summary, pp. 65 and 66; and in Parts 2 through 49 (State volumes), pp. XXVIII and XXIX. Similar material for the 3⅓-percent sample appears in each report based on that sample; for estimates of the sampling variability of the labor force data, see *1950 Census of Population*, Vol. IV, *Special Re-*

ports, Part 1, Chapter A, Employment and Personal Characteristics, pp. 1A–17 and 1A–18.

Estimates of the sampling variability of the statistics from the Current Population Survey are included in each published report presenting the survey results. The sample was redesigned and expanded from 68 to 230 areas in 1954, and from 230 to 330 areas in 1956. Accordingly, no single table of standard errors is applicable to data for all years. Estimates of the sampling variability of the major estimates for months prior to February 1954 may be found in *Current Population Reports,* Series P–57, No. 139; for months from February 1954 to April 1956, Series P–57, No. 166; and for months since May 1956, the current month's report in Series P–57. Estimates of the sampling variability of the annual averages are included in *Current Population Reports,* "Annual Report on the Labor Force," Series P–50.

A P P E N D I X   B

TECHNICAL NOTE ON PROJECTIONS

Tables B–1 through B–4 of this appendix present the four projections for the years 1960–1975. The method of estimating Projections I and II is an adaptation of the method used to prepare the earlier labor force projection published in the Bureau of the Census *Current Population Reports*, Series P–50, No. 42. This involves computation of the average annual rate of change between two base dates in the proportion of each age group in the labor force and calculating future estimates on the assumption that this rate of change will continue. (The formula used for computation is the so-called "compound interest" formula.) In age groups showing increasing proportions in the labor force, this method could lead eventually to impossible rates, in excess of 100 percent. For such age groups, therefore, the rates of change in the proportions *not* in the labor force were used to project for future dates.

TABLE **B–1.**—PROJECTION I—ESTIMATED TOTAL LABOR FORCE AND LABOR FORCE PARTICIPATION RATES, BY AGE AND SEX: ANNUAL AVERAGES, 1955 TO 1975

[Current survey levels. Projection of the average annual change in age-specific labor force participation rates from 1920 to the average of April 1954, 1955, and 1956]

Age and sex	Total labor force (thousands)					Labor force participation rates				
	1955 (actual)	1960	1965	1970	1975	1955 (actual)	1960	1965	1970	1975
Both sexes, 14 years and over.................	68,899	73,190	79,179	86,228	93,385	58.0	57.9	57.7	58.0	58.8
Male, 14 years and over....	48,040	49,947	52,974	56,832	60,856	82.3	81.0	79.3	78.7	78.9
14 to 19 years.................	3,378	3,898	4,903	5,220	4,994	49.0	47.5	46.1	44.7	43.4
20 to 24 years.................	4,832	5,085	6,054	7,798	8,663	89.5	89.3	89.1	88.9	88.7
25 to 34 years.................	11,462	10,855	10,757	12,098	15,079	96.5	96.5	96.6	96.6	96.6
35 to 44 years.................	10,835	11,351	11,466	10,834	10,729	96.9	96.9	97.0	97.0	97.0
45 to 54 years.................	8,879	9,686	10,191	10,667	10,766	95.1	95.2	95.4	95.5	95.6
55 to 64 years.................	6,129	6,469	6,965	7,561	7,923	86.4	86.3	86.2	86.1	86.0
65 years and over.............	2,525	2,603	2,638	2,654	2,702	38.5	36.5	34.6	32.8	31.1
Female, 14 years and over..	20,859	23,243	26,205	29,396	32,529	34.5	35.9	37.2	38.5	39.8
14 to 19 years.................	1,987	2,318	2,944	3,178	3,079	29.7	29.2	28.8	28.3	27.9
20 to 24 years.................	2,458	2,657	3,286	4,341	4,995	45.8	47.6	49.3	50.9	52.5
25 to 34 years.................	4,266	4,215	4,325	5,068	6,580	34.8	36.9	38.9	40.8	42.7
35 to 44 years.................	4,814	5,412	5,755	5,636	5,755	41.4	44.2	46.8	49.3	51.7
45 to 54 years.................	4,160	4,924	5,552	6,110	6,410	43.5	46.1	48.7	51.0	53.3
55 to 64 years.................	2,394	2,798	3,280	3,865	4,346	32.2	34.4	36.6	38.7	40.8
65 years and over.............	780	919	1,063	1,198	1,364	10.3	10.6	10.9	11.1	11.4

Source: U. S. Bureau of the Census, *Current Population Reports*, Series P–50, No. 69, table 1.

TABLE **B-2.**—PROJECTION II— ESTIMATED TOTAL LABOR FORCE AND LABOR FORCE PARTICIPATION RATES, BY AGE AND SEX: ANNUAL AVERAGES, 1955 TO 1975

[Current survey levels. Projection of rates of change in annual average labor force participation rates from 1950 to 1955]

Age and sex	Total labor force (thousands)					Labor force participation rates				
	1955 (actual)	1960	1965	1970	1975	1955 (actual)	1960	1965	1970	1975
Both sexes, 14 years and over..................	68,899	73,372	79,442	86,604	93,705	58.0	58.1	57.9	58.3	59.0
Male, 14 years and over....	48,040	49,751	52,536	56,213	60,104	82.3	80.7	78.7	77.9	77.9
14 to 19 years.................	3,378	3,771	4,651	4,897	4,638	49.0	46.2	43.7	41.9	40.3
20 to 24 years.................	4,832	5,022	5,912	7,518	8,253	89.5	88.2	87.0	85.7	84.5
25 to 34 years.................	11,462	10,889	10,802	12,186	15,220	96.5	96.8	97.0	97.3	97.5
35 to 44 years.................	10,835	11,398	11,549	10,946	10,873	96.9	97.3	97.7	98.0	98.3
45 to 54 years.................	8,879	9,737	10,276	10,801	10,934	95.1	95.7	96.2	96.7	97.1
55 to 64 years.................	6,129	6,552	7,143	7,834	8,292	86.4	87.4	88.4	89.2	90.0
65 years and over..............	2,525	2,382	2,203	2,031	1,894	38.5	33.4	28.9	25.1	21.8
Female, 14 years and over..	20,859	23,621	26,906	30,391	33,601	34.5	36.5	38.2	39.8	41.1
14 to 19 years.................	1,987	2,280	2,878	3,100	2,993	29.7	28.7	28.2	27.6	27.1
20 to 24 years.................	2,458	2,595	3,125	3,976	4,413	45.8	46.5	46.9	46.6	46.4
25 to 34 years.................	4,266	4,088	4,097	4,724	6,026	34.8	35.8	36.8	38.0	39.1
35 to 44 years.................	4,814	5,391	5,712	5,568	5,666	41.4	44.0	46.5	48.7	50.9
45 to 54 years.................	4,160	5,252	6,180	7,039	7,558	43.5	49.2	54.2	58.8	62.8
55 to 64 years.................	2,394	3,049	3,755	4,614	5,336	32.2	37.5	41.9	46.2	50.1
65 years and over..............	780	966	1,159	1,370	1,609	10.3	11.1	11.9	12.7	13.4

Source: U. S. Bureau of the Census, *Current Population Reports*, Series P–50, No. 69, table 2.

TABLE **B-3.**—PROJECTION III—ESTIMATED TOTAL LABOR FORCE AND LABOR FORCE PARTICIPATION RATES, BY AGE AND SEX: ANNUAL AVERAGES, 1955 TO 1975

[Current survey levels. For males 14 to 24 years and females 14 to 34 years of age, projection of rate of change in annual average labor force participation rates from 1950 to 1955; for other age groups, projection of rate of change in labor force participation rates from 1920 to the average of April 1954, 1955, and 1956]

Age and sex	Total labor force (thousands)					Labor force participation rates				
	1955 (actual)	1960	1965	1970	1975	1955 (actual)	1960	1965	1970	1975
Both sexes, 14 years and over..................	68,899	72,773	78,330	84,838	91,397	58.0	57.6	57.1	57.1	57.5
Male, 14 years and over....	48,040	49,757	52,580	56,229	60,090	82.3	80.7	78.7	77.9	77.9
14 to 19 years.................	3,378	3,771	4,651	4,897	4,638	49.0	46.0	43.7	41.9	40.3
20 to 24 years.................	4,832	5,022	5,912	7,518	8,253	89.5	88.2	87.0	85.7	84.5
25 to 34 years.................	11,462	10,855	10,757	12,098	15,079	96.5	96.5	96.6	96.6	96.6
35 to 44 years.................	10,835	11,351	11,466	10,834	10,729	96.9	96.9	97.0	97.0	97.0
45 to 54 years.................	8,879	9,686	10,191	10,667	10,766	95.1	95.2	95.4	95.5	95.6
55 to 64 years.................	6,129	6,469	6,965	7,561	7,923	86.4	86.3	86.2	86.1	86.0
65 years and over..............	2,525	2,603	2,638	2,654	2,702	38.5	36.5	34.6	32.8	31.1
Female, 14 years and over..	20,859	23,016	25,750	28,609	31,307	34.5	35.6	36.6	37.5	38.3
14 to 19 years.................	1,987	2,280	2,878	3,100	2,993	29.7	28.7	28.2	27.6	27.1
20 to 24 years.................	2,458	2,595	3,125	3,976	4,413	45.8	46.5	46.9	46.6	46.4
25 to 34 years.................	4,266	4,088	4,097	4,724	6,026	34.8	35.8	36.8	38.0	39.1
35 to 44 years.................	4,814	5,412	5,755	5,636	5,755	41.4	44.2	46.8	49.3	51.7
45 to 54 years.................	4,160	4,924	5,552	6,110	6,410	43.5	46.1	48.7	51.0	53.3
55 to 64 years.................	2,394	2,798	3,280	3,865	4,346	32.2	34.4	36.6	38.7	40.8
65 years and over..............	780	919	1,063	1,198	1,364	10.3	10.6	10.9	11.1	11.4

Source: U. S. Bureau of the Census, *Current Population Reports*, Series P–50, No. 69, table 3.

TABLE **B-4.**—PROJECTION IV—ESTIMATED TOTAL LABOR FORCE AND LABOR FORCE
PARTICIPATION RATES, BY AGE AND SEX: ANNUAL AVERAGES, 1955 TO 1975

[Current survey levels. Projection of 1955 labor force participation rates]

Age and sex	Total labor force (thousands)					Labor force participation rates				
	1955 (ac- tual)	1960	1965	1970	1975	1955 (ac- tual)	1960	1965	1970	1975
Both sexes, 14 years and over....................	68,899	72,298	77,446	83,686	89,782	58.0	57.2	56.5	56.3	56.5
Male, 14 years and over....	48,040	50,191	53,554	57,828	62,231	82.3	81.4	80.2	80.1	80.7
14 to 19 years.................	3,378	3,992	5,196	5,742	5,694	49.0	48.6	48.9	49.2	49.5
20 to 24 years.................	4,832	5,096	6,082	7,851	8,741	89.5	89.5	89.5	89.5	89.5
25 to 34 years.................	11,462	10,855	10,746	12,086	15,064	96.5	96.5	96.5	96.5	96.5
35 to 44 years.................	10,835	11,351	11,455	10,823	10,718	96.9	96.9	96.9	96.9	96.9
45 to 54 years.................	8,879	9,675	10,159	10,623	10,709	95.1	95.1	95.1	95.1	95.1
55 to 64 years.................	6,129	6,477	6,981	7,588	7,960	86.4	86.4	86.4	86.4	86.4
65 years and over.............	2,525	2,745	2,935	3,115	3,345	38.5	38.5	38.5	38.5	38.5
Female, 14 years and over..	20,859	22,107	23,892	25,858	27,551	34.5	34.2	33.9	33.9	33.7
14 to 19 years.................	1,987	2,347	3,030	3,359	3,329	29.7	29.6	29.6	29.9	30.2
20 to 24 years.................	2,458	2,557	3,053	3,906	4,357	45.8	45.8	45.8	45.8	45.8
25 to 34 years.................	4,266	3,975	3,869	4,323	5,362	34.8	34.8	34.8	34.8	34.8
35 to 44 years.................	4,814	5,069	5,091	4,733	4,609	41.4	41.4	41.4	41.4	41.4
45 to 54 years.................	4,160	4,647	4,959	5,211	5,232	43.5	43.5	43.5	43.5	43.5
55 to 64 years.................	2,394	2,619	2,886	3,215	3,430	32.2	32.2	32.2	32.2	32.2
65 years and over.............	780	893	1,004	1,111	1,232	10.3	10.3	10.3	10.3	10.3

Source: U. S. Bureau of the Census, *Current Population Reports*, Series P–50, No. 69, table 4.

The detailed procedure used for each projection follows:

1. *Projection I.*   Average annual rates of change in age-specific labor force rates between 1920[1] and the average of April 1954, 1955, and 1956 were computed.   As a preliminary step, the 1920 labor force participation rates for women in the age groups 14 to 44 years were standardized by marital status, using as a standard the marital status distribution of the female population in 1955, in order to eliminate from the estimates of changes in labor force rates the effects of changes in the proportion of women who were married.   This procedure also assumes, in effect, that the 1955 distribution of the female population by marital status would remain substantially unchanged for the next 20 years; a similar assumption was made for the previous projection, using the 1950 marital status distribution (*Current Population Reports,* Series P–50, No. 42).   In Projection II, allowance was made for projected changes in marital status (see later).

The rates of change computed for men and women were then used to project the annual average labor force participation rates for 1955 to obtain data for each fifth year up to 1975.   The use of annual averages, the average of 12 observations from the Current Population Survey, eliminates the effect of seasonal variation and reduces somewhat the sampling variability of the estimates.   If the present projections, like the earlier

---

[1] The data for 1920 were the original "gainful worker" statistics from the decennial census, adjusted roughly to make them comparable with the current labor force data.

ones, had projected data for April of each year, they would have been lower by perhaps 1 million or more.

In this and the other projections, estimates of the absolute numbers in the labor force were obtained by multiplying the projected labor force participation rates for each age-sex group by the projected population for July of each year, using in each case the Series A projection as published in *Current Population Reports*, Series P–25, No. 123. The use of any of the other population projections would not have changed the size of the projected labor force materially since the only age group affected by the varying assumptions about fertility is the 14-to-19-year group, beginning in 1970. The maximum difference would be about 725,000 in the 1975 labor force using Projection IV rates. With the Series AA population projection, this would be an increase; with the Series C projection, it would be a decrease.

It should be noted that the Census Bureau population projections do not allow for declines in mortality after 1960. To the extent that this is an unrealistic assumption, the size of the labor force among older age groups (but not the labor force participation rates) may be understated in these projections.

2. *Projection II.* This projection starts with annual average participation rates in 1950 and 1955 and projects the rates of change observed between the two years. The original data for 1950 from the Current Population Survey were in the form of sample estimates inflated to current population totals by age and sex, developed by extrapolating 1940 Census data to 1950. When the 1950 Census age statistics became available, it appeared advisable to substitute them for the earlier sample controls. The 1950 labor force data used in these computations, therefore, are revisions of those originally published in the *Monthly Report on the Labor Force*, Series P–57.

a. *Data for males.* Between 1950 and 1953 the Armed Forces were built up for the Korean conflict, and as a result the increase in labor force participation rates of males 20 to 24 years of age was much sharper than would be expected in subsequent five-year periods. A preliminary adjustment was made, therefore, in the 1950 average to raise the labor force by the number it was estimated would have been in the labor force if the Armed Forces had been at the 1953 level. The 1950 data for males 20 to 24 years and 25 to 34 years were also adjusted upward to compensate for the unusually large school enrollment of World War II veterans in that year. Both these adjustments had the effect of reducing the rate of increase between 1950 and 1955 shown by the original data.

It was possible, in this projection, to compute separate rates of change for the age groups 14 and 15, 16 and 17, and 18 and 19 years. Because of the changes in the relative size of the population in these age groups during the five-year base period, the use of rates for the separate groups was more satisfactory than would have been the rate for the group 14 to 19 years as a total. The projections to 1975 were made by detailed age groups; the rate for the age group 14 to 19 years is, therefore, based on the sum of the absolute figures derived from the detailed projections, divided by the total in the broad age group.

b. Data for females. In order to reflect the impact on the labor force of changes in the proportions of the female population who are married, the data for females were projected in three groups: single, married–spouse present, and all others. Until recent years, data on labor force participation by marital status were available only once a year, usually in April; since December 1954 this information has been collected each month. Thus it was possible to compute the annual average participation rates for 1955 by age and marital status, and to estimate the annual averages for 1950 on the basis of the relationship in 1955 between the annual average and the data for a single month. The distribution of the 1950 annual averages by marital status thus estimated was adjusted to add to the actual annual average for all women, by age. (As with the data for men, the original estimates were revised to reflect final 1950 Census statistics on the population by age.) The 1950–1955 rates of change in the annual average labor force participation rates by age and marital status were then projected from 1955 to 1975.

The projected labor force rates were multiplied by the appropriate population projections for single, married–spouse present, and other women, prepared in connection with household and family projections published by the Bureau of the Census in *Current Population Reports,* Series P–20, No. 69. Marital status projections underlying the Series II household projections were used as a basis for the labor force projections, since they assumed that the average annual rates of change in the percent single between 1950 and 1955 would continue until 1975—an assumption similar to that used in computing labor force Projection II. For single women, the age groups 14 to 17 years and 18 and 19 years were projected separately and then combined to give estimates for the total group 14 to 19 years.

It should be noted that labor force rates computed separately by marital status for Projection II, when combined to provide a rate for each age group, did not differ in any important way from rates that did not take marital status into account specifically. This would not have been the case if the direction and magnitude of the projected changes in the population by marital status had differed substantially from the direction and magnitude of the changes observed during the base period (1950–1955) for computing the change in labor force rates.

3. *Projection III.* The labor force participation rates developed for Projection II were used for the age groups 14 to 19 and 20 to 24 years for men, and for age groups 14 to 19, 20 to 24, and 25 to 34 years for women. The rates developed for Projection I were used for the remaining age groups.

4. *Projection IV.* Annual average labor force participation rates observed in 1955 were extended to 1975 without change. Within the age group 14 to 19 years, separate estimates were made for the groups 14 and 15 years, 16 and 17 years, and 18 and 19 years.

5. *Estimate of working mothers.* Because responsibility for the care of young children is an important factor in determining whether or not a married woman will enter the labor force, it would have been desirable to construct projections of the labor force separately for women with children and those without. This procedure would also have made it possible to take account of the differences in assumptions about future birth rates that underlie the various population projections. Unfortunately, sufficiently reliable data are not available on which to base projections of the number of women with children, by age, or the labor force participation rates of women with children, by age. Information from the Current Population Survey for a few dates, however, has been used to make rough estimates of the number of mothers of young children who might be in the labor force, assuming Projection II levels of labor force participation of women who are or have been married. The following estimation procedure was used:

Estimates of the ratio of children under 5 years of age to women ever married (married, widowed, or divorced) under 45 years, by age, were available from the April 1952 Current Population Survey. These data were projected forward on the basis of the rate of change in the total number of children under 5 in the population, according to the Series AA and A population projections. Estimates of women with and without young children were derived for 1960, 1965, 1970, and 1975, based on the projected number of women ever married by age at future dates developed in connection with the preparation of the Series II household projection and used for labor force Projection II by marital status.

Data on the labor force status of women ever married by age, with and without children under 6, were available from the Current Population Survey for April 1955. The proportions of women ever married in the population and in the labor force with children under 6 for April were applied to the annual average population and labor force to estimate the groups with children under 5. Those without children were obtained by subtraction from the total.

For 1950, data from the 1950 Census of Population were used (adjusted to an annual average basis) to provide information for women with and without children under 5.[2] The proportion of married women in the labor force with children under 6 from the 1950 Census was almost identical with the comparable proportion from the Current Population Survey for March 1950, although the labor force participation rates from the Current Survey were, of course, higher.[3] Therefore, it was decided to use the

---

[2] *1950 Census of Population*, Vol. IV, *Special Reports*, Part 5, Chapter C, Fertility, table 35.

[3] *1950 Census of Population*, Vol. IV, *Special Reports*, Part 2, Chapter A, General Characteristics of Families, table 12.

1950 Census proportions of women ever married in the labor force with children under 5 to estimate the number of working mothers by age in the annual average labor force for 1950, already estimated on the basis of Current Population Survey data.

Because the sampling variability of the estimates for women without children was less, the 1950–1955 changes in the labor force rates of this group were projected to 1975; the number of women in the labor force with young children was obtained by subtraction from the total women ever married in the labor force according to Projection II. The procedure used for estimating the number of working mothers is obviously rough and could understate the actual increase that may occur. Nevertheless, it is probably sufficiently reliable to indicate that, assuming Series AA or A fertility rates, the projected female labor force in these age groups cannot be achieved without a marked increase in the participation rates of women without children under 5 (but with older children in many cases), and some further increase in the labor force participation of women with preschool-age children.

TABLE **B–5.**—LABOR FORCE PARTICIPATION OF MARRIED, WIDOWED, AND DIVORCED WOMEN, BY AGE: ANNUAL AVERAGES, 1955 TO 1975

[Current survey levels. Projection of rates of change in annual average labor force participation rates from 1950 to 1955]

Age and marital status	Total labor force (thousands)					Labor force participation rates				
	1955 (actual)	1960	1965	1970	1975	1955 (actual)	1960	1965	1970	1975
MARRIED, WIDOWED, AND DIVORCED WOMEN										
Total, 14 years and over...	15,272	18,018	20,730	23,805	27,004	31.0	34.3	36.8	39.0	40.7
14 to 19 years..................	249	300	400	469	469	26.7	26.4	26.1	25.8	25.4
20 to 24 years..................	1,237	1,355	1,662	2,218	2,573	32.8	34.3	35.2	35.9	36.6
25 to 34 years..................	3,291	3,300	3,366	3,918	5,073	29.8	31.7	33.2	34.6	36.1
35 to 44 years..................	4,159	4,803	5,177	5,167	5,333	38.6	42.0	44.8	47.6	50.2
45 to 54 years..................	3,630	4,751	5,717	6,582	7,153	40.9	47.5	53.1	58.1	62.5
55 to 64 years..................	2,067	2,698	3,414	4,254	4,974	29.8	35.5	40.4	44.9	49.1
65 years and over..............	639	811	994	1,197	1,429	9.2	10.1	11.0	11.8	12.7
MARRIED WOMEN, HUSBAND PRESENT										
Total, 14 years and over...	10,813	12,614	14,626	16,886	19,282	28.5	31.8	35.0	38.1	40.9
14 to 19 years..................	194	227	301	351	348	24.7	24.2	23.7	23.3	22.8
20 to 24 years..................	1,009	1,036	1,243	1,629	1,861	30.1	30.2	30.3	30.4	30.5
25 to 34 years..................	2,652	2,617	2,686	3,146	4,096	26.5	28.1	29.6	31.1	32.6
35 to 44 years..................	3,241	3,749	4,111	4,162	4,345	34.4	37.9	41.2	44.4	47.3
45 to 54 years..................	2,539	3,367	4,138	4,839	5,323	35.4	42.0	48.0	53.3	58.1
55 to 64 years..................	1,008	1,415	1,910	2,487	2,998	21.6	28.2	34.2	39.8	44.8
65 years and over..............	170	203	237	272	311	6.6	6.8	7.0	7.2	7.4

Source: U. S. Bureau of the Census, *Current Population Reports*, Series P–50, No. 69, table 5.

APPENDIX C

SOME PROBLEMS OF CONCEPTS
AND MEASUREMENT

Development of present labor force concepts

The terms "labor force" and "labor force concepts" have been used in this study to relate only to the statistics produced through the decennial population census or the monthly Current Population Survey of the Bureau of the Census. Prior to 1940, the decennial census traditionally obtained a count of gainful workers, in answer to a question on occupation. Information was recorded for all persons 10 years of age and older. There was no particular time reference; seasonal workers, retired workers, and others whose attachment to the labor force may have been a thing of the past could have been reported as gainful workers along with persons currently at work full time or part time. New entrants into the labor force were not included. The 1930 Census instructions to enumerators warned them not to report occupations for persons no longer following an occupation on account of old age, permanent invalidism, or other reasons, or for persons who worked only occasionally or only a short time each day. Like many instructions, these were not always followed.

Under the gainful-worker concept, the occupational description was another demographic characteristic, like educational attainment, which served to classify the population into socio-economic groups. It provided a measure of the quality and general skills of the population—skills that might or might not be currently in use.

The change from the gainful-worker to the labor force concept is by now a familiar story. The Great Depression of the 1930's ran its course without a satisfactory statistical measurement of its greatest human and political problem—unemployment—but with extensive arguments over how to measure the problem. Toward the end of the decade, after a variety of experiments in individual States and cities and one nationwide survey, the 1937 Census of Unemployment, a generally acceptable set of concepts and procedures was developed.

These concepts had as their focus the *activity* of a person during a single calendar week and depended on a chain of priorities. Identification of the employed was essential to the identification of the unemployed, and the two groups together constituted the civilian labor force. In practice, the following groups were identified in sequence: (1) all persons who did any work for pay or profit (including unpaid work in a family business or on a family farm, except for incidental chores); (2) all persons who did not work but who were looking for work or were on emergency work relief programs; (3) all persons who did not work or look for work because (*a*) they had a job or business from which they were temporarily absent for reasons of vacation, illness, bad weather, etc.; (*b*) they were temporarily ill or on indefinite layoff, or they believed no work was available in the community or in their line of work. Groups 1 and 3*a* made up the employed, groups 2 and 3*b* the unemployed. The remainder of the population was considered to be outside the labor force and was classified as engaged in its own home housework, in school, unable to work, retired or voluntarily idle, or in institutions. Members of the Armed Forces were sometimes considered employed and sometimes as a third major category in the labor force.

In short, employed persons were those with jobs—either working at jobs or with claims to jobs apparently so firm that they were not looking for others. Unemployed persons were those who did no work at all but were looking for work or whose search for work was temporarily interrupted because of illness, postponed because they expected to be called back to their former jobs, or abandoned because of belief that no work was available. The labor force, then, consisted generally of all persons who during a given week had a job or were in search of one.

Much of the experimental work that led to the adoption of these concepts was done with public relief funds, in the framework of a national policy directed toward providing work relief for needy, employable persons without jobs. In the planning and administration of that program, there was a constant demand for a measure of the number of jobs that were required in the economy to take care of the jobless and the proportion of those jobless who were actually in need of relief. Accordingly a set of concepts that were oriented around the possession of a job at any given time was a logical one.

At the time of the preparatory work for the 1940 Census of Population, unemployment was still a major national problem, and in some areas a critical problem. The decennial census was considered an appropriate tool for providing information on unemployment in every type of area throughout the country and for delineating the characteristics of the unemployed in great detail. That many of the decennial statistics would quickly become outdated by the elimination of the unemployment problem seemed highly unlikely. The apparent need for statistics on this problem made it obviously desirable to change from the general gainful-worker concept to the carefully defined, activity-based labor force concept with a narrow time reference.

Adoption of these concepts for the 1940 Census of Population was agreed upon at about the same time that they were being tested for the first recurring survey of a sample of the population—the so-called Monthly Report on Unemployment, conducted by the Work Projects Administration.   The subsequent transfer of that survey to the Bureau of the Census in August 1942 consolidated under one sponsorship the decennial and monthly enumeration of the population, providing a tool for measuring both short-run, month-to-month changes in the economic activity of the entire population and longer-run trends in various social and demographic characteristics.

Meaning of labor force

The term "labor force" itself was originally used by the National Industrial Conference Board and other estimators of unemployment during the 1930's as synonymous with the total number of gainful workers.   It was essentially the "working population" or some equivalent that did not change in size except as the population and its basic characteristics changed.

> The labor force, viewed as a reservoir of potential workers having gainful occupations, must of necessity have an inertia with respect to its size and growth.   That is to say, the number of available persons on call plus the number engaged in remunerative pursuits does not fluctuate with business swings.   Each year there is an outflow of workers from the force through emigration, death, retirement, physical disability and the like; but there is also an inflow through immigration, increased age of young people, termination of education, increasing remunerative occupations for women, and so forth.   Underlying these flows in and out of the labor force are such basic factors as a changed standard of living, increased mechanization, population, age composition and growth.[1]

With such a concept, employment and unemployment had to move in opposite directions, for unemployment was the residual obtained by subtracting estimates of current employment from an almost stable labor force.   In fact, the idea that employment and unemployment could increase (or decrease) simultaneously because of seasonal changes in the size of the labor force was regarded as a piece of statistical nonsense by most nontechnical users of the current estimates until a few years ago.

Some of the early unemployment surveys had used the concept of persons "able and willing to work" as a crude measure of labor supply and had attempted to divide this total (obtained by direct questioning) into those who were already employed and those who were not—the latter then to be classified as unemployed.   The heterogeneity and vagueness of this latter category—those who were able and willing to work but not working —made it hard to defend as a measure of unemployment.   The notion of measuring the labor supply, or the unused portion of the labor supply as a residual, was abandoned.   National and local policy at that time required a measure of unemployment that would be equated with the minimum number of jobs needed.   There was no demand for a measure of total labor

---

[1] Leonard, Kuvin, *Conference Board Bulletin*, "Revised Estimates of Employment and Unemployment," National Industrial Conference Board, Inc., Vol. XII, No. 8, July 30, 1938.

supply as such, probably because labor supply seemed abundant for all possible demands. What was important was to distinguish the active, current, "legitimate" job seekers from all other persons who, under different circumstances, might become job seekers or might have been job seekers.

When the current activity concepts were finally accepted, the term "labor force" was used to describe the sum of the employed and the unemployed during a single week. With this definition, the idea was abandoned that the labor force was a slowly changing body of workers responsive chiefly to changes in population. Perhaps the greatest contribution that the monthly statistics on the labor force have made to knowledge of the behavior of the American people has been their demonstration of the flexibility of the working population. The amount of movement into and out of the labor force from week to week or year to year, the potential expansion or contraction in size under changing military demands, and the characteristics of persons entering or withdrawing in response to variations in demand had never been imagined prior to 1940.

In the system of labor force concepts, the labor force itself is a by-product. It has no independent definition or identification. Persons are not tagged as members of the labor force and then queried about their employment status. Rather, the labor force can be arrived at only as a summation of the various components—(1) persons at work, (2) those looking for work, and (3) those not looking for work but with a job attachment. (Members of the Armed Forces on active duty are also included in the total labor force whenever appropriate; definition of the civilian labor force is not affected by their treatment.) Apparently when the employment and unemployment concepts were developed, the only formulation of the labor force as an independent concept was a rather vague one—the total number of persons "exerting pressure in the labor market for jobs." Persons who had jobs even if they did no work or received no pay were to be counted as employed because they were not exerting pressure for other jobs. Only persons trying to find other jobs were to be classified as unemployed.

This summation of the number of persons with jobs and the number seeking them during a given week—the labor force—is being used in many ways, for example, to measure the current demand for jobs; the supply of and demand for labor; the population subject to unemployment, retirement, occupational hazard; the population engaged in some form of economic activity; and so forth. No single measurement could be expected to serve every purpose equally well. Hence, a brief review of the suitability of the present concept for some of its various uses might be in order before proceeding to discuss problems of measurement.

A measurement of the current demand for jobs is essential for the operation of the present Federal policy on employment, as expressed in the Employment Act of 1946. Under this Act, Congress declared that it was the Federal Government's responsibility to use all practicable means

to create and maintain conditions under which "there will be afforded useful employment opportunities, including self-employment, for those able,
willing, and seeking to work, and to promote maximum employment, production, and purchasing power." This suggests that national policy would
require information on the total number of jobs needed to accommodate
all would-be employed—those with jobs and those seeking them. In the
President's letter transmitting a reorganization plan for the Council of
Economic Advisers in 1953, the objective is restated.

> The legislative history of the Employment Act of 1946 makes it clear that it is the
> determination of the Congress to help develop a strong economy in the United States.
> . . . A strong economy means a free economy. . . . It means a stable economy—so
> that satisfying jobs are as numerous as the men and women seeking work, and the pro-
> duction of goods is abundant to meet our needs.[2]

Demand for jobs, to be recognized as such, must be expressed by some
action on the part of the worker; a person who wants to have a job but
makes this desire known to no one, makes no effort to inquire about jobs,
or, in short, does nothing that can be described as looking for work has
little reason to be counted among those in the market for a job. The
shortness of the time period of the labor force concept—working or seeking work during a calendar week—sharpens the measure of demand and
adds specificity. Members of the labor force are persons who have jobs
or who have made "bids" for jobs during a specified period and are still
available. Those who do not have jobs—the unemployed—constitute the
unfilled demand.[3]

The labor force as a measure of the current labor supply has some defects. If by labor supply we mean that part of the population that has
been drawn into the labor market, that is "job-oriented" in a broad sense,
and that is immediately and actively available for paid employment, then
a count of the labor force does provide some measure of labor supply. It
is not a measure of *total* labor supply except in the sense of the number of
workers who are or could be engaged immediately. Presumably, outside
the current labor force are many women and some men who could be put
to work tomorrow if communication could be established and they could
be offered exactly the right kind of job, or the appropriate arrangements
to take care of their other obligations. But because they have not taken
that critical step of looking for work or are not looking for work during
the week of reference, their availability is still speculative. As we shall

---

[2] Committee Print, 83d Congress, 2d Session—Employment Act of 1946, As Amended, and Related
Laws (60 Stat. 23), Public Law 304—79th Congress.

[3] Until 1957, persons on temporary layoff with definite instructions to return to work within 30 days
and persons who had made arrangements to start a new job within 30 days were classified as employed
—"with a job but not at work." Beginning in February 1957, their classification was changed to unemployed. (Persons who had arranged to start a new job but were still in school were to be classified
as not in the labor force.) It was decided to classify them as unemployed because their claims to jobs
during the survey week were somewhat dubious and their inability to work at their jobs generally reflected unfavorable economic factors.

see, at the margin it is sometimes difficult to distinguish between those who are in the labor force and those who are not, but for a large majority the distinction is clear.

It must be admitted that this concept tends to provide a minimum measurement of the number of individuals in the immediately available labor supply. And this is consistent with its origin—the need for a measurement of the number of required jobs. On the other hand, because in its crude form it gives as much weight to a family head working full time as to a teen-age babysitter who works three hours on Saturday night, the present concept of the labor force may give an exaggerated indication of changing labor supply, when part-time workers become proportionately more or less numerous. However, all crude measures are subject to weaknesses of this kind, and the survey apparatus that provides the data for classification of the population in and out of the labor force can also provide the further information to separate full-time from part-time workers.

Because the present set of labor force concepts has served pretty well as a framework for analyzing unemployment, and because an abundance of data based on these concepts has become available over the past 15 years, the use of the measurement of the current labor force to indicate supply has become customary. Projections of the labor force for future dates have been undertaken to provide estimates on the supply side for the further estimation of gross national product and other measures of economic activity. Variations among areas in the proportion of the population in the labor force have been used to indicate variations in the supply of experienced workers, in the degree of industrialization, and in comparative employment opportunities. The size of the population not in the labor force has been taken as a measure of available, uncommitted manpower, particularly in wartime.

For all these purposes, however, it can be argued that a concept with a broader base would have been more suitable. What is wanted, perhaps, is not just the number of persons who are working or looking for jobs at a single point in time, but those who have worked or tried to get work and are still available, and those who will become available with very little encouragement at an early date. In other words, the ideal measurement of current labor supply for many analytical purposes might include all persons who would be willing to work at something like current wage rates (including the potentially self-employed) and who are either at work, or available for jobs, except for temporary or accidental factors. This would include most seasonal workers in the offseason, married women who want a job but are not seeking one at the moment, women who have temporarily left the labor force because of family responsibilities, persons who have become discouraged about finding a job, those who are temporarily ill, etc. It would not include persons in full-time school, women who have family responsibilities of a long-range nature, those who do not want to work outside the home, the permanently retired, the seriously disabled, and the chronically ill.

The drawback of such a concept is that it is virtually impossible to translate into a measurement with any of the tools available at present. Experience with the measurement of availability for work has been discouraging, because of the large amount of speculation and personal opinion involved and because people tend to indicate some interest in gainful work if subjected to a series of questions on this point.

More important, perhaps, has been the strictness of the present concepts in which a member of the labor force who is not employed must be classified as unemployed. Vigorous objections have always been raised at the notion of calling a person unemployed who is only interested in working but who is not seeking work at a specific time. However, if the concept of labor supply could be separated entirely from the idea of unemployment, and if it were recognized universally that in the labor supply were employed and unemployed persons as now defined, plus other categories of potential workers, some progress toward a broader concept might be made. Its usefulness would be not as a current, economic indicator but as an occasional inventory of the population.

On the other side of the labor supply coin is labor demand. But the number of persons in the labor force is both an overstatement and an understatement of the demand for labor, for it includes workers without jobs, the unemployed, and can take no account of the number of persons who would be employed if possible recruits could be found to fill all the unfilled jobs. The *employed* sector of the labor force, its size and distribution among population groups, occupations, and industries, does, of course, reflect both the nature of the demand for labor that has been met and the supply of labor that is being utilized.

Although changes in the gross totals in the labor force have utility, one of the most satisfactory uses of the labor force measure is as a count of persons exposed to a risk such as the risk of unemployment. Here the currency of the measurement is a positive advantage, for the numerators of the rates are for the most part based on current classifications. For example, unemployment rates are computed by relating the persons unemployed in a current week to all persons in the labor force with similar characteristics that week. Unemployment rates by sex and age are computed by relating the number of unemployed men and women in specific age groups to all men and women in the labor force (the unemployed plus the employed) in those age groups during the given week. Thus the risk of being unemployed during the week is related to the precise group exposed to unemployment that week, not to persons who might have been exposed at some time over a period of weeks or months.

Again, unemployment rates by industry are computed by relating the number of unemployed persons whose last full-time job was in a specified industry to the sum of all persons employed in that industry during the week, plus the unemployed from that industry. In some ways, this gives a truer picture of the current incidence of unemployment by industry than could be obtained if the employment in the industry were for an earlier date, or at some time during a longer period but not necessarily at a current date. In a prolonged depression, however, the last job may have little relation to the usual job or to the job from which the worker was originally laid off; additional information on job history is needed for meaningful analysis at such times.

The one-week time reference of the labor force concept may be too restrictive for the analysis of occupational mortality rates, morbidity rates by occupation, and retirement rates by occupation or industry. However, for 90 percent or more of the employed the current job is the same as the longest job during an adjacent calendar year, so that many such diagnostic rates could be usefully computed with the current labor force as a base.

Analysis of the economic activity of the population concerns itself very often with examining changing patterns in relation to personal and family characteristics. For this purpose, a simple, two-way classification is needed which summarizes into one class persons who are currently in the economically productive group, and into the other class those who are not. The groups on which attention is generally focused—married women, school-age children, older workers—are usually not year-round full-time workers but move in and out of the labor force. Marital status and family status are current classifications; to relate them to economic activity in a period when there is a good deal of turnover, the analyst wants the current labor force status of the population. It is true that no single week will necessarily reflect the maximum or minimum extent of activity of any group, so that a weekly average over the year is to be preferred; but for any given week the marital status, family status, school enrollment, place of residence, or whatever factor is being examined, and the labor force activity are consistent. Conceivably, meaningful results could be obtained by examining *usual* activity in relation to these factors, but the vagueness of meaning of *usual* might offset the gains in widening the time reference. For example, the proportion of married women who usually work or look for work might be somewhat larger (or smaller) than the proportion in the labor force last week, but there would be many whose classification of "usually working" would be based on past history prior to marriage or on future hopes, not on the actual situation at the time of the inquiry.

For some purposes, the economic activity of the population is more adequately measured in terms of the distribution of income rather than by current employment status. To understand some of the reasons for differences in income, the analyst needs data on employment, or other activities, over the time period in which the income was being received—that is, over the course of a year. (In 1956, the Bureau of the Census inaugurated what it hoped would be an annual survey tying together work experience over a year and income for that year.) Many personal characteristics, of course, do not change. The relationship of income to race or to the sex of the recipient is unaffected by whether the characteristics are recorded for a week ago or for a year ago. Age, too, and educational attainment are only slightly affected. But marital status, family status, residence, occupation, and industry may change over a year. Thus, although the use of annual income or earnings data may offer many advantages over a classification based on one week, they are not free of other problems.

Finally, it should be remembered that the employment and unemployment concepts were developed for use as current indicators in a setting where measurement of change was of prime importance. Their adoption for use in a decennial census, as has been indicated, came about largely because of the desire for data on unemployment. Under present conditions of large-scale census taking in a country as vast as the United States, there is some question about whether the decennial census, characteristically an inventory of the population, is the vehicle for collecting timely information on unemployment. It would be possible to give high priority to the processing of the unemployment reports if this were held to be essential, but in a period of serious recession or developing unemployment, the data would tend to be out of date as measurements even if available within a few weeks or months of collection. Their primary usefulness is as a one-time reading of the employment status of the total labor force against which can be computed ratios for recurring statistics from other sources, such as unemployment insurance or payroll reports. These ratios can then serve to construct synthetic estimates of total employment, total unemployment, and the labor force for local areas and States in intercensal years.

As the unemployment insurance systems expand their coverage, the need for measures of total unemployment at benchmark dates may disappear. The labor force concept, whose unique value derives from its use in connection with the measurement of unemployment, may not be ideal for census purposes at that point. Perhaps a concept that would give a measurement of activity over a whole year so that seasonal factors would be eliminated would provide better benchmark data. For general analytical purposes, the number of persons who had done some gainful work during the preceding year, or 12-month period, or who had worked a minimum amount during that period would be useful. For individual areas, such a count would provide information on the characteristics and skills of a more extensive group than is included in the present labor force and should be free from seasonal influences which at present may introduce incomparabilities that are unknown in magnitude, as between one area and another.

One drawback is that such a measure of economic activity would have no relation either to current labor force measures or to data from other sources. Typically, employment reports from employers' payrolls refer to a specified pay period, in most cases a single week. Unemployment insurance statistics also relate to the number of beneficiaries during a single week. Where decennial census figures are used to develop relationships between the total labor force and segments that are measured currently by other sources, the use of an annual employment concept by the census might be unsatisfactory.

Another drawback has been indicated above. Some persons who worked at any time during the past 12 months or the preceding calendar year may have worked only in the early part of the period. Since then, they may have retired permanently, married and left the labor force, had a child and given up a job, gone back to full-time school, or left the labor force for other reasons. Over a 12-month period, major changes can take place in a person's life or in that of his family. Hence all the relationships of economic activity with current characteristics would become somewhat cloudy.

It is believed that a combination of two types of concepts would provide the best solution for decennial census purposes if both current and longer-run measures are desired. Persons in the current labor force plus those who have been in the labor force at some time during a longer period in the past might constitute the economically active population for census benchmark statistics.

Comparability of labor force concepts of employment and unemployment with other concepts

The urgent need for a generally acceptable measure of unemployment that would supersede the many conflicting estimates of business, labor unions, and various government sources led to the development of the labor force concepts and the establishment of the monthly sample survey. There is no evidence that the question of comparability with other measures of employment or unemployment was in the minds of the technicians who worked on this problem. The major emphasis seems to have been given to the development of a meaningful classification of the population on the basis of objective criteria, such as activity, that would give a defensible count of job seekers. The rigid activity criteria—working or seeking work—did seem likely to yield an incomplete count of persons with jobs or in the market for jobs, however. Accordingly, the classification was expanded to include, as employed, persons who were temporarily absent from their jobs but not seeking other ones and, as unemployed, certain persons whose search for work had been interrupted or become temporarily inactive. Most of these employed persons who had jobs but were not at work would not have appeared on an employer's payroll at that time, when paid vacations and paid sick leave benefits were relatively uncommon. The important point is that additional jobs were not needed for them; hence the lack of comparability with other measures of employment was disregarded, if considered at all.

The classification scheme was based not on *major* activity but on a series of priorities—working taking precedence over looking for work, and looking for work over having a job but being absent all week. Thus any work for pay or profit (including unpaid family work over and above incidental chores) would classify a person as employed. This simple and rather arbitrary procedure happened to be consistent with payroll reporting systems. Critics of the labor force concepts, who object to calling a person employed who works a few hours a week and spends the rest of the week looking for work, tend to ignore the fact that he would also appear in establishment statistics as employed. It must be admitted that the priority scheme in the past would have led to some understatement of the number of persons out of work for part of a specific week, but the information on part-time work now collected each month in the Current Population Survey provides the basis for adjustment, if needed. The questions on reason for working part time identify those persons who have been laid off during the week or, for some reason reflecting adverse economic conditions, have worked only part of a week. They can be combined with the unemployed or analyzed separately; this procedure makes it unnecessary for the respondent and interviewer to decide whether employment was the major status during the week. (In the Canadian labor force survey, the same system of priorities is observed, but persons who worked for less than 35 hours during the week are also asked whether they are looking for work.)

The State unemployment insurance systems had not been in operation very long at the time the present labor force concepts were developed, so the question of comparability with other unemployment figures probably did not arise. The "actively seeking work" test was common to both, but the inclusion of the "inactive" unemployed in the labor force concept was inconsistent with insurance definitions.

The United States, at the present time, has a wealth of statistics on the economic activity of its population: current statistics on the whole population of working age from the monthly sample survey of households (the Current Population Survey), statistics on those persons in business and industry who are reported on the payrolls of a sample of establishments (the Bureau of Labor Statistics series), statistics on persons working on farms, operated by a sample of farmers (the Agricultural Marketing Service series), and statistics on persons receiving unemployment benefits (the Bureau of Employment Security series). With the development of these statistics, users of the labor force and establishment or administrative data and even the general public have increasingly emphasized the need for comparability among the various series.[4] In part, this demand for similarity has arisen because people were puzzled when the statistics on

---

[4] In 1954, the Director of the Office of Statistical Standards of the U. S. Bureau of the Budget appointed a committee to make a review of the concepts used in current employment and unemployment statistics. The committee sought the opinions of as many users as possible and received many replies raising the question of comparability. Gladys Palmer points out, however, that the current concern over lack of agreement among the various series is mild compared with the confusion about the meaning and measurement of unemployment that existed prior to 1940.

employment or unemployment from different sources moved in opposite directions. It was thought that if all concepts were the same, differences would be eliminated. The demand for comparability has also come from technicians in the States and local areas who had no current data on the total labor force but were attempting to estimate the labor force from current establishment or administrative statistics.

Payroll data on nonfarm employment include all persons who draw any pay (whether or not they worked) for a specified pay period, usually a week but not necessarily a calendar week. A given individual may appear on more than one payroll during a pay period, if he holds more than one job or if he changes jobs, and thus may be counted more than once. In population-survey data, employed persons are those who do any work during a given calendar week or who are absent from their jobs all week and not seeking other jobs. Each person is counted once and only once. Not all persons on payrolls actually work any hours during the week (because of paid vacation, paid sick leave, etc.) and, conversely, not all persons who have jobs are on payrolls during a given week. Persons working in their own business or their family's business without pay are, of course, not counted in payroll statistics; they may be estimated from household statistics on the basis of other information about the job. More important, persons who report that they have jobs from which they are absent all week because of illness, vacation, bad weather, labor dispute, and other miscellaneous reasons are counted as employed in labor force statistics but only those receiving pay would be included in payroll statistics.

It is sometimes argued that the labor force concept should be altered to agree with payroll concepts, without much consideration of the losses. Changes in payroll counts between one week and the next may reflect layoffs or new hires, strikes, weather conditions, the vacation period, seasonal fluctuations, inventory shutdowns, natural catastrophes—in other words, both economic and noneconomic factors. Of this list only those factors involving separation of an individual from any form of employment or, conversely, the addition of an individual to the list of jobholders are reflected in the count of persons with jobs (working and not working) as measured by population surveys. Seasonal, cyclical, and secular changes affect the total number of employed persons, but temporary factors usually leave the total unchanged.

From the standpoint of usefulness of the data, then, the population survey concepts may add something which the establishment data cannot provide, since the reason for absence of a person's name from a payroll cannot easily be ascertained. Obviously, payroll data are important and essential for many purposes, chief among them the measurement of fluctuations in income of wage earners in individual industries. When the number of names on payrolls drops, it is clear that there has been a drop in earnings, and this is a fact of major importance in economic analysis. It does not mean, however, that there has been a corresponding increase in unemployment or that changes have taken place in the underlying demand for workers.

To meet the need for measurement of change in the basic demand for workers, a series of data concerning the number of persons with jobs is perhaps more useful than one showing changes in the number receiving pay. Occasional studies have shown that as many as 2.5 million workers may be absent from their jobs during a calendar week on an unpaid basis, and this number must fluctuate widely with the bad weather and the vacation seasons.[5]

On a seasonally adjusted basis, payroll counts and estimates of total wage and salary employment from household surveys would tend to show the same pattern of movement except for accidental factors, such as large-scale strikes (strikers are counted as employed in the population surveys), hurricanes and other disasters, and other nonrecurring events affecting the number of persons on payrolls. This is true, provided there are not at the same time changes in the numbers of persons with more than one job. Thus, an increasing number of two-job workers would appear as an increase in the total payroll count but not in the number of employed workers. Unfortunately, very little has been known about changes in multiple job holding, except from a few Bureau of the Census surveys. (Regular annual surveys were instituted in 1956.) Accordingly, when payroll and household data cannot agree in trend after adjustment for coverage, seasonality, etc., it is not possible to say whether the lack of agreement stems from sampling or reporting errors in one or both series, from changes in dual job holding, or from faulty seasonal adjustments.

Because with payroll statistics it is possible to compile detailed and relatively accurate data on type of industry, hours, earnings, and other data descriptive of the individual industry, they are a much better source of material for analysis of labor input or other aspects of productivity, of comparative earnings, or of any problem requiring that all persons on the payroll of a specific industry during the reference period be included. In population-survey statistics, much of this detail is impossible or too expensive to collect from direct interview; moreover, a person with two jobs is classified in the industry of his major job, so that a total count of all persons doing any work in a specified industry is usually not available unless special questions are asked. Thus, there are advantages in both types of data—population and payroll data—which should not be thrown away in order to achieve superficial consistency.

In the unemployed sector of the labor force, the question of comparability arises in connection with the count of persons drawing unemployment insurance (insured unemployment) and of all unemployed persons as

---

[5] Beginning in mid-1956, the Bureau of the Census recorded in the Current Population Survey whether or not a person who was absent from his job all week was receiving pay. Seasonal patterns are emerging from these data.

measured by the population survey (total unemployment). It would appear advantageous to define total unemployment in such a way that all persons drawing benefits and thus adjudged unemployed by an administrative agency are included. But the administrative system is really many systems. States vary in their requirements for eligibility, reasons for dis-qualification, seeking-work tests, and other aspects of the complicated process of determining whether or not a man is entitled to draw benefits at any given time.[6] Some States allow benefits to persons who are em-ployed, but at extremely low earnings (partial or part-total benefits); but a person who does any work at all is not classified as unemployed in the population survey. Some persons who are not seeking other jobs are eligible for benefits—persons who have not yet accumulated rights to paid vacations but must take unpaid vacations when a whole plant shuts down at the vacation season; persons in outdoor jobs that are temporarily af-fected by bad weather, etc. It may be argued that during the week of reference these persons, for all practical purposes, had no jobs. How-ever, in a population survey, they are asked if they had a job, and if they answer "yes," they are classified as employed (providing they are not look-ing for another job). And from the standpoint of assessing the number of new jobs that are needed in the economy to take care of the unemployed, it is largely true that these persons are already provided for.

A more puzzling type of discrepancy stems from the failure of some persons to report themselves to the survey interviewers as looking for work, although they are drawing unemployment compensation. This is not a serious problem except in periods of substantial withdrawal from the labor force—notably, for example, after World War II. On their way out of the labor force, many women claimed their unemployment insurance but made no serious effort to search out another job. Many World War II veterans also took advantage of their rights to readjustment allowances to rest awhile and survey the scene. Such persons were not looking for work in the popular sense and were generally reported to the survey in-terviewers as "taking it easy."

Again, it appears to the writer that much is gained from having both sets of data on unemployment. From the standpoint of measuring cur-rent unused labor supply that needs to be put to work, there seems to be no obvious advantage to the policy maker in the inclusion of persons on unpaid vacation or temporarily unable to work because of bad weather. Also, if persons are using up their unemployment benefits but are not seeking other jobs and are not likely to accept them if offered, they are not in the market for jobs or in the current labor force in any real sense. Therefore, to press the labor force concept of unemployment into the mold of the insurance statistics concept would distort the significance of the measurement of total unemployed.

---

[6] Herbert Parnes, "Unemployment Data from the Employment Security Program," in *The Measure-ment and Behavior of Unemployment,* National Bureau of Economic Research, Princeton University Press, 1957.

The preceding discussion relates primarily to the nonfarm labor force. Statistics on farm employment can be obtained from household surveys or from farmers themselves reporting on their own and their family's work and the work of hired workers on their farm.   The latter are "establishment" reports, with the reporting unit the farm; like nonfarm payroll statistics they provide a count of "filled positions" and not an unduplicated count of persons engaged in farm work.   On a current basis, establishment data on farm employment are compiled from a sample of crop reporters by the Agricultural Marketing Service of the U. S. Department of Agriculture.   Benchmark statistics of the same nature are provided by the quinquennial Censuses of Agriculture.   Because of the rather large number of workers who work on more than one farm in the busy season and are, theoretically, counted more than once in statistics originating from farms, there may be substantial discrepancies between population and establishment reports of farm employment.[7]   A further reason for difference stems from the fact that the labor force concepts require a person to be classified in only one category.   Therefore, if a person does both farm and nonfarm work during the week (an increasingly common arrangement for farm workers), he must be classified in one or the other and is customarily recorded in the type of work at which he spent most of his working time.   Establishment reports would include this person as a farm worker, regardless of any other job he might have.   Again, from the standpoint of measuring total labor input in farming (by type of farm, crop, etc.), establishment statistics on farm employment are preferable to population statistics.

If it were not for the information on family and personal characteristics that can be obtained from a population survey, statistics on farm employment from this source would have somewhat limited value as economic measures.   The increasing tendency of farm operators to have a nonfarm job as well means that the agricultural employment statistics from the labor force survey measure only changes in the number of persons whose *major* job during a week was in agriculture.   Because of temporary weather conditions, as well as seasonal factors, a change in the number of persons employed in agriculture is reported in the labor force survey, whereas the actual number may have been unchanged, or the change may have been considerably smaller than indicated.   It is possible, of course, with the addition of questions on dual employment in the Current Population Survey, to measure and take account of this expansion in off-the-farm work; but without such questions, the population statistics on agricultural employment may fall increasingly short of the complete total.   They are essential, however, in measuring the level and composition of total employment and the labor force, and thus in completing the picture of the economic activity of the population.

---

[7] The establishment statistics generally do not have a minimum age at 14 as the population survey statistics have had since 1940.   The inclusion of children under 14 in the farm employment figures may add a million or more at peak months.

Special problems in classification

Payroll statistics are not without their problems, but the basic count of the number of different names on a payroll during a specific pay period is comparatively simple and clear-cut. In population surveys, on the other hand, it is sometimes difficult to elicit the necessary information on which to base a classification; and, what is perhaps a more serious problem, it may not be possible to determine unequivocally what the classification should be. The controversial groups consist of intermittent or occasional workers, seasonal workers, and others who may or may not be in the labor force and unemployed when they are not working. These include family members who from time to time help out in the family business or on the family farm; married women who cannot work full time the year round but who take jobs as their family responsibilities permit or who undertake to earn pin money by selling on commission, dressmaking at home for pay, etc.; boys and girls going to school or college and carrying part-time jobs; semi-retired persons who need income or an activity, and work or seek to work at odd jobs or in some form of light work; seasonal workers qualified or interested only in work at certain times of the year—Christmas, Easter, the canning season, the fishing season, etc.; workers attached to one industry only; persons who want to work but whose efforts to find a job are mild and spasmodic; and workers of marginal employability.

Persons of these types present no real problems of classification while they are at work, although the fact they are working may require some diligence to discover. Farm housewives may not think of their farm chores as work, and women who do certain types of paid work at home (baby sitting, dressmaking, keeping boarders) may not report such activities because to them work means leaving home and going to an office or a factory. In an experimental program, the Bureau of the Census has tried the device of reading to a respondent a list of activities considered work, or of handing her a list to check. Marginal activities of the type described are brought to light as a result of the listing—marginal in the sense of taking only a few hours time and yielding only small amounts of money, or none at all in the case of farm chores. It is clear that if it is deemed important to get a complete count of persons doing only small amounts of work and to include them in the labor force, there are techniques for doing so.

At this time, techniques for determining that a person is unemployed have not been developed to the satisfaction of all users. Looking for work, the major criterion of unemployment, is defined as making efforts to find a job during the survey week or waiting to hear the results of some work-seeking activity undertaken within the preceding 60 days. Also to be classified as unemployed are the "inactive" groups: persons who would have been looking for work except that (1) they were temporarily ill, (2) they were on layoff, or waiting to start a new job, or (3) they believed no work was available in their line of work or in the community. This last clause is the most difficult of all to interpret, for although it was intended to cover workers in stranded communities, it can be taken to describe someone who never looked for work as well as any former job seeker who for many months may not have tried to find work.

For occasional and intermittent workers, job seeking may be halfhearted or not take place at all when work is plentiful and the employer seeks the employee. In connection with evaluating its measure of unemployment, the Census Bureau has questioned persons about their desire for work and their efforts to find work. Many reply that they want work but have not done anything specific about looking for work, or that they have looked in the recent past but at the moment are not available or interested. In other words, many of these intermittent workers do not stay in the current labor force but clearly move in and out. Generally, it is possible to distinguish between the one status and the other.

Others, such as certain seasonal workers or persons who work in a particular industry and nowhere else, present different problems. Presumably, if work were available in their trade, they would be employed, yet they do not look for other work. In some cases, as in some fishing or farming areas, there is no other work during the offseason; in other cases, as in centers of the garment industry, there is other work in the community but not in the specific occupation of the garment workers. Is it correct to call such persons in the current labor force and unemployed when they appear to be in the labor force only of a particular industry and are not looking for other work? For the most part they are probably eligible for unemployment insurance. The answer seems to be to some extent a question of *time*. A person who is laid off from a job may reasonably be thought of as a member of the labor force if he expects to go back to work in the comparatively near future. But if months go by during which he makes no effort to find other work, either by changing his occupation or his residence, it no longer seems reasonable to call him a member of the current labor force.

In between persons who work only occasionally and those who are firmly attached to a single industry and would prefer to work all the time is a group whose labor force activity may be extremely difficult to determine at any given time. They want to work and they may look for work actively for a time, but then their activity subsides. If a suitable job were offered, they would take it; or if they could arrange their home responsibilities, they would try again to find a job. These are not the chief earners of a family but other members who have not recently been part of the year-round labor force. The reader must know married women, for example, who would like to find an interesting or an easy job, or one that has a part-time schedule or is near home. Their search for work may be spasmodic— inquiring among friends, calling former employers, answering ads—until they find the suitable job. Weeks may go by without any kind of activity, or with interest at a low ebb. At what point have they entered the labor force? Should they be classified as unemployed through all these weeks, beginning with the first effort to find a job? They may or may not tell survey interviewers that they are looking for work, depending on the recency of their last effort and the intensity of their interest in paid employment at the time of interview. They are likely to report interest and activity, if asked probing questions.

A fourth type of problem is presented by the person of somewhat limited employability because of age, physical or mental condition, temperament, or lack of skill. Such persons may want to work or need to work but may have such difficulty finding a job that they give up the search. At this point, under present concepts and definitions, there is no provision for classifying them as unemployed and in the labor force. In times of business recession, this type of marginal worker has usually been the first to be laid off. As they are, in a sense, forced out of the labor force, the apparent size of the labor force will decrease. The number of persons for whom jobs are needed will be understated. Some of the decline in the proportion of men aged 65 and over in the labor force between 1930 and 1940 is generally attributed to this factor of discouragement.

These four groups present problems of classification in times of high employment. In times of depression or in depressed areas, the last group widens to include all kinds of workers who become discouraged after seeking work unsuccessfully for a long time. Some actually withdraw from the labor force voluntarily but continue to want to work, although they may give up the active search.

Undoubtedly, problems in labor force classifications will become relatively more numerous with the increasing employment of married women and the complex labor force attachments that are developing. Even though many women may hold full-time jobs when they do work, their greater tendency to move in and out of the labor force with changing family responsibilities and other factors will mean that the line between workers and nonworkers will be hard to draw in a large fraction of cases. The growing number of retired and semi-retired persons in the population will also tend to increase the frequency of problem cases in labor force classification.

APPENDIX D

SELECTED TABLES

TABLE D–1.—POPULATION AND LABOR FORCE, BY AGE, COLOR, AND SEX: 1890 TO 1955

[Adjusted data—decennial census levels. In thousands. Asterisk (*) denotes figures obtained by interpolation of data tabulated for different age groups]

Age, color, and sex	Labor force							Population						
	1890	1900	1920	1930	1940	1950	1955	1955	1950	1940	1930	1920	1900	1890
ALL CLASSES														
Total, 14 years and over	21,833	27,640	40,336	47,404	53,297	60,617	63,754	117,564	112,354	101,103	89,100	74,145	51,441	41,799
14 to 19 years	*2,981	*4,064	4,587	4,386	4,014	4,083	4,001	13,505	12,927	14,740	13,948	11,581	9,161	8,008
20 to 24 years	3,774	*4,481	5,865	7,063	7,723	7,185	6,206	10,031	11,474	11,589	10,882	9,296	7,365	6,222
25 to 34 years	5,732	7,072	10,381	11,634	13,683	14,641	15,139	24,002	23,732	21,339	18,974	17,190	12,132	9,844
25 to 29 years	....	....	*5,583	6,167	7,208	7,493	7,331	11,689	12,247	11,097	9,844	9,104	6,555	5,248
30 to 34 years	....	....	*4,798	5,467	6,475	7,148	7,808	12,313	11,485	10,242	9,130	8,087	5,577	4,596
35 to 44 years	3,997	5,279	8,340	10,268	11,241	13,827	14,988	22,721	21,349	18,332	17,218	14,150	9,248	7,078
35 to 39 years	....	....	*4,630	5,504	5,919	7,202	7,441	11,550	11,228	9,544	9,219	7,792	4,984	3,881
40 to 44 years	....	....	*3,710	4,764	5,322	6,625	7,547	11,171	10,121	8,788	7,999	6,358	4,264	3,197
45 to 54 years	2,783	3,599	6,163	7,615	9,072	10,823	12,315	18,805	17,269	15,513	13,030	10,519	6,424	5,079
45 to 49 years	....	....	*3,433	4,165	4,886	5,833	6,772	10,038	9,070	8,256	7,049	5,775	3,469	2,744
50 to 54 years	....	....	*2,730	3,450	4,186	4,990	5,543	8,767	8,199	7,257	5,981	4,744	2,955	2,335
55 to 64 years	1,630	2,031	3,437	4,400	5,431	7,125	8,101	14,480	13,258	10,571	8,407	6,545	4,018	3,142
55 to 59 years	....	....	*1,938	2,542	3,179	4,097	4,662	7,820	7,231	5,844	4,651	3,556	2,220	1,679
60 to 64 years	....	....	1,499	1,858	2,252	3,028	3,439	6,660	6,027	4,727	3,756	2,989	1,798	1,463
65 years and over	936	1,114	1,563	2,038	2,133	2,933	3,004	14,020	12,345	9,019	6,641	4,943	3,093	2,426
Male, 14 years and over	18,129	22,641	32,107	37,008	40,283	43,930	45,234	57,278	55,312	50,554	45,087	37,954	26,416	21,501
14 to 19 years	*1,997	*2,834	2,947	2,795	2,619	2,620	2,597	6,854	6,560	7,399	6,971	5,721	4,567	3,991
20 to 24 years	2,836	*3,302	4,080	4,747	5,035	4,630	3,899	4,666	5,611	5,693	5,343	4,538	3,643	3,121
25 to 34 years	4,943	5,933	8,370	9,053	10,077	10,748	11,137	11,739	11,584	10,521	9,433	8,689	6,255	5,148
25 to 29 years	....	....	*4,355	4,662	5,196	5,431	5,404	5,738	5,969	5,451	4,866	4,549	3,340	2,711
30 to 34 years	....	....	*4,015	4,391	4,881	5,317	5,733	6,001	5,615	5,070	4,567	4,141	2,915	2,437
35 to 44 years	3,570	4,627	7,037	8,445	8,741	10,008	10,593	11,127	10,512	9,164	8,827	7,378	4,896	3,723
35 to 39 years	....	....	*3,904	4,494	4,555	5,258	5,351	5,651	5,513	4,745	4,685	4,085	2,629	2,061
40 to 44 years	....	....	*3,133	3,951	4,186	4,750	5,242	5,476	4,999	4,419	4,142	3,293	2,267	1,662
45 to 54 years	2,479	3,172	5,294	6,391	7,381	7,948	8,668	9,291	8,588	7,963	6,811	5,667	3,419	2,641
45 to 49 years	....	....	*2,949	3,481	3,936	4,236	4,680	4,965	4,511	4,210	3,676	3,125	1,847	1,426
50 to 54 years	....	....	*2,345	2,910	3,445	3,712	3,988	4,326	4,077	3,753	3,135	2,542	1,572	1,215
55 to 64 years	1,458	1,786	2,996	3,782	4,572	5,557	6,030	7,082	6,626	5,408	4,373	3,471	2,073	1,638
55 to 59 years	....	....	*1,680	2,175	2,663	3,156	3,428	3,834	3,619	3,011	2,429	1,885	1,151	876
60 to 64 years	....	....	1,316	1,607	1,909	2,401	2,602	3,248	3,007	2,397	1,944	1,586	922	762
65 years and over	846	987	1,383	1,795	1,858	2,419	2,310	6,519	5,831	4,406	3,329	2,489	1,563	1,239

Note: The methods of adjusting the 1955 and 1950 labor force data are described in Appendix A, pp. 153–154. The adjustments used in connection with the statistics for 1940 and earlier are described in Durand, op. cit., Appendix A.

TABLE D-1.—POPULATION AND LABOR FORCE, BY AGE, COLOR, AND SEX: 1890 TO 1955—Cont.

[Adjusted data—decennial census levels. In thousands. Asterisk (*) denotes figures obtained by interpolation of data tabulated for different age groups]

Age, color, and sex	Population							Labor force						
	1955	1950	1940	1930	1920	1900	1890	1890	1900	1920	1930	1940	1950	1955
ALL CLASSES—Cont.														
Female, 14 years and over	60,286	57,042	50,549	44,013	36,191	25,025	20,298	3,704	4,999	8,229	10,396	13,014	16,687	18,520
14 to 19 years	6,651	6,367	7,341	6,977	5,780	4,594	4,017	*984	*1,230	1,640	1,591	1,395	1,463	1,404
20 to 24 years	5,365	5,863	5,896	5,539	4,758	3,722	3,101	938	*1,179	1,785	2,316	2,688	2,555	2,307
25 to 34 years	12,263	12,148	10,818	9,541	8,501	5,877	4,696	789	1,139	2,011	2,581	3,606	3,893	4,002
25 to 29 years	5,951	6,278	5,646	4,978	4,555	3,215	2,537	...	...	*1,228	1,505	2,012	2,062	1,927
30 to 34 years	6,312	5,870	5,172	4,563	3,946	2,662	2,159	...	...	*783	1,076	1,594	1,831	2,075
35 to 44 years	11,594	10,837	9,168	8,391	6,772	4,352	3,355	427	652	1,303	1,823	2,500	3,819	4,395
35 to 39 years	5,899	5,715	4,799	4,534	3,707	2,355	1,820	...	...	*726	1,010	1,364	1,944	2,090
40 to 44 years	5,695	5,122	4,369	3,857	3,065	1,997	1,535	...	...	*577	813	1,136	1,875	2,305
45 to 54 years	9,514	8,681	7,550	6,219	4,852	3,005	2,438	304	427	869	1,224	1,691	2,875	3,647
45 to 49 years	5,073	4,559	4,046	3,373	2,650	1,622	1,318	...	...	*484	684	950	1,597	2,092
50 to 54 years	4,441	4,122	3,504	2,846	2,202	1,383	1,120	...	...	*385	540	741	1,278	1,555
55 to 64 years	7,398	6,632	5,163	4,034	3,074	1,945	1,504	172	245	441	618	859	1,568	2,071
55 to 59 years	3,986	3,612	2,833	2,222	1,671	1,069	803	...	...	*258	367	516	941	1,234
60 to 64 years	3,412	3,020	2,330	1,812	1,403	876	701	...	...	*183	251	343	627	837
65 years and over	7,501	6,514	4,613	3,312	2,454	1,530	1,187	90	127	180	243	275	514	694
WHITE														
Total, 14 years and over	105,846	101,333	91,428	80,380	66,782	45,645	37,151	18,931	23,871	35,608	41,911	47,671	54,409	57,307
14 to 19 years	11,799	11,364	13,089	12,351	10,125	7,920	6,909	2,434	*3,322	3,924	3,712	3,460	3,602	3,528
20 to 24 years	8,817	10,175	10,341	9,622	8,201	6,355	5,467	3,252	*3,800	5,146	6,221	6,914	6,419	5,506
25 to 34 years	21,396	21,270	19,110	16,936	15,507	10,801	8,820	5,051	6,181	9,242	10,228	12,173	13,062	13,422
25 to 29 years	10,389	10,934	9,904	8,717	8,156	5,781	4,662	...	...	*4,938	5,392	6,405	6,676	6,494
30 to 34 years	11,007	10,336	9,206	8,219	7,352	5,020	4,158	...	...	*4,304	4,836	5,768	6,386	6,928
35 to 44 years	20,435	19,150	16,452	15,561	12,745	8,340	6,326	3,499	4,669	7,361	9,112	9,967	12,312	13,401
35 to 39 years	10,411	10,044	8,516	8,287	6,979	4,475	3,451	...	...	*4,063	4,856	5,218	6,392	6,750
40 to 44 years	10,024	9,106	7,936	7,274	5,766	3,865	2,875	...	...	*3,298	4,256	4,749	5,920	6,651
45 to 54 years	17,007	15,631	14,214	11,839	9,522	5,759	4,556	2,430	3,141	5,425	6,769	8,225	9,739	11,148
45 to 49 years	9,073	8,166	7,533	6,388	5,197	3,116	2,458	...	...	*3,002	3,698	4,406	5,222	6,113
50 to 54 years	7,934	7,465	6,681	5,451	4,325	2,643	2,098	...	...	*2,423	3,071	3,819	4,517	5,035
55 to 64 years	13,327	12,308	9,843	7,825	6,089	3,654	2,864	1,444	1,787	3,123	4,008	4,997	6,585	7,490
55 to 59 years	7,162	6,686	5,427	4,324	3,312	2,028	1,537	...	...	*1,766	2,315	2,920	3,770	4,292
60 to 64 years	6,165	5,622	4,416	3,501	2,777	1,626	1,327	...	...	*1,357	1,693	2,077	2,815	3,198
65 years and over	13,065	11,435	8,379	6,246	4,592	2,816	2,209	821	971	1,387	1,861	1,935	2,690	2,812

TABLE D-1.—POPULATION AND LABOR FORCE, BY AGE, COLOR, AND SEX: 1890 TO 1955—Cont.

[Adjusted data—decennial census levels. In thousands. Asterisk (*) denotes figures obtained by interpolation of data tabulated for different age groups]

Age, color, and sex	Population							Labor force						
	1955	1950	1940	1930	1920	1900	1890	1890	1900	1920	1930	1940	1950	1955
WHITE.—Cont.														
Male, 14 years and over.....	51,665	49,979	45,823	40,749	34,243	23,495	19,152	16,093	20,057	28,861	33,286	36,500	39,833	41,066
14 to 19 years.....	6,003	5,791	6,596	6,200	5,061	3,960	3,451	*1,664	*2,380	2,533	2,368	2,248	2,285	2,279
20 to 24 years.....	4,115	5,008	5,114	4,752	4,028	3,159	2,753	2,494	*2,860	3,613	4,204	4,522	4,141	3,478
25 to 34 years.....	10,520	10,434	9,465	8,450	7,887	5,585	4,627	4,444	5,306	7,607	8,118	9,104	9,752	10,053
25 to 29 years.....	5,136	5,357	4,892	4,329	4,103	2,955	2,417			*3,930	4,151	4,684	4,913	4,873
30 to 34 years.....	5,384	5,077	4,573	4,121	3,785	2,630	2,210			3,677	3,967	4,420	4,839	5,180
35 to 44 years.....	10,052	9,456	8,249	8,007	6,668	4,434	3,341	3,203	4,192	6,360	7,666	7,901	9,046	9,621
35 to 39 years.....	5,117	4,953	4,254	4,230	3,674	2,370	1,839			*3,511	4,061	4,101	4,750	4,864
40 to 44 years.....	4,935	4,503	3,995	3,777	2,994	2,064	1,502			*2,849	3,605	3,800	4,296	4,757
45 to 54 years.....	8,410	7,771	7,295	6,170	5,084	3,061	2,365	2,216	2,836	4,742	5,787	6,784	7,222	7,910
45 to 49 years.....	4,494	4,065	3,843	3,331	2,785	1,659	1,277			*2,626	3,155	3,604	3,833	4,259
50 to 54 years.....	3,916	3,706	3,452	2,839	2,299	1,402	1,088			*2,116	2,632	3,180	3,389	3,651
55 to 64 years.....	6,509	6,134	5,022	4,044	3,210	1,874	1,486	1,316	1,605	2,759	3,486	4,242	5,161	5,579
55 to 59 years.....	3,506	3,334	2,790	2,242	1,745	1,045	797			*1,551	2,004	2,468	2,918	3,165
60 to 64 years.....	3,003	2,800	2,232	1,802	1,465	829	689			*1,208	1,482	1,774	2,243	2,414
65 years and over.....	6,056	5,385	4,082	3,126	2,304	1,422	1,129	756	878	1,247	1,657	1,699	2,226	2,146
Female, 14 years and over...	54,181	51,354	45,605	39,631	32,539	22,150	17,999	2,838	3,814	6,747	8,625	11,171	14,576	16,241
14 to 19 years.....	5,796	5,573	6,493	6,151	5,064	3,960	3,458	*770	*942	1,391	1,344	1,212	1,317	1,249
20 to 24 years.....	4,702	5,167	5,227	4,870	4,173	3,196	2,714	758	*940	1,533	2,017	2,392	2,278	2,028
25 to 34 years.....	10,876	10,836	9,645	8,486	7,620	5,216	4,193	607	875	1,635	2,110	3,069	3,310	3,369
25 to 29 years.....	5,253	5,577	5,012	4,388	4,053	2,826	2,245			*1,008	1,241	1,721	1,763	1,621
30 to 34 years.....	5,623	5,259	4,633	4,098	3,567	2,390	1,948			*627	869	1,348	1,547	1,748
35 to 44 years.....	10,383	9,694	8,203	7,554	6,077	3,906	2,985	296	477	1,001	1,446	2,066	3,266	3,780
35 to 39 years.....	5,294	5,091	4,262	4,057	3,305	2,105	1,612			*552	795	1,117	1,642	1,787
40 to 44 years.....	5,089	4,603	3,941	3,497	2,772	1,801	1,373			*449	651	949	1,624	1,993
45 to 54 years.....	8,597	7,860	6,919	5,669	4,438	2,698	2,191	214	305	683	982	1,441	2,517	3,238
45 to 49 years.....	4,579	4,101	3,690	3,057	2,412	1,457	1,181			*376	543	802	1,389	1,854
50 to 54 years.....	4,018	3,759	3,229	2,612	2,026	1,241	1,010			*307	439	639	1,128	1,384
55 to 64 years.....	6,818	6,174	4,821	3,781	2,879	1,780	1,378	128	182	364	522	755	1,424	1,911
55 to 59 years.....	3,656	3,352	2,637	2,082	1,567	983	740			*215	311	452	852	1,127
60 to 64 years.....	3,162	2,822	2,184	1,699	1,312	797	638			*149	211	303	572	784
65 years and over.....	7,009	6,050	4,297	3,120	2,288	1,394	1,080	65	93	140	204	236	464	666

TABLE D-1.—POPULATION AND LABOR FORCE, BY AGE, COLOR, AND SEX: 1890 TO 1955—Cont.

[Adjusted data—decennial census levels. Asterisk (*) denotes figures obtained by interpolation of data tabulated for different age groups]

Age, color, and sex	Population							Labor force						
	1955	1950	1940	1930	1920	1900	1890	1955	1950	1940	1930	1920	1900	1890
NONWHITE														
Total, 14 years and over..	11,718	11,021	9,675	8,720	7,363	5,796	4,648	6,447	6,208	5,626	5,493	4,728	3,769	2,902
14 to 19 years............	1,706	1,563	1,651	1,597	1,376	1,241	1,099	473	481	554	674	663	*742	*547
20 to 24 years............	1,214	1,299	1,248	1,260	1,095	1,010	755	700	765	809	842	719	*681	522
25 to 34 years............	2,606	2,462	2,229	2,038	1,683	1,331	1,024	1,717	1,579	1,510	1,406	1,139	891	681
25 to 29 years............	1,300	1,313	1,193	1,127	948	774	586	837	817	803	775	*645	...	...
30 to 34 years............	1,306	1,149	1,036	911	735	557	438	880	762	707	631	*494	...	...
35 to 44 years............	2,286	2,199	1,880	1,657	1,405	908	752	1,587	1,517	1,274	1,156	979	610	498
35 to 39 years............	1,139	1,184	1,028	932	813	509	430	790	811	701	648	*567	...	...
40 to 44 years............	1,147	1,015	852	725	592	399	322	797	706	573	508	*412	...	...
45 to 54 years............	1,798	1,638	1,299	1,191	997	665	523	1,167	1,084	847	846	738	458	353
45 to 49 years............	965	904	723	661	578	353	286	659	611	480	467	*431	...	...
50 to 54 years............	833	734	576	530	419	312	237	508	473	367	379	*307	...	...
55 to 64 years............	1,153	950	728	582	456	364	278	611	539	434	392	314	244	186
55 to 59 years............	658	545	417	327	244	192	142	370	326	259	227	*172	...	...
60 to 64 years............	495	405	311	255	212	172	136	241	213	175	165	*142	...	...
65 years and over........	955	910	640	395	351	277	217	192	243	198	177	176	143	115
Male, 14 years and over....	5,613	5,333	4,731	4,338	3,711	2,921	2,349	4,168	4,097	3,783	3,722	3,246	2,584	2,036
14 to 19 years............	851	769	803	771	660	607	540	318	335	371	427	414	*454	*333
20 to 24 years............	551	603	579	591	510	484	368	421	489	513	543	467	*442	342
25 to 34 years............	1,219	1,150	1,056	983	802	670	521	1,084	997	973	935	763	627	499
25 to 29 years............	602	612	559	537	446	385	294	531	519	512	511	*425	...	...
30 to 34 years............	617	538	497	446	356	285	227	553	478	461	424	*338	...	...
35 to 44 years............	1,075	1,056	915	820	710	462	382	972	962	840	779	677	435	367
35 to 39 years............	534	560	491	455	411	259	222	487	508	454	433	*393	...	...
40 to 44 years............	541	496	424	365	299	203	160	485	454	386	346	*284	336	263
45 to 54 years............	881	817	668	641	583	358	276	758	726	597	604	552	336	263
45 to 49 years............	471	446	367	345	340	188	149	421	403	332	326	*323	...	...
50 to 54 years............	410	371	301	296	243	170	127	337	323	265	278	*229	...	...
55 to 64 years............	573	492	386	329	261	199	152	451	395	330	296	237	181	142
55 to 59 years............	328	285	221	187	140	106	79	263	237	195	171	*129	...	...
60 to 64 years............	245	207	165	142	121	93	73	188	158	135	125	*108	...	...
65 years and over........	463	446	324	203	185	141	110	164	193	159	138	136	109	90

TABLE D-1.—POPULATION AND LABOR FORCE, BY AGE, COLOR, AND SEX: 1890 TO 1955—Cont.

[Adjusted data—decennial census levels. In thousands. Asterisk (*) denotes figures obtained by interpolation of data tabulated for different age groups]

Age, color, and sex	Population							Labor force						
	1955	1950	1940	1930	1920	1900	1890	1890	1900	1920	1930	1940	1950	1955
NONWHITE—Cont.														
Female, 14 years and over...	6,105	5,688	4,944	4,382	3,652	2,875	2,299	866	1,185	1,482	1,771	1,843	2,111	2,279
14 to 19 years.............	855	794	848	826	716	634	559	*214	*288	249	247	183	146	155
20 to 24 years.............	663	696	669	669	585	526	387	180	*239	252	299	296	276	279
25 to 34 years.............	1,387	1,312	1,173	1,055	881	661	503	182	264	376	471	537	582	633
25 to 29 years.............	698	701	634	590	502	389	292	...	...	*220	264	291	298	306
30 to 34 years.............	689	611	539	465	379	272	211	...	...	*156	207	246	284	327
35 to 44 years.............	1,211	1,143	965	837	695	446	370	131	175	302	377	434	555	615
35 to 39 years.............	605	624	537	477	402	250	208	...	...	*174	215	247	303	303
40 to 44 years.............	606	519	428	360	293	196	162	90	122	*128	162	187	252	312
45 to 54 years.............	917	821	631	550	414	307	247	...	...	186	242	250	358	409
45 to 49 years.............	494	458	356	316	238	165	137	...	...	*108	141	148	208	238
50 to 54 years.............	423	363	275	234	176	142	110	...	...	*78	101	102	150	171
55 to 64 years.............	580	458	342	253	195	165	126	44	63	77	96	104	144	160
55 to 59 years.............	330	260	196	140	104	86	63	...	...	*43	56	64	89	107
60 to 64 years.............	250	198	146	113	91	79	63	...	...	*34	40	40	55	53
65 years and over..........	492	464	316	192	166	136	107	25	34	40	39	39	50	28

Source: Derived from unpublished tabulations of Current Population Survey data for April 1955 and 1950; *1950 Census of Population*, Vol. II, *Characteristics of the Population*, Part 1, U. S. Summary, tables 38, 39, and 50, and Vol. IV, *Characteristics of Population*, Vol. IV, *Characteristics by Age*, Part 1, U. S. Summary, table 24; *1930 Census of Population*, Vol. II, *General Report*, Chapter 10, table 21; *1920 Census of Population*, Vol. II, *General Report*, Chapter III, table 9; *1900 Census of Population*, Vol. II, table 1; *1890 Census of Population*, Part II, table 1; John D. Durand, *The Labor Force in the United States, 1890–1960*, Social Science Research Council, New York, 1948, table A–6.

TABLE **D-1a.**—LABOR FORCE PARTICIPATION RATES, BY AGE, COLOR, AND SEX: 1890 TO 1955

[Adjusted data—decennial census levels. Asterisk (*) denotes figures obtained by interpolation of data tabulated for different age groups]

Age and color	Both sexes							Male							Female						
	1955	1950	1940	1930	1920	1900	1890	1955	1950	1940	1930	1920	1900	1890	1955	1950	1940	1930	1920	1900	1890
ALL CLASSES																					
Total...........	54.2	54.0	52.7	53.2	54.4	53.7	52.2	79.0	79.4	79.7	82.1	84.6	85.7	84.3	30.7	29.3	25.7	23.6	22.7	20.0	18.2
14 to 19 years...	29.6	31.6	27.2	31.4	39.9	*44.4	*37.2	37.9	39.9	35.4	40.1	51.5	*62.1	*50.0	21.1	23.0	19.0	22.8	28.4	*26.8	*24.5
20 to 24 years...	61.9	62.6	66.6	64.9	63.1	*60.8	60.7	83.6	82.5	88.4	88.8	89.9	*90.6	90.9	43.0	43.6	45.6	41.8	37.5	*31.7	30.2
25 to 34 years...	63.1	61.7	64.1	61.3	60.4	58.3	58.2	94.9	92.8	95.8	96.0	96.3	94.9	96.0	32.6	32.0	33.3	27.1	23.7	19.4	16.8
25 to 29 years...	62.7	61.8	65.0	62.6	*61.3	...	...	94.2	91.0	95.8	95.9	*95.8	...	...	32.4	32.8	35.6	30.2	*27.0	...	...
30 to 34 years...	63.4	62.2	63.2	59.9	*59.3	...	...	95.5	94.7	96.3	96.1	*97.0	...	...	32.9	31.2	30.8	23.6	*19.8	...	...
35 to 44 years...	66.0	64.8	61.3	59.6	58.9	57.1	56.5	95.2	95.2	95.4	95.7	95.4	94.5	95.9	37.9	35.2	27.3	21.7	19.2	15.0	12.7
35 to 39 years...	64.4	64.1	62.0	59.7	*59.4	...	...	94.7	94.6	96.0	95.6	*95.6	...	...	35.4	34.0	28.4	22.3	*19.6	...	...
40 to 44 years...	67.6	65.5	60.6	59.6	*58.4	...	...	95.7	95.0	94.7	95.4	*95.1	...	...	40.5	36.6	26.0	21.1	*18.8	...	...
45 to 54 years...	65.5	62.7	58.5	58.4	58.6	56.0	54.8	94.1	93.9	92.7	93.8	93.4	92.8	93.9	38.3	33.1	22.4	19.7	17.9	14.2	12.5
45 to 49 years...	67.5	64.3	59.2	59.1	*59.4	...	...	94.3	93.9	93.5	93.4	*94.4	...	...	41.2	35.0	23.5	20.3	*18.3	...	...
50 to 54 years...	63.2	60.9	57.7	57.7	*57.5	...	...	92.2	91.0	91.8	92.8	*92.3	...	...	35.0	31.0	21.1	19.0	*17.5	...	...
55 to 64 years...	55.9	53.7	51.4	52.3	52.5	50.5	51.9	85.1	83.9	84.5	86.5	86.3	86.2	89.0	28.0	23.6	16.6	15.3	14.3	12.6	11.4
55 to 59 years...	59.6	56.7	54.4	54.7	*54.5	...	...	89.4	87.2	88.4	89.5	*89.1	...	...	31.0	26.1	18.2	16.5	*15.4	...	...
60 to 64 years...	51.6	50.2	47.6	49.5	*50.2	...	...	80.1	79.8	79.6	82.7	*83.0	...	...	24.5	20.8	14.7	13.9	*13.0	...	...
65 years and over..	21.4	23.8	23.7	30.7	31.6	36.0	38.6	35.4	41.5	42.2	53.9	55.6	63.1	68.3	9.3	7.9	6.0	7.3	7.3	8.3	7.6
WHITE																					
Total...........	54.1	53.7	52.1	52.1	53.3	52.3	51.0	79.5	79.7	79.7	81.7	84.3	85.4	84.0	30.0	28.4	24.5	21.8	20.7	17.2	15.8
14 to 19 years...	29.9	31.7	26.4	30.1	38.8	*41.9	*35.2	38.0	39.5	34.1	38.2	50.0	*60.1	*48.2	21.5	23.6	18.7	21.9	27.5	*23.8	*22.3
20 to 24 years...	62.4	63.1	66.9	64.7	62.7	*59.8	59.5	84.5	82.7	88.5	88.5	89.7	*90.5	90.6	43.1	44.1	45.8	41.4	36.7	*29.4	27.9
25 to 34 years...	62.7	61.4	63.7	60.4	59.6	57.2	57.3	95.6	93.5	96.2	96.1	96.4	95.0	96.0	31.0	30.5	31.8	24.9	21.5	16.8	14.5
25 to 29 years...	62.5	61.1	64.7	62.6	*60.5	...	...	94.9	91.7	95.9	95.9	*95.8	...	...	30.9	31.6	34.3	28.3	*24.9	...	...
30 to 34 years...	62.9	61.8	62.7	58.8	*58.5	...	...	96.2	95.3	96.7	96.3	*97.1	...	...	31.1	29.4	29.1	21.2	*17.6	...	...
35 to 44 years...	65.6	64.3	60.6	58.6	57.8	56.0	55.3	95.7	95.7	95.8	95.7	95.4	94.5	95.9	36.4	33.7	25.2	19.1	16.5	12.2	9.9
35 to 39 years...	63.9	63.6	61.3	58.6	*58.2	...	...	95.1	95.1	96.4	95.7	*95.6	...	...	33.8	32.3	26.2	19.6	*16.7	...	...
40 to 44 years...	67.3	65.0	59.8	58.5	*57.2	...	...	96.4	95.4	95.1	95.4	*95.2	...	...	39.2	35.3	24.1	18.6	*16.2	...	...
45 to 54 years...	65.5	62.3	57.9	57.2	57.0	54.5	53.3	94.8	94.3	93.0	93.8	93.3	92.6	93.7	37.7	33.0	21.7	17.3	15.4	11.3	9.8
45 to 49 years...	67.4	63.9	58.5	57.9	*57.8	...	...	94.1	94.3	93.8	94.7	*94.3	...	...	40.5	33.9	21.7	17.8	*15.6	...	...
50 to 54 years...	63.5	60.5	57.2	56.3	*56.0	...	...	93.2	91.4	92.1	92.7	*92.0	...	...	34.4	30.0	19.8	16.8	*15.2	...	...
55 to 64 years...	56.2	53.5	50.8	51.2	51.3	48.9	50.4	85.7	84.5	85.0	87.0	86.9	85.6	88.6	28.0	23.1	15.7	13.8	12.6	10.2	9.3
55 to 59 years...	59.9	56.4	53.8	53.5	*53.3	...	...	90.3	87.5	88.5	89.4	*88.9	...	...	30.8	25.4	17.1	14.9	*13.7	...	...
60 to 64 years...	51.9	50.1	47.0	48.4	*48.9	...	...	80.4	80.1	79.5	82.2	*82.5	...	...	24.8	20.3	13.9	12.4	*11.4	...	...
65 years and over..	21.5	23.5	23.1	29.8	30.2	34.5	37.2	35.4	41.3	41.6	53.0	54.1	61.7	67.0	9.5	7.7	5.5	6.5	6.1	6.7	6.0

TABLE **D-1a.**—LABOR FORCE PARTICIPATION RATES, BY AGE, COLOR, AND SEX: 1890 TO 1955—Cont.

[Adjusted data—decennial census levels. Asterisk (*) denotes figures obtained by interpolation of data tabulated for different age groups]

Age and color	Both sexes							Male							Female						
	1955	1950	1940	1930	1920	1900	1890	1955	1950	1940	1930	1920	1900	1890	1955	1950	1940	1930	1920	1900	1890
NONWHITE																					
Total................	55.0	56.3	58.1	63.0	64.2	65.0	62.4	74.3	76.8	80.0	85.8	87.5	88.5	86.7	37.3	37.1	37.3	40.4	40.6	41.2	37.7
14 to 19 years.....	27.7	30.8	33.6	42.2	48.2	*59.8	*49.8	37.4	43.6	46.2	55.4	62.7	*74.8	*61.7	18.1	18.4	21.6	29.9	34.8	*45.4	*38.3
20 to 24 years.....	57.7	58.9	64.8	66.8	65.7	*67.4	69.1	76.4	81.1	88.6	91.9	91.6	*91.3	92.9	42.1	39.7	44.2	44.7	43.1	*45.4	46.5
25 to 34 years.....	65.9	64.1	67.7	69.0	67.7	66.9	66.5	88.2	86.7	92.1	95.1	95.1	93.6	95.8	45.6	44.4	45.6	44.6	42.7	39.9	36.2
25 to 29 years.....	64.4	62.2	67.3	68.8	*68.0	.....	.....	88.2	84.8	91.6	95.2	*95.3	.....	.....	43.8	42.5	45.9	44.7	*43.8	.....	.....
30 to 34 years.....	67.4	66.3	68.2	69.3	*67.2	.....	.....	89.6	88.8	92.8	95.1	*94.9	.....	.....	47.5	46.5	45.6	44.5	*41.2	.....	.....
35 to 44 years.....	69.4	69.0	67.8	69.8	69.7	67.2	66.2	90.4	91.1	91.8	95.0	95.4	94.2	96.1	50.8	48.6	45.0	45.0	43.5	39.2	35.4
35 to 39 years.....	69.4	68.5	68.2	69.5	*69.7	.....	.....	91.2	90.7	92.5	95.2	*95.6	.....	.....	50.1	48.6	46.0	45.1	*43.3	.....	.....
40 to 44 years.....	69.5	69.6	67.3	70.1	*69.6	.....	.....	89.6	91.5	91.0	94.8	*95.0	.....	.....	51.5	48.6	43.7	45.0	*43.7	.....	.....
45 to 54 years.....	64.9	66.2	65.2	71.0	74.0	68.9	67.5	86.0	88.9	89.4	94.2	94.7	93.9	95.3	44.6	43.6	39.6	44.0	44.9	39.7	36.4
45 to 49 years.....	68.3	67.6	66.4	70.7	*74.6	.....	.....	89.4	90.4	90.5	94.5	*95.0	.....	.....	48.2	45.4	41.6	44.6	*45.4	.....	.....
50 to 54 years.....	61.0	64.4	63.7	71.5	*73.3	.....	.....	82.2	87.1	88.0	93.9	*94.2	.....	.....	40.4	41.3	37.1	43.2	*44.3	.....	.....
55 to 64 years.....	53.0	56.7	59.6	67.4	68.9	67.0	66.9	78.7	80.3	85.5	90.0	90.8	91.0	93.4	27.6	31.4	30.4	37.9	39.5	38.2	34.9
55 to 59 years.....	56.2	59.8	62.1	69.4	*70.5	.....	.....	80.2	83.2	88.2	91.4	*92.1	.....	.....	32.4	34.2	32.7	40.0	*41.3	.....	.....
60 to 64 years.....	48.7	52.6	56.3	64.7	*67.0	.....	.....	76.7	76.3	81.8	88.0	*89.3	.....	.....	21.2	27.8	27.4	35.4	*37.4	.....	.....
65 years and over..	20.1	26.7	30.9	44.8	50.1	51.6	53.0	35.4	43.3	49.1	68.0	73.5	77.3	81.8	5.7	10.8	12.3	20.3	24.1	25.0	23.4

Source: Same as table D-1.

TABLE D-2.—MAJOR OCCUPATION GROUP OF PERSONS IN THE LABOR FORCE, 1940 AND 1950, AND OF GAINFUL WORKERS, 1900 TO 1930, BY SEX

[Decennial census levels]

Major occupation group and sex[1]	Labor force		Gainful workers				Percent distribution					
							Labor force		Gainful workers			
	1950	1940	1930	1920	1910	1900	1950	1940	1930	1920	1910	1900
MALE												
Total workers	42,553,838	39,167,945	37,933,474	33,569,235	29,846,696	23,710,641	100.0	100.0	100.0	100.0	100.0	100.0
Professional, technical, and kindred workers	3,073,593	2,270,712	1,828,769	1,274,850	1,031,584	799,944	7.2	5.8	4.8	3.8	3.5	3.4
Farmers and farm managers	4,254,842	5,205,054	5,768,640	6,165,223	5,883,811	5,451,190	10.0	13.3	15.2	18.4	19.7	23.0
Managers, officials, and proprietors, exc. farm	4,455,540	3,355,962	3,320,790	2,611,388	2,311,294	1,621,984	10.5	8.6	8.8	7.8	7.7	6.8
Clerical and kindred workers	2,729,768	2,281,844	2,090,476	1,770,696	1,299,503	664,840	6.4	5.8	5.5	5.3	4.4	2.8
Sales workers	2,714,878	2,525,374	2,322,880	1,517,996	1,376,028	1,078,951	6.4	6.4	6.1	4.5	4.6	4.6
Craftsmen, foremen, and kindred workers	8,097,807	6,068,566	6,139,870	5,376,863	4,209,396	2,985,458	19.0	15.5	16.2	16.0	14.1	12.6
Operatives and kindred workers	8,743,362	7,066,629	5,822,347	4,839,850	3,739,881	2,456,710	20.6	18.1	15.3	14.4	12.5	10.3
Private household workers	79,729	134,907	88,693	50,968	67,291	52,694	0.2	0.3	0.2	0.1	0.2	0.2
Service workers, except private household	2,567,711	2,235,161	1,729,241	1,198,601	1,081,541	687,437	6.0	5.7	4.6	3.6	3.6	2.9
Farm laborers and foremen	2,097,054	3,281,861	3,645,069	4,056,192	4,474,794	4,428,943	4.9	8.4	9.6	12.1	15.0	18.7
Laborers, except farm and mine	3,739,554	4,741,875	5,176,699	4,706,608	4,371,573	3,482,490	8.8	12.1	13.7	14.0	14.7	14.7
FEMALE												
Total workers	16,445,105	12,574,078	10,752,116	8,636,510	7,444,787	5,319,397	100.0	100.0	100.0	100.0	100.0	100.0
Professional, technical, and kindred workers	2,006,989	1,607,906	1,481,937	1,007,725	725,951	434,418	12.2	12.8	13.8	11.7	9.7	8.2
Farmers and farm managers	119,851	157,114	263,242	276,249	279,249	311,340	0.7	1.3	2.4	3.2	3.8	5.9
Managers, officials, and proprietors, exc. farm	699,807	414,472	304,969	220,797	216,537	77,214	4.3	3.3	2.8	2.6	2.9	1.4
Clerical and kindred workers	4,502,009	2,700,383	2,245,824	1,614,246	687,811	212,184	27.4	21.4	20.9	18.7	9.2	4.0
Sales workers	1,418,337	924,916	736,228	540,501	378,915	227,782	8.6	7.4	6.8	6.3	5.1	4.3
Craftsmen, foremen, and kindred workers	252,669	134,823	106,432	104,974	106,092	76,128	1.5	1.1	1.0	1.2	1.4	1.4
Operatives and kindred workers	3,286,683	2,451,786	1,856,941	1,717,568	1,635,455	1,260,669	20.0	19.5	17.3	19.9	22.0	23.7
Private household workers	1,458,775	2,276,828	1,909,485	1,360,293	1,783,964	1,526,350	8.9	18.1	17.8	15.7	24.0	28.7
Service workers, except private household	2,073,311	1,422,150	1,044,632	702,795	629,292	359,319	12.6	11.3	9.7	8.1	8.5	6.7
Farm laborers and foremen	481,246	350,547	644,547	891,958	895,424	696,525	2.9	2.8	6.0	10.3	12.0	13.1
Laborers, except farm and mine	145,428	133,153	157,879	198,790	106,097	137,468	0.9	1.1	1.5	2.3	1.4	2.6

[1] Data adjusted for comparability of occupational classification but not for differences between gainful worker and labor force concepts.

Source: U. S. Bureau of the Census, Occupational Trends in the United States: 1900 to 1950, Working Paper No. 5, by David L. Kaplan and M. Claire Casey, Washington, D. C., 1958.

TABLE D-3.—EMPLOYMENT STATUS OF PERSONS 14 YEARS OLD AND OVER IN STANDARD METROPOLITAN AREAS OF 100,000 OR MORE, BY SEX: 1950 AND 1940

Standard metropolitan area and sex	1950 Total population 14 years and over	1950 Labor force	1950 Civilian labor force Total	1950 Employed	1950 Unemployed	1940 Total population 14 years and over	1940 Labor force	1940 Civilian labor force Total	1940 Employed	1940 Unemployed	Percent of population in labor force 1950	1940	Percent of civilian labor force unemployed 1950	1940
MALE														
Akron, Ohio	150,213	123,809	123,459	115,316	8,143	133,303	106,177	106,177	85,183	20,994	82.4	79.7	6.6	19.8
Albany-Schenectady-Troy, N. Y.	194,812	152,307	151,916	144,882	7,034	185,123	147,358	147,258	123,655	23,603	78.2	79.6	4.6	16.0
Albuquerque, N. Mex.	51,788	40,872	35,455	33,749	1,706	24,584	18,938	18,938	14,882	4,056	78.9	77.0	4.8	21.4
Allentown-Bethlehem-Easton, Pa.	167,257	133,306	133,209	126,792	6,417	155,740	124,974	124,974	107,536	17,438	79.7	80.2	4.8	14.0
Altoona, Pa.	49,952	37,964	37,909	36,068	1,841	52,936	39,482	39,482	32,450	7,032	76.0	74.6	4.9	17.8
Asheville, N. C.	43,339	32,142	32,097	30,647	1,450	38,860	29,503	29,503	25,216	4,287	74.2	75.9	4.5	14.5
Atlanta, Ga.	236,919	186,196	183,309	177,818	5,491	189,426	151,845	151,845	132,051	19,794	78.6	80.7	3.0	13.0
Atlantic City, N. J.	49,718	37,930	36,605	34,474	2,131	48,316	38,197	38,197	28,622	9,575	76.3	79.1	5.8	25.1
Augusta, Ga.	57,913	46,818	39,977	37,982	1,995	46,814	37,486	37,486	32,084	5,402	80.8	80.1	5.0	14.4
Austin, Texas	60,865	41,494	39,303	38,160	1,143	40,561	31,259	31,259	26,951	4,308	68.2	77.1	2.9	13.8
Baltimore, Md.	497,922	403,467	388,242	368,010	20,232	428,923	342,209	335,589	302,580	33,009	81.0	79.8	5.2	9.8
Baton Rouge, La.	55,212	41,326	41,244	38,960	2,284	32,133	25,682	25,682	22,925	2,757	74.8	74.8	5.5	10.7
Beaumont-Port Arthur, Texas	69,557	58,037	57,945	54,025	3,920	54,466	44,681	44,681	39,418	5,263	83.4	82.0	6.8	11.8
Binghamton, N. Y.	67,529	53,450	53,398	50,865	2,533	63,909	49,761	49,761	44,036	5,725	79.2	77.9	4.7	11.5
Birmingham, Ala.	190,409	152,245	151,455	142,977	8,478	166,423	134,064	134,064	112,655	21,409	80.0	80.6	5.6	16.0
Boston, Mass.	824,704	664,496	654,027	611,413	42,614	824,704	637,942	635,972	520,081	115,891	76.1	77.4	6.5	18.2
Bridgeport, Conn.	97,188	78,890	78,890	73,013	5,877	84,909	69,554	69,054	61,287	8,267	81.3	81.9	7.4	11.9
Brockton, Mass.	47,962	35,679	35,570	33,713	1,857	48,138	35,701	35,701	29,054	6,647	74.4	74.2	5.2	18.6
Buffalo, N. Y.	407,102	328,231	327,698	309,575	18,123	378,193	300,764	300,224	245,885	54,339	80.6	79.5	5.5	18.1
Canton, Ohio	104,676	86,161	86,051	82,332	3,719	93,135	73,060	73,060	62,851	10,209	82.3	78.4	4.3	14.0
Cedar Rapids, Iowa	38,218	31,728	31,691	31,241	450	34,572	27,685	27,685	25,101	2,584	83.0	80.1	1.4	9.3
Charleston, S. C.	56,196	44,470	36,600	33,574	3,026	41,485	34,675	32,018	26,866	5,152	79.1	83.6	8.3	16.1
Charleston, W. Va.	110,769	84,942	84,761	80,379	4,382	100,179	77,432	77,232	66,748	10,484	76.7	77.3	5.2	13.6
Charlotte, N. C.	68,202	56,887	56,046	54,628	1,418		44,730	44,730	41,488	3,242	83.4	82.0	2.5	7.2
Chattanooga, Tenn.	84,634	66,506	66,389	63,401	2,988	76,195	61,390	61,390	52,692	8,698	78.6	78.6	4.5	14.2
Chicago, Ill.	2,101,089	1,722,078	1,707,159	1,635,066	72,093	1,939,289	1,574,518	1,569,578	1,338,557	231,021	82.0	81.2	4.2	14.7
Cincinnati, Ohio	327,826	262,019	261,667	248,476	13,191	302,767	242,862	241,402	207,508	33,894	79.9	80.2	5.0	14.0
Cleveland, Ohio	547,644	453,914	453,102	432,523	20,579	507,709	412,265	411,815	339,505	72,310	82.9	82.9	4.5	17.6
Columbia, S. C.	50,100	35,765	33,613	32,361	1,252	37,873	27,202	27,202	23,787	3,415	71.4	71.8	3.7	12.6
Columbus, Ga.	63,914	55,650	35,630	34,263	1,367	48,892	42,070	42,070	26,715	3,515	87.1	86.0	3.8	11.6
Columbus, Ohio	190,568	143,803	142,488	135,127	7,361	152,175	115,032	113,822	97,902	15,920	75.5	75.6	5.2	14.0
Corpus Christi, Texas	56,412	47,833	42,929	40,121	2,808	33,960	29,004	29,004	25,341	3,663	84.8	85.4	6.5	12.6
Dallas, Texas	220,659	183,726	182,601	177,254	5,347	150,853	124,606	124,606	109,404	15,202	83.3	82.6	2.9	12.2
Davenport, Iowa—Rock Island-Moline, Ill.	87,656	71,540	71,444	69,576	1,868	79,756	64,511	64,207	58,811	5,396	81.6	80.9	2.6	8.4

TABLE D-3.—EMPLOYMENT STATUS OF PERSONS 14 YEARS OLD AND OVER IN STANDARD METROPOLITAN AREAS OF 100,000 OR MORE, BY SEX: 1950 AND 1940—Cont.

Standard metropolitan area and sex	1950					1940					Percent of population in labor force		Percent of civilian labor force unemployed	
	Total population 14 years and over	Labor force	Civilian labor force Total	Employed	Unemployed	Total population 14 years and over	Labor force	Civilian labor force Total	Employed	Unemployed	1950	1940	1950	1940
MALE—Continued														
Dayton, Ohio	167,582	136,400	133,221	128,799	4,422	131,818	103,012	101,402	89,462	11,940	81.4	78.1	3.3	11.8
Denver, Colo	208,294	164,700	155,087	148,993	6,094	159,193	122,104	118,904	98,944	19,960	79.1	76.7	3.9	16.8
Des Moines, Iowa	80,905	65,442	65,318	63,606	1,712	74,301	58,864	57,764	47,730	10,034	80.9	79.2	2.6	17.4
Detroit, Mich	1,137,249	947,889	943,608	885,297	58,311	949,642	793,063	790,783	681,536	109,247	83.3	83.5	6.2	13.8
Duluth, Minn.--Superior, Wis	96,575	75,740	75,557	70,884	4,673	105,242	81,708	81,708	56,325	25,383	78.4	77.6	6.2	31.1
Durham, N. C	36,514	27,054	26,996	25,817	1,179	28,595	23,099	23,099	19,992	3,107	74.1	80.8	4.4	13.5
El Paso, Texas	71,411	58,677	42,972	41,280	1,692	46,482	36,535	32,411	27,867	4,544	82.2	78.6	4.4	14.0
Erie, Pa	80,469	64,881	64,813	61,980	2,833	77,316	55,667	55,550	47,019	8,531	80.6	79.2	4.4	15.4
Evansville, Ind	57,144	46,762	46,705	44,879	1,826	49,728	39,488	39,488	33,527	5,961	81.8	79.4	3.9	15.1
Fall River, Mass	49,385	38,325	38,200	34,794	3,406	50,914	39,824	39,824	31,046	8,778	77.6	78.2	8.9	22.0
Flint, Mich	98,692	84,008	83,945	82,186	1,759	85,191	69,779	69,779	61,694	8,085	85.1	81.9	2.1	11.6
Fort Wayne, Ind	66,426	54,582	54,523	52,818	1,705	59,546	47,014	47,014	40,789	6,225	82.2	79.0	3.1	13.2
Fort Worth, Texas	132,895	110,396	105,258	102,440	2,818	86,147	68,643	68,643	57,511	11,132	83.1	79.7	2.7	16.2
Fresno, Calif	100,777	78,692	78,550	70,345	8,205	71,963	56,130	56,130	47,151	8,979	78.1	78.0	10.4	16.0
Galveston, Texas	41,193	34,473	34,066	31,796	2,270	32,536	27,348	26,252	23,300	2,952	83.7	84.1	6.7	11.2
Grand Rapids, Mich	103,787	84,731	84,653	81,753	2,900	92,860	72,992	72,992	63,600	9,392	81.6	78.6	3.4	12.9
Greensboro-High Point, N. C	66,355	54,661	54,600	53,401	1,199	55,313	45,357	45,357	42,164	3,193	82.4	82.0	2.2	7.0
Greenville, S. C	57,434	46,382	46,298	44,816	1,482	47,618	37,815	37,815	34,074	3,741	80.8	79.4	3.2	9.9
Hamilton-Middletown, Ohio	53,762	42,495	42,447	40,899	1,548	45,581	36,053	36,053	31,266	4,787	79.0	79.1	3.6	13.3
Harrisburg, Pa	109,104	86,598	84,450	82,095	2,355	97,839	77,048	76,328	65,288	11,040	79.4	78.7	2.8	14.5
Hartford, Conn	133,317	108,804	108,652	102,724	5,928	116,223	93,119	93,119	83,796	9,323	81.6	80.1	5.5	10.0
Houston, Texas	292,131	243,159	240,333	231,101	9,232	204,500	170,644	170,644	154,087	16,557	83.2	83.4	3.8	9.7
Huntington, W. Va.--Ashland, Ky	86,360	63,577	63,472	59,641	3,831	81,225	60,432	60,432	46,412	14,021	73.6	74.4	6.0	23.2
Indianapolis, Ind	199,381	165,313	164,561	158,801	5,760	177,992	144,167	141,317	121,850	19,467	82.9	81.0	3.5	13.8
Jackson, Mich	42,775	29,326	29,291	27,630	1,661	39,377	27,183	27,183	22,720	4,463	68.6	68.7	5.7	16.4
Jackson, Miss	47,916	38,316	38,150	36,819	1,331	37,279	31,088	31,088	27,789	3,299	80.0	83.4	3.5	10.6
Jacksonville, Fla	107,693	87,861	82,584	79,156	3,428	78,898	63,464	63,464	53,685	9,779	81.6	81.6	4.2	15.4
Johnstown, Pa	106,261	78,717	78,638	72,979	5,659	113,613	87,558	87,558	71,843	15,715	74.1	77.1	7.2	17.9
Kalamazoo, Mich	46,164	35,740	35,636	34,563	1,073	38,608	29,541	29,541	26,393	3,148	77.4	76.5	3.0	10.7
Kansas City, Mo	300,469	241,984	240,840	232,731	8,109	268,055	218,284	218,284	182,036	36,248	80.5	81.4	3.4	16.6
Knoxville, Tenn	116,004	87,503	87,299	82,808	4,491	86,960	68,404	68,404	59,249	9,155	75.4	78.7	5.1	13.4
Lancaster, Pa	84,972	69,850	69,734	68,207	1,527	79,270	63,489	63,489	57,948	5,541	82.2	80.1	2.2	8.7
Lansing, Mich	65,034	48,475	48,475	46,035	2,440	49,492	39,444	39,444	33,874	5,570	74.8	79.7	5.0	14.1
Lawrence, Mass	46,524	37,126	37,035	33,983	3,052	49,335	39,691	39,691	32,611	7,080	79.8	80.5	8.2	17.8

TABLE D-3.—EMPLOYMENT STATUS OF PERSONS 14 YEARS OLD AND OVER IN STANDARD METROPOLITAN AREAS OF 100,000 OR MORE, BY SEX: 1950 AND 1940—Cont.

Standard metropolitan area and sex	1950					1940					Percent of population in labor force		Percent of civilian labor force unemployed	
	Total population 14 years and over	Labor force	Civilian labor force Total	Employed	Unemployed	Total population 14 years and over	Labor force	Civilian labor force Total	Employed	Unemployed	1950	1940	1950	1940
MALE—Continued														
Lexington, Ky.	39,578	26,517	26,450	25,394	1,056	31,244	22,500	22,500	19,217	3,283	67.0	72.0	4.0	14.6
Lincoln, Nebr.	46,097	32,953	32,703	32,027	676	38,960	28,467	28,467	24,164	4,303	71.5	73.1	2.1	15.1
Little Rock-North Little Rock, Ark.	68,910	51,946	51,778	49,517	2,261	59,005	45,493	45,493	36,801	8,692	75.4	77.1	4.4	19.1
Lorain-Elyria, Ohio	55,850	46,567	46,505	45,081	1,424	45,362	36,362	36,362	32,223	4,139	83.4	80.2	3.1	11.4
Los Angeles, Calif.	1,621,437	1,267,154	1,250,436	1,160,461	89,975	1,172,661	901,200	895,600	769,471	126,129	78.2	76.9	7.2	14.1
Louisville, Ky.	205,351	165,240	164,227	157,080	7,147	170,647	136,826	136,666	117,067	19,599	80.5	80.2	4.4	14.3
Lowell, Mass.	48,713	35,880	35,707	33,106	2,601	50,245	36,568	36,568	28,163	8,405	73.7	72.8	7.3	23.0
Lubbock, Texas	37,846	30,564	28,467	27,582	885	19,733	15,900	15,900	14,168	1,732	80.8	80.6	3.1	10.9
Macon, Ga.	45,104	37,045	35,550	34,140	1,410	32,952	27,126	27,126	22,547	4,579	82.1	82.3	4.0	16.9
Madison, Wis.	65,378	48,912	48,786	47,413	1,373	50,290	39,129	39,129	34,888	4,241	74.8	77.8	2.8	10.8
Memphis, Tenn.	171,718	140,901	133,550	127,622	5,928	134,959	111,687	111,407	96,126	15,281	82.1	82.8	4.4	13.7
Miami, Fla.	189,691	145,906	144,303	135,446	8,857	107,279	84,384	84,384	75,822	8,562	76.9	78.7	6.1	10.1
Milwaukee, Wis.	328,554	269,813	268,651	260,999	7,652	299,071	239,291	239,171	196,709	42,462	82.1	80.0	2.8	17.8
Minneapolis-St. Paul, Minn.	405,689	321,726	320,280	307,250	13,030	363,999	285,102	282,552	233,707	48,845	79.3	78.3	4.1	17.3
Mobile, Ala.	77,032	61,891	60,257	53,769	6,488	50,934	41,270	40,979	34,779	6,200	80.3	81.0	10.8	15.1
Montgomery, Ala.	47,211	46,553	33,153	31,984	1,169	41,452	32,102	30,235	26,210	4,025	77.4	77.4	3.5	13.3
Nashville, Tenn.	115,743	86,529	85,981	83,205	2,776	94,503	72,884	72,884	63,558	9,326	74.8	77.1	3.2	12.8
New Bedford, Mass.	50,857	39,884	39,768	35,986	3,782	52,346	40,972	40,782	30,938	9,844	78.4	78.3	9.5	24.1
New Britain-Bristol, Conn.	55,349	46,207	46,171	43,429	2,742	50,622	41,273	41,273	36,765	4,508	83.5	81.5	5.9	10.9
New Haven, Conn.	101,818	77,324	77,203	72,985	4,218	94,282	75,225	75,225	64,097	11,128	75.9	79.8	5.5	14.8
New Orleans, La.	242,076	190,760	186,622	174,403	12,219	205,074	166,056	165,766	134,095	31,671	78.8	81.0	6.5	19.1
New York-Northeastern New Jersey	4,904,232	3,905,979	3,884,747	3,631,452	253,295	4,656,255	3,749,037	3,732,557	3,067,455	665,102	79.6	80.5	6.5	17.8
Norfolk-Portsmouth, Va.	185,455	161,999	101,978	95,917	6,061	103,235	86,312	77,472	70,291	7,181	87.4	83.6	5.9	9.3
Oklahoma City, Okla.	116,130	95,210	92,981	90,172	2,809	91,303	71,708	71,708	60,814	10,894	82.0	78.5	3.0	15.2
Omaha, Nebr.	136,287	108,758	106,192	103,209	2,983	125,444	99,451	98,001	81,191	16,810	79.8	79.3	2.8	17.2
Orlando, Fla.	41,526	31,191	31,085	29,651	1,434	26,550	20,740	20,740	18,408	2,332	75.1	78.1	4.6	11.2
Peoria, Ill.	94,208	77,137	77,052	73,909	3,143	83,804	67,498	67,498	60,060	7,438	81.8	80.5	4.1	11.0
Philadelphia, Pa.	1,379,654	1,085,331	1,057,404	994,040	63,364	1,250,151	1,000,211	995,831	821,188	174,643	81.7	80.0	6.0	17.5
Phoenix, Ariz.	117,426	88,220	84,997	77,838	7,159	69,920	53,379	53,379	41,757	11,622	75.1	76.3	8.4	21.8
Pittsburgh, Pa.	830,049	652,933	651,665	609,297	42,368	817,997	640,831	640,831	515,445	125,386	78.3	78.3	6.5	19.6
Portland, Maine	42,449	33,238	32,446	29,595	2,851	40,882	32,375	30,795	25,911	4,884	78.3	79.2	8.8	15.9
Portland, Oreg.	263,599	208,296	207,466	190,935	16,531	208,252	163,588	161,988	136,005	25,983	79.0	78.5	8.0	16.0
Providence, R. I.	275,677	214,894	208,797	191,976	16,821	259,172	206,426	206,426	167,183	39,243	78.0	78.6	8.1	19.0
Racine, Wis.	41,047	34,432	34,402	33,272	1,130	37,149	29,676	29,676	24,750	4,926	83.9	79.9	3.3	16.6

Table D-3.—Employment Status of Persons 14 Years Old and Over in Standard Metropolitan Areas of 100,000 or More, by Sex: 1950 and 1940—Cont.

Standard metropolitan area and sex	1950					1940					Percent of population in labor force		Percent of civilian labor force unemployed	
	Total population 14 years and over	Labor force	Civilian labor force Total	Employed	Unemployed	Total population 14 years and over	Labor force	Civilian labor force Total	Employed	Unemployed	1950	1940	1950	1940
MALE—Continued														
Raleigh, N. C.	50,079	35,724	35,589	34,935	654	39,642	30,162	30,162	27,902	2,260	71.3	76.1	1.8	7.5
Reading, Pa.	98,440	80,956	80,837	78,431	2,406	95,588	76,912	76,912	66,341	10,571	82.2	80.5	3.0	13.7
Richmond, Va.	118,752	95,138	94,723	90,912	3,811	99,008	80,433	80,373	72,181	8,252	80.1	81.2	4.0	10.3
Roanoke, Va.	49,023	37,821	37,755	36,525	1,230	41,837	32,571	32,571	29,066	3,505	77.1	77.9	3.3	10.8
Rochester, N. Y.	180,991	143,761	143,595	136,456	7,139	174,300	135,784	135,784	115,987	19,797	79.4	77.9	5.0	14.6
Rockford, Ill.	56,122	48,173	48,110	47,054	1,056	48,627	39,429	39,429	35,395	4,034	85.8	81.1	2.2	10.2
Sacramento, Calif.	108,367	84,906	80,648	74,578	6,070	75,412	57,356	56,645	46,793	9,852	78.4	76.1	7.5	17.4
Saginaw, Mich.	54,641	44,833	44,792	43,107	1,685	49,690	40,296	40,296	34,347	5,949	82.1	81.1	3.8	14.8
St. Louis, Mo.	624,001	500,673	490,050	469,662	20,388	556,899	455,386	453,076	381,708	71,368	80.2	81.8	4.2	15.8
Salt Lake City, Utah.	94,919	76,319	76,035	72,231	3,804	77,121	58,907	58,557	50,215	8,342	80.4	76.4	5.0	14.2
San Antonio, Texas.	180,787	145,460	115,815	110,884	4,931	129,653	104,179	86,519	71,074	15,445	80.5	80.4	4.3	17.9
San Bernardino, Calif.	105,246	77,574	73,625	68,547	5,078	64,221	46,377	46,377	38,022	8,355	73.7	72.2	6.9	18.0
San Diego, Calif.	224,035	181,764	126,859	118,686	8,173	121,298	93,084	76,316	66,080	10,236	81.1	76.7	6.4	13.4
San Francisco-Oakland, Calif.	884,053	704,369	643,313	593,501	49,812	630,561	496,769	481,189	415,067	66,122	79.7	78.8	7.7	13.7
San Jose, Calif.	108,404	79,861	77,682	71,702	5,980	72,230	53,498	50,153	41,237	8,916	73.7	74.1	7.7	17.8
Savannah, Ga.	51,620	41,861	39,304	36,419	2,885	42,569	34,351	33,774	28,667	5,107	81.1	80.7	7.3	15.1
Scranton, Pa.	95,041	68,579	68,507	62,799	5,708	115,518	89,496	89,496	58,610	30,886	72.2	77.5	8.3	34.5
Seattle, Wash.	281,848	221,932	213,009	195,914	17,095	212,977	165,978	164,678	139,157	25,521	78.7	77.9	8.0	15.5
Shreveport, La.	59,493	47,150	46,047	44,609	1,438	54,815	45,128	45,128	40,980	4,148	79.3	82.3	3.1	9.2
Sioux City, Iowa.	37,547	30,514	30,468	29,524	944	39,541	31,285	31,285	26,276	5,009	81.3	79.1	3.1	16.0
South Bend, Ind.	78,484	64,151	64,094	63,008	1,086	62,748	50,791	50,791	43,076	7,715	81.7	80.9	1.7	15.2
Spokane, Wash.	84,376	63,715	60,144	56,414	3,730	69,137	52,661	51,031	42,424	8,607	75.5	76.2	6.2	16.9
Springfield, Ill.	47,875	38,296	38,225	36,394	1,831	45,720	36,117	36,117	29,981	6,136	80.0	79.0	4.8	17.0
Springfield, Mo.	38,605	28,903	28,866	27,855	1,011	34,719	26,217	26,217	21,375	4,842	74.9	75.5	3.5	18.5
Springfield, Ohio.	40,400	32,777	32,581	31,275	1,306	37,149	29,420	29,240	25,271	4,149	81.1	79.2	4.0	14.1
Springfield-Holyoke, Mass.	151,923	121,630	117,351	111,566	5,785	142,993	112,570	112,570	93,607	18,963	80.1	78.7	4.9	16.8
Stamford-Norwalk, Conn.	71,404	58,318	58,253	56,082	2,171	62,149	49,642	49,642	43,178	6,464	81.7	79.9	3.7	13.0
Stockton, Calif.	80,358	62,559	62,354	55,848	6,506	62,441	48,435	48,435	39,391	9,044	77.9	77.6	10.4	18.7
Syracuse, N. Y.	129,745	100,670	100,500	95,032	5,468	116,880	90,670	90,670	76,849	13,821	77.6	77.6	5.4	15.2
Tacoma, Wash.	119,576	96,023	63,873	59,882	3,991	80,362	60,741	53,658	43,606	10,052	80.3	75.7	6.2	18.7
Tampa-St. Petersburg, Fla.	151,822	107,603	102,540	97,544	4,996	105,021	78,510	78,510	65,562	12,948	70.9	74.8	4.9	16.5
Terre Haute, Ind.	39,317	29,719	29,679	28,050	1,629	39,091	30,314	30,314	22,131	8,183	75.6	77.5	5.5	27.0
Toledo, Ohio.	148,289	121,226	121,090	113,497	7,593	136,388	108,268	108,268	86,689	21,579	81.7	79.4	6.3	19.9
Topeka, Kans.	38,752	30,169	30,059	29,172	887	34,532	26,064	26,064	22,402	3,662	77.9	75.6	3.0	14.1

TABLE D-3.—EMPLOYMENT STATUS OF PERSONS 14 YEARS OLD AND OVER IN STANDARD METROPOLITAN AREAS OF 100,000 OR MORE, BY SEX: 1950 AND 1940—Cont.

Standard metropolitan area and sex	1950 Total population 14 years and over	1950 Labor force	1950 Civilian labor force Total	1950 Civilian labor force Employed	1950 Civilian labor force Unemployed	1940 Total population 14 years and over	1940 Labor force	1940 Civilian labor force Total	1940 Civilian labor force Employed	1940 Civilian labor force Unemployed	Percent of population in labor force 1950	Percent of population in labor force 1940	Percent of civilian labor force unemployed 1950	Percent of civilian labor force unemployed 1940
MALE—Continued														
Trenton, N. J.	90,964	68,630	68,315	65,595	2,720	79,523	61,889	61,889	52,228	9,661	75.4	77.8	4.0	15.6
Tulsa, Okla.	89,888	72,069	71,955	69,002	2,953	72,688	57,927	57,927	50,367	7,560	80.2	79.7	4.1	13.1
Utica-Rome, N. Y.	106,510	81,415	80,887	74,477	6,410	106,062	80,537	80,537	69,194	11,343	76.4	75.9	7.9	14.1
Waco, Texas	49,078	35,692	33,755	32,525	1,230	37,813	28,279	28,279	24,172	4,107	72.7	74.8	3.6	14.5
Washington, D. C.	538,724	436,916	393,941	382,096	11,845	379,395	305,892	295,452	266,918	28,534	81.1	80.5	3.0	9.7
Waterbury, Conn.	57,856	47,783	47,747	44,412	3,335	55,656	46,005	46,005	40,178	5,827	82.6	82.7	7.0	12.7
Waterloo, Iowa	36,180	30,769	30,730	30,094	636	30,766	25,349	25,349	23,855	1,494	85.0	82.4	2.1	5.9
Wheeling, W. Va.—Steubenville, Ohio	131,765	102,110	102,048	97,104	4,944	142,927	110,092	110,092	89,375	20,717	77.5	77.0	4.8	18.8
Wichita, Kans.	77,977	64,737	64,637	63,039	1,598	54,177	42,467	42,467	37,621	4,846	83.0	78.4	2.5	11.4
Wilkes-Barre—Hazleton, Pa.	145,363	105,963	105,853	96,736	9,117	167,935	132,067	132,067	91,108	40,959	72.9	78.6	8.6	31.0
Wilmington, Del.	99,056	79,352	79,207	76,046	3,161	88,636	71,818	70,917	62,947	7,970	80.1	81.0	4.0	11.2
Winston-Salem, N. C.	50,345	40,660	40,624	39,458	1,166	44,360	36,191	36,191	31,432	4,759	80.8	81.6	2.9	13.1
Worcester, Mass.	103,705	77,149	77,020	72,100	4,920	98,795	74,039	74,039	62,630	11,409	74.4	74.9	6.4	15.4
York, Pa.	75,675	63,339	61,272	59,727	1,545	68,196	55,265	55,265	49,178	6,087	83.7	81.0	2.5	11.0
Youngstown, Ohio	198,685	163,053	162,926	154,878	8,048	189,038	149,785	149,785	120,560	29,225	82.1	79.2	4.9	19.5
FEMALE														
Akron, Ohio	157,668	45,757	45,731	43,127	2,604	133,956	33,170	33,170	27,373	5,797	29.0	24.8	5.7	17.5
Albany-Schenectady-Troy, N. Y.	208,762	65,840	65,825	63,501	2,324	195,428	57,884	57,884	50,682	7,202	31.5	29.6	3.5	12.4
Albuquerque, N. Mex.	50,628	13,464	13,419	13,015	404	25,538	5,962	5,962	5,168	794	26.6	23.3	3.0	13.3
Allentown-Bethlehem-Easton, Pa.	173,017	56,568	56,555	55,138	1,417	156,992	43,175	43,175	39,011	4,164	32.7	27.5	2.5	9.6
Altoona, Pa.	54,734	12,018	11,994	11,481	513	54,903	10,402	10,402	8,562	1,840	22.0	18.9	4.3	17.7
Asheville, N. C.	48,292	15,242	15,241	14,496	745	42,391	13,032	13,032	11,075	1,957	31.6	30.7	4.9	15.0
Atlanta, Ga.	267,144	97,872	97,690	94,734	2,956	213,449	79,000	79,000	69,688	9,688	36.6	37.0	3.0	12.3
Atlantic City, N. J.	55,502	17,470	17,448	16,283	1,165	53,367	17,325	17,325	13,830	3,495	31.5	32.5	6.7	20.2
Augusta, Ga.	58,873	21,021	20,787	19,775	1,012	51,032	18,965	18,965	16,345	2,620	35.7	37.2	4.9	13.8
Austin, Texas	61,480	20,460	20,444	19,908	536	44,967	14,075	14,075	12,146	1,929	33.3	31.3	2.6	13.7
Baltimore, Md.	519,899	168,787	168,453	160,240	8,213	434,530	134,656	134,656	122,007	12,649	32.5	31.0	4.9	9.4
Baton Rouge, La.	58,418	17,596	17,592	16,999	593	55,219	11,133	11,133	10,319	814	30.1	31.6	3.4	7.3
Beaumont-Port Arthur, Texas	72,565	20,769	20,766	19,691	1,075	55,496	14,383	14,383	12,391	1,992	28.6	25.9	5.2	13.8
Binghamton, N. Y.	73,309	24,856	24,851	23,889	962	66,299	21,943	21,943	20,013	1,930	33.9	33.1	3.9	8.8
Birmingham, Ala.	214,661	61,710	61,655	58,535	3,120	180,689	47,484	47,484	39,317	8,167	28.7	26.3	5.1	17.2
Boston, Mass.	975,578	316,094	315,652	303,305	12,347	913,936	285,095	285,095	245,319	39,776	32.4	31.2	3.9	14.0

TABLE D-3.—EMPLOYMENT STATUS OF PERSONS 14 YEARS OLD AND OVER IN STANDARD METROPOLITAN AREAS OF 100,000 OR MORE, BY SEX: 1950 AND 1940—Cont.

Standard metropolitan area and sex	1950					1940					Percent of population in labor force		Percent of civilian labor force unemployed	
	Total population 14 years and over	Labor force	Civilian labor force			Total population 14 years and over	Labor force	Civilian labor force			1950	1940	1950	1940
			Total	Employed	Unemployed			Total	Employed	Unemployed				
FEMALE—Continued														
Bridgeport, Conn.	102,375	34,539	34,527	32,158	2,369	86,691	29,510	29,510	26,654	2,856	33.7	34.0	6.9	9.7
Brockton, Mass.	51,579	16,325	16,325	15,712	613	48,902	14,995	14,995	12,885	2,110	31.7	30.7	3.8	14.1
Buffalo, N.Y.	427,492	121,498	121,465	114,194	7,271	381,438	99,868	99,868	83,145	16,723	28.4	26.2	6.0	16.7
Canton, Ohio	107,878	28,714	28,705	27,425	1,280	91,691	20,148	20,148	17,671	2,477	26.6	22.0	4.5	12.3
Cedar Rapids, Iowa	41,382	13,561	13,558	13,273	285	36,747	8,907	8,907	8,153	754	32.8	24.2	2.1	8.5
Charleston, S. C.	57,428	19,120	19,002	17,739	1,263	45,372	16,205	16,205	14,579	1,626	33.3	35.7	6.6	10.0
Charleston, W. Va.	74,127	25,505	25,496	24,500	996	96,106	17,911	17,911	16,095	1,816	22.3	18.6	3.9	10.1
Charlotte, N. C.	76,377	31,944	30,973	30,058	915	60,020	23,424	23,424	21,591	1,833	41.8	39.0	3.0	7.8
Chattanooga, Tenn.	95,153	30,897	30,875	29,638	1,237	82,295	25,578	25,578	22,619	2,959	32.5	31.0	4.0	11.6
Chicago, Ill.	2,184,813	760,739	759,623	727,485	32,138	1,970,094	613,270	613,270	536,792	76,478	34.8	31.1	4.2	12.5
Cincinnati, Ohio	368,834	113,296	113,252	108,862	4,390	330,027	91,746	91,746	80,399	11,347	30.7	27.8	3.9	12.4
Cleveland, Ohio	586,934	191,165	191,080	183,286	7,794	526,060	154,137	154,137	131,497	22,640	32.6	29.3	4.1	14.7
Columbia, S. C.	54,329	18,930	18,900	18,416	484	42,077	15,485	15,485	13,706	1,779	34.8	36.8	2.6	11.5
Columbus, Ga.	58,841	21,843	21,690	20,789	901	45,536	18,930	18,930	17,381	1,549	37.1	41.6	4.2	8.2
Columbus, Ohio	199,938	68,206	68,083	64,850	3,233	161,615	45,636	45,636	40,779	4,857	34.1	28.2	4.7	10.6
Corpus Christi, Texas	55,358	15,239	15,136	14,409	727	32,315	8,325	8,325	7,450	875	27.5	25.8	4.8	10.5
Dallas, Texas	244,868	93,436	93,399	90,838	2,561	167,511	59,788	59,788	52,615	7,173	38.2	35.7	2.7	12.0
Davenport, Iowa—Rock Island-Moline, Ill.	89,777	26,532	26,528	25,669	859	78,592	19,253	19,253	17,646	1,607	29.6	24.5	3.2	8.3
Dayton, Ohio	174,658	54,831	54,709	52,592	2,117	131,721	34,065	34,065	30,726	3,339	31.4	25.9	3.9	9.8
Denver, Colo.	220,859	71,943	71,352	69,005	2,347	167,493	47,039	47,039	41,215	5,824	32.6	28.1	3.3	12.4
Des Moines, Iowa	90,828	31,851	31,841	31,293	548	81,890	24,304	24,304	21,173	3,131	35.1	29.7	1.7	12.9
Detroit, Mich.	1,132,476	327,713	327,519	308,047	19,472	902,672	237,203	237,203	202,960	34,243	28.9	26.3	5.9	14.4
Duluth, Minn.—Superior, Wis.	93,514	26,242	26,226	25,294	932	96,781	22,489	22,489	17,841	4,648	28.1	23.2	3.6	20.7
Durham, N. C.	39,779	16,832	16,827	15,058	1,769	32,420	13,440	13,440	11,312	2,128	42.3	41.5	10.5	15.8
El Paso, Texas	65,810	18,765	18,535	17,936	599	47,231	13,294	13,294	11,636	1,658	28.5	28.1	3.2	12.5
Erie, Pa.	83,381	25,065	25,051	24,241	810	70,438	16,810	16,810	14,133	2,677	30.1	23.9	3.2	15.9
Evansville, Ind.	63,551	18,804	18,799	17,903	896	53,549	14,133	14,133	12,344	1,789	29.6	26.4	4.8	12.7
Fall River, Mass.	55,410	22,777	22,769	21,856	913	55,383	22,866	22,866	20,119	2,747	41.1	41.3	4.0	12.0
Flint, Mich.	98,525	27,877	27,863	26,339	1,524	82,915	19,102	19,102	16,576	2,526	28.3	23.0	5.5	13.2
Fort Wayne, Ind.	71,864	23,404	23,404	22,663	741	62,758	16,383	16,383	15,034	1,349	32.6	26.1	3.2	8.2
Fort Worth, Texas	139,345	45,835	45,802	44,258	1,544	92,730	28,278	28,278	23,562	4,716	32.9	30.5	3.4	16.7
Fresno, Calif.	97,965	25,205	25,190	22,542	2,648	66,122	13,751	13,751	11,665	2,086	25.7	20.8	10.5	15.2
Galveston, Texas	41,640	13,538	13,523	12,956	567	31,606	9,888	9,888	8,570	1,318	32.5	31.3	4.2	13.3

TABLE **D-3.**—EMPLOYMENT STATUS OF PERSONS 14 YEARS OLD AND OVER IN STANDARD METROPOLITAN AREAS OF 100,000 OR MORE, BY SEX: 1950 AND 1940—Cont.

Standard metropolitan area and sex	1950					1940					Percent of population in labor force		Percent of civilian labor force unemployed	
	Total population 14 years and over	Labor force	Civilian labor force			Total population 14 years and over	Labor force	Civilian labor force			1950	1940	1950	1940
			Total	Employed	Unemployed			Total	Employed	Unemployed				
FEMALE--Continued														
Grand Rapids, Mich.	110,848	33,619	33,605	32,213	1,392	97,469	24,331	24,331	22,066	2,265	30.3	25.0	4.1	9.3
Greensboro-High Point, N. C.	75,314	31,238	31,232	30,278	954	59,554	23,621	23,621	21,794	1,827	41.5	39.7	3.1	7.7
Greenville, S. C.	63,401	24,353	24,347	23,519	828	51,527	17,826	17,826	16,343	1,483	38.4	34.6	3.4	8.3
Hamilton-Middletown, Ohio	55,799	15,141	15,136	14,495	641	46,242	10,869	10,869	9,613	1,256	27.1	23.5	4.2	11.6
Harrisburg, Pa.	115,654	37,280	37,237	36,432	805	102,132	28,819	28,819	25,393	3,426	32.2	28.2	2.2	11.9
Hartford, Conn.	144,654	55,841	55,824	53,539	2,285	123,447	41,852	41,852	37,982	3,870	38.6	33.9	4.1	9.2
Houston, Texas	303,977	97,312	97,222	94,091	3,131	208,968	64,417	64,417	57,820	6,597	32.0	30.8	3.2	10.2
Huntington, W. Va.--Ashland, Ky.	91,394	21,094	21,081	20,181	900	82,962	16,383	16,383	13,396	2,987	23.1	19.7	4.3	18.2
Indianapolis, Ind.	221,719	77,664	77,645	75,158	2,487	191,684	57,087	57,087	50,611	6,476	35.0	29.8	3.2	11.3
Jackson, Mich.	38,692	11,285	11,281	10,635	646	34,277	8,550	8,550	7,472	1,078	29.2	24.9	5.7	12.6
Jackson, Miss.	54,936	20,779	20,772	19,969	803	42,542	16,653	16,653	15,059	1,594	37.8	39.1	3.9	9.6
Jacksonville, Fla.	118,128	40,472	40,331	38,578	1,753	85,570	29,638	29,638	25,690	3,948	34.3	34.6	4.3	13.3
Johnstown, Pa.	106,079	20,626	20,621	19,627	994	104,890	18,237	18,237	14,474	3,763	19.4	17.4	4.8	20.6
Kalamazoo, Mich.	48,988	15,099	15,098	14,614	484	39,601	9,989	9,989	9,244	745	30.8	25.2	3.2	7.5
Kansas City, Mo.	331,121	110,379	110,337	107,080	3,257	290,050	88,357	88,357	75,731	12,626	33.3	30.5	3.0	14.3
Knoxville, Tenn.	125,759	33,620	33,608	31,809	1,799	93,069	24,823	24,823	22,383	2,440	26.7	26.7	5.4	9.8
Lancaster, Pa.	91,179	29,895	29,891	29,302	589	83,646	23,492	23,492	21,787	1,705	32.8	28.1	2.0	7.3
Lansing, Mich.	65,271	20,546	20,533	19,580	953	50,741	13,135	13,135	11,848	1,287	31.5	25.9	4.6	9.8
Lawrence, Mass.	51,896	21,950	21,945	20,257	1,688	52,063	21,521	21,521	17,879	3,642	42.3	41.3	7.7	16.9
Lexington, Ky.	39,756	12,690	12,685	12,291	394	32,203	9,243	9,243	8,006	1,237	31.9	28.7	3.1	13.4
Lincoln, Nebr.	49,094	17,374	17,368	17,039	329	43,032	12,580	12,580	11,008	1,572	35.4	29.2	1.9	12.5
Little Rock-North Little Rock, Ark.	77,554	26,826	26,817	25,789	1,028	63,597	18,943	18,943	16,165	2,778	34.6	29.8	3.8	14.7
Lorain-Elyria, Ohio	54,583	13,715	13,711	13,178	533	43,487	9,197	9,197	7,904	1,293	25.1	21.1	3.9	14.1
Los Angeles, Calif.	1,784,360	574,104	573,301	529,955	43,346	1,237,495	347,674	347,674	303,977	43,697	32.2	28.1	7.6	12.6
Louisville, Ky.	226,961	69,947	69,926	67,364	2,562	186,396	54,161	54,161	46,595	7,566	30.8	29.1	3.7	14.0
Lowell, Mass.	53,515	18,466	18,454	17,290	1,164	52,577	17,047	17,047	14,008	3,039	34.5	32.4	6.3	17.8
Lubbock, Texas	35,208	10,354	10,342	10,009	333	19,370	4,773	4,773	4,157	616	29.4	24.6	3.2	12.9
Macon, Ga.	51,950	18,717	18,699	17,775	924	38,434	14,966	14,966	13,109	1,857	36.0	38.9	4.9	12.4
Madison, Wis.	64,864	23,335	23,320	22,756	564	52,152	15,306	15,306	14,065	1,241	36.0	29.3	2.4	8.1
Memphis, Tenn.	189,038	67,214	67,054	63,571	3,483	148,477	50,883	50,883	44,152	6,731	35.6	34.3	5.2	13.2
Miami, Fla.	202,825	68,151	68,090	64,446	3,644	111,922	38,936	38,936	35,180	3,756	33.6	34.8	5.4	9.6
Milwaukee, Wis.	347,915	116,643	116,610	113,756	2,854	309,757	87,653	87,653	76,261	11,392	33.5	28.3	2.4	13.0
Minneapolis-St. Paul, Minn.	445,134	158,455	158,375	154,099	4,276	395,729	124,529	124,529	108,346	16,183	35.6	31.5	2.7	13.0
Mobile, Ala.	84,581	28,632	28,566	26,845	1,721	55,594	17,411	17,411	14,430	2,981	33.9	31.3	6.0	17.1
Montgomery, Ala.	54,033	20,480	20,378	19,751	627	44,835	16,404	16,404	14,423	1,981	37.9	36.6	3.1	12.1

TABLE D–3.—EMPLOYMENT STATUS OF PERSONS 14 YEARS OLD AND OVER IN STANDARD METROPOLITAN AREAS OF 100,000 OR MORE, BY SEX: 1950 AND 1940—Cont.

Standard metropolitan area and sex	1950					1940					Percent of population in labor force		Percent of civilian labor force unemployed	
	Total population 14 years and over	Labor force	Civilian labor force Total	Employed	Unemployed	Total population 14 years and over	Labor force	Civilian labor force Total	Employed	Unemployed	1950	1940	1950	1940
FEMALE—Continued														
Nashville, Tenn.	130,494	45,680	45,655	44,393	1,262	106,482	34,482	34,482	30,621	3,861	35.0	32.4	2.8	11.2
New Bedford, Mass.	57,042	23,428	23,420	21,878	1,542	56,258	21,942	21,942	17,444	4,498	41.1	39.0	6.6	20.5
New Britain-Bristol, Conn.	57,734	21,427	21,424	20,242	1,182	49,937	16,216	16,216	14,689	1,527	37.1	32.5	5.5	9.4
New Haven, Conn.	105,823	36,183	36,170	34,766	1,404	100,039	33,097	33,097	29,373	3,724	34.2	33.1	3.9	11.3
New Orleans, La.	273,035	84,414	84,355	80,435	3,920	231,383	74,257	74,257	61,625	12,632	30.9	32.1	4.6	17.0
New York-Northeastern New Jersey	5,327,807	1,774,045	1,772,402	1,683,342	89,060	4,835,482	1,578,908	1,578,908	1,327,320	241,588	33.3	32.7	5.0	15.3
Norfolk-Portsmouth, Va.	152,197	46,357	45,880	42,856	3,024	100,639	29,160	29,160	25,337	3,823	30.5	29.0	6.6	13.1
Oklahoma City, Okla.	127,279	42,797	42,764	41,518	1,246	98,641	30,342	30,342	25,966	4,376	33.6	30.8	2.9	14.4
Omaha, Nebr.	142,926	45,364	45,223	44,281	942	131,018	35,949	35,949	31,051	4,898	31.7	27.4	2.1	13.6
Orlando, Fla.	46,356	14,678	14,665	13,984	681	28,933	10,132	10,132	8,864	1,268	31.7	35.0	4.6	12.5
Peoria, Ill.	95,194	27,840	27,831	26,772	1,059	83,357	20,089	20,089	18,384	1,705	29.2	24.1	3.8	8.5
Philadelphia, Pa.	1,469,044	464,894	463,871	443,911	19,960	1,310,949	406,379	406,379	339,189	67,190	31.6	31.0	4.3	16.5
Phoenix, Ariz.	188,894	33,032	33,000	30,585	2,415	65,937	14,697	14,697	12,739	1,958	27.8	22.3	7.3	13.3
Pittsburgh, Pa.	860,101	210,068	209,956	199,514	10,442	804,527	181,636	181,636	146,939	34,697	24.4	22.6	5.0	19.1
Portland, Maine	49,088	15,616	15,606	14,707	899	44,156	13,721	13,721	12,055	1,666	31.8	31.1	5.8	12.1
Portland, Oreg.	274,431	87,720	87,680	82,413	5,267	207,346	55,903	55,903	48,848	7,055	32.0	27.0	6.0	12.6
Providence, R. I.	297,135	106,821	106,716	101,035	5,681	279,525	98,512	98,512	83,293	15,219	36.0	35.2	5.3	15.4
Racine, Wis.	41,740	12,371	12,369	11,908	461	36,636	8,352	8,352	7,246	1,106	29.6	22.8	3.7	13.2
Raleigh, N. C.	51,172	17,064	17,059	16,696	363	42,224	12,564	12,564	11,242	1,322	33.3	29.8	2.1	10.5
Reading, Pa.	103,648	35,090	35,083	34,382	701	97,019	31,092	31,092	28,280	2,812	33.9	32.0	2.0	9.0
Richmond, Va.	135,641	52,385	52,366	49,816	2,550	112,399	43,423	43,423	38,541	4,882	38.6	38.6	4.9	11.2
Roanoke, Va.	52,736	16,915	16,908	16,390	518	45,046	13,071	13,071	11,580	1,491	32.1	29.0	3.1	11.4
Rochester, N. Y.	200,277	68,784	68,759	65,741	3,018	184,332	57,044	57,044	50,655	6,389	34.3	30.9	4.4	11.2
Rockford, Ill.	58,677	19,653	19,647	19,200	447	48,438	13,183	13,183	12,009	1,174	33.5	27.2	2.3	8.9
Sacramento, Calif.	100,655	33,861	33,824	31,522	2,302	64,373	19,257	19,257	16,581	2,676	33.6	29.9	6.8	13.9
Saginaw, Mich.	55,721	14,751	14,744	14,051	693	48,222	10,234	10,234	9,091	1,143	26.5	21.2	4.7	11.2
St. Louis, Mo.	681,008	215,404	215,082	207,255	7,827	597,449	176,814	176,814	153,313	23,501	31.6	29.6	3.6	13.3
Salt Lake City, Utah	98,591	29,006	28,988	27,552	1,436	79,723	18,110	18,110	16,146	1,964	29.4	22.7	5.0	10.8
San Antonio, Texas	181,715	52,039	50,667	49,082	1,595	129,407	35,987	35,987	30,374	5,613	28.6	27.8	3.1	15.6
San Bernardino, Calif.	103,596	25,080	25,059	23,395	1,664	61,352	13,564	13,564	11,392	2,172	24.2	22.1	6.6	16.0
San Diego, Calif.	202,843	55,491	54,971	50,144	4,827	114,682	28,058	28,058	24,448	3,610	27.4	24.5	8.8	12.9
San Francisco-Oakland, Calif.	867,081	295,059	293,643	271,066	22,577	604,712	178,992	178,992	155,435	23,557	34.0	29.6	7.7	13.2
San Jose, Calif.	112,252	32,663	32,587	29,120	3,467	71,561	18,369	18,369	15,193	3,176	29.1	25.7	10.6	13.3
Savannah, Ga.	58,404	19,527	19,514	18,295	1,219	48,648	16,857	16,857	13,448	3,409	33.4	34.7	6.2	20.2
Scranton, Pa.	106,171	30,553	30,542	29,533	1,009	118,554	30,923	30,923	22,555	8,368	28.8	26.1	3.3	27.1

TABLE D-3.—EMPLOYMENT STATUS OF PERSONS 14 YEARS OLD AND OVER IN STANDARD METROPOLITAN AREAS OF 100,000 OR MORE, BY SEX: 1950 AND 1940—Cont.

| Standard metropolitan area and sex | 1950 | | | | | | | 1940 | | | | | | Percent of population in labor force | | Percent of civilian labor force unemployed | |
| | Total population 14 years and over | Labor force | Civilian labor force | | | Total population 14 years and over | Labor force | Civilian labor force | | | | | 1950 | 1940 | 1950 | 1940 |
			Total	Employed	Unemployed			Total	Employed	Unemployed						
FEMALE—Continued																
Seattle, Wash.	281,485	91,669	91,367	85,913	5,454	208,288	58,175	58,175	51,783	6,392	32.6	27.9	6.0	11.0
Shreveport, La.	68,375	22,940	22,928	22,293	635	60,496	20,686	20,686	18,821	1,865	33.6	34.2	2.8	9.0
Sioux City, Iowa	40,995	12,825	12,822	12,564	258	41,279	11,206	11,206	9,903	1,303	31.7	27.1	2.0	11.6
South Bend, Ind.	76,851	23,871	23,863	23,272	591	63,215	17,551	17,551	15,736	1,815	31.1	27.8	2.5	10.3
Spokane, Wash.	84,011	24,119	24,074	22,933	1,141	66,176	17,188	17,188	15,039	2,149	28.7	26.0	4.7	12.5
Springfield, Ill.	53,495	17,138	17,131	16,572	559	48,743	13,218	13,218	11,705	1,513	32.0	27.1	3.3	11.4
Springfield, Mo.	42,020	11,432	11,429	11,058	371	36,941	7,959	7,959	6,919	1,040	27.2	21.5	3.2	13.1
Springfield, Ohio	43,342	12,403	12,398	11,888	510	38,171	8,834	8,834	7,710	1,124	28.6	23.1	4.1	12.7
Springfield-Holyoke, Mass	166,502	57,166	56,985	54,983	2,002	152,849	49,429	49,429	41,598	7,831	34.3	32.3	3.5	15.8
Stamford-Norwalk, Conn.	79,827	27,496	27,484	26,655	829	66,158	22,745	22,745	20,685	2,060	34.4	34.4	3.0	9.1
Stockton, Calif.	70,162	20,270	20,254	17,716	2,538	46,939	10,525	10,525	8,927	1,598	28.9	22.4	12.5	15.2
Syracuse, N. Y.	135,365	44,922	44,903	43,037	1,866	120,134	33,370	33,370	28,917	4,453	33.2	27.8	4.2	13.3
Tacoma, Wash.	93,294	24,745	24,417	23,155	1,262	69,170	15,096	15,096	12,670	2,426	26.5	21.8	5.2	16.1
Tampa-St. Petersburg, Fla.	167,127	49,506	49,454	46,815	2,639	112,480	37,758	37,758	31,760	5,998	29.6	33.6	5.3	15.9
Terre Haute, Ind.	42,154	12,274	12,273	11,784	489	41,292	9,829	9,829	8,256	1,573	29.1	23.8	4.0	16.0
Toledo, Ohio	154,606	47,798	47,782	45,082	2,700	138,540	37,662	37,662	31,505	6,157	30.9	27.2	5.7	16.3
Topeka, Kans.	43,182	15,060	15,054	14,729	325	38,882	10,794	10,794	9,458	1,336	34.9	27.8	2.2	12.4
Trenton, N. J.	91,297	33,161	33,145	31,974	1,171	79,862	26,645	26,645	23,629	3,016	36.3	33.4	3.5	11.3
Tulsa, Okla.	98,642	31,644	31,636	30,540	1,096	77,920	22,585	22,585	19,685	2,900	32.1	29.0	3.5	12.8
Utica-Rome, N. Y.	111,246	34,628	34,615	32,319	2,296	106,337	31,673	31,673	28,122	3,551	31.1	29.8	6.6	11.2
Waco, Texas	49,811	14,547	14,547	13,869	678	39,939	10,831	10,831	8,805	2,026	29.2	27.1	4.7	18.7
Washington, D. C.	586,440	249,151	246,786	238,807	7,979	404,711	165,155	165,155	150,657	14,498	42.5	40.8	3.2	8.8
Waterbury, Conn.	60,668	22,203	22,098	20,296	1,802	55,844	19,265	19,265	17,304	1,961	36.4	34.5	8.2	10.2
Waterloo, Iowa	38,360	12,389	12,386	12,034	352	31,737	7,954	7,954	7,483	471	32.3	25.1	2.8	5.9
Wheeling, W. Va.—Steubenville, Ohio	134,195	31,917	31,898	30,665	1,233	135,795	28,537	28,537	24,279	3,044	23.8	21.0	3.9	10.7
Wichita, Kans.	85,919	26,306	26,297	25,536	761	59,232	15,950	15,950	14,470	1,480	30.6	26.9	2.9	9.3
Wilkes-Barre—Hazleton, Pa.	158,358	43,903	43,891	42,137	1,754	168,667	41,223	41,223	28,843	12,380	27.7	24.4	4.0	30.0
Wilmington, Del.	103,785	31,148	31,138	30,123	1,015	87,183	25,196	25,196	22,564	2,632	30.0	28.9	3.3	10.4
Winston-Salem, N. C.	57,221	22,413	22,413	21,301	1,112	49,407	21,142	21,142	18,377	2,765	39.2	42.8	5.0	13.1
Worcester, Mass.	112,195	33,825	33,811	32,605	1,206	104,379	29,951	29,951	25,656	4,295	30.1	28.7	3.6	14.3
York, Pa.	77,631	25,336	25,322	24,738	584	69,509	19,810	19,810	18,023	1,787	32.6	28.5	2.3	9.0
Youngstown, Ohio	200,352	50,107	50,086	47,440	2,646	180,232	38,135	38,135	30,603	7,532	25.0	21.2	5.3	19.8

Source: Derived from *1950 Census of Population*, Vol. II, *Characteristics of the Population*, Part 1, U. S. Summary, table 89; *1940 Census of Population*, Vol. II, *Characteristics of the Population*, Parts 1–7, State table 23; and unpublished estimates.

TABLE D–4.—POPULATION AND LABOR FORCE, BY COLOR AND SEX, FOR SELECTED STANDARD METROPOLITAN AREAS: 1950 AND 1940

Standard metropolitan area and color	Male						Female					
	1950			1940			1950			1940		
	Population 14 years old and over	Labor force		Population 14 years old and over	Labor force		Population 14 years old and over	Labor force		Population 14 years old and over	Labor force	
		Number	Per-cent		Number	Per-cent	Change in percent in labor force, 1940 to 1950		Number	Per-cent		Number	Per-cent	Change in percent in labor force, 1940 to 1950

Re-organized with all columns:

Standard metropolitan area and color	Male 1950 Pop. 14+	Male 1950 LF Number	Male 1950 LF %	Male 1940 Pop. 14+	Male 1940 LF Number	Male 1940 LF %	Male Change % 1940–50	Female 1950 Pop. 14+	Female 1950 LF Number	Female 1950 LF %	Female 1940 Pop. 14+	Female 1940 LF Number	Female 1940 LF %	Female Change % 1940–50
WHITE														
Akron, Ohio	141,029	116,574	82.7	128,115	102,078	79.7	3.0	148,089	42,513	28.7	128,762	31,730	24.6	4.1
Amarillo, Texas	30,324	25,775	85.0	22,012	18,084	82.2	2.8	31,629	10,180	32.2	22,731	6,357	28.0	4.2
Asheville, N. C.	37,938	28,359	74.8	33,144	25,160	75.9	-1.1	42,189	12,040	28.5	35,669	9,341	26.2	2.3
Atlanta, Ga.	182,186	144,029	79.1	140,865	114,001	80.9	-1.8	199,779	67,356	33.7	152,386	46,572	30.6	3.1
Atlantic City, N. J.	41,853	32,303	77.2	40,617	32,090	79.0	-1.8	46,446	13,316	28.7	44,903	13,442	29.9	-1.2
Augusta, Ga.	40,275	32,764	81.4	28,710	22,184	77.3	4.1	38,041	12,543	33.0	29,853	8,814	29.5	3.5
Austin, Texas	53,257	36,261	68.1	33,982	26,214	77.1	-9.0	52,246	16,499	31.6	36,813	10,065	27.3	4.3
Baltimore, Md.	402,072	330,450	82.2	355,887	284,810	80.0	2.2	420,968	126,890	30.1	359,405	100,152	27.9	2.2
Baton Rouge, La.	38,209	29,267	76.6	20,484	16,390	80.0	-3.4	38,851	10,455	26.9	21,293	5,079	23.9	3.0
Beaumont-Port Arthur, Texas	54,606	45,923	84.1	42,396	34,804	82.1	2.0	56,399	13,840	24.5	42,138	8,424	20.0	4.5
Birmingham, Ala.	123,933	101,336	81.8	100,772	84,370	83.7	-1.9	135,992	36,214	26.6	109,383	23,415	21.4	5.2
Charleston, S. C.	37,225	30,358	81.6	23,813	20,092	84.4	-2.8	33,843	9,682	28.6	23,425	6,049	25.8	2.8
Charleston, W. Va.	100,859	78,242	77.6	90,495	69,952	77.3	0.3	104,261	22,829	21.9	86,838	15,217	17.5	4.4
Charlotte, N. C.	51,723	43,577	84.3	39,820	32,688	82.1	2.2	57,514	22,545	39.2	42,768	14,240	33.3	5.9
Chattanooga, Tenn.	69,561	55,108	79.2	61,270	49,335	80.5	-1.3	77,234	23,385	30.3	64,954	17,978	27.7	2.6
Chicago, Ill.	1,880,066	1,549,533	82.4	1,812,780	1,476,875	81.5	0.9	1,945,631	666,461	34.3	1,831,144	564,649	30.8	3.5
Cincinnati, Ohio	293,961	236,818	80.6	276,843	222,660	80.4	0.2	330,347	98,835	29.9	301,862	81,496	27.0	2.9
Cleveland, Ohio	491,327	409,308	83.3	474,270	385,813	81.3	2.0	526,070	168,164	32.0	490,367	141,598	28.9	3.1
Columbia, S. C.	33,511	24,782	73.2	23,538	17,232	73.2	0.8	36,065	11,941	33.1	25,965	8,172	31.5	1.6
Columbus, Ga.	46,854	41,690	89.0	33,000	28,592	86.6	2.4	39,002	12,819	32.9	26,591	9,085	34.2	-1.3
Columbus, Ohio	170,448	129,556	76.0	136,564	104,038	76.2	-0.2	180,120	60,330	33.5	146,551	40,336	27.5	6.0
Corpus Christi, Texas	53,512	45,386	84.8	31,801	27,084	85.2	-0.4	52,315	13,579	26.0	30,188	6,998	23.2	2.8
Dallas, Texas	191,247	160,199	83.8	128,325	105,760	82.4	1.4	211,808	76,080	35.9	140,919	44,048	31.3	4.6
Dayton, Ohio	151,248	124,520	82.3	121,646	95,828	78.8	3.5	158,463	48,754	30.8	121,973	30,674	25.1	5.7
Detroit, Mich.	1,004,170	840,901	83.7	882,402	736,925	83.5	0.2	996,934	288,709	29.0	836,142	217,501	26.0	3.0
Durham, N. C.	25,460	18,438	72.4	19,011	15,276	80.4	-8.0	26,599	10,367	39.0	20,814	7,375	35.4	3.6
El Paso, Texas	69,327	56,939	82.1	45,146	35,448	78.5	3.6	64,221	18,151	28.3	46,134	12,753	27.6	0.7
Evansville, Ind.	53,896	44,314	82.2	46,786	37,206	79.5	2.7	59,872	17,423	29.1	50,364	12,975	25.8	3.3
Flint, Mich.	93,456	79,588	85.2	82,637	67,695	81.9	3.3	93,428	26,260	28.1	80,347	18,375	22.9	5.2
Fort Worth, Texas	118,365	98,689	83.4	75,548	60,114	79.6	3.8	123,682	37,799	30.6	80,559	21,988	27.3	3.3
Fresno, Calif.	93,017	72,742	78.2	67,754	53,012	78.2	...	91,772	23,143	25.2	63,032	12,959	20.6	4.6

Note: Standard metropolitan areas shown are those in the South and those outside the South with more than 5 percent of population nonwhite in 1950.

TABLE D-4.—POPULATION AND LABOR FORCE, BY COLOR AND SEX, FOR SELECTED STANDARD METROPOLITAN AREAS: 1950 AND 1940—Cont.

Standard metropolitan area and color	Male							Female						
	1950			1940			Change in percent in labor force, 1940 to 1950	1950			1940			Change in percent in labor force, 1940 to 1950
	Population 14 years old and over	Labor force Number	Per-cent	Population 14 years old and over	Labor force Number	Per-cent		Population 14 years old and over	Labor force Number	Per-cent	Population 14 years old and over	Labor force Number	Per-cent	
WHITE—Continued														
Gadsden, Ala.	27,182	22,079	81.2	21,581	17,534	81.2	...	29,052	6,759	23.3	22,005	4,075	18.5	4.8
Galveston, Texas	32,572	27,354	84.0	25,656	21,501	83.8	0.2	32,564	9,345	28.7	24,072	5,845	24.3	4.4
Greensboro-High Point, N. C.	53,690	45,219	84.2	44,067	36,214	82.2	2.0	60,916	24,501	40.2	46,833	16,948	36.2	4.0
Greenville, S. C.	47,588	38,294	80.5	37,699	29,967	79.5	1.0	52,062	18,880	36.3	40,076	12,467	31.1	5.2
Hamilton-Middletown, Ohio	51,121	40,417	79.1	43,335	34,270	79.1	...	52,973	14,041	26.5	43,970	10,028	22.8	3.7
Harrisburg, Pa.	103,107	82,365	79.9	93,109	73,528	79.0	0.9	109,682	34,986	31.9	97,407	27,011	27.7	4.2
Houston, Texas	238,969	199,739	83.6	165,649	138,154	83.4	-0.7	245,636	71,714	29.2	165,544	42,187	25.5	3.7
Huntington, W. Va.—Ashland, Ky.	83,706	61,670	73.7	78,399	58,344	74.4	-0.7	88,535	20,027	22.6	80,035	15,109	18.9	3.7
Indianapolis, Ind.	176,119	146,962	83.4	158,557	128,581	81.1	2.3	195,520	67,103	34.3	169,960	48,859	28.7	5.6
Jackson, Miss.	27,788	22,514	81.0	19,255	15,844	82.3	-1.3	31,919	11,116	34.8	21,654	6,877	31.8	3.0
Jacksonville, Fla.	79,843	65,962	82.6	53,894	42,955	79.7	2.9	85,357	26,208	30.7	56,957	15,471	27.2	3.5
Kansas City, Mo.	268,292	218,024	81.3	242,126	196,951	81.3	...	295,325	96,283	32.6	260,980	76,402	29.3	3.3
Knoxville, Tenn.	106,738	80,514	75.4	79,416	62,426	78.6	-3.2	115,397	29,164	25.3	84,276	20,592	24.4	0.9
Laredo, Texas	17,383	12,776	73.5	14,935	11,919	79.8	-6.3	19,900	4,653	23.4	16,357	3,648	22.3	1.1
Lexington, Ky.	32,745	21,769	66.5	24,556	17,585	71.6	-5.1	32,841	9,725	29.6	25,346	6,040	23.8	5.8
Little Rock-North Little Rock, Ark.	53,394	40,834	76.5	43,826	33,639	76.8	-0.3	58,952	19,439	33.0	45,836	12,569	27.4	5.6
Los Angeles, Calif.	1,516,519	1,185,177	78.2	1,117,121	857,993	76.8	1.4	1,676,952	525,992	31.4	1,188,737	326,473	27.5	3.9
Louisville, Ky.	181,298	146,679	80.9	149,740	120,413	80.4	0.5	199,632	58,940	29.5	163,052	43,857	26.9	2.6
Lubbock, Texas	34,946	28,068	80.3	18,516	14,865	80.3	...	32,595	9,043	27.7	18,220	4,157	22.8	4.9
Macon, Ga.	30,193	25,217	83.5	19,077	15,385	80.6	2.9	33,571	10,475	31.2	21,376	6,330	29.6	1.6
Memphis, Tenn.	111,316	92,869	83.4	78,231	63,950	81.7	1.7	119,572	40,357	33.8	84,811	24,447	28.8	5.0
Miami, Fla.	166,373	126,252	75.9	88,199	67,708	76.8	-0.9	177,183	54,119	30.5	91,708	25,427	27.7	2.8
Mobile, Ala.	52,419	43,482	83.0	33,279	27,095	81.4	1.6	55,729	17,254	31.0	34,635	8,363	24.1	6.9
Montgomery, Ala.	28,249	23,128	81.9	22,817	18,022	79.0	2.9	30,579	10,087	33.0	22,417	6,524	29.1	3.9
Nashville, Tenn.	92,436	70,526	76.3	73,728	57,210	77.6	-1.3	103,356	33,852	32.8	81,653	22,404	27.4	5.4
New Orleans, La.	176,892	142,872	80.8	149,843	121,467	81.1	-0.3	194,692	56,494	29.0	164,969	45,736	27.7	1.3
New York-Northeastern New Jersey.	4,535,543	3,625,301	79.9	4,413,563	3,547,140	80.4	-0.5	4,886,813	1,561,485	32.0	4,547,394	1,433,226	31.5	0.5
Norfolk-Portsmouth, Va.	141,453	126,721	89.6	71,551	60,402	84.4	5.2	106,755	27,794	26.0	66,598	13,757	20.7	5.3
Oklahoma City, Okla.	106,598	87,699	82.3	82,756	64,962	78.5	3.8	116,453	37,911	32.6	89,089	25,200	28.3	4.3
Orlando, Fla.	33,327	24,333	73.0	20,164	15,274	75.7	-2.7	37,835	10,286	27.2	22,220	6,129	27.6	-0.4
Philadelphia, Pa.	1,208,193	961,408	79.6	1,127,329	904,556	80.2	-0.6	1,280,383	389,880	30.5	1,176,713	348,231	29.6	0.9
Phoenix, Ariz.	109,869	82,819	75.4	64,885	49,492	76.3	-0.9	111,854	30,767	27.5	61,801	13,554	21.9	5.6
Pittsburgh, Pa.	780,267	616,348	79.0	774,076	606,685	78.4	0.6	809,086	197,407	24.4	763,084	171,307	22.4	2.0

TABLE D-4.—POPULATION AND LABOR FORCE, BY COLOR AND SEX, FOR SELECTED STANDARD METROPOLITAN AREAS: 1950 AND 1940—Cont.

Standard metropolitan area and color	Male 1950 Population 14 years old and over	Male 1950 Labor force Number	Male 1950 Per cent	Male 1940 Population 14 years old and over	Male 1940 Labor force Number	Male 1940 Per cent	Male Change in percent in labor force, 1940 to 1950	Female 1950 Population 14 years old and over	Female 1950 Labor force Number	Female 1950 Per cent	Female 1940 Population 14 years old and over	Female 1940 Labor force Number	Female 1940 Per cent	Female Change in percent in labor force, 1940 to 1950
WHITE—Continued														
Raleigh, N. C.	36,876	25,688	69.7	27,268	20,514	75.2	-5.5	43,693	13,398	30.7	28,746	7,481	26.0	4.7
Richmond, Va.	87,959	72,039	81.9	72,688	59,382	81.7	0.2	100,628	36,330	36.1	81,263	26,547	32.7	3.4
Roanoke, Va.	42,373	35,048	80.3	35,879	28,019	78.1	-0.1	45,878	14,098	30.7	38,426	9,990	26.0	4.7
Sacramento, Calif.	100,396	79,013	78.7	68,452	52,179	76.2	2.5	94,950	31,349	33.0	60,735	17,978	29.6	3.4
Saginaw, Mich.	51,125	41,823	81.8	48,199	39,011	80.9	0.9	52,578	14,039	26.7	46,936	9,991	21.3	5.4
St. Louis, Mo.	548,447	445,134	81.2	500,800	410,427	82.0	-0.8	595,333	185,025	31.1	535,132	154,635	28.9	2.2
San Angelo, Texas	20,451	16,810	82.2	13,526	10,527	77.8	4.4	20,467	5,650	27.6	14,251	3,447	24.2	3.4
San Antonio, Texas	167,824	134,821	80.3	121,625	97,531	80.2	0.1	168,578	45,923	27.2	119,556	30,529	25.5	1.7
San Francisco-Oakland, Calif.	797,413	637,442	79.9	596,642	470,939	78.9	1.0	796,106	265,825	33.4	585,816	172,078	29.4	4.0
Savannah, Ga.	32,671	27,469	84.1	24,652	19,758	80.1	4.0	35,583	10,005	28.1	26,413	6,622	25.1	3.0
Shreveport, La.	39,256	32,193	82.0	33,015	26,930	81.6	0.4	43,472	12,263	28.2	34,647	8,577	24.8	3.4
Springfield, Ohio	36,800	30,010	81.5	33,891	26,893	79.4	2.1	39,411	11,000	27.9	34,705	7,865	22.7	5.2
Stockton, Calif.	70,094	53,926	76.9	53,558	40,626	75.9	1.0	65,404	18,509	28.3	44,715	9,956	22.3	6.0
Tampa-St. Petersburg, Fla.	131,646	91,658	69.6	87,355	63,677	72.9	-3.3	144,790	38,327	26.5	92,635	26,588	28.7	-2.2
Toledo, Ohio	138,574	113,556	81.9	130,536	103,613	79.4	2.5	144,592	43,990	30.4	132,591	35,521	26.8	3.6
Topeka, Kans.	35,883	28,052	78.2	31,965	24,184	75.7	2.5	40,085	13,958	34.8	36,046	9,862	27.4	7.4
Trenton, N. J.	83,029	63,018	75.9	74,145	58,083	78.3	-2.4	83,805	29,864	35.6	74,731	24,534	32.8	2.8
Tulsa, Okla.	82,245	66,341	80.7	65,628	52,587	80.1	0.6	89,422	27,352	30.6	69,564	18,088	26.0	4.6
Waco, Texas	41,431	30,628	73.9	31,226	23,381	74.9	-1.0	41,404	11,255	27.2	32,452	7,526	23.2	4.0
Washington, D. C.	414,741	340,804	82.2	293,448	237,653	81.0	1.2	451,530	182,015	40.3	310,991	117,703	37.8	2.5
Wheeling, W. Va.--Steubenville, Ohio	127,503	98,991	77.6	137,617	106,348	77.3	0.3	130,035	30,665	23.6	131,353	27,390	20.9	2.7
Wichita Falls, Texas	40,206	34,650	86.2	26,014	20,185	77.6	8.6	31,440	8,457	26.9	26,900	5,940	22.1	4.8
Wilmington, Del.	87,026	70,020	80.5	78,387	63,584	81.1	-0.6	92,002	26,104	28.4	77,528	20,558	26.5	1.9
Winston-Salem, N. C.	36,715	30,550	83.2	30,223	24,561	81.3	1.9	41,067	14,859	36.2	32,782	11,087	33.8	2.4
Youngstown, Ohio	185,337	152,270	82.2	179,986	142,580	79.2	3.0	187,656	47,016	25.1	171,766	36,074	21.0	4.1
NONWHITE														
Akron, Ohio	9,184	7,235	78.8	5,188	4,099	79.0	-0.2	9,579	3,244	33.9	5,194	1,440	27.7	6.2
Amarillo, Texas	1,323	1,123	84.9	1,085	968	89.2	-4.3	1,460	892	61.1	1,178	892	75.7	-14.6
Asheville, N. C.	5,401	3,783	70.0	5,716	4,343	76.0	-6.0	6,103	3,202	52.5	6,722	3,691	54.9	-2.4
Atlantic City, N. J.	7,865	5,894	74.9	7,699	6,107	79.3	-4.4	9,056	4,154	45.9	8,464	3,883	45.9	...

TABLE D-4.—POPULATION AND LABOR FORCE, BY COLOR AND SEX, FOR SELECTED STANDARD METROPOLITAN AREAS: 1950 AND 1940—Cont.

Standard metropolitan area and color	Male							Female						
	1950			1940			Change in percent in labor force, 1940 to 1950	1950			1940			Change in percent in labor force, 1940 to 1950
	Population 14 years old and over	Labor force Number	Per-cent	Population 14 years old and over	Labor force Number	Per-cent		Population 14 years old and over	Labor force Number	Per-cent	Population 14 years old and over	Labor force Number	Per-cent	
NONWHITE—Continued														
Atlanta, Ga.	54,733	42,167	77.0	48,561	38,804	79.9	-2.9	67,365	30,516	45.3	61,063	32,428	53.1	-7.8
Augusta, Ga.	17,638	14,054	79.7	18,104	15,302	84.5	-4.8	20,832	8,478	40.7	21,179	10,151	47.9	-7.2
Austin, Texas	7,608	5,233	68.8	6,579	5,045	76.7	-7.9	9,234	3,961	42.9	8,154	4,010	49.2	-6.3
Baltimore, Md.	95,850	73,017	76.2	73,036	57,399	78.6	-2.4	98,931	41,897	42.3	75,125	34,504	45.9	-3.6
Baton Rouge, La.	17,003	12,059	70.9	11,649	9,292	79.8	-8.9	19,567	7,141	36.5	13,926	6,054	43.5	-7.0
Beaumont-Port Arthur, Texas	14,951	12,114	81.0	12,070	9,877	81.8	-0.8	16,166	6,929	42.9	13,358	5,959	44.6	-1.7
Birmingham, Ala.	66,476	50,909	76.6	65,651	49,694	75.7	0.9	78,669	25,496	32.4	71,306	24,069	33.8	-1.4
Charleston, S. C.	18,971	14,112	74.4	17,672	14,583	82.5	-8.1	23,585	9,438	40.0	21,947	10,156	46.3	-6.3
Charleston, W. Va.	9,910	6,700	67.6	9,684	7,480	77.2	-9.6	9,866	2,676	27.1	9,268	2,694	29.1	-2.0
Charlotte, N. C.	16,479	13,310	80.8	14,750	12,042	81.6	-0.8	18,863	9,399	49.8	17,252	9,184	53.2	-3.4
Chattanooga, Tenn.	15,073	11,398	75.6	14,925	12,055	80.8	-5.2	17,919	7,512	41.9	17,341	7,600	43.8	-1.9
Chicago, Ill.	221,023	172,545	78.1	126,509	97,643	77.2	0.9	239,182	94,278	39.4	138,950	48,621	35.0	4.4
Cincinnati, Ohio	33,865	25,201	74.4	25,924	20,202	77.9	-3.5	38,487	14,461	37.6	28,165	10,250	36.4	1.2
Cleveland, Ohio	56,317	44,606	79.2	33,439	26,452	79.1	0.1	60,864	23,001	37.8	35,693	12,439	34.8	3.0
Columbia, S. C.	16,589	10,983	66.2	14,335	9,970	69.6	-3.4	18,264	6,989	38.3	16,112	7,313	45.4	-7.1
Columbus, Ga.	17,060	13,960	81.8	15,892	13,478	84.8	-3.0	19,839	9,024	45.5	18,945	9,845	52.0	-6.5
Columbus, Ohio	20,120	14,247	70.8	15,611	10,994	70.4	0.4	19,818	7,876	39.7	15,064	5,300	35.2	4.5
Corpus Christi, Texas	2,900	2,447	84.4	2,159	1,920	88.9	-4.5	3,043	1,660	54.6	2,127	1,327	62.4	-7.8
Dallas, Texas	29,412	23,527	80.0	22,528	18,846	83.7	-3.7	33,060	17,356	52.5	26,592	15,740	59.2	-6.7
Dayton, Ohio	16,334	11,880	72.7	10,172	7,184	70.6	2.1	16,195	6,077	37.5	9,748	3,391	34.8	2.7
Detroit, Mich.	133,079	106,988	80.4	67,240	56,138	83.5	-3.1	135,542	39,004	28.8	66,530	19,702	29.6	-0.8
Durham, N. C.	11,054	8,616	77.9	9,584	7,823	81.6	-3.7	13,180	6,465	49.1	11,606	6,065	52.3	-3.2
El Paso, Texas	2,084	1,738	83.4	1,336	1,087	81.4	2.0	1,589	614	38.6	1,097	541	49.3	-10.7
Evansville, Ind.	3,248	2,448	75.4	2,942	2,282	77.6	-2.2	3,679	1,381	37.5	3,185	1,158	36.4	1.1
Flint, Mich.	5,236	4,420	84.4	2,554	2,084	81.6	2.8	5,097	1,617	31.7	2,568	727	28.3	3.4
Fort Worth, Texas	14,530	11,707	80.6	10,599	8,529	80.5	0.1	15,663	8,036	51.3	12,171	6,290	51.7	-0.4
Fresno, Calif.	7,760	5,950	76.7	4,209	3,118	74.1	2.6	6,193	2,062	33.3	3,090	792	25.6	7.7
Gadsden, Ala.	4,461	3,517	78.8	3,776	3,036	80.4	-1.6	4,789	1,850	38.6	4,003	1,615	40.3	-1.7
Galveston, Texas	8,621	7,119	82.6	6,880	5,847	85.0	-2.4	9,076	4,193	46.2	7,534	4,043	53.7	-7.5
Greensboro-High Point, N. C.	12,665	9,442	74.6	11,246	9,143	81.3	-6.7	14,398	6,737	46.8	12,721	6,673	52.5	-5.7
Greenville, S. C.	9,846	8,088	82.1	9,919	7,848	79.1	3.0	11,339	5,473	48.3	11,451	5,359	46.8	1.5
Hamilton-Middletown, Ohio	2,641	2,078	78.7	2,246	1,783	79.4	-0.7	2,826	1,100	38.9	2,272	841	37.0	1.9
Harrisburg, Pa.	5,997	4,233	70.6	4,730	3,520	74.4	-3.8	5,972	2,294	38.4	4,725	1,808	38.3	0.1

TABLE D-4.—POPULATION AND LABOR FORCE, BY COLOR AND SEX, FOR SELECTED STANDARD METROPOLITAN AREAS: 1950 AND 1940—Cont.

Standard metropolitan area and color	Male							Female						
	1950			1940			Change in percent in labor force, 1940 to 1950	1950			1940			Change in percent in labor force, 1940 to 1950
	Population 14 years old and over	Labor force Number	Per cent	Population 14 years old and over	Labor force Number	Per cent		Population 14 years old and over	Labor force Number	Per cent	Population 14 years old and over	Labor force Number	Per cent	
NONWHITE—Continued														
Houston, Texas	53,162	43,420	81.7	38,851	32,490	83.6	-1.9	58,341	25,598	43.9	43,424	22,230	51.2	-7.3
Huntington, W. Va.—Ashland, Ky.	2,654	1,907	71.9	2,826	2,088	73.9	-2.0	2,859	1,067	37.3	2,927	1,274	43.5	-6.2
Indianapolis, Ind.	23,262	18,351	78.9	19,435	15,586	80.2	-1.3	26,199	10,561	40.3	21,724	8,228	37.9	2.4
Jackson, Miss.	20,128	15,802	78.5	18,024	15,244	84.6	-6.1	23,017	9,663	42.0	20,888	9,776	46.8	-4.8
Jacksonville, Fla.	27,850	21,899	78.6	25,004	20,509	82.0	-3.4	32,771	14,264	43.5	28,613	14,167	49.5	-6.0
Kansas City, Mo.	32,177	23,960	74.5	25,929	21,333	82.3	-7.8	35,796	14,096	39.4	29,070	11,955	41.1	-1.7
Knoxville, Tenn.	9,266	6,989	75.4	7,544	5,978	79.2	-3.8	10,362	4,456	43.0	8,793	4,231	48.1	-5.1
Laredo, Texas	46	25	54.3	70	58	82.9	-28.6	45	12	26.7	61	30	49.2	-22.5
Lexington, Ky.	6,833	4,748	69.5	6,688	4,915	73.5	-4.0	6,915	2,965	42.9	6,857	3,203	46.7	-3.8
Little Rock-North Little Rock, Ark.	15,516	11,112	71.6	15,179	11,854	78.1	-6.5	18,602	7,387	39.7	17,761	6,374	35.9	3.8
Los Angeles, Calif.	104,918	81,977	78.1	55,540	43,607	78.5	-0.4	107,408	48,112	44.8	48,758	21,201	43.5	1.3
Louisville, Ky.	24,053	18,561	77.2	20,907	16,413	78.5	-1.3	27,329	11,007	40.3	23,344	10,304	44.1	-3.8
Lubbock, Texas	2,900	2,496	86.1	1,217	1,035	85.0	1.1	2,613	1,311	50.2	1,150	616	53.6	-3.4
Macon, Ga.	14,911	11,828	79.3	13,875	11,741	84.6	-5.3	18,379	8,242	44.8	17,058	8,636	50.6	-5.8
Memphis, Tenn.	60,402	48,032	79.5	56,728	47,737	84.2	-4.7	69,466	26,857	38.7	63,666	26,436	41.5	-2.8
Miami, Fla.	23,318	19,654	84.3	19,080	16,676	87.4	-3.1	25,642	14,032	54.7	20,214	13,509	66.8	-12.1
Mobile, Ala.	24,613	18,409	74.8	17,655	14,175	80.4	-5.5	28,852	11,378	39.4	20,959	9,048	43.2	-3.8
Montgomery, Ala.	18,962	13,425	70.8	18,635	14,080	75.6	-4.8	23,454	10,393	44.3	22,418	9,880	44.1	0.2
Nashville, Tenn.	23,307	16,003	68.7	20,775	15,674	75.4	-6.7	27,138	11,828	43.6	24,829	12,078	48.6	-5.0
New Orleans, La.	65,184	47,888	73.5	55,231	44,589	80.7	-7.2	78,343	27,920	35.6	66,414	28,521	42.9	-7.3
New York-Northeastern New Jersey	368,689	280,678	76.1	242,692	201,897	83.2	-7.1	440,994	212,560	48.2	288,088	145,682	50.6	-2.4
Norfolk-Portsmouth, Va.	44,002	35,278	80.2	31,684	25,910	81.8	-1.6	45,442	18,563	40.8	34,041	15,403	45.2	-4.4
Oklahoma City, Okla.	9,532	7,511	78.8	8,547	6,746	78.9	-0.1	10,826	4,886	45.1	9,552	5,142	53.8	-8.7
Orlando, Fla.	8,199	6,858	83.6	6,386	5,466	85.6	-2.0	8,521	4,392	51.5	6,713	4,003	59.6	-8.1
Philadelphia, Pa.	171,461	123,923	72.3	122,822	95,655	77.9	-5.6	188,661	75,014	39.8	134,236	58,148	43.3	-3.5
Phoenix, Ariz.	7,557	5,401	71.5	5,035	3,887	77.2	-5.7	7,040	2,265	32.2	4,136	1,143	27.6	4.6
Pittsburgh, Pa.	49,782	36,585	73.5	43,921	34,146	77.7	-4.2	51,015	12,661	24.8	41,443	10,329	24.9	-0.1
Raleigh, N. C.	13,203	10,036	76.0	12,374	9,648	78.0	-2.0	7,479	3,666	49.0	13,478	5,083	37.7	11.3
Richmond, Va.	30,793	23,099	75.0	26,320	21,051	80.0	-5.0	35,013	16,055	45.9	31,136	16,876	54.2	-8.3
Roanoke, Va.	6,650	4,773	71.8	5,958	4,552	76.4	-4.6	6,858	2,817	41.1	6,620	3,081	46.5	-5.4
Sacramento, Calif.	7,971	5,893	73.9	6,960	5,177	74.4	-0.5	5,705	2,512	44.0	3,638	1,279	35.2	8.8
Saginaw, Mich.	3,516	3,010	85.6	1,491	1,285	86.2	-0.6	3,143	712	22.7	1,286	243	18.9	3.8
St. Louis, Mo.	75,554	55,539	73.5	56,099	44,959	80.1	-6.6	85,675	30,379	35.5	62,317	22,179	35.6	-0.1

TABLE D-4.—POPULATION AND LABOR FORCE, BY COLOR AND SEX, FOR SELECTED STANDARD METROPOLITAN AREAS: 1950 AND 1940—Cont.

Standard metropolitan area and color	Male							Female						
	1950			1940			Change in percent in labor force, 1940 to 1950	1950			1940			Change in percent in labor force, 1940 to 1950
	Population 14 years old and over	Labor force Number	Per-cent	Population 14 years old and over	Labor force Number	Per-cent		Population 14 years old and over	Labor force Number	Per-cent	Population 14 years old and over	Labor force Number	Per-cent	
NONWHITE--Continued														
San Angelo, Texas	1,130	901	79.7	749	622	83.0	-3.3	1,151	545	47.4	903	577	63.9	-16.5
San Antonio, Texas	12,963	10,639	82.1	8,028	6,648	82.8	-0.7	13,137	6,116	46.6	9,851	5,458	55.4	-8.8
San Francisco-Oakland, Calif	86,640	66,927	77.2	33,919	25,830	76.2	1.0	70,975	29,234	41.2	18,896	6,914	36.6	4.6
Savannah, Ga	18,949	14,392	76.0	17,917	14,593	81.4	-5.4	22,821	9,522	41.7	22,235	10,235	46.0	-4.3
Shreveport, La	20,237	14,957	73.9	21,800	18,198	83.5	-9.6	24,903	10,677	42.9	25,849	12,109	46.8	-3.9
Springfield, Ohio	3,600	2,767	76.9	3,258	2,527	77.6	-0.7	3,931	1,403	35.7	3,466	969	28.0	7.7
Stockton, Calif	10,264	8,633	84.1	8,883	7,809	87.9	-3.8	4,758	1,761	37.0	2,224	569	25.6	11.4
Tampa-St. Petersburg, Fla	20,176	15,945	79.0	17,666	14,833	84.0	-5.0	22,337	11,179	50.0	19,845	11,170	56.3	-6.3
Toledo, Ohio	9,715	7,670	79.0	5,852	4,655	79.5	-0.5	10,014	3,808	38.0	5,949	2,141	36.0	2.0
Topeka, Kans	2,869	2,117	73.8	2,567	1,880	73.2	0.6	3,097	1,102	35.6	2,836	932	32.9	2.7
Trenton, N. J	7,935	5,612	70.7	5,378	3,806	70.8	-0.1	7,492	3,297	44.0	5,131	2,111	41.1	2.9
Tulsa, Okla	7,643	5,728	74.9	7,060	5,340	75.6	-0.7	9,220	4,292	46.6	8,356	4,497	53.8	-7.2
Waco, Texas	7,647	5,064	66.2	6,587	4,898	74.4	-8.2	8,407	3,296	39.2	7,487	3,305	44.1	-4.9
Washington, D. C	123,983	96,112	77.5	86,507	68,239	78.9	-1.4	134,910	67,136	49.8	93,720	47,452	50.6	-0.8
Wheeling, W. Va--Steubenville, Ohio	4,262	3,119	73.2	5,310	3,744	70.5	2.7	4,160	1,252	30.1	4,442	1,147	25.8	4.3
Wichita Falls, Texas	2,791	2,431	87.1	1,668	1,384	83.0	4.1	2,164	1,264	58.4	1,929	1,292	67.0	-8.6
Wilmington, Del	12,030	9,332	77.6	10,249	8,234	80.3	-2.7	11,783	5,044	42.8	9,655	4,638	48.0	-5.2
Winston-Salem, N. C	13,630	10,110	74.2	14,137	11,630	82.3	-8.1	16,154	7,564	46.8	16,625	10,055	60.5	-13.7
Youngstown, Ohio	13,348	10,783	80.8	9,052	7,205	79.6	1.2	12,696	3,091	24.3	8,466	2,061	24.3	...

Source: Derived from *1950 Census of Population*, Vol. II, *Characteristics of the Population*, Parts 2-48, tables 35 and 36; *1940 Census of Population*, Vol. II, *Characteristics of the Population*, Parts 1-7, State table 23.

TABLE D-5.—LABOR FORCE PARTICIPATION RATES FOR MARRIED WOMEN, HUSBAND PRESENT, BY AGE, AND STANDARDIZED RATES, FOR CITIES OF 100,000 OR MORE: 1950 AND 1940

City	1950					1940					Standardized rates[1]	
	Total married women, husband present	14 to 24 years	25 to 34 years	35 to 44 years	45 years and over	Total married women, husband present	14 to 24 years	25 to 34 years	35 to 44 years	45 years and over	1950	1940
Akron, Ohio	22.3	27.2	22.6	27.3	17.4	14.1	14.6	19.3	15.7	8.3	22.4	13.9
Albany, N. Y.	22.4	34.5	24.0	26.0	16.6	14.6	21.3	22.0	15.2	8.3	23.0	15.3
Atlanta, Ga.	35.0	37.5	37.0	41.2	26.1	30.0	31.0	37.1	31.7	17.7	34.2	28.1
Baltimore, Md.	25.5	31.6	27.1	30.7	18.1	18.9	24.5	24.9	20.2	10.3	25.3	18.4
Birmingham, Ala.	24.6	24.7	25.1	30.4	19.1	18.7	17.5	22.6	20.7	12.0	24.2	17.7
Boston, Mass.	18.7	29.3	17.7	20.4	15.9	10.8	17.0	14.2	10.8	7.6	19.0	11.3
Bridgeport, Conn.	26.6	38.5	27.9	30.5	20.0	21.6	33.6	30.5	23.6	11.0	26.9	22.1
Buffalo, N. Y.	18.3	26.9	19.6	21.4	13.2	11.1	14.8	15.4	11.8	6.7	18.6	11.3
Cambridge, Mass.	24.3	38.7	24.6	25.7	18.9	14.7	20.1	20.2	15.0	9.4	24.4	15.0
Camden, N. J.	24.2	29.0	26.0	30.7	17.0	17.7	23.3	24.6	19.5	9.8	24.3	17.8
Canton, Ohio	19.9	26.1	20.4	25.0	14.7	10.3	12.4	13.9	11.9	6.0	20.1	10.4
Charlotte, N. C.	38.4	44.7	39.6	42.8	28.5	32.5	38.8	39.8	31.2	16.6	37.0	29.2
Chattanooga, Tenn.	30.9	27.6	34.5	37.2	23.9	24.4	22.5	30.6	26.5	14.9	30.6	23.0
Chicago, Ill.	27.3	37.1	28.7	31.7	20.3	17.7	28.6	23.6	18.4	9.5	27.4	17.8
Cincinnati, Ohio	22.1	27.5	24.1	26.7	15.9	13.5	17.3	17.9	15.2	8.0	22.2	13.6
Cleveland, Ohio	24.2	31.9	25.5	29.5	17.4	15.0	19.2	19.9	16.8	8.6	24.3	15.0
Columbus, Ohio	28.6	37.9	30.1	33.5	20.0	17.3	21.6	24.1	19.4	9.4	28.2	17.3
Dallas, Texas	32.9	38.3	33.8	37.4	24.7	27.3	27.5	32.9	30.4	16.9	31.9	25.9
Dayton, Ohio	25.7	32.0	27.5	30.8	18.1	16.3	21.0	21.8	17.2	9.2	25.4	16.0
Denver, Colo.	25.3	32.8	25.7	29.3	19.7	15.8	18.3	19.8	17.8	10.6	25.2	15.8
Des Moines, Iowa	27.8	39.1	27.1	31.6	22.1	15.8	20.1	19.9	17.5	10.3	27.8	15.9
Detroit, Mich.	21.6	27.1	23.7	25.4	15.1	14.6	18.3	19.0	15.3	8.2	21.4	14.1
Duluth, Minn.	20.6	26.2	19.2	25.2	17.5	10.0	11.6	13.0	11.3	6.8	20.9	10.2
Elizabeth, N. J.	24.9	39.5	28.3	28.0	16.9	15.8	27.6	22.5	16.7	7.4	25.4	16.2
Erie, Pa.	21.1	29.2	23.0	25.6	14.1	9.5	14.1	12.6	10.0	5.8	21.1	9.7
Fall River, Mass.	36.6	52.1	44.4	42.7	23.4	30.3	51.5	46.5	33.1	12.7	37.3	31.5
Flint, Mich.	22.9	23.9	25.1	27.4	17.5	15.8	19.1	19.1	17.7	9.3	22.8	15.1
Fort Wayne, Ind.	25.1	36.7	25.7	29.7	17.8	14.6	22.6	20.9	14.2	7.8	25.1	14.7
Fort Worth, Texas	28.5	34.2	29.2	33.9	22.3	21.7	22.3	26.6	24.2	13.9	28.2	20.9
Gary, Ind.	20.1	24.2	20.8	24.5	14.3	9.1	12.4	10.4	9.8	5.3	19.8	8.6
Grand Rapids, Mich.	22.4	32.5	22.1	26.2	17.3	13.2	20.0	18.4	14.4	7.4	22.6	13.6
Hartford, Conn.	33.6	40.1	32.5	37.1	29.9	17.9	22.4	22.4	20.2	11.0	33.6	18.1
Houston, Texas	27.3	31.8	28.0	30.5	20.0	22.1	21.5	26.5	23.8	13.7	26.2	20.7

[1] Age distribution of married women, husband present, in all cities of 100,000 or more in 1950 used as standard.

Table D–5.—Labor Force Participation Rates for Married Women, Husband Present, by Age, and Standardized Rates, for Cities of 100,000 or More: 1950 and 1940—Cont.

City	1950					1940					Standardized rates[1]	
	Total married women, husband present	14 to 24 years	25 to 34 years	35 to 44 years	45 years and over	Total married women, husband present	14 to 24 years	25 to 34 years	35 to 44 years	45 years and over	1950	1940
Indianapolis, Ind.	28.4	33.5	29.8	33.9	21.9	18.7	22.7	24.9	20.3	11.2	28.4	18.6
Jacksonville, Fla.	30.2	30.7	32.7	35.7	22.3	24.8	25.3	30.3	25.9	15.6	29.5	23.3
Jersey City, N. J.	21.2	33.7	20.8	26.6	14.9	14.4	26.0	21.1	13.8	7.1	21.6	14.8
Kansas City, Kans.	24.9	31.0	24.8	32.6	17.9	15.9	18.0	20.8	17.8	10.0	25.0	15.8
Kansas City, Mo.	26.7	32.5	28.3	31.5	20.2	19.2	22.5	24.4	21.2	12.4	26.6	19.1
Knoxville, Tenn.	27.9	28.4	30.2	32.1	22.0	25.5	25.9	32.5	27.3	15.1	27.5	24.3
Long Beach, Calif.	23.5	25.1	25.9	28.6	18.0	14.5	13.0	15.7	17.5	12.1	23.6	14.6
Los Angeles, Calif.	27.1	31.2	28.9	32.8	20.6	19.9	20.6	24.4	23.3	13.7	27.1	19.8
Louisville, Ky.	24.3	26.4	25.8	30.5	17.5	18.1	19.7	24.0	20.0	10.8	24.0	17.8
Memphis, Tenn.	30.1	32.1	30.4	35.1	24.1	24.2	23.8	29.8	25.6	15.5	29.5	22.9
Miami, Fla.	29.6	38.4	33.9	35.1	20.1	28.3	33.6	35.9	30.8	15.8	29.7	27.1
Milwaukee, Wis.	24.7	33.1	25.9	30.7	17.9	14.0	18.5	19.0	15.6	7.9	25.0	14.1
Minneapolis, Minn.	26.9	40.4	27.1	30.3	21.1	14.9	21.1	20.2	16.0	9.1	27.2	15.2
Nashville, Tenn.	32.3	35.6	35.1	40.1	22.4	23.8	23.9	31.0	26.0	14.3	31.8	22.9
Newark, N. J.	25.9	38.0	28.4	30.2	17.3	16.8	26.3	23.1	17.3	8.8	25.9	16.8
New Bedford, Mass.	38.1	50.8	46.6	47.8	25.2	30.0	48.7	43.6	35.2	15.7	39.7	32.0
New Haven, Conn.	25.4	39.5	27.4	28.9	18.4	17.4	29.8	24.6	18.9	9.2	25.9	18.2
New Orleans, La.	23.0	25.8	23.5	29.0	16.1	18.7	19.8	24.1	20.0	10.9	22.5	17.8
New York, N. Y.	21.9	34.4	21.4	24.8	17.6	16.7	28.7	22.1	16.8	9.3	22.3	16.9
Norfolk, Va.	25.0	24.7	25.8	29.9	20.0	17.7	17.3	20.8	20.2	12.2	24.6	17.2
Oakland, Calif.	27.5	32.9	29.9	32.9	20.4	17.0	19.6	21.5	19.6	11.4	27.6	17.2
Oklahoma City, Okla.	28.5	30.7	28.1	32.3	24.4	20.6	19.6	24.5	22.2	14.3	28.1	19.7
Omaha, Nebr.	23.6	29.2	23.4	28.8	18.7	14.3	17.7	18.2	15.7	9.2	23.7	14.3
Paterson, N. J.	26.7	39.7	28.3	33.6	18.0	18.8	29.8	25.3	20.8	10.5	27.2	19.3
Peoria, Ill.	25.6	35.1	25.9	30.2	18.9	15.8	19.9	20.4	17.5	9.2	25.5	15.6
Philadelphia, Pa.	21.9	30.3	22.9	25.8	16.0	16.2	24.0	22.0	17.3	9.2	22.0	16.4
Pittsburgh, Pa.	15.6	22.7	16.3	19.5	10.7	8.3	10.2	11.2	9.2	5.0	15.8	8.4
Portland, Oreg.	27.4	35.9	28.4	32.0	22.0	17.5	22.8	22.8	19.3	11.8	27.8	18.0
Providence, R. I.	25.4	34.2	27.6	30.8	18.4	16.7	28.1	24.3	17.6	9.1	25.8	17.6
Reading, Pa.	28.9	39.7	32.7	39.5	17.8	23.3	37.1	36.0	25.8	10.3	29.8	24.3
Richmond, Va.	32.6	41.2	36.3	38.0	22.5	28.6	35.5	38.2	30.3	14.8	32.3	27.5
Rochester, N. Y.	27.3	35.7	26.8	32.2	23.0	18.8	26.2	25.4	22.2	11.5	27.8	19.7
Sacramento, Calif.	31.4	37.4	32.5	37.0	25.1	22.0	29.8	28.5	23.3	13.1	31.5	21.8

[1] Age distribution of married women, husband present, in all cities of 100,000 or more in 1950 used as standard.

TABLE D-5.—LABOR FORCE PARTICIPATION RATES FOR MARRIED WOMEN, HUSBAND PRESENT, BY AGE, AND STANDARDIZED RATES, FOR CITIES OF 100,000 OR MORE: 1950 AND 1940—Cont.

City	1950					1940					Standardized rates[1]	
	Total married women, husband present	14 to 24 years	25 to 34 years	35 to 44 years	45 years and over	Total married women, husband present	14 to 24 years	25 to 34 years	35 to 44 years	45 years and over	1950	1940
St. Louis, Mo.	25.0	30.6	27.5	30.2	18.1	17.0	23.7	23.8	17.7	9.0	25.1	16.9
St. Paul, Minn.	23.0	32.3	24.0	27.4	17.1	11.8	16.4	16.8	12.8	6.8	23.3	12.2
Salt Lake City, Utah	24.2	33.7	24.0	26.8	18.5	12.6	16.8	15.2	13.4	8.0	23.8	12.3
San Antonio, Texas	20.2	21.0	19.0	25.6	16.5	16.6	14.9	20.4	19.1	11.3	20.0	16.2
San Diego, Calif.	23.6	25.4	23.8	30.2	17.6	16.7	13.9	18.3	20.2	14.0	23.3	16.7
San Francisco, Calif.	29.7	34.9	32.1	34.8	22.7	20.2	24.9	26.1	23.1	12.5	29.7	20.3
Scranton, Pa.	15.4	29.4	16.2	20.4	9.2	8.0	11.8	11.5	7.9	4.6	16.2	8.1
Seattle, Wash.	27.5	35.2	28.5	31.7	22.2	16.1	18.8	19.7	18.2	11.8	27.8	16.4
Somerville, Mass.	21.0	35.0	21.5	23.1	16.1	9.9	14.8	13.2	11.1	5.9	21.5	10.2
South Bend, Ind.	24.3	29.2	25.0	29.2	18.9	17.7	22.5	23.8	20.0	9.7	24.3	17.6
Spokane, Wash.	23.3	28.3	21.9	29.9	18.7	14.8	17.6	19.2	16.7	10.0	23.5	15.1
Springfield, Mass.	23.4	37.6	23.8	28.1	17.2	13.2	18.0	18.5	14.5	8.3	24.0	13.8
Syracuse, N.Y.	25.6	39.5	26.0	30.7	18.8	15.1	20.6	20.8	16.8	9.2	26.1	15.6
Tacoma, Wash.	23.3	24.4	22.9	29.2	19.5	12.1	13.6	14.8	13.6	9.1	23.4	12.3
Tampa, Fla.	30.3	26.7	31.1	39.6	24.0	31.1	27.0	38.7	37.6	20.1	30.2	30.4
Toledo, Ohio	24.9	30.4	25.7	31.3	18.9	16.1	19.8	22.8	18.6	8.6	25.2	16.3
Trenton, N.J.	30.4	41.2	35.4	35.7	20.6	21.7	34.2	32.0	22.9	10.5	30.8	22.2
Tulsa, Okla.	26.7	31.5	26.3	30.2	22.0	19.5	18.8	22.9	21.9	13.5	26.3	18.8
Utica, N.Y.	25.3	34.5	25.3	32.8	19.2	19.6	26.1	26.7	20.2	12.3	26.0	19.8
Washington, D.C.	37.0	41.5	39.7	42.6	27.9	31.2	34.1	40.3	33.7	18.4	36.4	30.1
Wichita, Kans.	24.3	28.8	23.3	29.0	19.8	15.9	15.5	19.0	18.1	11.7	24.1	15.8
Wilmington, Del.	23.9	32.6	27.0	28.2	16.4	17.6	25.6	23.4	19.0	9.6	24.1	17.6
Worcester, Mass.	19.4	32.0	20.7	24.5	13.4	10.9	18.2	14.9	12.2	6.4	20.3	11.5
Yonkers, N.Y.	21.6	32.2	21.1	24.8	18.2	16.8	26.1	22.2	18.1	10.0	22.0	17.2
Youngstown, Ohio	16.1	24.6	17.6	19.5	10.7	8.2	9.6	11.7	8.9	4.6	16.4	8.2

[1] Age distribution of married women, husband present, in all cities of 100,000 or more in 1950 used as standard.

Source: Derived from *1950 Census of Population*, Vol. II, *Characteristics of the Population*, Parts 2-49, table 57, and unpublished data; *1940 Census of Population*, Vol. III, *The Labor Force*, Parts 2-5, table 8, and Vol. IV, *Characteristics by Age*, Parts 2-4, table 11.

TABLE D-6.—WOMEN AS PERCENT OF TOTAL EMPLOYED IN SPECIFIC OCCUPATIONS WITH AT LEAST 10 PERCENT WOMEN IN 1950: 1950 AND 1940

[Decennial census levels. "N.e.c." means not elsewhere classified]

Occupation	1950	1940
PROFESSIONAL, TECHNICAL, AND KINDRED WORKERS		
Accountants and auditors	14.8	8.3
Actors and actresses	34.1	40.2
Artists and art teachers	38.2	34.3
Authors	38.7	32.6
Chemists	10.0	3.1
Chiropractors	14.3	17.6
College presidents, professors, and instructors (n.e.c.)	23.2	26.5
Dancers and dancing teachers	71.1	80.6
Designers	26.5	27.0
Editors and reporters	32.0	25.0
Entertainers (n.e.c.)	28.7	19.7
Farm and home management advisors	49.3	47.5
Librarians	88.6	89.9
Musicians and music teachers	50.7	46.3
Nurses, professional and student	97.6	97.9
Osteopaths	15.2	18.3
Photographers	17.3	14.0
Religious workers	69.6	77.0
Social, welfare, & rec. group wkrs.	64.4	63.8
Sports instructors and officials	24.7	18.1
Teachers (n.e.c.)	74.5	75.6
Technicians, med., dental, & testing.	39.6	35.3
Technicians (n.e.c.)	15.8	9.1
Therapists and healers (n.e.c.)	49.4	44.0
MANAGERS, OFFICIALS, AND PROPRIETORS, EXC. FARM		
Buyers and department heads, store	25.4	25.1
Credit men	21.7	12.3
Floormen and floor managers, store	46.2	32.0
Managers and superintendents, bldg.	34.1	41.4
Officials & administrators (n.e.c.), public administration	17.1	13.6
Federal pub. admin. & postal serv.	10.7	8.5
State public administration	12.1	8.5
Local public administration	22.4	18.7
Officials, lodge, soc., union, etc.	10.8	16.3
Postmasters	43.1	42.4
Managers, offs., & propr's (n.e.c.)	12.8	10.0
Retail trade	16.6	13.2
Food and dairy products stores, and milk retailing	16.7	13.5
General merchandise and five and ten cent stores	21.9	14.3
Apparel and accessories stores	31.1	23.3
Eating and drinking places	26.7	23.8
Other retail trade	17.3	12.4
Insurance and real estate	15.2	9.1
Business services	16.0	13.0
Personal services	29.2	25.0
CLERICAL AND KINDRED WORKERS		
Agents (n.e.c.)	15.5	10.4
Attendants and assistants, library	74.4	78.2
Attendants, phys., and dent. office	95.0	95.7
Bookkeepers and cashiers	78.1	67.1
Collectors, bill and account	14.8	8.0
Messengers and office boys	18.2	4.5
Office machine operators	82.3	86.1
Stenographers, typists, and secys	94.4	93.4
Telegraph messengers	10.5	1.5
Telegraph operators	21.7	21.3
Telephone operators	95.5	94.6
Ticket, station, and express agents	12.9	4.7

Occupation	1950	1940
SALES WORKERS		
Advertising agents and salesmen	14.1	6.9
Demonstrators	81.9	80.7
Hucksters and peddlers	14.0	4.8
Real estate agents and brokers	14.4	9.2
CRAFTSMEN, FOREMEN, AND KINDRED WORKERS		
Bakers	11.7	7.8
Decorators and window dressers	30.0	22.6
Engravers, except photoengravers	12.7	7.9
Foremen (n.e.c.), textiles, textile products, & apparel manufacturing	30.5	27.1
Furriers	14.4	13.9
Opt., & lens grinders & polishers	13.1	8.9
Paperhangers	14.0	6.0
Tailors and tailoresses	19.5	14.0
OPERATIVES AND KINDRED WORKERS		
Dressmakers & seamstr., exc. factory.	97.2	98.3
Fruit, nut, and vegetable graders and packers, except factory	60.2	57.2
Laundry and dry cleaning operatives	67.1	66.8
Milliners	89.4	95.1
Painters, exc. const. & maintenance.	11.4	8.2
Photographic process workers	44.5	35.0
Operatives & kindred wkrs. (n.e.c.)	38.9	38.8
Miscellaneous wood products	25.2	20.6
Furniture and fixtures	21.2	15.5
Stone, clay, and glass products	25.7	22.6
Glass and glass products	30.1	25.6
Structural clay products	18.8	10.8
Pottery and related products	42.5	38.6
Miscellaneous nonmetallic mineral and stone products	22.3	15.4
Metal industries	17.6	15.1
Prim. iron & steel, exc. blast furnaces, & fab'd steel prod.	21.4	18.7
Primary nonferrous and fabricated nonferrous metal prod.	22.6	19.7
Machinery, exc. electrical.	17.9	14.7
Office & store mach. & devices.	33.6	30.0
Miscellaneous machinery	17.8	13.5
Electrical mach., equip., & sup.	53.8	47.3
Transportation equipment	15.5	11.7
Motor vehicles & mtr. veh. eqp.	16.7	13.9
Aircraft and parts	12.5	4.4
Profess'l & photo. equip. & sup.	43.1	42.8
Nondurable goods	52.8	51.6
Food and kindred products	38.0	37.0
Meat products	28.7	22.8
Dairy products	16.0	16.2
Canning and preserving fruits, vegetables, and sea foods	62.6	63.7
Grain-mill products	15.1	15.1
Bakery products	52.9	51.2
Confectionery & related prod.	65.4	67.1
Beverage industries	17.1	18.6
Tobacco manufactures	70.1	71.7
Textile mill products	53.3	49.9
Knitting mills	72.1	67.1
Dyeing and finishing textiles, except knit goods	22.3	24.4
Carpets, rugs, and other floor coverings	43.3	45.3
Yarn, thread, & fabric mills	49.9	44.5
Misc. textile mill products	46.8	37.8

TABLE **D–6.**—WOMEN AS PERCENT OF TOTAL EMPLOYED IN SPECIFIC OCCUPATIONS WITH AT LEAST 10 PERCENT WOMEN IN 1950: 1950 AND 1940—Cont.

[Decennial census levels. "N.e.c." means not elsewhere classified]

Occupation	1950	1940	Occupation	1950	1940
OPERATIVES AND KINDRED WORKERS --Continued			SERVICE WORKERS, EXCEPT PRIVATE HOUSEHOLD--Continued		
Operatives & kindred wkrs. (n.e.c.) --Continued			Boarding and lodging house keepers...	73.0	85.4
Nondurable goods--Continued			Charwomen and cleaners.............	60.4	54.3
Apparel & other fab'd text. prod.	80.7	77.6	Cooks, except private household.....	55.8	42.1
Apparel and accessories........	81.4	77.8	Elevator operators.................	30.2	16.5
Misc. fabricated text. prod....	71.8	74.0	Housekeepers and stewards, except		
Paper and allied products........	32.4	33.5	private household.................	78.3	76.7
Pulp, paper, & paperbd. mills..	15.5	19.5	Janitors and sextons...............	11.7	10.8
Paperboard containers & boxes..	45.4	51.3	Midwives and practical nurses.......	95.7	95.7
Misc. paper and pulp products..	49.1	52.7	Ushers, recreation and amusement.....	33.7	21.4
Printing, pub., and allied ind...	44.2	46.9	Waiters, waitresses, counter and fountain workers...................	78.5	67.6
Chemicals and allied products....	22.6	26.2			
Synthetic fibers...............	32.4	33.8			
Paints, varnishes, & rel. prod.	15.1	14.4	FARM LABORERS AND FOREMEN		
Drugs, medicines, & misc. chemicals & allied products...	21.7	24.8	Farm laborers, unpaid family wkrs....	34.9	19.2
Rubber products..................	30.4	29.2	LABORERS, EXCEPT FARM AND MINE		
Leather and leather products.....	49.4	43.1			
Leather: tanned, curried, and finished......................	15.8	12.1	Laborers (n.e.c.): Pottery and related products.......	11.2	11.6
Footwear, except rubber........	52.8	46.1	Electrical, mach. equip., & sup...	16.6	15.4
Leather prod., exc. footwear...	55.3	52.0	Profess'l, photo. equip. & sup.....	16.0	15.6
Transportation, except railroad....	13.4	6.9	Canning and preserving fruits, vegetables, and sea foods.........	16.0	19.1
Wholesale and retail trade........	37.9	34.1			
Business and repair services.......	13.4	11.0	Bakery products....................	13.2	13.2
Personal services................	56.2	55.6	Confectionery and related products..	16.2	27.9
Public administration.............	12.3	11.0	Tobacco manufactures..............	23.7	22.6
			Textile mill products..............	13.9	15.3
PRIVATE HOUSEHOLD WORKERS			Knitting mills................	30.2	32.7
			Yarn, thread, and fabric mills...	14.3	15.6
Housekeepers, private household......	96.2	99.2	Misc. textile mill products......	13.6	10.1
Laundresses, private household.......	96.9	98.2	Apparel & other fab'd text. prod...	37.3	40.4
Private household workers (n.e.c.)....	94.5	92.8	Apparel and accessories..........	42.0	46.1
			Misc. fabricated textile prod....	22.3	23.6
SERVICE WORKERS, EXCEPT PRIVATE HOUSEHOLD			Paperboard containers and boxes....	14.9	18.0
			Misc. paper and pulp products......	12.4	16.4
Attendants, hospital & other inst....	59.3	41.6	Printing, pub., & allied ind.......	10.6	11.3
Attendants, professional and personal service (n.e.c.)...................	66.4	63.3	Rubber products....................	13.2	14.1
			Leather and leather products.......	19.7	17.6
Barbers, beauticians, & manicurists..	49.6	49.7	Footwear, except rubber..........	30.6	29.3
			Leather products, exc. footwear..	26.0	23.3

Source: Derived from *1950 Census of Population*, Vol. II, *Characteristics of the Population*, Part 1, U. S. Summary, table 125.

TABLE D-7.—EMPLOYED WOMEN BY OCCUPATION AND AGE: 1950 AND 1940

[Decennial census levels. "N.e.c." means not elsewhere classified]

Year and occupation[1]	Total, 14 years and over	14 and 15 years	16 and 17 years	18 and 19 years	20 to 24 years	25 to 34 years	35 to 44 years	45 to 54 years	55 to 64 years	65 years and over	Median age (years)
1950											
Total employed women	15,715,164	91,674	304,887	875,828	2,381,711	3,683,301	3,657,577	2,755,620	1,488,543	476,023	36.4
Professional, technical, and kindred workers	1,938,985	1,479	4,890	58,323	298,117	445,315	487,209	385,632	199,761	58,259	38.3
Accountants and auditors	55,660	...	...	1,902	8,268	14,418	14,365	11,196	4,536	975	37.3
Actresses	5,077	...	...	239	926	1,523	1,045	687	508	149	34.0
Artists and art teachers	29,566	31	100	681	5,510	7,996	6,500	4,871	2,713	1,164	35.7
Authors, editors, and reporters	34,654	46	134	586	5,155	9,654	8,049	5,995	3,327	1,708	37.2
College presidents, prof'rs, & instructors (n.e.c.)	28,907	12	...	143	2,780	6,856	7,235	6,827	3,970	1,096	41.5
Designers and draftsmen	18,573	...	37	527	3,592	5,686	4,141	2,974	1,263	341	34.0
Lawyers and judges	6,256	...	...	17	269	1,435	1,836	1,592	786	321	42.7
Librarians	49,027	201	591	1,937	5,900	8,763	11,457	10,069	6,803	3,306	41.2
Musicians and music teachers	77,844	436	902	1,469	8,275	15,034	17,661	16,677	11,732	5,658	42.3
Nurses and student nurses	463,495	...	1,257	35,705	103,104	119,699	95,082	63,669	34,647	10,332	32.7
Physicians and surgeons	11,714	...	...	61	691	3,291	3,012	2,439	1,429	791	41.0
Social, welfare, and recreation workers	58,917	30	73	441	7,651	13,484	15,433	12,674	7,264	1,867	40.0
Teachers (n.e.c.)	834,996	140	546	6,949	96,078	162,223	245,766	204,951	97,810	20,533	41.2
Other professional, technical, and kindred workers	264,299	583	1,250	7,666	49,918	75,253	55,627	41,011	22,973	10,018	34.7
Farmers and farm managers	116,371	604	732	1,026	3,517	12,107	23,659	29,666	26,935	18,125	50.6
Managers, officials, & proprietors, exc. farm	676,778	409	1,081	4,272	29,679	110,325	197,622	189,224	106,331	37,835	44.7
Specified managers and officials	126,594	106	267	1,352	8,470	21,263	32,939	32,694	21,124	8,379	44.7
Managers, off'ls, & propr's (n.e.c.), by industry:											
Manufacturing	40,806	...	29	316	1,953	6,691	12,434	11,802	5,743	1,838	44.2
Eating and drinking places	95,234	...	62	246	2,739	16,375	34,751	27,456	10,989	2,616	43.1
Other trade	241,254	213	397	1,161	8,772	38,880	70,226	67,525	39,945	14,635	45.2
Personal services	61,030	31	122	397	1,557	8,610	17,035	17,890	11,083	4,305	46.5
Miscellaneous industries and services	111,860	59	204	800	6,688	18,506	30,237	31,857	17,447	6,062	44.8
Clerical and kindred workers	4,291,764	2,955	52,230	391,459	1,058,441	1,135,467	835,218	557,464	214,782	43,748	30.6
Bookkeepers, cashiers, etc.	747,471	761	9,965	55,219	152,860	195,464	170,705	111,054	42,198	9,245	32.9
Office machine operators	116,917	60	784	12,337	32,879	36,168	20,753	11,131	2,624	181	28.4
Stenographers, typists, and secretaries	1,501,090	265	14,172	146,269	419,843	435,406	263,031	158,020	53,503	10,581	28.9
Telegraph operators	7,440	...	31	367	1,806	1,225	1,592	1,745	582	92	36.8
Telephone operators	341,706	322	4,430	34,567	92,498	72,344	67,172	51,015	17,214	2,144	30.4
Other clerical workers	1,577,140	1,547	22,848	142,700	358,555	394,860	311,965	224,499	98,661	21,505	31.7

[1] Original 1950 and 1940 data revised where necessary to give comparable occupation classification.

TABLE D-7.—EMPLOYED WOMEN BY OCCUPATION AND AGE: 1950 AND 1940—Cont.

[Decennial census levels. "N.e.c." means not elsewhere classified]

Year and occupation[1]	Total, 14 years and over	14 and 15 years	16 and 17 years	18 and 19 years	20 to 24 years	25 to 34 years	35 to 44 years	45 to 54 years	55 to 64 years	65 years and over	Median age (years)
1950—Continued											
Sales workers...........	1,329,724	9,330	66,049	97,474	159,546	260,432	317,752	252,589	131,855	34,697	37.3
Insurance agents and brokers........	25,913	...	116	641	3,028	5,619	5,561	5,998	3,727	1,223	41.4
Real estate agents and brokers.......	20,277	167	112	...	530	2,315	4,714	6,861	4,100	1,478	48.4
Other specified sales workers........	24,008	1,362	1,188	906	2,579	5,678	5,347	4,130	2,187	631	35.5
Other sales workers (n.e.c.).........	1,259,526	7,801	64,633	95,927	153,409	246,820	302,130	235,600	121,841	31,365	37.0
Craftsmen, foremen, and kindred workers.........	235,544	213	1,612	6,253	23,524	54,921	65,824	49,802	26,095	7,300	39.7
Compositors and typesetters.........	11,077	28	83	580	1,796	2,348	2,761	1,906	1,188	387	37.5
Foremen (n.e.c.)................	67,955	5	204	776	3,862	15,421	23,766	16,008	6,552	1,361	40.8
Other craftsmen and kindred workers....	156,512	180	1,325	4,897	17,866	37,152	39,297	31,888	18,355	5,552	39.3
Operatives and kindred workers.........	3,018,787	2,109	39,304	130,567	392,255	806,787	792,634	522,590	265,585	66,956	36.7
Dressmakers and seamstresses, except factory.....	134,310	18	270	1,092	4,020	13,008	25,085	33,511	36,829	20,477	52.1
Laundry and dry cleaning operatives........	287,533	488	4,461	11,714	33,370	68,909	76,828	54,763	29,510	7,490	38.2
Other specified operatives and kindred workers....	119,550	393	1,897	5,301	16,320	32,279	30,869	20,013	9,848	2,730	36.2
Operatives and kindred workers (n.e.c.):											
lumber, furniture, and lumber products.....	41,878	...	418	1,759	5,839	12,816	11,568	5,991	3,039	448	35.1
Stone, clay, and glass products.......	46,815	...	467	2,459	7,502	15,251	11,486	6,257	2,677	716	33.5
Metal and machinery............	333,140	43	2,625	13,684	50,631	116,214	87,839	44,531	15,467	2,106	33.6
Transportation equipment.........	66,097	...	151	1,179	6,165	23,181	20,763	10,578	3,596	484	36.1
Food and kindred products........	186,337	214	2,896	9,162	26,608	50,844	48,983	30,988	14,163	2,479	35.7
Tobacco manufactures...........	43,200	30	516	1,489	4,770	11,180	13,276	7,808	3,615	516	37.7
Textile mill products...........	453,968	118	4,675	18,196	57,790	124,454	131,083	77,979	33,730	5,943	36.7
Apparel and other fabricated products.....	655,351	131	10,239	31,864	84,473	165,097	169,185	121,244	60,962	12,156	37.1
Paper, paper products, and printing.......	103,965	122	1,614	6,390	16,276	27,410	25,827	16,889	7,519	1,918	35.1
Chemicals and petroleum and coal products....	42,818	29	350	1,491	6,699	13,773	11,427	6,034	2,461	554	34.3
Rubber products...............	36,259	...	408	1,100	4,336	11,343	10,683	5,718	2,451	220	35.9
Leather and leather products........	140,199	31	2,916	7,996	20,023	34,371	35,744	24,271	12,251	2,596	36.3
Other manufacturing............	164,344	42	2,112	7,539	27,020	47,499	40,423	26,077	11,402	2,030	34.5
Nonmanufacturing..............	163,223	450	3,289	8,152	20,513	39,158	41,565	29,938	16,065	4,093	37.4
Private household workers............	1,334,310	33,795	47,031	49,789	108,745	244,166	299,492	268,559	190,752	91,981	41.1

[1] Original 1950 and 1940 data revised where necessary to give comparable occupation classification.

Table D-7.—Employed Women by Occupation and Age: 1950 and 1940—Cont.

[Decennial census levels. "N.e.c." means not elsewhere classified]

Year and occupation¹	Total, 14 years and over	14 and 15 years	16 and 17 years	18 and 19 years	20 to 24 years	25 to 34 years	35 to 44 years	45 to 54 years	55 to 64 years	65 years and over	Median age (years)
1950—Continued											
Service workers, except private household	1,914,293	10,419	51,163	92,707	211,992	426,519	446,631	354,216	240,385	80,261	38.7
Attendants, ushers, and bootblacks	165,905	1,457	8,291	14,313	23,927	34,061	33,277	28,194	17,419	4,966	35.3
Barbers, beauticians, and manicurists	189,870	65	667	5,184	23,625	65,568	56,569	27,286	9,095	1,811	35.0
Boarding and lodging house keepers	21,052	...	27	134	1,020	2,739	4,350	6,687	6,095		58.4
Charwomen, janitors, and porters	128,941	650	1,046	1,567	4,207	15,433	28,538	35,222	32,198	10,080	48.7
Cooks, except private household	242,422	197	1,082	2,917	10,436	38,038	67,738	67,121	44,437	10,456	45.1
Elevator operators	26,929	63	664	2,434	5,658	7,395	5,879	3,382	1,233	221	31.3
Housekeepers and stewards, exc. private household	82,904	42	180	668	3,838	8,169	13,561	22,184	24,301	9,961	51.8
Practical nurses and midwives	131,695	164	688	2,507	8,609	16,251	24,577	32,079	31,953	14,867	49.1
Protective service	10,555	31	66	184	602	2,073	2,333	2,562	1,960	744	45.0
Waitresses, bartenders, and counter workers	603,419	5,568	31,670	51,905	105,333	182,223	138,148	61,661	22,510	4,401	30.9
Other serv. wkrs., exc. priv. hshld. & protective	310,601	2,182	6,782	11,028	25,623	56,288	73,272	70,175	48,592	16,659	42.3
Farm laborers and foremen	449,336	21,578	26,355	23,571	46,517	95,361	100,968	76,974	43,692	14,320	36.1
Farm laborers (wage) and foremen	131,758	5,534	8,030	8,713	17,738	28,700	27,443	20,175	11,117	4,308	34.0
Farm laborers, unpaid family workers	317,578	16,044	18,325	14,858	28,779	66,661	73,525	56,799	32,575	10,012	36.9
Laborers, except farm and mine	126,979	744	2,793	6,516	17,242	32,073	31,268	21,375	11,509	3,459	36.3
Manufacturing	67,454	30	1,311	3,964	9,575	19,884	17,138	9,423	5,123	1,006	34.5
All other	59,525	714	1,482	2,552	7,667	12,189	14,130	11,952	6,386	2,453	38.7
Occupation not reported	282,293	8,039	11,647	13,871	32,136	59,828	59,300	47,529	30,861	19,082	37.6
1940											
Total employed women	11,138,178	39,441	187,401	712,415	2,271,450	3,243,910	2,218,615	1,474,905	738,966	251,075	32.3
Professional, technical, and kindred workers	1,486,446	133	2,288	46,537	267,195	507,845	324,307	208,574	100,142	29,425	33.4
Accountants and auditors	18,265	...	...	521	3,277	6,524	4,658	2,418	734	133	33.2
Actresses	4,761	13	52	203	1,020	1,682	884	555	261	91	31.5
Artists and art teachers	18,007	...	36	541	3,428	6,063	3,735	2,310	1,263	631	33.2
Authors, editors, and reporters	18,536	5	66	365	2,350	5,387	4,613	3,195	1,754	801	37.4
College presidents, prof'rs, & instructors (n.e.c.)	19,884	...	...	12	1,304	4,959	5,942	4,631	2,372	664	41.2
Designers and draftsmen	9,105	4	34	260	1,612	2,978	2,330	1,311	471	105	33.9

¹ Original 1950 and 1940 data revised where necessary to give comparable occupation classification.

TABLE D-7.—EMPLOYED WOMEN BY OCCUPATION AND AGE: 1950 AND 1940—Cont.

[Decennial census levels. "N.e.c." means not elsewhere classified]

Year and occupation[1]	Total, 14 years and over	14 and 15 years	16 and 17 years	18 and 19 years	20 to 24 years	25 to 34 years	35 to 44 years	45 to 54 years	55 to 64 years	65 years and over	Median age (years)
1940—Continued											
Profess'l, technical, and kindred workers—Cont.											
Lawyers and judges	4,187	...	...	7	226	1,503	1,217	746	319	169	37.9
Librarians	32,366	...	32	453	3,463	10,002	7,153	5,632	3,916	1,715	38.1
Musicians and music teachers	59,456	47	316	1,175	6,615	15,990	14,597	12,081	6,211	2,424	38.8
Nurses and student nurses	344,977	...	345	31,424	93,928	110,504	54,906	35,223	15,194	3,453	29.2
Physicians and surgeons	7,608	...	...	12	277	2,215	2,065	1,428	935	676	41.3
Social, welfare, and recreation workers	44,389	...	...	89	4,395	16,646	10,875	7,812	3,640	932	36.0
Teachers (n.e.c.)	767,769	...	768	7,678	122,075	281,002	182,729	110,559	51,441	11,517	34.0
Other professional, technical, and kindred workers	137,136	64	639	3,797	23,225	42,390	28,603	20,673	11,631	6,114	34.6
Farmers and farm managers	151,899	...	152	608	3,190	12,000	29,165	43,594	38,127	25,063	52.1
Managers, officials, & proprietors, exc. farm	399,098	3	257	2,038	17,232	75,638	112,140	108,435	61,730	21,625	44.3
Specified managers and officials	92,288	...	...	553	5,440	19,914	24,432	22,864	14,106	4,979	43.3
Managers, off'ls, & propr's (n.e.c.), by industry:											
Manufacturing	17,862	3	12	86	794	3,694	5,358	4,686	2,458	771	43.1
Eating and drinking places	61,829	...	62	309	2,532	12,909	19,827	17,357	7,227	1,606	42.6
Other trade	151,626	...	152	757	5,604	26,205	41,958	42,565	24,993	9,392	45.3
Personal services	31,055	...	31	155	994	4,286	7,577	9,130	6,273	2,609	47.7
Miscellaneous industries and services	44,438	...	...	178	1,868	8,630	12,988	11,833	6,673	2,268	43.9
Clerical and kindred workers	2,364,288	194	13,590	164,182	632,607	835,656	448,336	192,483	64,145	13,095	29.4
Bookkeepers, cashiers, etc	432,544	89	2,349	24,199	100,449	152,872	92,100	42,624	14,845	3,017	30.8
Office machine operators	51,454	2	2,134	3,052	15,446	20,503	9,817	2,150	304	46	28.5
Stenographers, typists, and secretaries	988,081	100	5,280	73,277	297,481	364,430	167,789	59,325	16,744	3,155	28.2
Telegraph operators	8,228	3	15	161	824	3,293	2,706	885	287	54	34.4
Telephone operators	189,202	...	949	11,385	39,848	69,449	44,611	18,216	4,174	570	31.1
Other clerical workers	694,779	...	4,863	52,108	178,559	225,109	131,313	68,783	27,791	6,253	30.0
Sales workers	801,881	842	10,840	61,632	182,710	224,828	159,116	106,334	45,110	10,469	31.4
Insurance agents and brokers	13,081	...	11	138	866	2,426	3,305	3,475	2,118	742	44.4
Real estate agents and brokers	10,254	1	3	21	168	905	2,626	3,564	2,208	758	48.9
Other specified sales workers	13,023	76	120	292	1,194	2,776	3,292	2,936	1,781	556	41.2
Other sales workers (n.e.c.)	765,523	765	10,706	61,181	180,482	218,721	149,893	96,359	39,003	8,413	30.9

[1] Original 1950 and 1940 data revised where necessary to give comparable occupation classification.

TABLE D-7.—EMPLOYED WOMEN BY OCCUPATION AND AGE: 1950 AND 1940—Cont.

[Decennial census levels. "N.e.c." means not elsewhere classified]

Year and occupation[1]	Total, 14 years and over	14 and 15 years	16 and 17 years	18 and 19 years	20 to 24 years	25 to 34 years	35 to 44 years	45 to 54 years	55 to 64 years	65 years and over	Median age (years)
1940—Continued											
Craftsmen, foremen, and kindred workers	113,120	144	579	3,493	16,014	31,567	27,914	20,931	9,613	2,865	36.7
Compositors and typesetters	7,425	7	33	272	1,060	2,071	1,892	1,314	589	187	36.4
Foremen (n.e.c.)	35,790	9	97	630	4,145	11,596	9,633	6,452	2,620	608	36.5
Other craftsmen and kindred workers	69,905	128	449	2,591	10,809	17,900	16,389	13,165	6,404	2,070	36.9
Operatives and kindred workers	2,029,674	352	28,757	139,477	462,173	639,670	402,613	237,079	93,656	25,897	31.0
Dressmakers and seamstresses, except factory	131,127	...	262	1,705	6,556	18,227	29,766	36,846	26,488	11,277	47.5
Laundry and dry cleaning operatives	188,289	...	2,446	9,781	34,235	58,687	44,392	26,710	9,969	2,069	33.1
Other specified operatives and kindred workers	63,242	178	1,006	3,973	12,787	19,156	13,560	8,248	3,469	865	32.1
Operatives and kindred workers (n.e.c.):											
Lumber, furniture, and lumber products	18,834	...	207	1,206	4,355	6,542	3,714	1,942	717	151	30.6
Stone, clay, and glass products	25,423	...	305	1,960	7,024	8,958	4,275	2,036	687	178	28.8
Metal and machinery	134,778	...	1,078	11,591	45,690	46,634	19,408	7,817	2,156	404	26.9
Transportation equipment	27,665	...	83	830	6,999	11,481	5,810	2,020	387	55	30.2
Food and kindred products	111,710	112	1,787	9,384	31,614	37,311	18,544	9,495	3,016	447	28.5
Tobacco manufactures	51,753	...	414	2,072	9,636	19,686	12,329	5,647	1,658	311	32.0
Textile mill products	416,845	...	5,419	26,261	89,205	151,315	87,537	42,518	12,089	2,501	30.8
Apparel and other fabricated products	453,041	...	8,608	34,884	104,652	135,460	92,873	54,365	18,122	4,077	30.8
Paper, paper products, and printing	71,761	...	646	5,310	18,299	23,897	13,491	6,889	2,583	646	29.9
Chemicals and petroleum and coal products	28,421	...	284	2,188	8,526	11,085	3,979	1,648	597	114	27.9
Rubber products	22,171	...	133	1,132	5,837	8,611	4,305	1,687	399	67	27.6
Leather and leather products	114,706	...	3,100	12,516	32,151	31,920	18,371	11,252	4,363	1,033	28.0
Other manufacturing	106,566	1	2,181	10,797	32,171	32,316	16,919	8,513	3,021	647	27.5
Nonmanufacturing	63,342	61	798	3,887	12,436	18,384	13,340	9,446	3,935	1,055	32.9
Private household workers	1,971,483	13,814	74,991	161,824	337,461	463,763	376,930	292,071	179,585	71,044	33.6
Service workers, except private household	1,224,639	1,251	16,385	75,237	238,985	319,898	242,194	192,342	105,776	32,571	33.8
Attendants, ushers, and bootblacks	63,861	124	1,346	5,928	15,162	15,938	11,137	8,729	4,372	1,125	30.9
Barbers, beauticians, and manicurists	206,592	31	1,030	11,439	58,047	71,984	41,821	17,240	4,290	710	29.5
Boarding and lodging house keepers	61,355	...	61	245	1,351	5,896	11,669	17,873	15,723	8,537	51.4
Charwomen, janitors, and porters	73,505	...	369	884	2,946	9,428	11,959	24,157	12,374	3,388	46.3
Cooks, except private household	116,310	59	438	1,976	8,298	23,164	32,646	31,749	15,108	2,872	42.4
Elevator operators	12,686	3	96	1,004	3,419	4,518	2,310	945	316	75	29.0

[1] Original 1950 and 1940 data revised where necessary to give comparable occupation classification.

TABLE D-7.—EMPLOYED WOMEN BY OCCUPATION AND AGE: 1950 AND 1940—Cont.

[Decennial census levels. "N.e.c." means not elsewhere classified]

Year and occupation [1]	Total, 14 years and over	14 and 15 years	16 and 17 years	18 and 19 years	20 to 24 years	25 to 34 years	35 to 44 years	45 to 54 years	55 to 64 years	65 years and over	Median age (years)
1940—Continued											
Service workers, exc. private household—Cont.											
Housekeepers and stewards, exc. private household	59,576	...	119	596	2,919	7,685	12,332	17,754	13,643	4,528	48.5
Practical nurses and midwives	87,198	239	762	2,173	7,677	13,961	15,864	21,982	18,560	5,980	46.3
Protective service	5,396	9	15	59	273	864	1,314	1,472	1,023	367	46.1
Waitresses, bartenders, and counter workers	364,036	364	9,110	41,542	113,693	123,167	51,380	18,949	5,102	729	26.4
Other serv. wkrs., exc. priv. hshld. & protective	174,124	422	3,039	9,391	25,200	43,293	41,762	31,492	15,265	4,260	36.4
Farm laborers and foremen	320,830	20,214	32,470	35,964	60,861	67,349	48,635	34,170	15,747	5,420	26.6
Farm laborers (wage) and foremen	97,551	3,609	7,121	8,975	18,437	22,925	16,681	11,804	5,658	2,341	29.6
Farm laborers, unpaid family workers	223,279	16,605	25,349	26,989	42,424	44,424	31,954	22,366	10,089	3,079	25.1
Laborers, except farm and mine	101,835	216	1,828	8,672	27,108	31,667	17,205	9,846	4,086	1,207	29.1
Manufacturing	76,086	76	1,217	6,848	22,293	24,957	12,098	6,010	2,054	533	28.0
All other	25,749	140	611	1,824	4,815	6,710	5,107	3,836	2,032	674	33.2
Occupation not reported	172,985	2,278	5,264	12,751	25,914	34,029	30,060	29,046	21,249	12,394	37.1

[1] Original 1950 and 1940 data revised where necessary to give comparable occupation classification.

Source: Derived from *1950 Census of Population*, Vol. II, *Characteristics of the Population*, Part 1, U. S. Summary, table 127, and Vol. IV, *Special Reports*, Part 1, Chapter B, Occupational Characteristics, table 6; *1940 Census of Population*, Vol. III, *The Labor Force*, Part 1, U. S. Summary, table 65.

TABLE D-8.—EMPLOYED WOMEN BY INDUSTRY AND AGE: 1950 AND 1940

[Decennial census levels]

Year and industry	Total, 14 years and over	14 and 15 years	16 and 17 years	18 and 19 years	20 to 24 years	25 to 34 years	35 to 44 years	45 to 54 years	55 to 64 years	65 years and over	Median age (years)
1950											
Total employed women	15,715,164	91,465	304,530	876,093	2,382,464	3,682,450	3,659,820	2,752,650	1,490,272	475,420	36.4
Agriculture, forestry, and fisheries	589,625	22,203	27,477	25,946	53,228	113,054	130,819	111,105	72,888	32,905	39.0
Agriculture	584,144	22,177	27,391	25,708	52,536	111,707	129,332	110,132	72,387	32,774	39.1
Forestry and fisheries	5,481	26	86	238	692	1,347	1,487	973	501	131	37.4
Mining	23,178	39	108	1,204	5,129	7,276	4,853	3,063	1,197	309	32.0
Coal mining	5,555	17	34	283	1,135	1,678	1,119	777	428	84	32.8
Crude petroleum and natural gas extraction	12,417	6	39	570	2,960	4,214	2,649	1,435	433	111	31.2
Mining and quarrying, except fuel	5,206	16	35	351	1,034	1,384	1,085	851	336	114	33.4
Construction	98,356	156	786	4,805	15,919	26,165	23,742	16,659	7,740	2,384	35.6
Manufacturing	3,641,052	2,559	40,963	192,870	605,774	1,031,374	902,350	566,804	248,941	49,417	34.5
Logging	2,197	30	67	123	330	549	482	389	188	39	35.0
Sawmills, planing mills, and mill work	20,056	56	223	1,195	3,493	5,617	5,116	2,989	1,101	266	34.0
Miscellaneous wood products	17,012	14	167	821	2,683	4,773	4,649	2,602	1,071	232	35.1
Furniture and fixtures	51,369	20	578	3,112	9,080	14,521	12,771	7,522	3,161	604	33.9
Glass and glass products	33,769	10	260	1,849	7,057	11,338	7,804	3,712	1,485	254	31.8
Stone and clay products	46,539	24	309	2,396	8,285	13,331	11,324	6,896	3,247	727	34.2
Primary iron and steel industries	223,584	63	1,312	11,769	43,067	70,690	52,569	30,300	11,802	2,012	32.9
Primary nonferrous industries											
Fabricated met. industries (incl. not spec. metal)											
Machinery, except electrical	173,255	31	837	9,222	34,778	54,211	39,634	23,805	9,088	1,649	32.7
Electrical machinery, equipment, and supplies	275,424	34	2,370	15,444	55,284	96,373	63,174	31,375	10,102	1,268	31.7
Motor vehicles and motor vehicle equipment	109,429	11	291	4,384	18,186	38,014	28,340	14,777	4,785	641	33.4
Aircraft and parts	32,632	4	27	855	5,015	12,887	8,348	4,195	1,182	119	33.1
Ship and boat building and repairing	9,309	3	29	324	1,455	2,986	2,172	1,677	574	89	34.5
Railroad and misc. transportation equipment	6,652	3	33	301	1,296	1,993	1,564	976	416	70	33.5
All other durable goods	236,992	77	3,261	13,798	42,208	69,133	55,462	34,440	15,215	3,398	33.6
Meat products	55,977	29	569	2,860	9,149	16,890	14,946	8,167	3,003	364	34.1
Bakery products	62,658	140	1,372	4,262	10,661	16,400	15,410	9,362	4,227	824	34.1
Other food industries	199,645	213	2,615	11,337	32,097	51,452	49,508	33,692	15,657	3,074	35.4
Tobacco manufactures	49,757	14	504	1,908	6,107	12,425	14,521	9,290	4,224	764	37.7
Knitting mills	120,544	14	2,068	8,225	20,136	33,175	31,634	16,853	7,014	1,425	34.0
Yarn, thread, and fabric mills											
Other textile mill products	408,076	123	3,172	14,498	52,983	112,057	116,651	71,867	31,211	5,514	36.8

TABLE **D–8.**— EMPLOYED WOMEN BY INDUSTRY AND AGE: 1950 AND 1940—Cont.

[Decennial census levels]

Year and industry	Total, 14 years and over	14 and 15 years	16 and 17 years	18 and 19 years	20 to 24 years	25 to 34 years	35 to 44 years	45 to 54 years	55 to 64 years	65 years and over	Median age (years)
1950--Continued											
Manufacturing--Cont.											
Apparel and other fabricated textile products	754,227	165	11,468	38,796	101,991	189,391	192,829	137,556	68,121	13,910	36.8
Paper and allied products	109,498	23	1,229	6,792	20,749	30,958	25,793	15,713	6,810	1,431	33.4
Printing, publishing, and allied industries	214,185	1,337	3,120	14,816	40,455	49,817	46,176	35,253	17,844	5,367	34.5
Chemicals and allied products	128,796	52	857	7,051	27,768	39,919	28,777	16,485	6,580	1,307	32.2
Petroleum and coal products	32,248	3	106	1,460	8,150	10,988	6,527	3,806	1,064	144	30.8
Rubber products	60,203	9	372	2,397	9,991	19,062	15,463	9,064	3,386	459	34.1
Footwear, except rubber	133,512	30	2,671	8,709	21,375	32,199	33,212	22,322	10,809	2,185	35.5
Leather and leather products, except footwear	37,861	12	719	2,164	5,525	9,958	9,036	6,350	3,283	814	35.6
Not specified manufacturing industries	35,646	15	357	2,002	6,420	10,267	8,458	5,369	2,291	467	33.8
Transport., communication, & other pub. util.	681,323	503	6,447	60,526	182,337	163,580	128,665	96,922	36,845	5,498	30.6
Railroads and railway express service	72,753	28	107	1,384	9,684	17,935	15,397	18,087	8,632	1,499	39.7
Street railways and bus lines	25,973	27	193	1,131	3,949	6,788	6,750	4,651	2,020	464	36.3
Trucking service and warehousing	47,357	70	580	3,813	9,678	12,998	10,305	6,647	2,614	652	32.3
Water transportation	11,122	11	77	532	2,290	3,049	2,493	1,805	693	172	33.7
Air transportation	19,264	9	48	658	6,107	8,469	2,552	1,052	313	56	28.3
All other transportation	17,892	34	239	873	2,991	5,119	4,236	2,976	1,170	254	34.4
Telecommunications	391,585	290	4,601	43,474	121,896	85,818	69,136	48,720	16,071	1,579	28.0
Electric and gas utilities. / Water supply, sanitary services, & other utilities.	95,377	34	602	8,661	25,742	23,404	17,796	12,984	5,332	822	30.4
Wholesale and retail trade	3,550,919	15,512	114,655	235,642	504,070	807,366	859,343	619,407	312,350	82,574	36.1
Wholesale trade	380,372	340	4,176	25,822	76,022	101,238	86,257	57,752	23,604	5,161	33.3
Food and dairy products stores, and milk retailing	480,798	3,502	16,860	27,398	53,479	103,035	128,462	90,685	44,757	12,620	37.8
General merchandise and five and ten cent stores	768,000	2,928	38,478	68,370	117,141	150,174	168,332	131,868	71,797	18,912	35.4
Apparel and accessories stores	337,748	595	6,906	15,735	34,966	60,206	82,342	76,238	46,188	14,572	41.1
Furniture, home furnishings, and equipment stores	100,436	98	1,142	5,930	15,436	24,492	25,534	17,626	8,104	2,074	36.2
Motor vehicles and accessories retailing	60,569	36	662	4,637	13,303	17,608	14,073	7,612	2,238	400	31.6
Gasoline service stations	21,844	73	304	913	2,500	5,391	6,272	4,070	1,822	499	37.8
Drug stores	127,354	1,666	10,374	14,812	22,023	28,234	26,718	15,901	6,248	1,378	30.2
Eating and drinking places	863,077	5,248	26,916	46,128	111,078	228,701	223,585	140,581	66,816	14,024	35.6
Hardware, farm implement, and bldg. material ret.	76,565	100	851	5,130	12,748	17,152	18,680	13,822	6,311	1,771	36.2
All other retail trade	334,156	926	7,986	20,767	43,374	71,135	79,088	63,252	34,465	11,163	37.6
Finance, insurance, and real estate	780,299	307	9,575	93,094	198,036	163,170	131,433	108,055	57,556	19,073	30.5
Banking and other finance	285,446	72	3,310	36,647	85,403	66,856	44,631	33,120	12,675	2,732	27.6
Insurance and real estate	494,853	235	6,265	56,447	112,633	96,314	86,802	74,935	44,881	16,341	32.5

TABLE D-8.—EMPLOYED WOMEN BY INDUSTRY AND AGE: 1950 AND 1940—Cont.

[Decennial census levels]

Year and industry	Total, 14 years and over	14 and 15 years	16 and 17 years	18 and 19 years	20 to 24 years	25 to 34 years	35 to 44 years	45 to 54 years	55 to 64 years	65 years and over	Median age (years)
1950—Continued											
Business and repair services......	182,836	157	1,973	11,519	34,700	48,395	42,169	28,354	12,032	3,537	33.9
Business services......	158,398	101	1,625	9,928	30,535	42,136	35,843	24,431	10,632	3,167	33.8
Miscellaneous repair services......											
Automobile repair services and garages......	24,438	56	348	1,591	4,165	6,259	6,326	3,923	1,400	370	34.7
Personal services......	2,328,872	35,472	57,475	80,725	206,111	465,988	548,661	466,290	322,547	145,603	40.8
Private households......	1,426,774	34,141	47,651	50,782	112,242	252,630	314,606	291,376	217,249	106,097	41.9
Hotels and lodging places......	254,529	453	2,188	5,746	18,996	43,972	59,395	60,633	44,862	18,284	44.4
Laundering, cleaning, and dyeing services......	361,529	583	5,997	16,388	44,107	87,529	97,557	67,271	33,954	8,143	37.7
All other personal services......	286,040	295	1,639	7,809	30,766	81,857	77,103	47,010	26,482	13,079	37.7
Entertainment and recreation services......	141,059	2,149	10,356	11,806	23,723	33,953	27,393	19,112	9,729	2,838	31.6
Professional and related services......	2,716,581	3,783	21,706	120,469	419,828	571,284	634,960	536,387	311,232	96,932	38.5
Medical and other health services......	1,039,888	1,645	11,976	70,195	196,658	242,014	212,682	169,101	102,618	32,999	34.9
Educational services, government......	1,321,660	1,503	6,419	33,103	170,180	251,005	348,772	302,969	164,577	43,132	40.7
Educational services, private......											
Welfare, religious, & misc. membership organizations......	233,404	538	2,136	8,821	28,528	46,256	47,635	46,069	35,687	17,734	41.4
Legal, engineering, & misc. professional services......	121,629	97	1,175	8,350	24,462	32,009	25,871	18,248	8,350	3,067	33.4
Public administration......	652,088	146	1,453	19,558	90,896	179,166	157,418	127,334	62,760	13,357	37.2
Postal service......	52,508	17	74	493	2,817	8,904	13,382	15,112	9,488	2,221	45.4
Federal public administration......											
State and local public administration......	599,580	129	1,379	19,065	88,079	170,262	144,036	112,222	53,272	11,136	36.4
Industry not reported......	328,976	8,479	11,556	17,929	42,713	71,679	68,014	53,158	34,455	20,993	36.8
1940[1]											
Total employed women......	11,138,178	40,775	186,592	706,525	2,259,135	3,240,536	2,222,769	1,482,321	745,670	253,855	32.3
Agriculture, forestry, and fisheries......	488,569	20,352	32,869	37,528	66,946	83,800	81,177	80,085	54,902	30,910	35.3
Agriculture......	486,393	20,331	32,826	37,432	66,581	83,143	80,690	79,778	54,753	30,859	35.4
Forestry and fisheries......	2,176	21	43	96	365	657	487	307	149	51	33.6

[1] Original 1940 data revised where necessary to conform to 1950 classification.

TABLE **D-8.**—EMPLOYED WOMEN BY INDUSTRY AND AGE: 1950 AND 1940—Cont.

[Decennial census levels]

Year and industry	Total, 14 years and over	14 and 15 years	16 and 17 years	18 and 19 years	20 to 24 years	25 to 34 years	35 to 44 years	45 to 54 years	55 to 64 years	65 years and over	Median age (years)
1940¹—Continued											
Mining............	10,939	13	58	447	2,261	3,823	2,536	1,244	417	140	32.0
Coal mining............	3,236	7	28	155	719	956	735	416	156	64	32.4
Crude petroleum and natural gas extraction......	5,097	1	10	186	1,053	2,056	1,204	447	113	27	31.3
Mining and quarrying, except fuel............	2,606	5	20	106	489	811	597	381	148	49	33.4
Construction............	36,367	41	273	2,314	8,055	10,450	7,771	4,750	2,127	586	32.2
Manufacturing............	2,324,542	940	28,958	167,315	586,324	785,685	442,591	222,311	73,958	16,460	29.8
Logging............	1,262	12	34	81	225	324	291	200	79	16	33.6
Sawmills, planing mills, and mill work......	8,487	21	85	513	1,952	2,871	1,771	872	316	86	30.8
Miscellaneous wood products............	10,903	6	112	775	2,708	3,808	2,041	967	388	98	29.9
Furniture and fixtures............	24,739	11	219	1,739	6,342	8,212	4,716	2,441	866	193	29.9
Glass and glass products............	19,280	4	236	1,472	6,035	7,303	2,811	1,034	317	68	27.6
Stone and clay products............	24,144	10	184	1,690	5,843	7,974	4,778	2,480	924	261	30.4
Primary iron and steel industries............	115,634	34	766	8,976	34,268	39,356	19,710	8,935	2,924	665	28.5
Primary nonferrous industries............											
Fabricated met. industries (incl. not spec. metal)...											
Machinery, except electrical............	64,760	11	304	4,727	19,500	22,280	11,412	4,738	1,457	331	28.5
Electrical machinery, equipment, and supplies......	100,401	17	658	8,490	34,592	36,287	14,068	4,917	1,200	172	26.8
Motor vehicles and motor vehicle equipment......	49,321	18	128	2,000	12,875	20,239	10,053	3,250	655	103	29.8
Aircraft and parts............	4,605	2	19	408	1,720	1,630	556	202	53	15	25.9
Ship and boat building and repairing............	3,099	...	7	140	630	901	820	416	155	30	33.6
Railroad and misc. transportation equipment......	2,302	1	7	139	630	736	453	239	83	14	30.1
All other durable goods............	128,631	7	2,093	11,962	38,394	40,613	20,917	10,095	3,643	907	27.9
Meat products............	31,741	8	241	2,187	8,687	11,303	5,730	2,844	631	110	29.2
Bakery products............	39,121	24	520	3,371	11,241	13,318	6,072	3,114	1,172	289	28.3
Other food industries............	127,032	136	1,923	9,584	32,932	41,348	23,330	12,506	4,391	882	29.6
Tobacco manufactures............	58,819	17	476	2,370	11,020	22,258	13,879	6,465	1,919	415	32.0
Knitting mills............	128,413	14	1,681	10,459	34,480	48,236	21,389	8,868	2,706	580	28.6
Yarn, thread, and fabric mills............	349,288	175	4,342	19,995	70,372	124,692	77,329	38,664	11,397	2,322	31.4
Other textile mill products............											
Apparel and other fabricated textile products...	516,910	133	9,393	39,662	121,129	155,912	104,448	61,275	20,699	4,259	30.7
Paper and allied products............	71,722	14	603	5,262	19,397	25,156	12,737	5,952	2,082	519	29.2
Printing, publishing, and allied industries......	132,454	208	974	7,998	29,889	42,233	26,846	15,265	6,902	2,139	31.4
Chemicals and allied products............	74,934	16	499	4,949	20,728	28,344	12,622	5,402	1,950	424	29.0

¹ Original 1940 data revised where necessary to conform to 1950 classification.

TABLE **D-8.**—EMPLOYED WOMEN BY INDUSTRY AND AGE: 1950 AND 1940—Cont.

[Decennial census levels]

Year and industry	Total, 14 years and over	14 and 15 years	16 and 17 years	18 and 19 years	20 to 24 years	25 to 34 years	35 to 44 years	45 to 54 years	55 to 64 years	65 years and over	Median age (years)
1940¹—Continued											
Manufacturing--Cont.											
Petroleum and coal products	14,659	4	35	511	2,948	6,144	3,515	1,180	279	43	31.2
Rubber products	36,802	6	181	2,015	9,833	14,250	7,071	2,670	655	121	29.5
Footwear, except rubber	107,436	27	1,727	8,195	25,029	36,399	20,761	10,811	3,687	800	30.1
Leather and leather products, except footwear	29,878	4	700	3,111	8,514	8,623	4,783	2,787	1,092	264	28.0
Not specified manufacturing industries	47,765	...	811	4,534	14,411	14,935	7,682	3,722	1,336	334	27.8
Transport., communication, & other pub. util.	340,344	87	1,440	17,011	69,139	119,131	81,587	37,840	11,924	2,185	31.9
Railroads and railway express service	35,658	14	58	475	2,942	7,424	12,548	8,280	3,320	597	40.5
Street railways and bus lines	8,307	5	35	286	1,321	2,269	2,061	1,341	773	216	36.2
Trucking service and warehousing	20,952	15	163	1,488	5,373	6,868	4,260	1,895	703	187	30.0
Water transportation	5,470	4	23	189	1,001	1,850	1,416	658	259	70	33.2
Air transportation	2,297	...	10	104	867	955	270	76	13	2	26.8
All other transportation	4,972	3	33	257	1,031	1,666	1,193	553	191	45	32.0
Telecommunications	205,445	37	985	11,896	43,754	76,651	47,187	19,382	4,818	735	31.0
Electric and gas utilities	57,243	9	133	2,316	12,850	21,448	12,652	5,655	1,847	333	31.2
Water supply, sanitary services, & other utilities											
Wholesale and retail trade	2,028,040	1,812	23,876	140,791	447,766	592,520	405,941	268,702	116,711	29,921	31.7
Wholesale trade	181,847	100	1,381	11,515	44,777	62,866	36,365	17,421	6,203	1,219	30.3
Food and dairy products stores, and milk retailing	282,755	518	4,110	18,203	50,100	70,576	62,107	47,968	22,462	6,711	34.7
General merchandise and five and ten cent stores	485,667	161	5,100	39,196	125,804	148,634	84,192	53,169	23,461	5,950	29.9
Apparel and accessories stores	219,693	41	1,182	8,586	33,031	57,558	53,311	41,657	19,270	5,057	36.8
Furniture, home furnishings, and equipment stores	48,444	17	306	2,876	10,182	14,220	10,669	6,589	2,874	711	32.6
Motor vehicles and accessories retailing	30,148	5	183	2,247	8,095	10,779	6,121	2,125	499	94	29.2
Gasoline service stations	13,664	33	130	640	2,083	3,924	3,316	2,217	1,042	279	35.1
Drug stores	53,899	59	1,109	5,680	15,727	16,406	8,237	4,415	1,780	486	27.7
Eating and drinking places	477,640	713	8,537	37,243	109,362	143,338	93,535	59,043	21,824	4,045	30.8
Hardware, farm implement, and bldg. material ret.	38,798	12	191	2,428	8,601	11,362	8,392	5,017	2,187	608	32.2
All other retail trade	195,485	153	1,647	12,177	40,004	52,857	39,696	29,081	15,109	4,761	33.3
Finance, insurance, and real estate	456,050	51	1,953	26,134	100,570	140,692	92,282	58,078	27,611	8,679	32.1
Banking and other finance	145,496	15	596	8,111	34,998	51,118	31,754	13,522	4,423	959	30.7
Insurance and real estate	310,554	36	1,357	18,023	65,572	89,574	60,528	44,556	23,188	7,720	32.8

¹ Original 1940 data revised where necessary to conform to 1950 classification.

TABLE D-8.—EMPLOYED WOMEN BY INDUSTRY AND AGE: 1950 AND 1940—Cont.

[Decennial census levels]

Year and industry	Total, 14 years and over	14 and 15 years	16 and 17 years	18 and 19 years	20 to 24 years	25 to 34 years	35 to 44 years	45 to 54 years	55 to 64 years	65 years and over	Median age (years)
1940¹—Continued											
Business and repair services...	78,677	33	543	5,154	18,318	25,700	16,358	8,186	3,409	976	30.9
Business services...	65,390	18	431	4,255	15,369	21,495	13,240	6,773	2,952	857	30.9
Miscellaneous repair services...	13,287	15	112	899	2,949	4,205	3,118	1,413	457	119	31.4
Automobile repair services and garages...											
Personal services...	2,838,212	14,327	81,319	194,322	474,067	682,829	564,881	445,866	273,819	106,782	34.6
Private households...	2,059,936	13,970	76,058	163,318	345,492	476,267	392,862	315,047	199,200	77,722	34.1
Hotels and lodging places...	248,650	164	1,347	5,834	22,054	48,635	56,092	57,135	39,891	17,498	43.3
Laundering, cleaning, and dyeing services...	216,870	107	2,408	11,400	40,786	69,025	50,980	29,603	10,503	2,058	32.8
All other personal services...	312,756	86	1,506	13,770	65,735	88,902	64,947	44,081	24,225	9,504	33.5
Entertainment and recreation services...	84,271	183	1,804	7,455	20,846	26,783	15,042	7,972	3,294	892	29.4
Professional and related services...	1,866,303	545	6,974	78,322	353,386	595,797	390,433	264,672	135,184	40,990	33.3
Medical and other health services...	599,344	174	2,919	49,297	152,060	180,769	101,531	68,743	33,880	9,971	30.3
Educational services, government...	1,032,016	234	2,554	17,047	159,143	349,265	241,409	160,743	80,286	21,335	34.6
Educational services, private...	139,991	123	780	4,389	18,329	34,777	29,049	26,489	17,593	8,462	39.0
Welfare, religious, and membership organizations...	94,952	14	721	7,589	23,854	30,986	18,444	8,697	3,425	1,222	29.9
Legal, engineering, & misc. professional services...											
Public administration...	308,598	40	395	7,804	53,197	100,922	72,838	47,214	21,474	4,714	34.2
Postal service...	33,267	10	43	570	2,778	6,716	9,061	8,139	4,861	1,089	42.2
Federal public administration...	275,331	30	352	7,234	50,419	94,206	63,777	39,075	16,613	3,625	33.5
State and local public administration...											
Industry not reported...	277,266	2,351	6,130	21,928	58,260	72,404	49,332	35,401	20,840	10,620	30.4

¹ Original 1940 data revised where necessary to conform to 1950 classification.

Source: Derived from *1950 Census of Population*, Vol. II, *Characteristics of the Population*, Part 1, U. S. Summary, table 132; *1940 Census of Population*, Vol. III, *The Labor Force*, Part 1, U. S. Summary, table 80.

TABLE D-9.—EMPLOYED NEGRO WOMEN BY OCCUPATION, BY REGIONS: 1950 AND 1940

[Decennial census levels. "N.e.c." means not elsewhere classified]

Occupation[1]	United States 1950	United States 1940	Northeast 1950	Northeast 1940	North Central 1950	North Central 1940	South 1950	South 1940	West 1950	West 1940
Total employed Negro women	1,869,956	1,542,273	321,835	194,057	269,649	130,366	1,203,850	1,195,485	74,622	22,365
Professional, technical, and kindred workers	104,728	65,888	13,736	5,787	13,230	6,184	74,480	53,127	3,282	790
Nurses, professional and student	14,871	6,617	5,020	1,938	2,736	935	6,243	3,601	872	143
Teachers (n.e.c.)	67,857	50,112	3,178	1,588	5,191	3,086	58,491	45,253	997	185
Farmers and farm managers	30,949	46,216	84	35	222	162	30,572	46,009	71	10
Managers, officials, and proprietors, except farm	24,557	10,914	3,544	1,392	4,087	1,826	15,491	7,285	1,435	411
Clerical and kindred workers	74,255	13,145	21,106	3,345	19,777	3,242	27,963	6,108	5,409	450
Stenographers, typists, and secretaries	21,593	4,110	6,340	1,155	5,478	1,106	8,043	1,664	1,732	185
Sales workers	25,492	7,620	4,874	1,227	6,102	1,891	13,325	4,322	1,191	180
Craftsmen, foremen, and kindred workers	11,629	2,374	3,602	558	3,069	426	4,368	1,329	590	61
Operatives and kindred workers	274,000	96,190	93,931	23,954	57,366	11,728	112,091	59,832	10,612	676
Dressmakers and seamstresses, except factory	10,248	11,270	2,090	2,101	1,848	1,529	5,739	7,328	571	312
Laundry and drycleaning operatives	98,998	43,135	18,523	9,024	19,476	6,222	57,546	27,749	3,453	140
Operatives and kindred workers (n.e.c.)—mfg.:										
Food and kindred products	18,710	5,638	2,453	250	5,836	646	9,609	4,728	812	14
Apparel and other fabricated textile products	52,910	11,343	36,268	7,613	6,897	1,400	6,398	2,250	3,347	80
Private household workers	773,590	917,942	122,398	132,745	82,385	73,915	538,431	696,042	30,376	15,240
Service workers, except private household	351,856	159,805	48,700	22,256	69,698	28,115	214,823	105,231	18,635	4,203
Attendants, hospital and other institution	19,324	1,666	6,425	334	5,190	239	6,128	1,063	1,581	30
Barbers, beauticians, and manicurists	26,584	14,782	5,297	3,698	5,030	2,979	14,766	7,562	1,491	543
Charwomen, janitors, and porters	35,456	12,457	6,066	2,567	8,005	2,344	18,628	7,018	2,757	528
Cooks, except private household	60,385	26,738	3,078	1,712	6,998	2,518	48,722	22,109	1,587	399
Practical nurses and midwives	16,141	11,015	3,211	570	1,575	287	10,717	10,054	638	104
Waitresses, bartenders, and counter workers	42,139	15,293	6,560	2,855	8,958	3,001	24,437	9,042	2,184	395
Farm laborers and foremen	139,657	198,549	1,059	191	891	369	137,122	197,950	585	39
Farm laborers, unpaid family workers	72,751	128,338	32	11	178	94	72,509	128,222	32	11
Farm laborers, except unpaid, and farm foremen	66,906	70,211	1,027	180	713	275	64,613	69,728	553	28
Laborers, except farm and mine	28,414	12,959	4,325	989	7,813	1,514	14,753	10,349	1,523	107
Occupation not reported	30,829	10,671	4,476	1,578	5,009	994	20,431	7,901	913	198

[1] Major occupation group plus any specific occupation in which as many as 0.5 percent of employed Negro women were reported in 1950. Original 1940 data revised where necessary to conform to 1950 classification.

TABLE D-9.—EMPLOYED NEGRO WOMEN BY OCCUPATION, BY REGIONS: 1950 AND 1940—Cont.

[Decennial census levels. "N.e.c." means not elsewhere classified]

Occupation[1]	United States		Northeast		North Central		South		West	
	1950	1940	1950	1940	1950	1940	1950	1940	1950	1940
PERCENT DISTRIBUTION										
Total employed Negro women.........	100.0	100.0	100.0	100.0	100.0	100.0	100.0	100.0	100.0	100.0
Professional, technical, and kindred workers......	5.7	4.3	4.3	3.0	5.0	4.8	6.3	4.5	4.5	3.6
Nurses, professional and student......	0.8	0.4	1.6	1.0	1.6	0.7	0.5	0.3	1.2	0.6
Teachers (n.e.c.)......	3.7	3.3	1.0	0.8	2.0	2.4	4.9	3.8	1.4	0.8
Farmers and farm managers......	1.7	3.0	(2)	(2)	0.1	0.1	2.6	3.9	0.1	(2)
Managers, officials, and proprietors, except farm.	1.3	0.7	1.1	0.7	1.5	1.4	1.3	0.6	1.9	1.9
Clerical and kindred workers......	4.0	0.9	6.7	1.7	7.5	2.5	2.4	0.5	7.3	2.0
Stenographers, typists, and secretaries......	1.2	0.3	2.0	0.6	2.1	0.9	0.7	0.1	2.3	0.8
Sales workers......	1.4	0.5	1.5	0.6	2.3	1.5	1.1	0.4	1.6	0.8
Craftsmen, foremen, and kindred workers......	0.6	0.2	1.1	0.3	1.2	0.3	0.4	0.1	0.8	0.3
Operatives and kindred workers......	14.9	6.3	29.6	12.4	21.7	9.1	9.5	5.0	14.4	3.0
Dressmakers and seamstresses, except factory......	0.6	0.7	0.7	1.1	0.7	1.2	0.5	0.6	0.8	1.4
Laundry and drycleaning operatives......	5.3	2.8	5.8	4.7	7.2	4.8	4.8	2.3	4.6	0.6
Operatives and kindred workers (n.e.c.)—mfg.:										
Food and kindred products......	1.0	0.4	0.8	0.1	2.2	0.5	0.8	0.4	1.1	0.1
Apparel and other fabricated textile products......	2.9	0.7	11.4	4.0	2.6	1.1	0.5	0.2	4.5	0.4
Private household workers......	42.2	59.9	38.7	69.1	31.1	57.1	45.5	58.5	41.2	68.7
Service workers, except private household......	19.1	10.4	15.3	11.6	26.3	21.7	18.1	8.9	25.3	19.0
Attendants, hospital and other institution......	1.0	0.1	2.0	0.2	0.5	0.2	0.5	0.1	2.1	0.1
Barbers, beauticians, and manicurists......	1.4	1.0	1.7	1.9	1.9	2.3	1.2	0.6	2.0	2.4
Charwomen, janitors, and porters......	1.9	0.8	1.9	1.3	3.0	1.8	1.6	0.6	3.7	2.4
Cooks, except private household......	3.3	1.7	1.0	0.9	2.6	1.9	4.1	1.9	2.2	1.8
Practical nurses and midwives......	0.9	0.7	1.0	0.3	0.6	0.2	0.9	0.8	0.9	0.5
Waitresses, bartenders, and counter workers......	2.3	1.0	2.1	1.5	3.4	2.3	2.1	0.8	3.0	1.8
Farm laborers and foremen......	7.6	13.0	0.3	0.1	0.3	0.3	11.6	16.7	0.8	0.2
Farm laborers, unpaid family workers......	4.0	8.4	(2)	(2)	0.1	0.1	6.1	10.8	(2)	(2)
Farm laborers, except unpaid, and farm foremen.	3.6	4.6	0.3	0.1	0.3	0.2	5.5	5.9	0.8	0.1
Laborers, except farm and mine......	1.5	0.8	1.4	0.5	3.0	1.2	1.2	0.9	2.1	0.5
Occupation not reported......	...	...	...	...	...	...	...	...	...	...

[1] Major occupation group plus any specific occupation in which as many as 0.5 percent of employed Negro women were reported in 1950. Original 1940 data revised where necessary to conform to 1950 classification. [2] Less than 0.05 percent.

Source: Derived from *1950 Census of Population*, Vol. II, *Characteristics of the Population*, Part 1, U. S. Summary, tables 125, 128, and 159; *1940 Census of Population*, Vol. III, *The Labor Force*, Part 1, U. S. Summary, tables 58, 62, and 63.

TABLE D-10.—SELECTED DATA FOR CITIES OF 100,000 OR MORE IN 1940

[1950 unstandardized rates based on 20-percent sample data. Rates standardized for age on basis of distribution of male and female population by age in all cities of 100,000 in 1950]

City	Median wage or salary income of persons in experienced labor force with $100 or more income				Labor force participation rates of persons 14 years old and over							
	Male		Female		Male				Female			
					Unstandardized		Standardized for age		Unstandardized		Standardized for age	
	1949	1939	1949	1939	1950	1940	1950	1940	1950	1940	1950	1940
Akron, Ohio	$3,120	$1,362	$1,748	$790	83.2	80.2	82.9	81.6	31.5	26.7	31.1	25.6
Albany, N. Y.	2,765	1,280	1,952	808	80.1	81.0	80.9	81.9	35.3	34.3	36.3	34.7
Atlanta, Ga.	2,233	858	1,394	509	78.9	82.7	78.7	82.2	43.1	42.2	42.3	39.6
Baltimore, Md.	2,694	1,121	1,468	613	80.7	80.6	80.2	80.9	34.8	33.0	34.8	32.1
Birmingham, Ala.	2,414	918	1,179	417	81.2	81.9	81.4	82.4	33.3	32.0	32.6	30.1
Boston, Mass.	2,657	1,156	1,733	793	75.2	77.2	77.1	79.1	35.1	34.0	35.9	34.1
Bridgeport, Conn.	2,708	1,172	1,833	716	81.9	82.3	81.8	83.4	36.7	37.2	37.0	35.6
Buffalo, N. Y.	2,968	1,234	1,690	702	80.4	79.6	80.9	80.8	30.8	28.4	31.1	27.6
Cambridge, Mass.	2,656	1,209	1,771	791	66.0	77.7	71.7	79.8	38.6	36.2	39.6	36.4
Camden, N. J.	2,690	1,103	1,668	665	80.2	82.3	80.8	83.6	34.0	33.7	33.7	32.0
Canton, Ohio	2,791	1,252	1,545	674	84.9	81.2	85.8	83.0	30.2	25.3	30.6	24.3
Charlotte, N. C.	2,471	913	1,342	494	85.5	83.7	84.1	83.1	45.8	44.1	43.2	39.6
Chattanooga, Tenn.	2,176	850	1,220	537	79.5	81.5	80.2	81.9	38.1	35.3	37.4	33.4
Chicago, Ill.	3,277	1,253	2,047	764	82.0	82.0	81.4	81.6	37.7	33.5	37.4	31.8
Cincinnati, Ohio	2,789	1,203	1,574	709	78.7	79.6	79.8	80.8	33.0	29.8	33.9	30.1
Cleveland, Ohio	3,057	1,159	1,827	707	82.3	81.2	81.9	81.3	34.7	30.6	34.4	28.8
Columbus, Ohio	2,860	1,171	1,701	720	75.7	75.4	76.0	76.4	36.2	30.2	36.4	30.0
Dallas, Texas	2,822	1,033	1,645	601	84.5	83.1	82.8	82.4	41.2	39.3	39.8	36.9
Dayton, Ohio	3,344	1,332	2,019	748	83.3	80.9	82.9	81.6	35.5	29.6	35.3	28.9
Denver, Colo.	2,887	1,180	1,758	715	79.2	76.7	80.2	78.8	34.6	30.1	35.3	30.2
Des Moines, Iowa	2,995	1,247	1,688	780	81.0	79.0	82.5	81.1	37.4	32.2	38.0	31.4
Detroit, Mich.	3,442	1,355	2,069	782	83.5	84.7	82.3	83.7	31.3	28.3	30.2	26.1
Duluth, Minn.	2,926	1,230	1,562	729	78.9	77.2	81.8	80.7	33.0	28.2	33.3	27.5
Elizabeth, N. J.	3,032	1,344	1,841	734	83.9	82.3	83.2	83.0	36.7	33.2	36.5	30.8
Erie, Pa.	3,042	1,184	1,697	660	81.1	79.6	82.4	82.2	32.5	27.0	32.6	26.2
Fall River, Mass.	2,272	819	1,513	587	78.2	78.4	79.5	81.3	42.7	43.1	44.1	42.5
Flint, Mich.	3,622	1,520	2,042	812	86.1	82.6	86.2	83.4	30.9	26.8	30.1	25.1
Fort Wayne, Ind.	3,308	1,349	1,766	748	82.2	79.3	82.7	81.3	35.2	29.0	35.4	28.3
Fort Worth, Texas	2,667	1,203	1,400	534	83.8	80.8	83.0	81.7	35.5	33.3	34.9	31.9
Gary, Ind.	3,264	1,397	1,730	673	85.8	83.7	84.3	82.3	28.2	20.2	27.0	17.8
Grand Rapids, Mich.	3,183	1,149	1,733	677	82.6	78.5	84.7	81.6	33.1	27.9	32.9	27.8
Hartford, Conn.	2,751	1,254	1,863	846	82.1	80.8	81.8	81.8	44.2	37.9	44.0	36.3
Houston, Texas	2,846	1,128	1,745	532	83.1	83.8	81.0	81.8	35.1	34.6	33.4	31.8

TABLE D-10.—SELECTED DATA FOR CITIES OF 100,000 OR MORE IN 1940—Cont.

[1950 unstandardized rates based on 20-percent sample data. Rates standardized for age on basis of distribution of male and female population by age in all cities of 100,000 in 1950]

City	Median wage or salary income of persons in experienced labor force with $100 or more income				Labor force participation rates of persons 14 years old and over							
	Male		Female		Male				Female			
					Unstandardized		Standardized for age		Unstandardized		Standardized for age	
	1949	1939	1949	1939	1950	1940	1950	1940	1950	1940	1950	1940
Indianapolis, Ind	$3,038	$1,197	$1,814	$745	83.3	80.9	83.8	82.0	37.6	31.2	37.8	30.9
Jacksonville, Fla	2,261	820	1,195	452	81.3	81.1	80.6	80.6	38.4	36.9	37.4	34.8
Jersey City, N. J.	2,929	1,303	2,019	834	81.1	82.9	80.9	83.6	35.3	34.1	35.0	31.8
Kansas City, Kans	2,895	1,118	1,612	648	79.7	79.9	81.3	82.5	32.3	28.0	32.9	27.6
Kansas City, Mo.	2,923	1,143	1,777	680	80.6	82.8	80.8	83.4	37.0	34.9	37.3	34.5
Knoxville, Tenn.	2,271	835	1,342	583	75.2	81.0	77.0	81.7	34.3	36.6	34.1	34.8
Long Beach, Calif.	3,262	1,358	1,877	722	78.9	75.3	79.8	77.3	29.2	23.7	30.8	24.9
Los Angeles, Calif.	3,157	1,251	1,932	820	78.1	78.0	77.5	77.7	35.8	31.6	36.5	31.9
Louisville, Ky.	2,654	1,014	1,555	617	80.9	81.5	81.1	82.7	33.8	32.3	34.1	32.0
Memphis, Tenn.	2,358	804	1,203	409	81.8	83.7	81.1	83.1	38.2	36.7	37.4	34.9
Miami, Fla.	2,422	970	1,432	511	78.4	80.1	77.7	78.8	37.9	38.5	37.5	36.5
Milwaukee, Wis.	3,315	1,341	1,757	766	82.7	80.6	83.0	81.3	35.6	29.9	35.7	29.0
Minneapolis, Minn.	3,122	1,350	1,729	776	79.0	78.6	80.4	80.4	40.4	34.1	40.4	33.2
Nashville, Tenn.	2,027	801	1,253	495	73.5	80.1	76.0	81.5	40.3	36.9	40.4	35.9
Newark, N. J.	2,714	1,132	1,774	701	79.9	80.8	79.6	81.3	37.4	34.4	36.7	32.1
New Bedford, Mass.	2,244	827	1,430	576	78.7	78.2	80.7	80.8	42.9	40.5	45.7	41.0
New Haven, Conn.	2,723	1,126	1,733	692	72.3	79.4	75.3	81.9	36.6	36.0	37.3	35.4
New Orleans, La.	2,923	810	1,291	468	78.4	81.0	78.2	81.4	31.7	33.2	31.5	32.3
New York, N. Y.	2,083	1,245	1,968	790	79.4	81.1	78.9	80.5	34.5	33.7	34.4	32.0
Norfolk, Va.	3,303	940	1,186	434	89.3	84.2	85.0	83.6	33.8	31.8	32.5	30.5
Oakland, Calif.	2,733	1,432	2,129	886	80.3	79.0	80.1	79.4	34.8	28.0	35.4	28.4
Oklahoma City, Okla.	2,900	1,104	1,604	646	82.4	79.4	82.7	79.2	36.6	33.4	36.1	31.6
Omaha, Nebr.	2,729	1,149	1,673	703	79.2	79.8	80.5	81.6	34.1	30.9	34.3	30.2
Paterson, N. J.	3,017	980	1,650	605	82.2	82.2	83.4	83.2	37.4	34.7	38.2	33.8
Peoria, Ill.		1,378	1,708	700	81.7	82.6	82.5	82.6	35.2	30.5	35.7	29.8
Philadelphia, Pa.	2,826	1,187	1,711	692	77.8	80.6	78.2	81.8	33.8	33.4	34.1	32.8
Pittsburgh, Pa.	2,825	1,237	1,657	724	78.4	79.5	79.0	81.1	29.5	28.4	29.5	27.0
Portland, Oreg.	3,223	1,297	1,892	774	79.5	79.1	80.8	80.4	36.7	31.3	38.0	31.7
Providence, R. I.	2,370	1,008	1,498	659	75.5	80.2	77.6	82.9	37.3	37.1	38.2	36.9
Reading, Pa.	2,606	1,002	1,488	609	83.1	81.3	84.7	83.6	38.6	37.1	40.2	37.5
Richmond, Va.	2,469	1,061	1,588	599	79.0	81.1	79.0	81.6	41.4	42.3	41.2	40.7
Rochester, N. Y.	3,002	1,308	1,899	798	78.4	77.6	79.8	79.5	37.3	33.7	38.7	33.9
Sacramento, Calif.	3,372	1,375	2,199	940	79.3	79.7	79.7	79.9	39.0	34.2	39.6	33.5

TABLE D–10.—Selected Data for Cities of 100,000 or More in 1940—Cont.

[1950 unstandardized rates based on 20-percent sample data. Rates standardized for age on basis of distribution of male and female population by age in all cities of 100,000 in 1950]

City	Median wage or salary income of persons in experienced labor force with $100 or more income				Labor force participation rates of persons 14 years old and over							
	Male		Female		Male				Female			
					Unstandardized		Standardized for age		Unstandardized		Standardized for age	
	1949	1939	1949	1939	1950	1940	1950	1940	1950	1940	1950	1940
St. Louis, Mo.	$2,773	$1,103	$1,716	$662	79.0	82.7	79.5	83.2	35.6	33.4	36.1	33.0
St. Paul, Minn.	3,203	1,320	1,810	762	79.0	79.3	80.5	81.2	35.3	31.8	35.7	31.0
Salt Lake City, Utah.	3,051	1,327	1,638	756	80.1	76.2	81.7	79.7	32.5	25.9	32.4	25.0
San Antonio, Texas.	2,201	687	1,351	472	79.5	80.5	80.0	81.2	29.6	30.3	29.2	29.5
San Diego, Calif.	2,772	1,074	1,781	707	81.6	77.7	80.7	77.7	30.2	25.9	30.7	26.6
San Francisco, Calif.	3,132	1,372	2,248	977	79.1	79.7	78.4	78.5	40.1	34.7	40.4	34.7
Scranton, Pa.	2,507	942	1,497	591	74.5	78.9	76.5	80.9	29.8	29.0	31.0	27.7
Seattle, Wash.	3,334	1,386	2,093	829	78.7	78.3	79.4	79.3	36.7	31.2	37.4	31.3
Somerville, Mass.	2,820	1,278	1,701	809	80.3	79.6	82.2	82.4	34.6	29.5	35.5	29.7
South Bend, Ind.	3,802	1,369	1,906	702	86.1	82.1	86.4	83.6	33.0	30.4	32.8	29.2
Spokane, Wash.	3,294	1,235	1,773	730	77.0	77.8	79.7	80.9	30.6	29.1	31.8	29.1
Springfield, Mass.	2,926	1,299	1,628	755	79.9	79.8	80.9	81.9	35.0	32.0	36.1	32.1
Syracuse, N. Y.	2,797	1,222	1,685	725	76.3	78.1	78.2	80.3	36.9	30.4	37.3	30.6
Tacoma, Wash.	3,187	1,284	1,929	783	78.5	78.1	80.9	81.1	29.4	24.7	30.3	25.1
Tampa, Fla.	1,992	705	1,177	441	77.2	80.1	78.0	81.2	36.5	40.4	36.5	39.5
Toledo, Ohio.	3,379	1,230	1,862	708	81.3	79.2	82.2	80.7	33.3	28.9	33.9	28.8
Trenton, N. J.	2,791	1,066	1,799	636	76.9	76.7	76.4	77.7	38.7	36.0	39.2	34.8
Tulsa, Okla.	3,087	1,266	1,700	596	82.3	81.3	82.2	81.4	35.1	33.0	34.6	31.3
Utica, N. Y.	2,650	1,075	1,540	620	77.1	76.9	79.4	79.4	35.1	33.3	36.8	33.6
Washington, D. C.	2,772	1,342	2,404	1,051	78.8	80.8	77.1	79.2	48.0	45.3	46.8	43.6
Wichita, Kans.	2,932	1,108	1,628	633	83.8	78.3	83.5	79.9	33.3	29.8	33.3	29.1
Wilmington, Del.	2,769	1,193	1,636	672	80.4	82.0	81.3	82.7	36.6	34.5	36.9	33.4
Worcester, Mass.	2,782	1,270	1,630	711	74.2	76.0	76.4	78.6	32.2	29.9	33.6	30.0
Yonkers, N. Y.	3,425	1,415	2,027	848	81.4	80.5	81.6	81.7	32.7	32.0	33.1	31.3
Youngstown, Ohio.	2,937	1,241	1,537	657	83.9	80.5	84.3	82.6	28.3	24.6	27.9	22.9

Source: Derived from *1950 Census of Population*, Vol. II, *Characteristics of the Population*, Parts 2–49, tables 66 and 94; *1940 Census of Population*, Vol. III, *The Labor Force*, Parts 2–5, tables 5 and 15.

TABLE **D-11.**—SELECTED DATA FOR STANDARD METROPOLITAN AREAS OF 250,000
OR MORE IN 1950

Standard metropolitan area	Median income in 1949 of male family heads, married, spouse present	Year-round workers				Percent of families with 2 or more members in labor force
		Male		Female		
		Percent of population 14 years and over who worked 50 to 52 weeks in 1949	Median income	Percent of population 14 years and over who worked 50 to 52 weeks in 1949	Median income	
Akron, Ohio.....................	$3,271	54.9	$3,389	15.5	$2,050	34.0
Albany-Schenectady-Troy, N. Y...	3,238	55.2	3,276	19.7	2,163	35.8
Allentown-Bethlehem-Easton, Pa..	2,924	50.4	2,979	16.6	1,799	40.6
Atlanta, Ga.....................	2,718	53.5	2,896	21.7	1,889	37.4
Baltimore, Md...................	3,117	52.4	3,136	18.5	1,861	37.9
Birmingham, Ala.................	2,601	43.7	3,033	16.0	1,513	32.8
Boston, Mass....................	3,187	52.3	3,212	19.6	2,010	35.0
Bridgeport, Conn................	3,117	52.8	3,231	19.2	2,125	39.8
Buffalo, N. Y...................	3,274	51.8	3,340	16.3	2,022	34.6
Canton, Ohio....................	3,114	45.6	3,310	13.5	1,820	34.6
Charleston, W. Va...............	3,018	39.4	3,495	11.8	1,962	27.3
Chicago, Ill....................	3,565	55.5	3,584	19.8	2,311	39.6
Cincinnati, Ohio................	3,155	53.4	3,261	17.9	1,922	33.4
Cleveland, Ohio.................	3,473	55.4	3,555	18.7	2,206	35.2
Columbus, Ohio..................	3,206	51.0	3,350	20.5	2,039	37.0
Dallas, Texas...................	3,096	58.3	3,266	21.5	2,020	37.0
Dayton, Ohio....................	3,455	58.0	3,544	17.9	2,294	32.6
Denver, Colo....................	3,209	53.6	3,297	18.2	2,104	32.3
Detroit, Mich...................	3,575	47.3	3,792	14.6	2,395	34.6
Duluth, Minn.--Superior, Wis....	3,024	44.0	3,219	14.8	1,792	31.2
Flint, Mich.....................	3,500	53.8	3,628	12.1	2,361	33.9
Fort Worth, Texas...............	2,981	58.9	3,108	17.7	1,878	33.4
Fresno, Calif...................	2,973	44.9	3,402	11.8	2,209	31.3
Grand Rapids, Mich..............	3,305	53.3	3,431	14.6	2,099	34.7
Harrisburg, Pa..................	2,929	55.2	2,967	19.8	1,850	35.8
Hartford, Conn..................	3,290	57.5	3,306	23.8	2,163	42.1
Houston, Texas..................	3,291	56.1	3,461	17.6	2,032	32.1
Indianapolis, Ind...............	3,311	56.7	3,420	20.0	2,162	35.9
Jacksonville, Fla...............	2,731	54.7	2,891	18.7	1,689	32.9
Johnstown, Pa...................	2,605	26.7	2,847	9.4	1,357	28.9
Kansas City, Mo.................	3,200	54.9	3,323	18.6	2,084	32.0
Knoxville, Tenn.................	2,470	43.7	2,900	13.1	1,854	30.7
Los Angeles, Calif..............	3,378	48.6	3,650	16.0	2,349	31.0
Louisville, Ky..................	2,962	53.7	3,107	17.4	1,883	33.4
Memphis, Tenn...................	2,608	56.4	2,770	19.8	1,650	35.4
Miami, Fla......................	3,004	43.4	3,303	14.6	2,071	31.8
Milwaukee, Wis..................	3,513	58.6	3,532	19.8	2,085	38.8
Minneapolis-St. Paul, Minn......	3,380	54.7	3,455	20.1	2,082	35.1
Nashville, Tenn.................	2,621	49.5	2,810	19.2	1,698	37.7
New Haven, Conn.................	3,164	48.4	3,214	17.8	2,021	37.9
New Orleans, La.................	2,576	53.9	2,762	18.5	1,629	33.9
New York-Northeastern New Jersey	3,353	53.1	3,397	19.1	2,274	37.3
Norfolk-Portsmouth, Va..........	2,966	63.2	2,617	15.9	1,651	31.8
Oklahoma City, Okla.............	2,998	56.5	3,135	18.5	2,017	31.6
Omaha, Nebr.....................	3,141	56.1	3,160	18.2	1,938	33.7
Peoria, Ill.....................	3,300	53.8	3,339	15.6	2,042	34.0
Philadelphia, Pa................	3,213	53.2	3,231	18.1	2,018	38.0
Phoenix, Ariz...................	2,774	41.9	3,182	11.9	2,094	28.4
Pittsburgh, Pa..................	3,130	39.4	3,346	13.6	1,901	31.3
Portland, Oreg..................	3,257	47.3	3,542	16.4	2,251	30.9
Providence, R. I................	2,764	48.4	2,916	17.8	1,913	42.3
Reading, Pa.....................	2,924	55.2	2,949	18.2	1,799	44.1
Richmond, Va....................	3,005	57.6	3,001	22.9	1,938	42.6
Rochester, N. Y.................	3,329	53.3	3,388	18.4	2,206	38.5
Sacramento, Calif...............	3,463	50.7	3,630	18.8	2,495	33.9
St. Louis, Mo...................	3,190	54.0	3,242	17.7	2,017	34.3
Salt Lake City, Utah............	3,301	54.4	3,430	15.7	1,978	32.2
San Antonio, Texas..............	2,495	54.5	2,508	16.7	1,727	30.8

TABLE **D-11.**—Selected Data for Standard Metropolitan Areas of 250,000 or More in 1950—Cont.

Standard metropolitan area	Median income in 1949 of male family heads, married, spouse present	Year-round workers				Percent of families with 2 or more members in labor force
		Male		Female		
		Percent of population 14 years and over who worked 50 to 52 weeks in 1949	Median income	Percent of population 14 years and over who worked 50 to 52 weeks in 1949	Median income	
San Bernardino, Calif...........	$3,049	45.6	$3,333	10.6	$2,225	26.0
San Diego, Calif................	3,257	53.4	3,170	13.3	2,245	25.6
San Francisco-Oakland, Calif....	3,581	52.2	3,671	19.2	2,511	32.0
San Jose, Calif.................	3,352	46.3	3,618	13.0	2,328	30.1
Scranton, Pa....................	2,649	37.8	2,848	14.2	1,669	36.0
Seattle, Wash...................	3,520	49.5	3,729	17.9	2,408	30.3
Springfield-Holyoke, Mass.......	3,087	54.6	3,146	19.1	1,952	39.4
Syracuse, N. Y..................	3,118	50.3	3,221	17.9	2,014	37.0
Tacoma, Wash....................	3,236	52.1	2,912	13.7	2,311	27.2
Tampa-St. Petersburg, Fla.......	2,291	41.9	2,572	13.4	1,609	30.4
Toledo, Ohio....................	3,457	52.2	3,630	15.9	2,199	35.9
Tulsa, Okla.....................	3,139	56.6	3,375	18.4	2,087	31.3
Utica-Rome, N. Y................	2,878	48.8	3,043	15.8	1,966	36.9
Washington, D. C................	3,568	60.6	3,444	28.3	2,692	40.1
Wheeling, W. Va.--Steubenville, Ohio........................	2,894	41.1	3,134	12.6	1,672	30.8
Wilkes-Barre--Hazleton, Pa......	2,675	34.9	2,887	12.1	1,653	37.2
Wilmington, Del.................	3,340	56.2	3,346	17.7	1,964	33.4
Worcester, Mass.................	3,043	49.0	3,127	17.6	1,904	37.0
Youngstown, Ohio................	3,191	41.4	3,368	13.3	1,900	34.8

Source: Derived from *1950 Census of Population*, Vol. II, *Characteristics of the Population*, Parts 2-49, tables 72, 90, and 91; and Vol. IV, *Special Reports*, Part 2, Chapter A, General Characteristics of Families, table 40.

INDEX